POLITICAL GAME THEORY

Political Game Theory is a self-contained introduction to game theory and its applications to political science. The book presents choice theory, social choice theory, static and dynamic games of complete information, static and dynamic games of incomplete information, repeated games, bargaining theory, mechanism design, and a mathematical appendix covering logic, real analysis, calculus, and probability theory. The methods employed have many applications in various subdisciplines including comparative politics, international relations, and American politics. *Political Game Theory* is tailored to students without extensive backgrounds in mathematics and traditional economics; however, many special sections present technical material appropriate for more advanced students. A large number of exercises are also provided for practice with the skills and techniques discussed.

Nolan McCarty is Associate Dean and Professor of Politics and Public Affairs at the Woodrow Wilson School at Princeton University. His recent publications include *Polarized America: The Dance of Ideology and Unequal Riches* (2006, with Keith Poole and Howard Rosenthal) and *The Realignment of National Politics and the Income Distribution* (1997, with Keith Poole and Howard Rosenthal), as well as many articles in periodicals such as the *American Political Science Review* and the *American Journal of Political Science*.

Adam Meirowitz is Associate Professor of Politics and Jonathan Dickenson Bicentennial Preceptor at Princeton University. He has published in periodicals such as the *American Political Science Review*, the *American Journal of Political Science, Games and Economic Behavior*, and *Social Choice and Welfare*.

ANALYTICAL METHODS FOR SOCIAL RESEARCH

Analytical Methods for Social Research presents texts on empirical and formal methods for the social sciences. Volumes in the series address both the theoretical underpinnings of analytical techniques and their application in social research. Some series volumes are broad in scope, cutting across a number of disciplines. Others focus mainly on methodological applications within specific fields such as political science, sociology, demography, and public health. The series serves a mix of students and researchers in the social sciences and statistics.

Series Editors:

R. Michael Alvarez, *California Institute of Technology*
Nathaniel L. Beck, *New York University*
Lawrence L. Wu, *New York University*

Other Titles in the Series:

Event History Modeling: A Guide for Social Scientists, by Janet M. Box-Steffensmeier and Bradford S. Jones

Ecological Inference: New Methodological Strategies, edited by Gary King, Ori Rosen, and Martin A. Tanner

Spatial Models of Parliamentary Voting, by Keith T. Poole

Essential Mathematics for Political and Social Research, by Jeff Gill

Data Analysis Using Regression and Multilevel/Hierarchical Models, by Andrew Gelman and Jennifer Hill

Political Game Theory

AN INTRODUCTION

NOLAN McCARTY
Princeton University

ADAM MEIROWITZ
Princeton University

CAMBRIDGE
UNIVERSITY PRESS

CAMBRIDGE UNIVERSITY PRESS
Cambridge, New York, Melbourne, Madrid, Cape Town, Singapore, São Paulo

Cambridge University Press
32 Avenue of the Americas, New York, NY 10013-2473, USA

www.cambridge.org
Information on this title: www.cambridge.org/9780521841078

First published 2007

Printed in the United States of America

A catalog record for this publication is available from the British Library.

Library of Congress Cataloging in Publication Data
McCarty, Nolan M.
Political game theory : an introduction / Nolan McCarty, Adam Meirowitz.
        p. cm. – (Analytical methods for social research)
Includes bibliographical references.
ISBN 0-521-84107-0 (hardback)
1. Political games.   2. Game theory.   3. Political science – Mathematical models.
I. Meirowitz, Adam.   II. Title.   III. Series.
JA72.5.M33   2006
320.01′5193 – dc22   2006042596

ISBN-13   978-0-521-84107-8 hardback
ISBN-10   0-521-84107-0 hardback

To Moms and Dads, Liz, Janis, Lachlan, and Delaney

Contents

Acknowledgments

The origin of this book is the utter inability of either of its authors to write legibly on a blackboard (or any other surface, for that matter). To save our students from what would have been the most severe form of pedagogical torture, we were forced to commit our lecture notes to an electronic format. Use of this medium also compensated for our inability to spell without the aid of a spell checker.[1] Ultimately we decided that all of the late nights spent typesetting game theory notes should not go in vain. So we undertook to turn them into this book, which, of course, led to more late nights spent typing. We hope these weren't wasted either.

We are most grateful to our students at Columbia and Princeton, on whom we inflicted early versions of our notes and manuscript. Puzzled looks and panicked office hours helped us learn how to convey game theory to students of politics. We also benefited from early conversations with Chris Achen, Scott Ashworth, Larry Bartels, Cathy Hafer, Keith Krehbiel, David Lewis, Kris Ramsay, and Thomas Romer on what a book on political game theory ought to look like. Along the way Stuart Jordan and Natasha Zharinova have provided valuable assistance and feedback. We especially thank John Londregan and Mark Fey for noting mistakes in earlier drafts. Finally, our greatest debts are to those who taught us political game theory:

---

[1] Our misspelling styles are quite distinctive, however. For a given word, McCarty uses completely random spellings whereas Meirowitz consistently misspells the word in exactly the same way.

David Austen-Smith, Jeffrey Banks, David Baron, Bruce Bueno de Mesquito, Thomas Romer, and Howard Rosenthal.

Nolan McCarty
Adam Meirowitz

Princeton, NJ

1 Introduction

In a rather short period of time, game theory has become one of the most powerful analytical tools in the study of politics. From their earliest applications in electoral and legislative behavior, game theoretic models have proliferated in such diverse areas as international security, ethnic cooperation, and democratization. Indeed all fields of political science have benefited from important contributions originating in game theoretic models. Rarely does an issue of the *American Political Science Review*, the *American Journal of Political Science*, or *International Organization* appear without at least one article formulating a new game theoretic model of politics or one providing an empirical test of existing models.

Nevertheless, applications of game theory have not developed as fast in political science as they have in economics. One of the consequences of this uneven development is that most political scientists who wish to learn game theory are forced to rely on textbooks written by and for economists. Although there are many excellent economic game theory texts, their treatments of the subject are often not well suited to the needs of political scientists. First and perhaps most important, the applications and topics are generally those of interest to economists. For example, it is not always obvious to novice political scientists what duopoly or auction theory tells us about political phenomena. Second, there are topics such as voting theory that are indispensable to political game theorists but receive scant coverage in economics texts. Third, many economics treatments presume some level of exposure to ideas in classical price theory. Consequently, the entry barriers to political scientists include not only mathematics but also knowledge of demand curves, marginal rates of substitution, and the like.

Certainly, there have been a few texts by and for political scientists such as those by Ordeshook (1986) and Morrow (1994). We feel, however, that each is dated both in terms of the applications and in terms of the needs of modern political science. Ordeshook remains an outstanding treatment of social choice and spatial theory, yet it was written well before the emergence of noncooperative theory as the dominant paradigm in political game theory. Morrow provides an accessible introduction to the tools of noncooperative game theory, but the analytical level falls short of the contemporary needs of students. Further, it has been a decade since its publication – a decade in which there have been hundreds of important articles and books deploying the tools of game theory. In a more recent series of books, Austen-Smith and Banks (1999 and 2005) address part of this need. The first book, *Positive Political Theory I*, provides a thorough treatment of social choice theory, a topic to which we devote only one chapter. The second book, *Positive Political Theory II*, deals with strategy and institutions, but presumes a knowledge of game theory atypical of first-year students in political science. It is also organized by substantive topics rather than game theoretic ones.

So we have several goals in writing this book. First, we want to write a textbook on political game theory instead of a book on abstract or economic game theory. Consequently, we focus on applications of interest to political scientists and present topics unique to political analysis. Second, in writing a book for political scientists, we want to be cognizant of the diversity of backgrounds and interests of young political scientists. We recognize that most doctoral students in political science enter graduate school with limited mathematical and modeling backgrounds. We feel, however, that it does not serve even those students to ignore the mathematical rigor and key theoretical concepts on which contemporary political models are based. For students needing more remediation, we include a detailed mathematical appendix covering some necessary tools ranging from set theory and analysis to basic optimization and probability theory. Some students enter graduate study in political science with stronger backgrounds in mathematics and economics. We want our book to be useful to this audience as well. Thus, we provide in-depth coverage of some of the more difficult and subtle concepts. We include a number of advanced sections (denoted by * or **) that provide more detail about the analytical and mathematical structure of the models we encounter. These sections can be safely skipped upon first readings by those not quite ready for the more technical material.

1. Organization of the Book

Organizationally, our book departs from standard treatments, because it includes a number of topics that are either directly relevant for political science or designed for remediation in areas in which students of political science have limited backgrounds. Chapter 2 is a self-contained exposition of classical choice theory under conditions of certainty. In this chapter, we introduce the basic ideas of preferences and utility theory. We prove a few key results. Some of these proofs are quite simple, and others appeal to more advanced mathematics and appear in starred sections. The focus of this chapter, however, is on providing the intuition and language of rational choice theory. We also include a section on spatial or Euclidean preferences. This class of preferences plays a central role in voting theory and its application to electoral and legislative politics.

In Chapter 3, we describe how game theorists model choices under uncertainty. The focus is the standard von Neumann-Morgenstern expected utility model, but we also consider some of the most serious criticisms leveled against it. In addition to a standard treatment of risk preferences, we discuss the special implications for risk when actors have spatial preferences.

Chapter 4 provides a cursory review of social choice theory. The chapter is not intended to be a replacement for full-length texts such as those by Peter Ordeshook (1986) and David Austen-Smith and Jeff Banks (1999). Instead it is primarily a reference for those ideas and concepts that have become integral parts of formal political science. These include Arrow's impossibility theorem, the emptiness of the majority core, and the role of single-peaked preferences. This chapter also presents Gibbard-Sattherwaite's theorem about the ubiquity of strategic behavior in social decisions.

Chapter 5 begins our treatment of the heart of contemporary formal political theory: noncooperative game theory. We examine normal form games with complete information and present the most fundamental solution concepts, dominance and Nash equilibrium. Our theoretical development is fairly standard, but we include a number of important political applications. We review the standard Downsian model of electoral competition as well as the extensions developed by Donald Wittman and Randy Calvert. We also present several models of private contributions to public goods based on the work of Thomas Palfrey and Howard Rosenthal. In Chapter 6, we extend the normal form model to cases where agents are uncertain about the payoffs associated with different strategy combinations. After presenting solution concepts for such games, Bayesian Nash equilibria, we consider incomplete information versions of many of the models reviewed in Chapter 5. These comparisons aid understanding of the strategic implications of uncertainty.

Chapter 7 considers dynamic, multistage games of complete information and develops the notion of subgame perfection. Here we focus on a number of applications from legislative politics, democratic transitions, coalition formation, and international crisis bargaining. In Chapter 8, we consider dynamic games in which some players are imperfectly informed about the payoffs of different strategic choices. After explaining how these models are solved, we explore applications drawn from legislative politics, campaign finance, and international bargaining. Signaling games, which have increasingly important applications in political science, are the focus of much of this chapter.

Chapter 9 reviews the theory of repeated games and its application to political science. The role of time discounting and the structure of folk theorems in repeated games are the primary focus of the chapter. Applications include interethnic cooperation and trade wars.

In Chapter 10 we consider applications of bargaining theory. Beginning with the canonical models of Nash and Rubinstein, we focus on the majority-rule bargaining game developed by Baron and Ferejohn. We then consider several examples of bargaining with incomplete information.

In Chapter 11, we illustrate the mechanism design approach to modeling institutions. Our focus is the selection of games that induce equilibrium behavior that meets certain prespecified goals. After presenting the revelation principle and incentive compatibility conditions, we trace out a number of recent applications to electoral politics and organizational design. Building on Chapter 8, we then draw connections between signaling games and mechanism design.

Finally, to keep the book as self-contained as possible, Chapter 12 provides a review of all of the mathematics used. Topics that are integral to the development of key theoretical results or tools for analyzing applications are drawn from the fields of set theory, real analysis, linear algebra, calculus, optimization, and probability theory. Indeed this chapter may serve as a basis for review or self-study. Students interested in working at the frontier of political game theory are encouraged to seek additional course work in order to gain comfort with the mathematical concepts summarized in this appendix.

2 The Theory of Choice

Much of political game theory is predicated on the idea that people rationally pursue goals subject to constraints imposed by physical resources and the expected behavior of other actors. The assumption of rationality is often controversial. Indeed one of the most lively debates in the social sciences is the role of rationality and intentionality as a predictor of behavior. Nevertheless, we omit the debate between *Homo economicus* and *Homo sociologicus* and jump immediately into the classical model of rational choice.

For almost all of our purposes, it is sufficient to define rationality on a basis of two simple ideas:

(1) Confronted with any two options, denoted x and y, a person can determine whether he does not prefer option x to option y, does not prefer y to x, or does not prefer either. When preferences satisfy this property, they are *complete*.

(2) Confronted with three options x, y, and z, if a person does not prefer y to x and does not prefer z to y, then she must not prefer z to x. Preferences satisfying this property are *transitive*.

Roughly speaking, our working definition of rational behavior is behavior consistent with complete and transitive preferences. Sometimes we call such behavior *thinly* rational, as properties 1 and 2 contain little or no substantive content about human desires. Thin rationality contrasts with *thick* rationality whereby analysts specify concrete goals such as wealth, status, or fame. The thin characterization of rationality is consistent with a very large number of these substantive goals. In principal, thinly rational agents could be motivated by any number of factors including ideology, normative values, or even religion. As long as these belief systems produce complete and transitive orderings over personal and social outcomes, we can use the classical theory of choice to model behavior.

Although it is appealing to avoid explicit assumptions about substantive goals, it is often necessary to make stronger assumptions about preferences. For example, a model might assume that an interest group wishes to maximize the wealth of its members or that a politician wishes to maximize her reelection chances. In subsequent chapters, we explore models that make such assumptions about agent preferences. But rational models may be just as useful in developing models of activists who wish to minimize environmental degradation or the number of abortions for principled, nonmaterial reasons.

In the following sections, we develop the classical theory of choice under *certainty*. By certainty, we mean simply that each agent has sufficient information about her available set of actions that she can perfectly predict the consequences of each. Later we examine choice under uncertainty – where the actor's lack of information forces her to choose among actions with uncertain consequences.

1. Finite Sets of Actions and Outcomes

We begin with the simplest description of a choice problem: an agent chooses an action from a finite list. We denote these alternatives as a set $A = \{a_1, \ldots, a_k\}$. A leader involved in an international crisis might face the following set of alternatives: $A = \{send\ troops,\ negotiate,\ do\ nothing\}$. An American voter might choose among $A = \{vote\ Democrat,\ vote\ Republican,\ abstain\}$.

As mentioned, we assume, for now, that agents have *complete* information – they are sufficiently knowledgeable that they perfectly predict the consequences of each action. To formalize this idea, we define outcome sets as $X = \{x_1, \ldots, x_n\}$. In our crisis example, let $X = \{win\ major\ concessions\ and\ lose\ troops,\ win\ minor\ concessions,\ status\ quo\}$. The assumption of certainty implies that each action $a \in A$ maps directly onto one and only one $x \in X$. Formally, certainty implies that there exists a function $x : A \to X$ that maps each action into a specific outcome. For convenience, we also assume that all of the outcomes listed in X are feasible – each outcome is the consequence of at least one action. Thus, x_i is feasible if there exists an $a \in A$ such that $x(a) = x_i$. With certainty and feasibility, it makes no difference whether we speak of an agent's preferences over actions or his preferences over outcomes. Consequently, we concentrate on the agent's preferences over outcomes. In Chapter 3, the assumption of uncertainty or *incomplete* information makes the distinction between actions and outcomes relevant.

To generate predictions about choice behavior, we require a more formal notion of preferences. *Weak preference* is captured by a binary relation R where the notation $x_i R x_j$ means that outcome x_j is not preferred to policy x_i. If $x_i R x_j$, x_i is "weakly" preferred to x_j.[1] By way of analogy, note that R is similar to the binary relation $\geq$ (greater than or equal) that operates on real numbers.

Beyond the weak preference relation R, we define two other important binary relations: strict preference and indifference.

DEFINITION 2.1 *For any $x, y \in X$, $x P y$ (x is strictly preferred to y) if and only if $x R y$ and not $y R x$. Alternatively, $x I y$ (x is indifferent to y) if and only if $x R y$ and $y R x$.*

Accordingly, P denotes strict preference and I denotes indifference. Returning to the analogy of $\geq$, the strict relation derived from $\geq$ is equivalent to the relation $>$ and the indifference relation derived from $\geq$ is equivalent to the relation $=$.

Although preferences expressed in the form of binary relations are useful concepts, we are ultimately interested in behavior. Given a set of preferences, an agent's behavior is rational so long as she selects an outcome that she values at least as much as any other. Consequently, a rational agent chooses an $x^* \in X$ (read x^* in X) such that $x^* R y$ for every $y \in X$. Without adding more structure to preferences, however, there is no guarantee that such an optimal outcome exists. We now turn to the conditions on X and R to ensure that such a best choice is meaningful and well defined. We begin with the following formal definition.

DEFINITION 2.2 *For a weak preference relation R on a choice set X, the maximal set $M(R, X) \subset X$ is defined as $M(R, X) = \{x \in X : x R y \forall y \in X\}$ (read as $M(R, X)$ is the set of x's in X such that $x R y$ for all y in X).*

The fundamental tenet of rationality is that *agents choose outcomes from the maximal set*. Of course, this requirement is meaningful only if

---

[1] Formally, a binary relation R is a subset of $X \times X$ such that if $(x, y) \in R$ then $x R y$.

the maximal set contains at least one outcome. Consequently, we are interested in the properties of preferences that guarantee that $M(R, X)$ is nonempty.

The easiest way for the maximal set to be empty is for R to be silent between a pair of outcomes. If neither $x R y$ or $y R x$, it is not clear what a rational choice is. Two conditions ensure that all elements of X are ordered.

DEFINITION 2.3 *A binary relation R on X is*

(1) complete if for all $x, y \in X$ with $x \neq y$, either $x R y$ or $y R x$ or both.
(2) reflexive if for all $x \in X$, $x R x$.

Completeness means simply that the agent can compare any two outcomes. This may not be a terribly controversial assumption, but we all know people who cannot seem to make up their minds.[2] Reflexivity is a more technical condition. Some authors choose to define completeness in a slightly different manner that also captures reflexivity.[3]

Although these properties rule out the noncomparability problem, completeness and reflexivity do not ensure that rational choices exist. We also must rule out the following problem: $x P y$, $y P z$, and $z P x$. The problem is that there is no reasonable choice – why choose y when you can choose x, why choose x when you can choose z, and why choose z when you can choose y? Each of the following restrictions on preferences resolves this problem.

DEFINITION 2.4 *A binary relation R on X is*

(1) transitive if $x R y$ and $y R z$ implies $x R z$ for all $x, y, z \in X$.
(2) quasi-transitive if $x P y$ and $y P z$ implies $x P z$ for all $x, y, z \in X$.
(3) acyclic if on any finite set $\{x_1, x_2 \dots , x_n\} \in X$ $x_i P x_{i+1}$ for all $i < n$ implies $x_1 R x_n$.

Note the subtle differences among these definitions. Transitivity and quasi transitivity may seem innocuous, but they are strong assumptions that might be violated even by very reasonable behavior. For example,

---

[2] Many economists and psychologists, however, have been concerned about the assumption of completeness. A theory of choice without this condition has been derived.
[3] For all $x, y \in X$, either $x R y$ or $y R x$ or both.

suppose X is a set of 1,000 different bottles of beer. Beer b_1 has had one drop of beer replaced with one drop of plain water, b_2 has had two drops replaced, and so on, to $b_{1,000}$. Unless one is a master brewer, $b_1 I b_2$, and $b_2 I b_3, \ldots,$ and $b_{999} I b_{1,000}$. Because $x I y$ implies $x R y$ (by the definition of I), then $b_{1,000} R b_{999}, \ldots, b_2 R b_1$. If the relation is transitive, we derive $b_{1,000} R b_1$. But clearly, $b_1 P b_{1,000}$.[4] The assumption of acyclicity does not suffer from this problem, however, and is typically sufficient for our purposes. Despite the problems associated with transitivity, we maintain it as an assumption (rather than acyclicity) to simplify many of the results that follow.

The properties of completeness, reflexivity, and transitivity together form the basis of a *weak ordering*.

DEFINITION 2.5 *Given a set X, a weak ordering is a binary relation that is complete, reflexive, and transitive.*

Our recurring analogy of $\geq$ satisfies all of the conditions for a weak ordering. We now state our first result.

THEOREM 2.1 *If X is finite and R is a weak ordering then $M(R, X) \neq \emptyset$.*

Theorem 2.1 guarantees that there is a best choice so long as the choice set is finite and that R is complete, reflexive, and transitive. Its proof follows.

Proof Let X be finite and R be complete, reflexive, and transitive. We establish the result by induction (see Mathematical Induction in the Mathematical Appendix) on the number of elements in X.

Step 1: If X has one element, $X = \{x\}$. From reflexivity $x R x$, $M(R, X) = \{x\}$.

Step 2: We show that if the statement of the theorem is true that for any set X' with n elements and weak ordering R' on X' then it must be true for any X with $n + 1$ elements and weak ordering R on X.

Proof of Step 2: Assume that $M(R', X') \neq \emptyset$ for any X' with n elements and weak ordering R'. Now consider a set X with $n + 1$ elements and any weak ordering R. For an arbitrary $x \in X$, $X = X' \cup \{x\}$ with X' a set having n elements. Let R' denote the restriction of R to X' (i.e.,

---

[4] This is approximately the difference between Guinness and Coors Light.

$R \cap \{X' \times X'\}$). By assumption $M(R', X') \neq \emptyset$. So for an arbitrary $y \in M(R', X')$ either yRx or xRy or both by completeness.

If yRx, then yRz for all $z \in X' \cup \{x\}$ and thus $y \in M(R, X)$ and we have proved step 2. Now assume xRy. Note that $y \in M(R', X')$ implies that yRz for any $z \in X'$. Thus for any $z \in X'$, xRy and yRz. Because R is transitive, xRz for any $z \in X'$. This implies that xRw for any $w \in X'$. Thus $x \in M(R, X)$, and we have proved step 2.

By mathematical induction, steps 1 and 2 establish the theorem. $\square$

It turns out that a weak preference ordering is unnecessary for establishing that $M(R, X)$ is nonempty. The statement of this Theorem follows. Because the proof is a bit more complicated, we leave it as an exercise.

THEOREM 2.2 *Let X be finite and R be a complete and reflexive binary relation on X. $M(R, S) \neq \emptyset$ on any $S \subset X$ (except $S = \emptyset$) if and only if R is acyclic.*

Even with a finite choice space and no uncertainty the theory of choice is fairly rich. Austen-Smith and Banks (1999) is a good first source for students interested in further study. In the next, more technical, section, we consider rational choice when the set of outcomes is not finite. We derive an analog to Theorem 2.1 for such choice sets. Although the results are conceptually similar, additional mathematical structure on the choice sets and preferences is required.

2. Continuous Choice Spaces*

2.1. Nonemptiness of $M(R, X)$. The assumption of a finite choice space is crucial for the proof of Theorem 2.1 because it allows us to use mathematical induction. For an infinite number of choices, however, this approach does not work. If agents choose from a continuum (e.g., the set of real numbers denoted $\mathbb{R}$ or the set $[0, 1] = \{x \in \mathbb{R} : x \geq 0$ and $x \leq 1\}$), we need more structure on preferences to ensure that $M(R, S) \neq \emptyset$. Two simple examples demonstrate how matters can go wrong.

EXAMPLE 2.1 *Let $X = (0, 1)$ (or let $X = \mathbb{R}^1$) and let R be equivalent to $\geq$ so that xRy if and only if $x \geq y$. The set $M(\geq, X)$ is empty.*

To see why $M(\geq, (0, 1))$ is empty, note that for every $x \in X$ there exists some $y \in X$ for which $y > x$. There is no x such that $x R y$ for all $y \in X$. That $(0, 1)$ has no biggest element is the key to this example. If X were a closed interval such as $[0, 1]$, however, there would be no problem: $M(\geq, [0, 1]) = \{1\}$. This is a strong hint that the nonemptiness of the maximal set may depend on the choice set's being "closed." Another example provides additional clues.

EXAMPLE 2.2 *Let* $X = [0, 1]$ *and define* R *as follows:* $x R y$ *if* $\max\{x, y\} \leq 1/2$ *and* $x \geq y$ *or if* $\min\{x, y\} > 1/2$ *and* $x \leq y$ *or if* $x > 1/2$ *and* $y \leq 1/2$. *The set* $M(R, X)$ *is empty.*

No element of $[0, 1/2]$ is a member of $M(R, X)$ – any element of $[0, 1/2]$ is defeated by every element of $(1/2, 1]$. Elements of $(1/2, 1]$ also cannot be elements of $M(R, X)$ because the preference ordering increases as the choice gets closer to $1/2$ but $1/2$ is not in this set. Thus, the problem is quite similar to that of the first example. In this example, however, the problem is not with X; it is a closed interval. Instead, the problem is with R. It jumps at $1/2$. Outcomes slightly less than or equal $1/2$ are among the least preferred, but those slightly greater are among the most preferred. It is this discontinuity in preferences that generates the empty maximal set.

Before turning these examples and intuitions into general axioms, we review a few mathematical concepts.[5] We begin with the assumption that preferences are defined on n-dimensional Euclidean space and consider choices from subsets, $X \subset \mathbb{R}^n$. A point in such a space is written as a vector $x = (x^1, x^2, \ldots, x^n)$ where each coordinate x^i is a point in $\mathbb{R}^1$.

One of our primary concerns is whether the set X is *open* or *closed*. Openness can be demonstrated with the simplest example of $\mathbb{R}^1$. A set $A \subset \mathbb{R}^1$ is open if for every point $x \in A$ there is some number $\varepsilon > 0$ such that $y \in A$ for any $y \in X$ satisfying $|x - y| < \varepsilon$. Therefore, a set is open if all the points close to any given point in the set are also elements of the set. Clearly, the set $(0, 1)$ is open. For each point in the set, there are some points higher and some points lower that are also in the set. Thus, for any point $x \in (0, 1)$, there is a number ε such

---

[5] More precisely we use a few topological concepts. Students interested in further study of choice theory would be well served by a tour of the Mathematical Appendix to this book or, better yet, a text on real analysis. An approachable introductory text is Gaughan (1993). A more complete text is A. N. Kolmogorov and S. V. Fomin (1970).

that $x - \varepsilon$ and $x + \varepsilon$ are also in $(0, 1)$. A set is closed if its complement is open. Therefore, because $(0, 1)$ is open, $(-\infty, 0] \cup [1, \infty)$ is closed. Intervals such as $[0, 1]$ are also closed. Some sets may be neither open nor closed such as $[0, 1)$.

To generalize these concepts to the n-dimensional Euclidean space, we use a measure of distance called the *norm*:

$$\|x - y\| = \sqrt{\sum_{i=1}^{n} (x^i - y^i)^2}.$$

The quantity $\|x - y\|$ is the distance between points x and y and generalizes the absolute value used in $\mathbb{R}^1$. Given this definition of distance, we generalize the interval into a *ball*.

DEFINITION 2.6 *An open ball of radius $\varepsilon > 0$ and center $x \in X$ is denoted $B(x, \varepsilon) = \{y \in X : \|x - y\| < \varepsilon\}$.*

Now it is easy to define openness.

DEFINITION 2.7 *A set $A \subset \mathbb{R}^n$ is open if for every $x \in A$ there is some $\varepsilon > 0$ such that $B(x, \varepsilon) \subset A$.*

Just as before, a set is closed if its complement is open. Consequently, closed sets have the property that some points are on the boundary so that all open balls contain points outside the set.

DEFINITION 2.8 *A set $A \subset \mathbb{R}^n$ is closed if its complement $C = \mathbb{R}^n \backslash A$ is an open set.*

Recall our first example. Because X is an open set, there is an open ball around each x in X that is contained in X. As each of these balls contains points weakly preferred to X, no maximal set can exist. If $X = [0, 1]$, any open ball around 1 contains points outside X. Because all of the points preferred to 1 lie outside $[0, 1]$, $M(\geq, [0, 1]) = 1$. Closed outcome sets are not sufficient for nonempty maximal sets, however. Recall that $(-\infty, 0] \cup [1, \infty)$ is a closed set, but $M(\geq, (-\infty, 0] \cup [1, \infty))$ is empty. The problem, of course, is that there is no upper bound on this set, so for any x there is a $y > x$ so that yPx. Therefore, another important condition is *boundedness*.

DEFINITION 2.9 *A set $A \subset \mathbb{R}^n$ is bounded if there exists a finite number b such that for every $x \in A$ it is the case that $\|x\| < b$.*

The set $(-\infty, 0] \cup [1, \infty)$ clearly fails this criterion so we can rule it out by requiring that choice sets be bounded. It is easy to see in example 2.1 so long as X is closed and bounded $M(\geq, X)$ is nonempty. In $\mathbb{R}^n$, the following definition is used often.

DEFINITION 2.10 *A set $A \subset \mathbb{R}^n$ is compact if it is closed and bounded.*

Because all examples and problems in this book deal with subsets of Euclidean spaces, we could stop here. In arbitrary choice spaces, however, the equivalence between compactness and closedness and boundedness does not hold. Ironically, the proof of nonemptiness of the maximal set result is easier using a more general definition of compactness (even if we lose some of the intuition of our examples). The more general definition of compactness is based on sets known as *open covers*. An open cover for a set A is a collection of open sets whose union contains A.

DEFINITION 2.11 *Given a set A, an open covering of A is a collection of sets $\{O_\theta\}_{\theta \in \Theta}$ where Θ is an arbitrary index set and the sets O_θ are open for every $\theta \in \Theta$ such that $A \subset \{\cup_{\theta \in \Theta} O_\theta\}$ (in other words, if $x \in A$, then there is some $\theta \in \Theta$ such that $x \in O_\theta$).*

The general definition of compactness can now be given.

DEFINITION 2.12 *A set A is compact if for any open covering $\{O_\theta\}_{\theta \in \Theta}$ of A there exists some finite set $B \subset \Theta$, such that the finite covering $\{O_\theta\}_{\theta \in B}$ is a covering of A (i.e., $A \subset \cup_{\theta \in B} O_\theta$).*

These definitions are subtle for those not familiar with analysis so an example is surely warranted. Consider $\mathbb{R}^1$ and two subsets $[0, 1]$ and $(0, 1)$. We already know that $(0, 1)$ is not compact because it is not closed. To demonstrate that $(0, 1)$ is not compact using Definition 2.12, consider the following open covering of $(0, 1)$. For each $\theta \in \Theta = \{3, 4, 5, \ldots\}$, let $O_\theta = (1/\theta, 1 - 1/\theta)$. This is a collection of open intervals centered at $1/2$, and the width of the intervals approaches 1 as θ gets larger. Is $\{O_\theta\}_{\theta \in \Theta}$ an open covering of $(0, 1)$? Yes, for any element in $x \in (0, 1)$ there is a θ big enough that $x \in (1/\theta, 1 - 1/\theta)$. So we have constructed an open covering of $(0, 1)$. Definition 2.12 requires that there be a finite subset $B \subset \{3, 4, 5, \ldots \ldots\}$ so that $(0, 1) \subset \cup_{\theta \in B} O_\theta$. But for any finite set B, there is a finite largest element $\theta^* \in B$.[6] The value $\frac{1}{\theta^*}$ is strictly larger than 0 and because $(0, 1)$ contains points arbitrarily close to 0, $\frac{1}{\theta^*}$ is strictly larger than some element of $(0, 1)$. Accordingly, for any finite collection of subsets in the open covering, we can find an element of $(0, 1)$ that is not contained in any set O_θ for $\theta \in B$. Definition 2.12 demonstrates that $(0, 1)$ is not compact. The reader should try to prove that $[0, 1]$ is compact using the open covering definition.[7]

Having specified some desirable properties of X, we turn to properties of R. Not surprisingly, given example 2.2, it is useful for R not to have jumps. We use the definition of upper and lower contour sets to define continuity of R.[8]

DEFINITION 2.13 *Given a binary relation R on $\mathbb{R}^n$ the strict upper contour set of a point $x \in \mathbb{R}^n$ is $P(x) \equiv \{y \in \mathbb{R}^n : yPx\}$. The strict lower contour set of point x is the set $P^{-1}(x) \equiv \{y \in \mathbb{R}^n : xPy\}$. The level set of x is the set of points for which the agent is indifferent to x or $I(x) \equiv \{y \in \mathbb{R}^n : yRx \text{ and } xRy\}$.*

For any x, the upper contour set contains the points that are strictly preferred to x, the lower contour contains the points that x is preferred to, and the level set contains the points indifferent to x.

DEFINITION 2.14 *A binary relation R on $\mathbb{R}^n$ is*

(1) upper continuous if $P(x)$ is open for all $x \in \mathbb{R}^n$
(2) lower continuous if $P^{-1}(x)$ is open for all $x \in \mathbb{R}^n$
(3) continuous if it is both lower and upper continuous.

---

[6] The reader can prove this sentence by noting that $\geq$ is a weak ordering and applying our result about the nonemptiness of the maximal set for finite sets.

[7] We direct the reader to the Heine-Borel theorem that relates the topological open-covering and Euclidean closed-and-bounded definitions of compactness for $\mathbb{R}^n$. Gaughan (1993) presents a particularly detailed proof of the result for $\mathbb{R}^1$.

[8] In political science, the upper contour set is often referred to as the "preferred to set." Keith Krehbiel has pointed out to both authors on numerous occasions that this terminology (along with many others) contains a redundancy. Thus, he and we implore all readers to use our preferred term *preferred set*.

Consider the implications of these conditions. Given a point x, completeness implies that any other point y is an element of either $P(x)$, $P^{-1}(x)$, or $I(x)$. Continuity implies that if $y \in P(x)$ then all points sufficiently close to y are in $P(x)$ as well. Similarly, if $y \in P^{-1}(x)$ nearby points are also in $P^{-1}(x)$. This implies that small perturbations of y should not affect its preference ordering with respect to x.

Example 2.2 illustrates how continuity helps rule out anomalous behavior. In that example $P^{-1}(1/2 + \varepsilon) = (-\infty, 1/2] \cup (1/2 + \varepsilon, 1]$. So the lower contour set is not open. If the preferences were lower continuous, there would be no jump in the preference ordering.

We now state sufficient conditions for a nonempty maximal set.

THEOREM 2.3 *If X is nonempty and compact, and R on X is complete, reflexive, transitive, and lower continuous, then $M(R, X) \neq \emptyset$.*

The proof of this result is more technical than most other sections of this book. But the result holds very generally. This allows us to apply it to choice problems in which x is an infinite sequence of outcomes, a function, or a probability distribution.

Proof Let X be nonempty and compact, and let R be complete, reflexive, transitive, and lower continuous. To establish a contradiction, assume that $M(R, X) = \emptyset$. Consequently, every point in X is contained in $P^{-1}(\alpha)$ for some $\alpha \in X$. Because R is lower continuous every such $P^{-1}(\alpha)$ is open. This means that $\{P^{-1}(\alpha)\}_{\alpha \in X}$ is an open covering of X. Because X is compact, there exists a finite set of points $B \subset X$ for which the collection $\{P^{-1}(\alpha)\}_{\alpha \in B}$ is also a covering of X. So for all $x \in X$ it is the case that $x \in P^{-1}(\alpha)$ for some $\alpha \in B$ (an appropriate α is chosen for each X). But from Theorem 2.1, $M(R, B) \neq \emptyset$ because B is finite and R is complete, reflexive, and transitive. Thus, $x^* \in M(R, B)$ exists. Now consider any arbitrary point $y \in X$. Either y is an element of $M(R, B)$ or it is not. By definition, $x^* I y$ if $y \in M(R, B)$ so that $x^* R y$. Now suppose $y \notin M(R, B)$. Because $\{P^{-1}(\alpha)\}_{\alpha \in B}$ covers X, there is some $\alpha \in B$ such that $y \in P^{-1}(\alpha)$. This means that $\alpha R y$. Because $x^* \in M(R, B)$, however, we know that $x^* R \alpha$. Because R is transitive on X, this implies that $x^* R y$. Thus, we have shown that for all $y \in X$, $x^* R y$. This implies that $x^* \in M(R, X)$ contradicting the emptiness of $M(R, X)$. □

Theorem 2.3 establishes sufficient, but not necessary, conditions. Sometimes we encounter situations in which X is either unbounded or not closed, and R is discontinuous. In each of these possibilities, the nonemptiness of $M(R, X)$ must be established by other means. Violations of the compactness of X generally require stronger assumptions about R whereas violations of continuity require more structure on X.

2.2. Uniqueness of $M(R, X)$. It is valuable to know whether or not $M(R, X)$ has a unique element. If the choice set is finite, we can guarantee a unique element of $M(R, X)$ by assuming that all preferences are strict. Without indifference, $M(R, X)$ cannot contain more than a single element if X is finite.

If the choice space is not finite, however, additional structure is needed to ensure that $M(R, X)$ contains a single element. Many applications impose an additional condition on X and an additional condition on R. Typically, we assume that X is a convex set. Convexity requires that if x and y are points in X all the points on the line segment between x and y must also be in X.

DEFINITION 2.15 *A set $X \subset \mathbb{R}^n$ is convex if for any $x, y \in X$ the point $\lambda x + (1 - \lambda)y$ is an element of X for every $\lambda \in [0, 1]$.*

The point $\lambda x + (1 - \lambda)y$ is often called a convex combination (or a weighted average) of x and y. For example, the set $[0, 1]$ is convex because any point between two points in the set is also in the set. Alternatively, $X = [0, 1/4] \cup [3/4, 0]$ is not convex because $\lambda/4 + (1 - \lambda)3/4 \notin X$ for any $\lambda \in (0, 1)$. Informally, convexity requires that there are no "holes" in the outcome set. If the outcome set has more than one dimension, convexity also requires that its surface not have any appendages. Look at your hand. Convex combinations of points on your thumb and index finger are not part of it.[9] Your hand is not convex.

The sufficient condition on preferences is also called convexity.

DEFINITION 2.16 *Preference relation R defined on the convex set X is convex if $x R y$ implies $[\lambda x + (1 - \lambda)y] R y$ for any $\lambda \in (0, 1)$ and all distinct points $x, y \in X$. Preference relation R is strictly convex if $x R y$ implies $[\lambda x + (1 - \lambda)y] P y$ for any $\lambda \in (0, 1)$ and all distinct points $x, y \in X$.*

Essentially, convex preferences have the property that if the agent prefers x to y she also prefers convex combinations of x and y to y.

---

[9] Game theorists spend a lot of time contemplating such ironies.

Strict convexity goes a step further. Even if the agent is only indifferent between x and y, she still prefers the convex combination to either x or y. We leave it as an exercise to show that convexity of R implies that the upper contour sets $P^{-1}(x)$ are convex. Because the upper contour sets are convex, they cannot have holes or appendages. Strict convexity also rules out flat spots on the boundaries of the upper contours.

The following result is easy to establish.

THEOREM 2.4 *If X is convex and R (defined on X) is strictly convex then $M(R, X)$ contains at most one element.*

Proof To establish a contradiction assume that X is convex, R is strictly convex, and two distinct policies x, y are both in $M(R, X)$. For arbitrary $\lambda \in (0, 1)$ the point $[\lambda x + (1 - \lambda)y]$ is in X because X is convex. But R is strictly convex so that $[\lambda x + (1 - \lambda)y] \, Py$. But this contradicts the assumptions that $y \in M(R, X)$. $\square$

Theorem 2.3 guarantees that a rational choice exists if the choice set is compact and the weak ordering is lower continuous. If the choice set is convex and the preference ordering is strictly convex, the rational choice is unique.

3. Utility Theory

The model of choice and rationality described previously is based on the use of binary preferences and the maximal set. Binary operators, however, can be hard to work with except in the most trivial models. Numbers on the other hand are easy to work with. If we can associate a number with each element of the outcome set, then we can just use the $\geq$ operator to compare alternatives. In this section we explore the conditions under which it is possible to represent outcome sets as sets of real numbers and use $\geq$ as the preference operator. In other words, we would like to represent preferences using a utility function (a real-valued function with domain X) such that

$$u(x) \geq u(y) \text{ implies } x\,Ry,$$
$$u(x) > u(y) \text{ implies } x\,Py, \text{ and}$$
$$u(x) = u(y) \text{ implies } x\,Iy.$$

The idea of utility has been the subject of philosophical and moral debates over the past 300 years, but again we use a narrow definition. Utilities are simply numerical representations of preferences for which $\geq$ is the appropriate preference operator – we imbue them with no additional normative content.

At our current level of generality, utility functions are ordinal: they are used only to rank alternatives. In particular, they do not tell us how much something is preferred to something else. The value $u(x) - u(y)$ has no meaning. Any function w such that $w(x) \geq w(y)$ if and only if $u(x) \geq u(y)$ represents exactly the same preferences as u. This indicates that comparing utilities across agents is generally not a meaningful exercise. As we discuss in the next chapter, however, the standard model of choice under uncertainty presumes that utility functions contain more than ordinal information.

The following is a formal definition of a utility function.

DEFINITION 2.17 *Given X and R on X, we say the utility function $u : X \to \mathbb{R}^1$ represents R if for all $x, y \in X$, $u(x) \geq u(y)$ if and only if $x R y$.*

Using this definition it is quite easy to show that $u(x) > u(y)$ if and only if $x P y$ and $u(x) = u(y)$ if and only if $x I y$. If X is finite the existence of a utility representation of R hinges only on R's being complete, reflexive, and transitive.

Just as in the last section, we can characterize the agent's optimal choice. Let x be a maximizer of $u : X \to \mathbb{R}^1$ if $u(x) \geq u(y)$ for all $y \in X$. As the next result shows the existence of a maximizer and the nonemptiness of $M(R, X)$ are equivalent.

THEOREM 2.5 *If the function $u(\cdot)$ is a utility representation of R on choice set X then $M(R, X) = \arg\max_{x \in X}\{u(x)\}$.*

Proof To show that $M(R, X) \subset \arg\max_{x \in X}\{u(x)\}$, assume that $u(\cdot)$ represents R and that $x' \in M(R, X)$. Because $x' \in M(R, X)$, $x' R y$ for all $y \in X$. Consequently, $u(x') \geq u(y)$ for all $y \in X$. Thus $x \in \arg\max_{x \in X}\{u(x)\}$. To show that $\arg\max_{x \in X}\{u(x)\} \subset M(R, X)$ assume that $u(\cdot)$ represents R and that $x' \in \arg\max_{x \in X}\{u(x)\}$. Then $u(x') \geq u(y)$ for all $y \in X$, which implies that $x' R y$ for all $y \in X$. Thus $x \in M(R, X)$. $\square$

If X is finite and R is complete, reflexive, and transitive, $M(R, X)$ is nonempty (e.g., Theorem 2.1); thus a maximizer of $u(x)$ must exist. If X is not finite, however, further conditions on X and the utility function are required to ensure the existence of maximizers. In the next advanced section we consider utility functions on nonfinite outcome spaces.

4. Utility Representations on Continuous Choice Spaces*

For the same reasons that continuity of preferences is important in establishing uniqueness of $M(R, X)$, we often assume utility functions are continuous.

DEFINITION 2.18 *A function $f : X \to \mathbb{R}^1$ is continuous if the following statement is true for every $x \in X$. For every $\varepsilon > 0$ there exists some $\delta > 0$ such that $\left| f(x) - f(y) \right| < \varepsilon$ if $\|x - y\| < \delta$.*

As is often taught to high school students, a continuous function is one that can be drawn without lifting the pencil. Substantively, a continuous utility function is one that produces almost identical utilities for outcomes that are close together.

The following sufficient conditions on preferences ensure that a continuous utility representation exists.

THEOREM 2.6 *(Debreu, 1959) If $X \subset \mathbb{R}^n$ and R is complete, reflexive, transitive, and continuous, then there exists a continuous utility function $u : X \to \mathbb{R}^1$ that represents R.*

We do not prove this claim.[10] Nevertheless the converse is not difficult to establish, and we leave it as an exercise. A result analogous to theorem 2.3 is the following.

THEOREM 2.7 *If $X \subset \mathbb{R}^n$ is compact and $u : X \to \mathbb{R}^1$ is continuous, then a maximizer exists.*

---

[10] We do, however, encourage the interested student to look at Debreu's monograph (1959).

This result is sometimes known as the Weierstrass Theorem. We do not prove the result here (see Royden (1988) for a proof); Theorem 2.3 is actually a stronger result requiring only lower continuity (i.e., for every x the set $\{y : u(y) < u(x)\}$ is open) and compactness.

As noted earlier, utility functions are somewhat arbitrary; they contain ordinal but not cardinal information. Consequently, there is nothing intrinsically meaningful about any particular value of a utility function. All that matters is the ordering of $u(x)$ and $u(y)$ for any two $x, y \in X$. We say that $f : \mathbb{R}^1 \to \mathbb{R}^1$ is a strictly increasing function if for all $x, y \in X$ $x > y$ implies that $f(x) > f(y)$. Utility functions are defined only up to strictly increasing transformations. This means that if $u : X \to \mathbb{R}^1$ represents R and $f(\cdot)$ is a strictly increasing transformation, then $f \circ u : X \to \mathbb{R}^1$ represents R where $f \circ u : X \to \mathbb{R}^1$ is a nice way to write the function that maps x into $f(u(x))$. Rescaling a utility function has no consequence for choice, and the magnitude of a utility function has no natural meaning.

Although we have listed conditions sufficient to guarantee a maximizer of a utility function, we have not characterized the maximizer. If utility functions are differentiable, however, the tools of calculus allow us to characterize optimal choices. The Mathematical Appendix reviews key results from calculus and optimization theory.

5. Spatial Preferences

In most economic applications, outcomes are denominated in money (incomes, wealths, wages, profits, etc.) or commodities (widgets, gizmos, chili burritos). It is sensible to assume that larger outcomes are preferred to smaller outcomes (except perhaps in the case of chili burritos). In other words, many of the preferences considered in economics are nonsatiable in that agents believe either that more is always better (i.e., money) or that less is always better (air pollution). In political game theory, however, many of the outcomes we want to study are policies in which at least some agents have a most preferred outcome that is neither 0 or infinite (e.g., taxes, welfare benefits, or abortion restrictions). A voter's utility may be increasing in tax rates below some level and decreasing for higher levels. A voter may prefer restrictions on abortion only so stringent as outlawing them in the third trimester but not otherwise. Thus, in applications it is often necessary to assume that

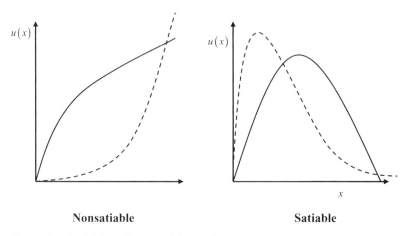

Figure 2.1. Satiable and Nonsatiable Utility Functions.

political actors have satiable preferences. Formally, an agent has satiable preferences if $M(X, R)$ contains elements that are interior to the
outcome space X. Similarly, preferences are satiable when the maximizer of $u : X \to \mathbb{R}$ is in the interior of X. Figure 2.1 illustrates the
difference between satiable and nonsatiable preferences.

The most common application of satiable preferences is the *spatial
model* that represents policy outcomes as points in a subset of $\mathbb{R}^d$. In
principle, one could specify very general preferences of this sort, but
in practice (and most applications in this book) it is generally assumed
that voters have *single-peaked* and *symmetric* preferences. We discuss
single peakedness in more detail in Chapter 4, but for now we simply
note that it implies that the agent's maximal set has a single element
and that the utility function has a single maximizer. This most preferred
policy outcome is the agent's *ideal point*. The assumption of symmetry
requires that the agent's utility declines at the same rate regardless
of direction. This implies that preferences are a decreasing function
of the distance between the policy outcome and the agent's ideal
point.

If the policy space is one-dimensional, single-peaked, symmetric
preferences are represented by utility functions of the form $u_i(x) =
h(-|x - z_i|)$ where z_i is agent i's ideal point and h is an increasing func-
tion. The two most popular examples are the linear, $u_i(x) = -|x - z_i|$
and quadratic utility functions $u_i(x) = -(x - z_i)^2$. These functions are
plotted in Figure 2.2.

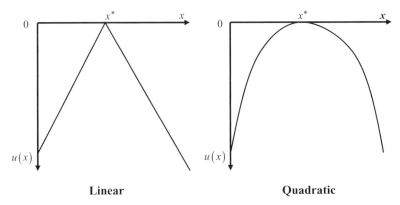

Linear   **Quadratic**

Figure 2.2. Linear and Quadratic Preferences.

In outcome spaces with more than one dimension (i.e., $X \subset \mathbb{R}^d$), distances are generally measured by the Euclidean norm defined as

$$\|x - y\| = \sqrt{\sum_{j=1}^{n}\left(x^j - z_i^j\right)^2}.$$

Thus, symmetric, single-peaked preferences take the form

$$u_i(x) = h(-\|x - z_i\|)$$

where again, $z_i \in \mathbb{R}^d$ is the ideal point of agent i, and h is an increasing function.

It is difficult to visualize utility functions over multidimensional spaces. For two dimensions, however, graphical analysis is simplified because each agent's preferred sets (i.e., $P(y) = \{x \in X | x\,Ry\}$) form circular regions centered on the agent's ideal point. Similarly, given a policy y, an agent is indifferent between y and all of the points on the circle through y centered on her ideal point. These sets are illustrated in Figure 2.3. For any indifference curve, an agent prefers an outcome inside the circle to any outside it.

One of the reasons that single-peaked, symmetric preferences are so popular in applied political game theoretic models is the ease with which the predicted choices of agents can be characterized. As long as one is willing to make the appropriate assumptions, choice over a pair

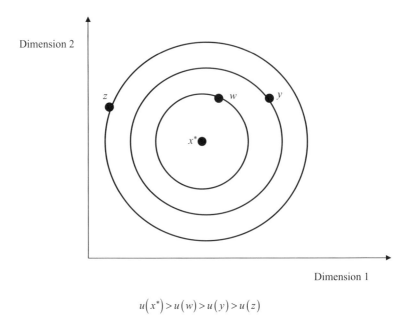

$$u\left(x^*\right) > u\left(w\right) > u\left(y\right) > u\left(z\right)$$

Figure 2.3. Indifference Curves for Two-Dimensional Quadratic Preferences.

of outcomes can be characterized by an agent's ideal point and a "cut point" in $\mathbb{R}^1$ or a "cutting plane" in $\mathbb{R}^d$.

To see this, consider an agent with symmetric single-peaked preferences over $\mathbb{R}^1$. Thus, agent i prefers x to y if and only if $h(-|x - z_i|) > h(-|y - z_i|)$. Assuming that $x > y$, this condition becomes

$$z_i > c \equiv \frac{x + y}{2}.$$

Conversely, yPx if and only if $z_i < c$. Thus, given a set of agents and outcomes $x > y$, the model predicts that all agents with ideal points greater than the midpoint of x and y prefer x, and those with ideal points lower than the midpoint prefer y. Note that this prediction is completely independent of the function h.

This logic extends to $\mathbb{R}^d$ as well. Now agent i prefers x to y if and only if $h(-\|x - z_i\|) > h(-\|y - z_i\|)$. Now we can define a *separating hyperplane* as follows. Let $C = \{c \mid \|x - c\| - \|y - c\|\}$. This hyperplane is equivalent to the cut point in $\mathbb{R}^1$. It divides the ideal points into those who prefer x to y and those who prefer y to x. Again armed only with knowledge of ideal points and C, we can confidently characterize the choices of the agents.

6. Exercises

EXERCISE 2.1 *Prove the following statement. If X is finite and R is a complete and reflexive binary relation on X, then $M(R, S) \neq \emptyset$ on any $S \subset X$ (except $S = \emptyset$) if and only if R is acyclic.*

EXERCISE 2.2 *Prove that if R on X is transitive then the weak and strict preferences I and P derived from R are also transitive.*

EXERCISE 2.3 *In this chapter we first defined the weak ordering R and then defined P as $x P y$ if and only if $x R y$ and $\tilde{\ } y R x$. Suppose instead we first define a strict preference P relation and define R as $x R y$ if and only if $\tilde{\ } y P x$.*

   (1) A relation P is called asymmetric if there are no distinct points $x, y \in X$ where $x P y$ and $y P x$ are both true. Show that P is asymmetric if and only if R is complete.

   (2) A relation P is called negatively transitive if for any $x, y, z \in X$, $x P y$ implies either $x P z$ or $z P y$ or both. Show that P is negatively transitive if and only if R is transitive.

EXERCISE 2.4 *For the following utility functions, describe the preferred set. This can be done either graphically or by formally characterizing $P(x) = \{y : y R x\}$ for all $x \in X$. Plot the utility curve if possible.*

   (1) $u(x) = -|1 - x|$ for $x \in [0, 1]$.
   (2) $u(x) = -x^2$ for $x \in [0, 1]$.
   (3) $u(x) = \sqrt{x}$ for $x \in [0, 1]$.
   (4) $u(x) = -\alpha x_1^2 - (1 - \alpha)x_2^2$ for $x \in \mathbb{R}^2$.

EXERCISE 2.5 *An agent has spatial preferences R over $\mathbb{R}^d$ represented by the utility function $u_i(x) = h(-\|x - z_i\|)$.*

   (1) Prove that for any compact $X \subset \mathbb{R}^d$, $M(R, X)$ is nonempty.
   (2) Give a characterization of $M(R, X)$.
   (3) Show that if X is also convex, $M(R, X)$ has a unique element.
   (4) Now assume that X is a ball of the form $\{x \in \mathbb{R}^d : \|x - w\| < k\}$ for a fixed $w \in \mathbb{R}^d$ and $k > 0$. Characterize the set $M(R, X)$ as a function of the vectors z_i and w and the scalar k.

EXERCISE 2.6 (*) *Suppose that X is convex and R is a weak ordering. Prove that if R is strictly convex the upper contour sets $P(x)$ are convex.*

EXERCISE 2.7 (*) *Use Definition 2.12 to show that $[0, 1]$ is compact.*

EXERCISE 2.8 (*) *Let $X \subset \mathbb{R}^n$ and $u : X \to \mathbb{R}^1$ be a continuous utility function representing the binary ordering R on X. Prove that R is complete, reflexive, transitive, and continuous.*

EXERCISE 2.9 (*) *Use Theorem 2.7 to prove the Weierstrass Theorem: if X is compact and $u(\cdot)$ is a continuous, real-valued function on X, then there exists at least one point $x = \arg\max_{x \in X} u(x)$ that maximizes $u(\cdot)$ on X.*

3 Choice Under Uncertainty

In this chapter we relax the assumption that agents can perfectly predict the consequences of their actions. Instead agents understand that the outcomes are generated probabilistically from their choice of action – certain actions increase or decrease the likelihood of particular outcomes. People know which actions are more or less likely to produce specific outcomes. Recall the example from the last chapter where $A =$ {*send in the troops*, *try negotiating*, *do nothing*} and $X =$ {*win large concessions*, *win minor concessions*, *status quo*}. The agent might believe that large concessions are more likely when the troops are deployed than when negotiation is initiated. Thus, in her decision, she balances this likelihood of generating a better outcome against the costs of each action. Deploying the troops would be rational if it is much more likely to lead to large concessions, if the additional concessions are valuable to the agent, or if the costs of deployment are low. These are the basic trade-offs underlying the classical theory of choice under uncertainty.

There are two key elements of this model of uncertainty. The first are *beliefs* that we model as probability distributions or *lotteries* over the outcomes associated with each action. The second are the payoffs associated with each outcome. These two elements combine to generate von Neumann-Morgenstern utility functions over actions. This naming convention honors two pioneers of classical decision theory. As we will see, the von Neumann-Morgenstern functions rely on a much stronger concept of utility than the ordinal functions discussed in Chapter 2.

1. The Finite Case

We begin with models in which the number of actions and outcomes is finite. As in the previous chapter, we denote the feasible actions and outcomes as sets $A = \{a_1, \ldots, a_I\}$ and $X = \{x_1, \ldots, x_J\}$. Actions and outcomes are now linked probabilistically rather than deterministically. To model this link, outcomes now depend both on the action taken and on the state of the world, s. From the point of view of the agent, s is a random variable like rainfall on election day or missile precision in a war. In decision theoretic models (or in game theoretic models where agents choose actions randomly), s can also represent the actions of other agents. The set of states is $S = \{s_1, \ldots, s_K\}$. Agents have beliefs about the likelihood of each state represented by the probability function $\pi(s_k) \equiv \pi_k$. These probabilities must satisfy the basic axioms of probability theory – each must be between 0 and 1 and together they must sum to 1. Formally, these probabilities satisfy

$$0 \leq \pi_k \leq 1 \text{ for each } k$$

$$\pi_1 + \pi_2 + \cdots + \pi_K = \sum_{k=1}^{K} \pi_k = 1.$$

An outcome function, written as $\chi(a, s) : A \times S \to X$, links actions, states, and outcomes.[1] Consider the example in Table 3.1 where an outcome is specified for each combination of states and actions.

Outcome x_1 occurs in state s_1 regardless of the chosen action. In states s_2 and s_3, however, the outcome depends on the action chosen by the agent. For agents it is not the state that matters so much as the likelihood of the outcomes following each action. Because the agent does not know the state when she chooses a_i, the probability of receiving outcome x is the probability that the state takes on a value s such that $\chi(a_i, s) = x$. Let p_{ij} be the probability that outcome x_j follows action a_i.

Table 3.1

$A\backslash S$	s_1	s_2	s_3
a_1	x_1	x_1	x_2
a_2	x_1	x_2	x_3

One can easily compute these probabilities from Table 3.1: $p_{11} = \pi_1 + \pi_2$, $p_{12} = \pi_3$, $p_{13} = 0$, $p_{21} = \pi_1$, $p_{22} = \pi_2$, and $p_{23} = \pi_3$. The general formula for these probabilities is

$$p_{ij} = \sum_{\{k\,:\,\chi(a_i, s_k) = x_j\}} \pi_k.$$

[1] Because we focus only on outcomes that can occur for some combination of a and s, we require that the total number of action-state combinations be no less than the number of outcomes or $I \cdot K \geq J$.

These p_{ij} inherit the following properties from the π_k:

$$0 \leq p_{ij} \leq 1 \text{ for each } i, j$$

$$p_{i1} + p_{i2} + \cdots + p_{iJ} = \sum_{j=1}^{J} p_{ij} = 1 \text{ for each } i.$$

Consequently, we simplify the notation by suppressing the dependence of the outcome probabilities on s and focus solely on p_{ij}. In later chapters, however, we do use the action-state representation of the agent's problem more explicitly.

Also to minimize notation, we define the *vector* $\mathbf{p}_i = (p_{i1}, \ldots, p_{iJ})$ as the *lottery* over the outcomes associated with action a_i. Because of the correspondence between an action and the lottery it generates, we refer interchangeably to an agent's choosing action a_i or simply choosing the lottery $\mathbf{p}_i$. Let $\mathbf{P}$ be the set of all lotteries. Given that there are J possible outcomes, the set $\mathbf{P}$ consists of the set of vectors with J elements that satisfy the preceding conditions (each element is between 0 and 1, and all coordinates sum to 1). This set is denoted Δ^J and termed the J-dimensional simplex.[2] For two dimensions, the simplex is simply the straight line from coordinate $(0, 1)$ to $(1, 0)$ as in Figure 3.1. For three dimensions, it is the triangular segment of the plane with the following corners (vertices) $(1, 0, 0)$, $(0, 1, 0)$, and $(0, 0, 1)$ as in the lower panel of Figure 3.1.

Another way to visualize lotteries is to use *trees* as in Figure 3.2. Beginning from the initial node, each branch corresponds to a specific outcome and is labeled with the probability of that outcome. Lottery $\mathbf{p}$ generates a larger probability of x_1 and a lower probability of x_3 than the lottery $\mathbf{q}$, whereas both lotteries generate the same probability of x_2. To build some intuition for our subsequent discussion, let us consider how an agent might choose between an action that generates $\mathbf{p}$ and one that generates $\mathbf{q}$. First, it seems unreasonable for the agent to base her decision on her preferences for x_2 – both lotteries generate this outcome with identical probabilities. Because these lotteries differ in the likelihoods of x_1 and x_3, a rational agent chooses $\mathbf{p}$ only if $x_1 R x_3$. Using these two intuitive arguments (which we formalize shortly), we anticipate that the agent chooses $\mathbf{p}$ if $x_1 P x_3$, chooses $\mathbf{q}$ if $x_3 P x_1$, and is indifferent if $x_1 I x_3$.

---

[2] We refer those readers who are unfamiliar with vectors and coordinate systems to the Mathematical Appendix.

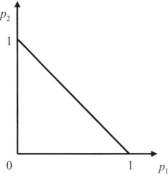

Two-Dimensional Simplex

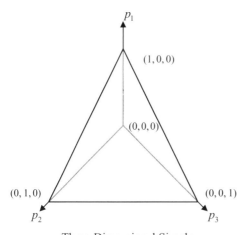

Three-Dimensional Simplex

Figure 3.1. The Simplex.

A feature of this example, one that facilitated our intuitive predic-tion, is that the lotteries are *simple*. In other words, each outcome is associated with a single probability number. It is often necessary, how-ever, to consider more complicated situations where agents choose between lotteries over lotteries over lotteries,..., ad infinitum. Such choices are called *compound* lotteries. A compound lottery over **P** is represented by $\{\alpha_1, \ldots, \alpha_I\}$ where α_i represents the probability of playing lottery $\mathbf{p}_i$. For example, consider how a rational agent eval-uates a lottery in which she gets lottery **p** with probability 1/4 and lottery **q** with probability 3/4. We abuse the notation slightly and la-bel this lottery $\mathbf{r} = (1/4)\mathbf{p} + (3/4)\mathbf{q}$. Figure 3.3 represents this lottery

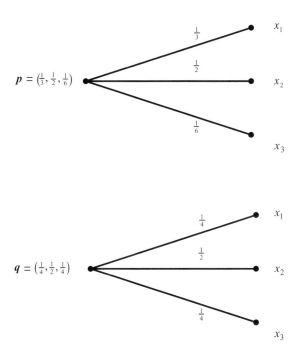

$$p = \left(\tfrac{1}{3}, \tfrac{1}{2}, \tfrac{1}{6}\right)$$

$$q = \left(\tfrac{1}{4}, \tfrac{1}{2}, \tfrac{1}{4}\right)$$

Figure 3.2. Tree Representations of Lotteries.

as a tree. How does an agent choose among **p**, **q**, and **r**? First, the availability of **r** should not change the preference ranking between **p** and **q** so we only need consider comparisons of **r** versus **p** and **r** versus **q**. But these comparisons seem difficult because of **r**'s compound structure. Fortunately, preferences over **r** are easy to analyze. Rational agents should care only about the probabilities associated with each outcome, not the paths traveled to reach those outcomes. Therefore, the agent computes that the probability of receiving outcome x_1 is the probability of receiving lottery **p** (1/4) times 1/3 plus the probability of receiving **q** (3/4) times 1/4. She computes the probabilities of x_2 and x_3 similarly. Because the agent computes a single probability number for each outcome, **r** is represented as a simple lottery as in the second panel of Figure 3.3. Formally, any compound lottery $\{\alpha_1, \ldots, \alpha_I\}$ over **P** that assigns probability α_i to lottery $\mathbf{p}_i$ can be represented as a simple lottery with the probability of x_j given by $\sum_{i=1}^{I} \alpha_i p_{ij}$.

Once **r** is reduced to a simple lottery, which lottery does the agent prefer? In the simplification of **r**, the probability of x_2 is remains 1/2 as it is in **p** and **q**. So preferences over x_2 are again irrelevant – only

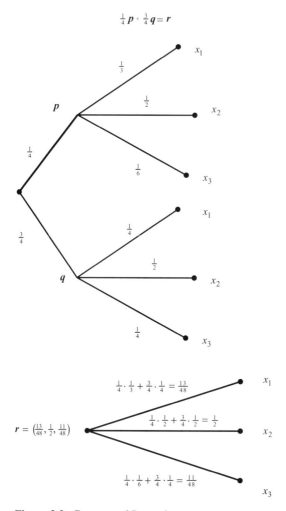

Figure 3.3. Compound Lotteries.

the comparison of x_1 to x_3 matters. Because under **r** the outcome x_1 is more likely than x_3, any agent for whom $x_1 P x_3$ prefers **r** to **q**. The agent prefers **p** to **r** because outcome x_1 is also more likely under **p**.

This discussion of how agents with preferences over the outcomes X evaluate lotteries illustrates some of the key features of the standard model of choice under uncertainty. This model formalizes weak preferences on **P** to deal with choice under uncertainty. Just as utility functions greatly simplify the analysis of choice under certainty, the model of *expected utility* simplifies the analysis of choice under uncertainty. All of the intuition used in our example is succinctly summarized by four axioms about weak preferences R on $\mathbf{P}$.

AXIOM 3.1. *Completeness and Transitivity:* *The weak preference relation R over $\mathbf{P}$ is complete, reflexive, and transitive.*

AXIOM 3.2. *Reduction of Compound Lotteries:* *For any $\alpha \in [0,1]$ and $\mathbf{p} \in \mathbf{P}$, $\mathbf{p} I [\alpha \mathbf{p} + (1 - \alpha) \mathbf{p}]$.*

AXIOM 3.3. *Continuity:* *Let $\mathbf{p}, \mathbf{q}$, and $\mathbf{r}$ be three lotteries in $\mathbf{P}$. The set of scalars $\alpha \in [0,1]$ such that $[\alpha \mathbf{p} + (1 - \alpha) \mathbf{r}] R \mathbf{q}$ is a closed interval. The set of scalars $\beta \in [0,1]$ such that $\mathbf{q} R [\beta \mathbf{p} + (1 - \beta) \mathbf{r}]$ is a closed interval.*[3]

AXIOM 3.4. *Independence:* *Let $\mathbf{p}, \mathbf{q}$, and $\mathbf{r}$ be three lotteries in $\mathbf{P}$. For any scalar $\alpha \in (0,1)$, $\mathbf{p} R \mathbf{q}$ if and only if $[\alpha \mathbf{p} + (1 - \alpha) \mathbf{r}] R [\alpha \mathbf{q} + (1 - \alpha) \mathbf{r}]$.*

The meaning of each of the axioms is pretty straightforward. First, as in the case of outcomes, any two lotteries can be compared, and preferences over lotteries do not cycle. This axiom is critical in our example. As in the Chapter 1, transitivity may be extended to indifference and strict preference. The second axiom simply formalizes Figure 3.3 to guarantee that agents care only about the probabilities of outcomes, not the representation of the probabilistic process generating those outcomes.[4]

The continuity axiom is more abstract than the previous two, but it implies that small changes in the probabilities of outcomes do not generate large changes in the preferences. It requires that if $\mathbf{p} P \mathbf{q}$ then all lotteries sufficiently close to $\mathbf{p}$ are also preferred to $\mathbf{q}$. If $\mathbf{p} P \mathbf{q}$, a modification of $\mathbf{p}$ that adds a very small probability of a really bad outcome does not reverse the preference ordering. The continuity axiom has the following straightforward and useful implication.

---

[3] The Mathematical Appendix has a detailed discussion of closed sets. For the present purposes, however, it is sufficient to know that a closed interval $[a, b]$ is one that includes points a and b and all points in between.

[4] In some texts this assumption is implicit when authors define preferences over lotteries. We choose to make the assumption explicit to highlight that this theory ignores details regarding the representation of lotteries.

LEMMA 3.1 *If* $\mathbf{p}\,Rq\,R\mathbf{r}$ *then there exists some* $\lambda \in [0,1]$ *such that* $[\lambda\mathbf{p} + (1-\lambda)\mathbf{r}]\,I\mathbf{q}$.

Proof Let $\mathbf{p}\,Rq\,R\mathbf{r}$. For every $\lambda \in [0,1]$, either $[\lambda\mathbf{p} + (1-\lambda)\mathbf{r}]\,P\mathbf{q}$ or $\mathbf{q}\,P\,[\lambda\mathbf{p} + (1-\lambda)\mathbf{r}]$ or $[\lambda\mathbf{p} + (1-\lambda)\mathbf{r}]\,I\mathbf{q}$. If $\mathbf{p}\,I\mathbf{q}$ or $\mathbf{r}\,I\mathbf{q}$, the claim is true at $\lambda = 1$ or $\lambda = 0$. The case where $\mathbf{p}\,P\mathbf{q}\,P\mathbf{r}$ remains. This statement implies that the sets $\{\alpha : [\alpha\mathbf{p} + (1-\alpha)\mathbf{r}]\,R\mathbf{q}\}$ and $\{\beta : \mathbf{q}\,R\,[\beta\mathbf{p} + (1-\beta)\mathbf{r}]\}$ are nonempty. The continuity axiom implies that these sets must be closed. Consequently, the first set contains a smallest element, $\underline{\alpha}$, and the second set contains a largest element, $\overline{\beta}$. Because the strict preference relation is not reflexive, it cannot be simultaneously true that $[\lambda\mathbf{p} + (1-\lambda)\mathbf{r}]\,P\mathbf{q}$ and $\mathbf{q}\,P\,[\lambda\mathbf{p} + (1-\lambda)\mathbf{r}]$ for any value of λ. Thus, $\overline{\beta} \le \underline{\alpha}$. But then neither $[\lambda\mathbf{p} + (1-\lambda)\mathbf{r}]\,P\mathbf{q}$ nor $\mathbf{q}\,P\,[\lambda\mathbf{p} + (1-\lambda)\mathbf{r}]$ is true for $\lambda \in [\overline{\beta}, \underline{\alpha}]$. Thus, by completeness $[\lambda\mathbf{p} + (1-\lambda)\mathbf{r}]\,I\mathbf{q}$ for all $\lambda \in [\overline{\beta}, \underline{\alpha}]$. □

Now consider the independence axiom – perhaps the most controversial of the four.[5] Suppose an agent has a preference ranking between two lotteries. If those lotteries are mixed with a third (using the same probabilities), the independence axiom holds that the preference ordering is the same as that over the original lotteries. For example, consider two lotteries. The first pays $100 with probability .5 and $0 otherwise. The second pays $75 for sure. If we compound each of these lotteries with a .5 chance of $1,000,000 for sure and .5 chance of playing the original lottery, the independence axiom says that the preferences over the compound lotteries correspond to the original lotteries. Using the tree metaphor for lotteries, the independence axiom says that the comparison of two lotteries is based only on the comparison of the outcome branches that are distinct across lotteries. This axiom, therefore, justifies ignoring x_2 in our first example. The next two lemmas extend the independence axiom to the case of indifference and strict preference.

LEMMA 3.2 *For any scalar* $\alpha \in (0,1)$ *and lotteries* $\mathbf{r}, \mathbf{p}, \mathbf{q} \in \mathbf{P}$, $\mathbf{p}\,I\mathbf{q}$ *if and only if* $[\alpha\mathbf{p} + (1-\alpha)\mathbf{r}]\,I\,[\alpha\mathbf{q} + (1-\alpha)\mathbf{r}]$.

Proof To establish sufficiency, suppose that $\mathbf{p}\,I\mathbf{q}$. The independence axiom requires both $[\alpha\mathbf{p} + (1-\alpha)\mathbf{r}]\,R\,[\alpha\mathbf{q} + (1-\alpha)\mathbf{r}]$ and

---

[5] In some texts and articles the independence axiom is called the substitution axiom.

$[\alpha\mathbf{q} + (1 - \alpha)\mathbf{r}]\,R\,[\alpha\mathbf{p} + (1 - \alpha)\,\mathbf{r}]$. Consequently, $[\alpha\mathbf{p} + (1 - \alpha)\mathbf{r}]\,I\,[\alpha\mathbf{q} + (1 - \alpha)\mathbf{r}]$ is the only possibility. The proof of necessity is similar. □

LEMMA 3.3 *For any scalar* $\alpha \in (0, 1)$ *and lotteries* $\mathbf{r}, \mathbf{p}, \mathbf{q} \in \mathbf{P}$, $\mathbf{p}P\mathbf{q}$ *if and only if* $[\alpha\mathbf{p} + (1 - \alpha)\,\mathbf{r}]\,P\,[\alpha\mathbf{q} + (1 - \alpha)\,\mathbf{r}]$.

Proof To establish sufficiency, suppose that $\mathbf{p}P\mathbf{q}$. The independence axiom requires that $[\alpha\mathbf{p} + (1 - \alpha)\,\mathbf{r}]\,R\,[\alpha\mathbf{q} + (1 - \alpha)\,\mathbf{r}]$. To show that indifference violates the independence axiom, assume that $[\alpha\mathbf{q} + (1 - \alpha)\,\mathbf{r}]\,I\,[\alpha\mathbf{p} + (1 - \alpha)\,\mathbf{r}]$. Lemma 3.2 implies that $\mathbf{q}I\mathbf{p}$, contradicting the assumption that $\mathbf{p}P\mathbf{q}$. The proof of necessity is very similar. □

An equally important, but less direct, implication of the independence axiom is the following lemma.

LEMMA 3.4 *If* $\mathbf{p}R\mathbf{q}$ *and* $\alpha \in (0, 1)$, *then* $\mathbf{p}R\,[\alpha\mathbf{p} + (1 - \alpha)\,\mathbf{q}]\,R\mathbf{q}$.

Proof Suppose $\mathbf{p}P\mathbf{q}$. The reduction of compound lotteries, Lemma 3.3, and transitivity imply that
$\mathbf{p}I\,[\alpha\mathbf{p} + (1 - \alpha)\,\mathbf{p}]\,P\,[\alpha\mathbf{p} + (1 - \alpha)\,\mathbf{q}]\,P\,[\alpha\mathbf{q} + (1 - \alpha)\,\mathbf{q}]\,I\mathbf{q}$.
If $\mathbf{p}I\mathbf{q}$, Lemma 3.2 implies that $\mathbf{p}I\,[\alpha\mathbf{p} + (1 - \alpha)\,\mathbf{q}]\,I\mathbf{q}$ by alternating the use of $\mathbf{r} = \mathbf{p}$ and $\mathbf{r} = \mathbf{q}$. Consequently, $\mathbf{p}R\,[\alpha\mathbf{p} + (1 - \alpha)\,\mathbf{q}]\,R\mathbf{q}$. □

This lemma establishes that given a weighted average of two lotteries, the resulting lottery has an intermediate preference ranking. The independence and continuity axioms have another implication that is crucial for the existence of expected utility functions.

LEMMA 3.5 *Suppose the alternatives are indexed so that* $x_1 Rx_j$ *for all* j *and* $x_j Rx_J$ *for all* j. *Then for all* $\alpha, \beta \in [0, 1]$,
$[\alpha x_1 + (1 - \alpha)\,x_J]\,R\,[\beta x_1 + (1 - \beta)\,x_J]$ *if and only if* $\alpha \geq \beta$.

Proof Suppose $\alpha \geq \beta$. We can write $\alpha x_1 + (1 - \alpha)\,x_J$ as
$\gamma x_1 + (1 - \gamma)\,[\beta x_1 + (1 - \beta)\,x_J]$ where $\gamma = (\alpha - \beta)/(1 - \beta) \in (0, 1]$. From Lemma 3.4, $x_1 R\,[\beta x_1 + (1 - \beta)\,x_J]$. Applying Lemma 3.4 again, $[\gamma x_1 + (1 - \gamma)\,[\beta x_1 + (1 - \beta)\,x_J]]\,R\,[\beta x_1 + (1 - \beta)\,x_J]$. The proof of necessity is identical to the earlier proof where the roles of α and β are reversed. □

Intuitively, in comparing lotteries over the best and worst outcomes, the agent prefers the one with the greatest likelihood of producing the best outcome. These axioms and lemmas are used to prove that preferences over lotteries can be represented by *expected utility functions*. We state the theorem in terms of preferences over lotteries. Because actions induce lotteries over outcomes, an analogous statement can be made about preferences over actions.

THEOREM 3.1 *(von Neumann-Morgenstern) If Axioms 3.1.–3.4. hold, then there exists a function $u(x_j)$ that assigns a number u_j for each outcome such that the expected utility of a lottery $\mathbf{p}_i$ induced by action i is given by*

$$EU(\mathbf{p}_i) = p_{i1}u_1 + p_{i2}u_2 + \cdots + p_{iJ}u_J = \sum_{j=1}^{J} p_{ij}u_j$$

and $\mathbf{p}_i \, R \mathbf{p}_j$ if and only if $EU(\mathbf{p}_i) \geq EU(\mathbf{p}_j)$.

The function $u(x_j)$ is sometimes called a Bernoulli utility function to distinguish it from the expected utility function $EU(\mathbf{p})$. The Bernoulli and expected utility functions are very different. The Bernoulli functions are defined over outcomes, whereas expected utility functions are defined over lotteries.

Theorem 3.1 shows that expected utility of a lottery is simply the weighted average of the utilities over outcomes where the weights are the probabilities of each outcome. Returning to our earlier example, if we assign utilities to outcomes x_1, x_2, and x_3 of $u(x_1)$, $u(x_2)$, and $u(x_3)$, then the expected utility of lottery $\mathbf{p}$ is $EU(\mathbf{p}) = (1/3)u(x_1) + (1/2)u(x_2) + (1/6)u(x_3)$, but that of $\mathbf{q}$ is $EU(\mathbf{q}) = (1/4)u(x_1) + (1/2)u(x_2) + (1/4)u(x_3)$. One of the most attractive properties of expected utility functions is that they are linear functions of the Bernoulli utilities. Among other things this result implies that if $\mathbf{r}$ is a compound lottery resulting in $\mathbf{p}$ with probability $1/2$ and $\mathbf{q}$ with probability $3/4$ then $EU(\mathbf{r}) = EU((1/4)\mathbf{p} + (3/4)\mathbf{q}) = (1/4)EU(\mathbf{p}) + (3/4)EU(\mathbf{q}) = (13/48)u(x_1) + (1/2)u(x_2) + (11/48)u(x_3)$: exactly what one gets from computing the expected utility of the reduced lottery.

We do not prove the von Neumann-Morgenstern Theorem formally. Rather we sketch the argument for the case of three outcomes and leave the proof of the general result as an exercise in the use of mathematical induction. Let $X = \{x_1, x_2, x_3\}$ where $x_1 R x_2 R x_3$ and assume that at least one of the preferences is strict: $x_1 I x_2 I x_3$ is a trivial case. We represent lotteries over X as a vector (p_1, p_2, p_3). From Lemma 3.1, there exist an α such that $x_2 I(\alpha, 0, 1 - \alpha)$. Similarly, $x_1 I(1, 0, 0)$ and $x_3 I(0, 0, 1)$ Therefore, let $u_1 = 1$, $u_2 = \alpha$, and $u_3 = 0$. Now consider any lottery $\mathbf{p} = (p_1, p_2, p_3)$. From this lottery, a compound lottery $(p_1 + u_2 p_2, 0, p_3 + p_2 (1 - u_2))$ is formed by substituting the lottery $(u_2, 0, 1 - u_2)$ for the degenerate lottery that reaches x_2. From Lemma 3.2, the agent must be indifferent between this compound lottery and $\mathbf{p}$. Using similar substitutions for x_1 and x_2, the indifference between $\mathbf{p}$ and $\{p_1 u_1 + p_2 u_2 + p_3 u_3, 0, p_1 (1 - u_1) + p_2 (1 - u_2) + p_3 (1 - u_3)\}$ is established. Now consider an alternative lottery $\mathbf{q}$. From the replication of the preceding arguments, the agent is indifferent between $\mathbf{q}$ and $(q_1 u_1 + q_2 u_2 + q_3 u_3, 0, q_1 (1 - u_1) + q_2 (1 - u_2) + q_3 (1 - u_3))$.

For the proof's grand finale, the application of Lemma 3.5 says that $\mathbf{p} R \mathbf{q}$ if and only if $p_1 u_1 + p_2 u_2 + p_3 u_3 \geq q_1 u_1 + q_2 u_2 + q_3 u_3$. Consequently, preferences over lottery $\mathbf{p}$ are represented by the scalar $p_1 u_1 + p_2 u_2 + p_3 u_3$. The theorem does not claim that any $\alpha \in [0, 1]$ works, however. Rather the theorem ensures that there exists at least one such α so that the outcome utilities $u_1 = 1$, $u_2 = \alpha$, and $u_3 = 0$ work.

1.1. Cardinal Utility. In the previous chapter, we assuaged utility skeptics with the argument "Relax, utility functions do nothing more than represent preference orderings." For expected utilities, however, such a defense is no longer tenable. The utility functions over outcomes $u(x_j)$ are no longer simply ordinal, but *cardinal* because they represent information about *relative* preferences over outcomes. Just as the Fahrenheit temperature scale says the difference between $212°$ and $32°$ is twice the difference between $122°$ and $32°$, cardinal utility functions allow one to say that "my preference for steak over chicken is 3.8 times my preference for chicken over fish." Unlike ordinal utilities, the value $u(x_j) - u(x_k)$ has a meaningful interpretation.

It is easy to see why expected utility theory depends on cardinal Bernoulli utility functions. Suppose that an agent were choosing between two lotteries over the three outcomes x_1, x_2, x_3 where $x_1 P x_2 P x_3$. Lottery 1 provides a .5 shot at x_1 and a .5 shot at x_3 whereas lottery 2 generates x_2 with certainty. Suppose $u(x_1) = 1$, $u(x_2) = \alpha \in (0, .5)$, and $u(x_3) = 0$. This utility representation suggests that the agent would choose lottery 1. If this representation were simply ordinal, we could apply any order-preserving transformation to the utility functions, and the resulting function would represent the exact same preferences. But consider the following transformation of the Bernoulli utilities: $v(x_1) = 1$, $v(x_2) = 1 - \alpha$, and $v(x_3) = 0$. This transformation preserves the preference ordering over outcomes, but now the agent prefers lottery 2.

Just as Fahrenheit is not the only temperature scale that produces identical relative information about heat, expected utility representations are not unique. To see this, consider two cardinal utility functions $u(x_j)$ and $v(x_j) = a + bu(x_j)$ where $b > 0$. Given a lottery **p**, these produce expected utility functions of $\sum_{j=1}^{J} p_j u(x_j)$ and $a + b \sum_{j=1}^{J} p_j u(x_j)$, respectively. Because the ordering produced by $\sum_{j=1}^{J} p_j u(x_j)$ and $\sum_{j=1}^{J} q_j u(x_j)$ is the same as the ordering of $a + b \sum_{j=1}^{J} p_j u(x_j)$ and $a + b \sum_{j=1}^{J} q_j u(x_j)$, each cardinal utility function produces exactly the same behavior. This also implies that $u(x_j) - u(x_k)$ is unique up to a scale factor b while relative differences $(u(x_j) - u(x_k)) / (u(x_l) - u(x_m))$ are uniquely determined. The conclusion, then, is that while Bernoulli utility functions are not just ordinal, they are, however, defined only up to positive linear (or affine) transformations.

2. Risk Preferences

One aspect of choice under uncertainty not determined by the axioms of the previous section is the amount of risk a rational agent is willing to tolerate. Some agents are willing to accept a substantial probability of a bad outcome in exchange for moderately higher probabilities of good outcomes, while others prefer to minimize the probability of bad outcomes by forgoing certain opportunities for high payoffs. Recall that the continuity axiom says that given three outcomes $x P y P z$, an agent prefers a lottery between x and z to y for certain if the probability of z is sufficiently small. The axiom, however, is silent about how small this risk needs to be.

A common way to characterize an agents's preference for risk is to ask whether the agent is willing to accept a *fair bet*. A fair bet is one that pays its price or stake in expectation. Suppose for now that the price and rewards (i.e., outcomes) are denominated in money or some other commodity of which agents prefer to have more. In later sections, we return to the case of agents that have *satiable* preferences where more is better only up to a certain point.

Let w be the stake or wager, $x_1 > x_2$ be distinct monetary outcomes, p be the probability of x_1, and $1 - p$ be the probability of x_2. Consider the following definitions:

DEFINITION 3.1 *A bet is fair if $w = px_1 + (1 - p)x_2$. A bet is favorable if $w < px_1 + (1 - p)x_2$. A bet is unfair if $w > px_1 + (1 - p)x_2$*

For example, a fair bet would be buying a \$1 lottery ticket that pays \$100 with probability 1/100 and nothing with probability 99/100. The bet would be favorable if the ticket cost less than a dollar and unfair if it cost more. Needless to say, nearly all lotteries that are called "lotteries" in the real world (especially those run by state governments) are of the unfair variety. Using the notion of fair bets, we characterize preferences for risk.

DEFINITION 3.2 *An agent is risk averse if she does not accept unfair bets, that is, $u(px_1 + (1 - p)x_2) > pu(x_1) + (1 - p)u(x_2)$ for all p, x_1, x_2.*

DEFINITION 3.3 *An agent is risk acceptant if she accepts unfair bets, that is, $u(px_1 + (1 - p)x_2) < pu(x_1) + (1 - p)u(x_2)$ for all p, x_1, x_2.*

DEFINITION 3.4 *An agent is risk neutral if she is indifferent between any fair bet and its stake, that is, $u(px_1 + (1 - p)x_2) = pu(x_1) + (1 - p)u(x_2)$ for all p, x_1, x_2.*

It turns out that an agent's preference for risk is closely related to the shape of her utility function for money. Consider Figure 3.4, which demonstrates the utility comparison for the fair bet $w = px_1 + (1 - p)x_2$. The line connecting the coordinates $(u(x_1), x_1)$ and $(u(x_2), x_2)$ must travel through the point $(pu(x_1) + (1 - p)u(x_2), px_1 + (1 - p)x_2)$. Thus, we know that the value of $pu(x_1) + (1 - p)u(x_2)$ lies at the intersection of the line between $u(x_1)$ and $u(x_2)$ and the vertical line beginning at w. Consequently, we can see that $u(w) > pu(x_1) + (1 - p)u(x_2)$ so that the agent is risk averse and rejects the fair bet. Obviously, the feature of the utility function generating this result is that the utility function always lies above any line connecting two utilities. This property is called *concavity*.

In Figure 3.5, we can see that the utility function always lies below lines connecting two utility values. For a *convex* utility function,

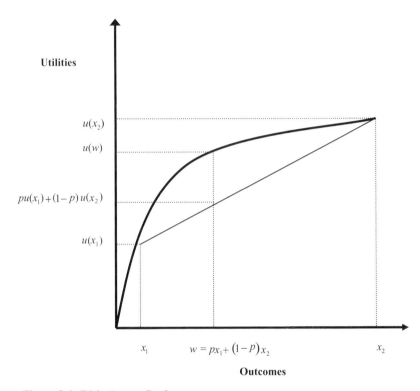

Figure 3.4. Risk-Averse Preferences.

such as this one, the agent always accepts the fair bet as $pu(x_1) + (1 - p)u(x_2) > u(px_1 + (1 - p)x_2)$. Figure 3.6 illustrates that linear utility functions produce risk-neutral behavior; under this type of utility function the expected utility of a gamble is identical to the utility of the expected outcome.

2.1. Risk Preferences and Stochastic Dominance*. It is not difficult to extend these ideas to lotteries that assign positive probability to an arbitrary number (finite) of possible outcomes.

DEFINITION 3.5 *A preference relation exhibits risk aversion if for any nondeterministic lottery* $\mathbf{p}$, $u(\sum_j p_j x_j) > \sum_j p_j u(x_j)$.

DEFINITION 3.6 *A preference relation exhibits risk acceptance if for any nondeterministic lottery* $\mathbf{p}$, $u(\sum_j p_j x_j) < \sum_j p_j u(x_j)$.

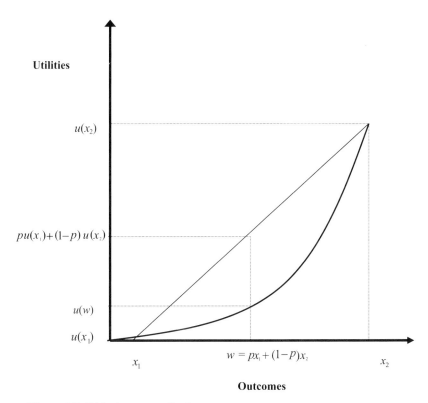

Figure 3.5. Risk-Acceptant Preferences.

To link risk aversion to behavior, we require additional definitions. For lottery **p** the *expected value* is $E(\mathbf{p}) = \sum_j p_j x_j$, and the *variance* of this lottery is $V(\mathbf{p}) = \sum_j p_j (E(\mathbf{p}) - x_j)^2$. For lottery **p** and expected utility representation $u = (u_1, \ldots, u_J)$, the *certainty equivalent* $C(\mathbf{p})$ is the outcome that the agent values just as much as the lottery. That is,

$$u(C(\mathbf{p})) = EU(\mathbf{p}).$$

The behavior of risk-averse agents is somewhat predictable. They sacrifice expected value for a reduction in variance so that the certainty equivalent is less than the expected value. In addition if there are two lotteries **p** and **q** where **q** has the same expected value as **p** but a greater variance, the agent prefers **p**. In this case **q** is a *mean-preserving spread* of **p**.

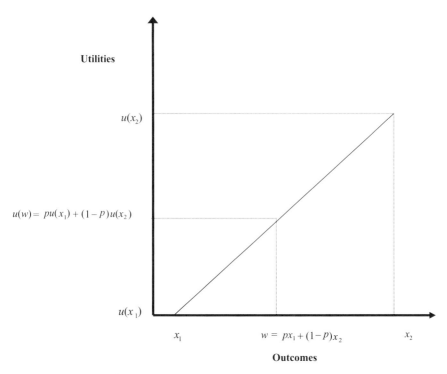

Figure 3.6. Risk-Neutral Preferences.

DEFINITION 3.7 *Lottery* **q** *is a mean-preserving spread of* **p** *if* **q** *is a compound lottery that first takes the realization of* **p** *and then adds to it a random term* ε *with distribution* **z** *having* $E(\mathbf{z}) = 0$ *and* $V(\mathbf{z}) > 0$.

THEOREM 3.2 *Given a preference relation R on lotteries and the Bernoulli utility function u(x) representing R, the following statements are equivalent.*

(1) *The preference relation R exhibits risk aversion.*

(2) *The utility function u(x) is strictly concave.*

(3) *For any lottery* **p**, $C(\mathbf{p}) \leq E(\mathbf{p})$ *(and if* $V(\mathbf{p}) > 0$ *the inequality is strict).*

(4) *For any two lotteries* **q** *and* **p** *where* **q** *is a mean-preserving spread of* **p**, $EU(\mathbf{q}) < EU(\mathbf{p})$.

Proof The equivalence of statements 1 and 2 is immediate. To show that statement 2 implies 3, assume that R exhibits risk aversion. This implies that for any nondeterministic lottery $\mathbf{p}$ (e.g., $V(\mathbf{p}) > 0$), $u(E(\mathbf{p})) > \sum_j p_j u(x_j)$. But $u(C(\mathbf{p})) = EU((\mathbf{p}))$ imply that $u(E(\mathbf{p})) > u(C(\mathbf{p}))$. Because $u(x)$ is an increasing function, this last statement implies that $E(\mathbf{p}) > C(\mathbf{p})$.

To see that statement 3 implies 2, assume that 3 is true and consider any two outcomes x_1 and x_2 with $p_1 \in (0, 1)$. In this case, statement 3 and that $u(x)$ is increasing imply that $u(px_1 + (1 - p)x_2) > pu(x_1) + (1 - p)u(x_2)$ so that the function $u(x)$ is concave. Because $V(\mathbf{p}) = 0$ (i.e., $\mathbf{p}$ is deterministic) results in equality, this case is trivial.

To see that 2 implies 4, consider $\mathbf{p}$ and a mean-preserving spread $\mathbf{q}$ that results in $x + \varepsilon$ with x having the distribution $\mathbf{p}$ and $\varepsilon \in \{\varepsilon_1, \ldots, \varepsilon_T\}$ having the distribution $\mathbf{z}$. Thus,

$$EU(\mathbf{q}) = \sum_t \sum_j z_t p_j u(x_j + \varepsilon_t).$$

By statement 2, for each value of x_j,

$$\sum_t z_t p_j u(x_j + \varepsilon_t) < u\left(\sum_t z_t p_j(x_j + \varepsilon_t) \right).$$

Rearranging the right-hand side yields

$$\sum_t z_t p_j u(x_j + \varepsilon_t) < u\left(p_j x_j + \sum_t z_t \varepsilon_t \right) = u(p_j x_j).$$

Summing over j yields

$$EU(\mathbf{q}) = \sum_t \sum_j z_t p_j u(x_j + \varepsilon_t) < \sum_j u(p_j x_j) = EU(\mathbf{p}).$$

To see that statement 4 implies 3, consider lottery $\mathbf{q}$. The lottery $\mathbf{q}$ is a mean-preserving spread of the lottery $\mathbf{p}$ that assigns probability 1 to $E(\mathbf{q})$. Statement 4 implies that $EU(\mathbf{p}) > EU(\mathbf{q})$. Because p is a deterministic lottery, $u(E(\mathbf{p})) = EU(\mathbf{p})$ so we have $u(E(\mathbf{p})) > EU(\mathbf{q})$. The monotonicity of $u(x)$ and $u(C(\mathbf{q})) = EU(\mathbf{q})$ imply that $E(\mathbf{p}) = E(\mathbf{q}) > C(\mathbf{q})$. $\qquad\square$

If lottery **q** is a mean-preserving spread of **p**, lottery **q** is *second-order stochastically dominated* by **p**. An additional result, proved by reapplying the logic of the last proof, provides a convenient characterization of second-order stochastic dominance.

THEOREM 3.3 *Lottery* **q** *is second-order stochastically dominated by* **p** *if and only if for every concave increasing function* $u(x)$,

$$\sum_j p_j u(x_j) \geq \sum_j q_j u(x_j).$$

Consequently, the preferences of risk-averse agents conform with second-order stochastic dominance – if **p** second-order stochastically dominates **q**, a risk-averse agent prefers **p** to **q**. In some cases the choice over lotteries is trivial. One common notion of such a "no-brainer" decision involves the choice between a lottery and another that *first-order stochastically* dominates it.

DEFINITION 3.8 *Lottery* **q** *is first-order stochastically dominated by* **p** *if for any nondecreasing function* $u(x)$

$$\sum_j p_j u(x_j) \geq \sum_j q_j u(x_j).$$

So in choosing between lotteries that are ordered by first-order stochastic dominance, risk attitudes are irrelevant.

2.2. Risk Preferences with Satiable Preferences. As discussed in Chapter 2, many utility functions used in political science are satiable because agents have most preferred outcomes. Such preferences have important implications for risk tolerance. Consider the utility function in Figure 3.7 and a lottery over x_1 and x_2. Note that x_1 is less than the agent's ideal point whereas x_2 is greater. Again the expected utility of such a lottery is the intersection of the line between $u(x_1)$ and $u(x_2)$ and the vertical line beginning at w. Because the ideal point lies between x_1 and x_2, there must be at least one outcome w_1 in this interval such that $u(w_1) > pu(x_1) + (1 - p)u(x_2)$. As a result, satiable preferences produce risk-averse behavior near the ideal point. Satiable preferences need not produce global risk aversion, however. Gambles over a set of outcomes bounded away from the ideal point over a region where

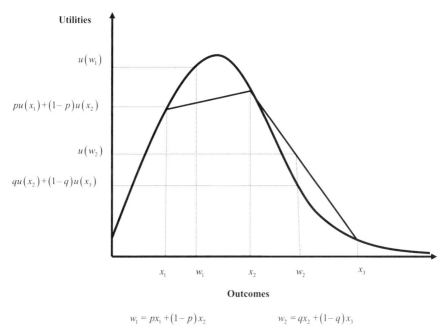

Figure 3.7. Risk and Spatial Preferences.

the agent's utility function is convex produce risk-acceptant behavior. The next section elaborates this point in more detail.

2.3. Risk and Higher-Dimension Euclidean Preferences*. In this section we consider choice over lotteries on $\mathbb{R}^n$. Bendor and Meirowitz (2004) show that we can extend notions of risk aversion developed for the case of strictly increasing preferences to that of Euclidean preferences. Recall that preferences over $x \in \mathbb{R}^n$ are Euclidean if we can represent them with a utility function of the form

$$u(x) = h(-\|x - x^*\|)$$

where x^* is a point in $\mathbb{R}^n$ and $h(\cdot)$ is a strictly increasing function. If the function $h(\cdot)$ is strictly convex, it is not difficult to see that the utility function $u(x)$ is itself strictly concave. In this case the Bernoulli utility function represents risk-averse preferences. Even if the function h is not convex, however, the preferences exhibit a form of risk aversion.

To extend the concept of a mean-preserving spread to $\mathbb{R}^n$, we simply apply Definition 3.7 with the relevant states in $\mathbb{R}^n$.

THEOREM 3.4 *If $u(x)$ is Euclidean with ideal point x^* then for any two lotteries $\mathbf{q}$ and $\mathbf{p}$ on $\mathbb{R}^n$ with expected value x^* in which $\mathbf{q}$ is a mean-preserving spread of $\mathbf{p}$, $EU(\mathbf{q}) < EU(\mathbf{p})$.*

Proof Let $\mathbf{q}$ and $\mathbf{p}$ be lotteries on $\mathbb{R}^n$, each with expected value x^*. Lottery $\mathbf{q}$ is a mean-preserving spread of $\mathbf{p}$. Define $d_j \equiv \| x_j - x^* \|$ as the distance between realization x_j and the point x^*. Because preferences are Euclidean, $EU(\mathbf{q}) < EU(\mathbf{p})$ if and only if

$$\sum_j q_j h(-d_j) < \sum_j p_j h(-d_j)$$

for some increasing function $h(\cdot)$. Because q is a mean-preserving spread of p, it must be the case that

$$\sum_j q_j d_j > \sum_j p_j d_j.$$

This requires that

$$\sum_j q_j g(-d_j) < \sum_j p_j g(-d_j)$$

for any increasing function $g(\cdot)$ including $h(\cdot)$. □

This theorem establishes that for lotteries centered at the agent's ideal point, second-order stochastic dominance in outcomes corresponds to first-order stochastic dominance in disutility. Alternatively, all agents with Euclidean preferences are risk averse over lotteries centered at their ideal point.

3. Learning

It is important to model how rational agents respond to new information about the likelihood of different outcomes. Again it is convenient to begin the discussion with an example. Consider Figure 3.8 where the agent believes that the incumbent politician is "good" with probability 3/4 and "bad" with probability 1/4. Suppose that the agent

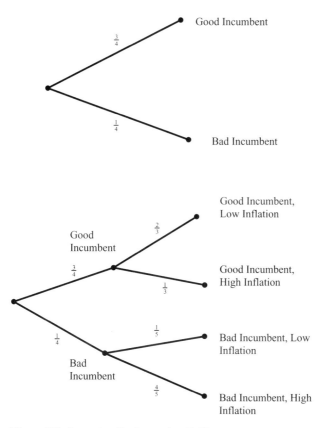

Figure 3.8. Learning the Incumbent's Type.

incorporates information about the incumbent's performance in office such as the inflation rate generated by his economic policies. How does this information change her probability assessment of the incumbent's quality?

Suppose the agent knows that good incumbents produce low inflation with a greater likelihood than bad incumbents. To be specific the agent knows that good incumbents produce low inflation with probability 2/3 and that bad incumbents produce low inflation with only a 1/5 probability. Intuition tells us is that when inflation is low the agent should increase her probability assessment that the incumbent is good beyond her original belief of 3/4. Conversely, when inflation is high, the agent should lower the probability that the incumbent is good. Fortunately, we can take the analysis a step further and compute the exact probability of a good incumbent after each realization of the inflation rate.

First, consider the case where inflation is low. A rational agent knows that the outcome is either the top or the third node of the second panel of Figure 3.8. Further, she knows that there is a $(3/4)(2/3) = 1/2$ probability of reaching the top node and a $(1/4)(1/5) = 1/20$ probability of reaching the third node. Therefore, after observing low inflation, it is ten times more likely that the incumbent is good than it is that he is bad. Let $p(l)$ be the probability of a good incumbent conditional on low inflation. Because probabilities must sum to 1, $p(l) + p(l)/10 = 1$ so that $p(l) = 10/11$. Similar reasoning leads to $p(h) = 4/9$. This confirms our intuition that low inflation raises the probability that the incumbent is good whereas high inflation lowers it.

Generalizing this example into a model of learning requires more precise statements from probability theory. Let A and B represent two events (such as the terminal nodes in Figure 3.8). Suppose an agent observes that event B has occurred and computes the probability that event A occurs. This estimate is the *conditional probability of A given event B*. We write it as

$$\Pr(A \mid B) = \frac{\Pr(A\& B)}{\Pr(B)} \text{ assuming } \Pr(B) > 0$$

where $\Pr(A)$ is the probability of event A, $\Pr(B)$ is the probability of event B, and $\Pr(A \& B)$ is the probability that both events occur (the joint probability). This formula, known as Bayes' rule, is defined only if $\Pr(B) \neq 0$. A special case, *independent* events, has the property that $\Pr(A \& B) = Pr(A)Pr(B)$ so that

$$\Pr(A \mid B) = \frac{\Pr(A)\Pr(B)}{\Pr(B)} = \Pr(A).$$

To see Bayes' rule in action, note that the probability of low inflation and a good incumbent $(1/2)$ is the probability of low inflation conditional on a good incumbent $(2/3)$ times the probability of a good incumbent $(3/4)$. Given these definitions, we state the main result.

THEOREM 3.5 *(Bayes' Rule)* *Let $A_1 \ldots A_N$ be disjoint events (i.e., no two can occur simultaneously) such that $\sum \Pr(A_n) = 1$ and $Pr(A_n) > 0$ for* *all n. Let B be some other event. Then*

$$\Pr(A_j \mid B) = \frac{\Pr(B \mid A_j)\Pr(A_j)}{\sum_{n=1}^{N}\Pr(B \mid A_n)\Pr(A_n)}.$$

Bayes' rule provides an easy to use formula to compute how rational agents update their probability assessments after new information. We can apply it easily to the voter's problem we saw earlier. Let A_1 be the event that the incumbent is good and A_2 be the event that she is bad. Because the incumbent cannot be both good and bad, these events satisfy the requirement of disjointedness. Event B is low inflation. For two events the formulae are

$$\Pr(A_1 \mid B) = \frac{\Pr(B \mid A_1)\Pr(A_1)}{\Pr(B \mid A_1)\Pr(A_1) + \Pr(B \mid A_2)\Pr(A_2)}$$

and

$$\Pr(A_2 \mid B) = \frac{\Pr(B \mid A_2)\Pr(A_2)}{\Pr(B \mid A_1)\Pr(A_1) + \Pr(B \mid A_2)\Pr(A_2)}.$$

We obtain all of the following probabilities from Figure 3.8:

$$\Pr(A_1) = \frac{3}{4}$$

$$\Pr(A_2) = \frac{1}{4}$$

$$\Pr(B \mid A_1) = \frac{2}{3}$$

$$\Pr(B \mid A_2) = \frac{1}{5}.$$

Thus, we can plug these numbers into Bayes' rule to get

$$\Pr(A_1 \mid B) = \frac{\frac{2}{3} \cdot \frac{3}{4}}{\frac{2}{3} \cdot \frac{3}{4} + \frac{1}{5} \cdot \frac{1}{4}} = \frac{10}{11}$$

and

$$\Pr(A_2 \mid B) = \frac{\frac{1}{5} \cdot \frac{1}{4}}{\frac{2}{3} \cdot \frac{3}{4} + \frac{1}{5} \cdot \frac{1}{4}} = \frac{1}{11}.$$

Voila!

Although seemingly straightforward and logical, Bayes' rule is often criticized as a poor model of learning. Not only can the rule be computationally challenging and exceed the typical person's grasp of conditional probability, its predictions are often counterintuitive. Consider the following scenario from the *Let's Make a Deal* game show hosted by Monte Hall. Monte offers contestants the choice of opening three doors. Behind one door is a luxury car, but the other doors hide prizes of little pecuniary value (goats seem to have been a favorite). Once a door is selected but before it is opened, Monte opens one of the remaining two doors to reveal a goat. He then asks the contestant whether he would like to switch his selection to the remaining closed door. Should a rational contestant switch? Most people intuitively say there is nothing to gain from switching: getting the car from a subsequent switch is just as likely as getting it on the original try. The probability of winning the car is 1/3 either way. Indeed a number of mathematicians and statisticians took this position in response to the publication of this problem in a popular newspaper column. Nevertheless, this logic is incompatible with Bayes' rule.

To simplify, suppose the contestant chooses door 3. Because the doors are ex ante the same, the analysis of the other cases is identical. First, consider the probability of winning if the contestant does not switch to the remaining door. Obviously, this is the same as the original probability that a car is behind door 3, and thus the probability is just 1/3. Now consider the probability of winning by switching. To formalize, let A_1, A_2, A_3 correspond to the car's being located behind doors 1, 2, and 3, respectively. Let B_1, B_2 corresponds to the event that Monte opens door 1 or 2. Because $\Pr(A_1) = \Pr(A_2) = \Pr(A_3) = 1/3$, we simply need to compute $\Pr(B_i|A_j)$ for all of the events. Because Monte never exposes a car, $\Pr(B_1|A_1) = \Pr(B_2|A_2) = 0$. We also assume that in the event A_3 Monte randomly selects which goat to expose. Therefore, $\Pr(B_1|A_2) = \Pr(B_2|A_1) = 1$ and $\Pr(B_1|A_3) = \Pr(B_2|A_3) = 1/2$.

Suppose Monte opens door 2; then the probability that a switching contestant wins is

$$\Pr(A_1 \mid B_2)$$
$$= \frac{\Pr(B_2 \mid A_1)\Pr(A_1)}{\Pr(B_2 \mid A_1)\Pr(A_1) + \Pr(B_2 \mid A_2)\Pr(A_2) + \Pr(B_2 \mid A_3)\Pr(A_3)}$$
$$= \frac{1 \cdot \frac{1}{3}}{1 \cdot \frac{1}{3} + 0 \cdot \frac{1}{3} + \frac{1}{2} \cdot \frac{1}{3}} = \frac{2}{3}.$$

Similarly, if Monte opens door 1, the probability of winning is $\Pr(A_2 \mid B_1) = 2/3$. So a switching contestant wins with probability $2/3$ whereas a sticking one only wins $1/3$ of the time.[6]

So why does the intuition that switching does not pay fail so badly? Because most people do not appreciate the implication of the fact that Monte never reveals a car. Observing that he does not open a particular door is information that a switcher uses in his decision that a stand-patter cannot.

Although the Monte Hall problem does expose an important set of problems with Bayesian learning, the objections can be carried too far. Bayes' rule does tell us correctly that switchers win $2/3$ of the time. Thus, a frequent viewer of the show can learn that one should switch without ever doing a conditional probability calculation. So one can justify the use of Bayes' rule by appealing to the notion that agents are acting as if they had performed the calculation even if they are simply following rules that they learn from experience.

4. Critiques of Expected Utility Theory

Whereas most of the models used in this book rely heavily on expected utility theory, a large and influential body of work is critical of expected utility theory. The application of these critical insights and alternative models to political game theory, however, is still in its infancy.[7]

4.1. Risk, Uncertainty, and Subjective Probability. One of the basic criticisms of expected utility theory is based on a distinction between risk and uncertainty. The economist Frank Knight (1921) originally argued that expected utility theory models risk rather than uncertainty. In his formulation, uncertainty implies that agents lack sufficient statistical information to form estimates of the probabilities of various outcomes. Formally, uncertainty implies that agents do not know the true set of lotteries **P**. The standard response to this distinction, proposed by the statistician Leonard Savage (1954), argues that agents

---

[6] The solution we present to this problem is somewhat convoluted in order to provide an additional demonstration of Bayes' rule. An easier proof is to note that a switcher only loses if he picked the right door in the first place. Thus, a switcher loses $1/3$ of the time and wins $2/3$.

[7] "Behavioral models" (as opposed to those based on expected utility theory) have become far more common in economics in recent years (see Camerer 2003).

have subjective beliefs about **P** that can be used to formulate (subjective) probability distributions over outcomes.

Nevertheless, experimental evidence has cast doubt as to whether uncertainty is reducible to beliefs about beliefs. Consider the paradox first formulated by Daniel Ellsberg (1961). There are two urns containing red and black balls. In urn 1, there are 100 red and black balls where the proportion of red balls is unknown. Urn 2, however, contains 50 red balls and 50 black balls.

Subjects are given $100 for selecting a red ball. Most subjects choose urn 2. But when offered $100 for selecting a black ball, the modal choice is again urn 2. Choosing urn 2 for both gambles, however, violates the axioms of expected utility theory. According to expected utility theory, choosing urn 2 in search of a red ball indicates a belief that urn 1 has fewer than 50 red balls whereas selecting urn 2 for a black ball suggests that the subject believes that urn 1 has fewer than 50 black balls. Obviously, these beliefs are inconsistent with the knowledge that urn 1 contains 100 balls. Selecting urn 1 in both gambles similarly violates expected utility theory.

4.2. The Allais Paradox. Other predictions of expected utility theory have been tested in experimental settings. These studies provide robust evidence for a number of decision-making anomalies inconsistent with expected utility theory. One of the earliest and most studied anomalies was first uncovered by the French economist Maurice Allais. His experiment finds that subjects often make choices inconsistent with the independence axiom.

Initially, subjects are asked to choose between lotteries **a** and **b** where

Lottery **a**: .33 chance of $2500, .66 chance of $2400, and .01 chance of 0

Lottery **b**: $2400 for sure

When given these choices, subjects overwhelmingly choose lottery **b**. For example, Kahneman and Tversky (1979) find that 82 percent choose lottery **b** when given this hypothetical choice.

Next the subjects are given the choice between lotteries **c** and **d**.

Lottery **c**: .33 chance of $2500, .67 chance of 0

Lottery **d**: .34 chance of $2400 and .66 chance of 0

Experimental subjects generally choose **c**. Kahneman and Tversky find that 83 percent choose this lottery. It can easily be shown that choosing **b** in the first experiment and **c** in the second violates the independence axiom and therefore expected utility theory. The choices of **b** and **c** imply that

$$u(2400) > .33u(2500) + .66u(2400) + .01u(0)$$

and

$$.33u(2500) + .67u(0) > .34u(2400) + .66u(0).$$

Rearranging the top inequality, we get $.34u(2400) > .33u(2500) + .01u(0)$ for the first inequality and $.33u(2500) + .01u(0) > .34u(2400)$ for the second. Therefore, we derive a contradiction. The contradiction is attributable to a violation of the independence axiom. Lottery **a** is the compound lottery $.34(33/34, 0, 1/34) + .66(0, 1, 0)$ over the outcomes $(2500, 2400, 0)$ while **b** is $.34(0, 1, 0) + .66(0, 1, 0)$. If $\mathbf{a}P\mathbf{b}$, then the independence axiom holds that $(33/34, 0, 1/34)$ P $(0, 1, 0)$. But this in turn implies that $.34(33/34, 0, 1/34) + .66(0, 0, 1)$ P $.34(0, 1, 0) + .66(0, 0, 1)$, which means that $\mathbf{c}P\mathbf{d}$.

4.3. Prospect Theory. In their classic article, Kahneman and Tversky (1979) propose an alternative model of decision making to account for the Allais paradox and other experimental anomalies. Whereas many previous authors attributed the Allais paradox to a preference for certainty, Kahneman and Tversky note that the independence axiom is often violated when all of the lotteries are far from sure things. Consider the following pairs of lotteries:

Lottery **a**: .45 chance of $6000, .55 chance of 0
Lottery **b**: .90 chance of $3000, .10 chance of 0
Lottery **c**: .001 chance of $6000, .999 chance of 0
Lottery **d**: .002 chance of $3000, .998 chance of 0

They find that the modal choices were **b** over **a** and **c** over **d**, choices that violate the independence axiom. Because the large payoffs in lotteries **c** and **d** have minuscule probabilities, subjects seem inclined to go for the one with the bigger prize. But when both probabilities are reasonably high, subjects are still inclined to take the one that is relatively more certain.

Kahneman and Tversky note, however, that this preference for certainty does not hold when gambles are over losses rather than gains. Consider the following pairs of lotteries:

Lottery **a**: .80 chance of −$4000, .20 chance of 0
Lottery **b**: −$3000 for sure
Lottery **c**: .20 chance of −$4000, .80 chance of 0
Lottery **d**: .25 chance of −$3000, .75 chance of 0

If the Allais paradox were simply due to a preference for certainty, **b** and **c** would be the modal choices. Kahneman and Tversky, however, find that **a** and **d** are the modal choices. Their interpretation is that even though people are risk averse over gains, they are risk acceptant over losses.

Kahneman and Tversky also argue that the presentation of the lotteries affects the choices that people make. Suppose that a person has been given $1000 and then offered

Lottery **a**: .5 chance of an additional $1000, .5 chance of 0
Lottery **b**: $500 for sure

Next consider a person who has been given $2000 and offered the choice of

Lottery **c**: .5 chance of losing $1000, .5 chance of 0
Lottery **d**: Loss of $500 for sure

Kahneman and Tversky find that **b** and **c** are the modal choices.

To account for these findings, Kahneman and Tversky propose prospect theory as an alternative to expected utility theory. According to their model, choice involves two distinct phases: editing and evaluation. In the editing phase, people "organize and reformulate the options so as to simplify subsequent evaluation and choice."

4.3.1. The Editing Phase. Kahneman and Tversky identify six distinct operations that occur during the editing phase.

(1) Coding: Because Kahneman and Tversky argue that people evaluate gains and losses separately, the first stage of editing involves determining a reference point and coding outcomes as either gains or losses.
(2) Combination: People combine probabilities associated with identical outcomes.

(3) Segregation: People identify and segregate the riskless components of a choice. For example, a lottery that produces $200 with probability .7 and $100 with .3 is interpreted as a riskless $100 gain and a lottery over an addition $100.

(4) Cancellation: When comparing two lotteries, people ignore the common elements of both lotteries. For example, the $2000 bonus in the last example "cancels out" and does not affect the choice between **c** and **d**.

(5) Simplification: People may simplify the tasks by rounding probabilities such as recoding .49 to even odds or by dropping extremely unlikely outcomes from consideration.

(6) Detection of dominance: People drop from consideration any lottery that is first-order stochastically dominated.

4.3.2. The Evaluation Phase. Kahneman and Tversky's model of evaluation is very similar to expected utility theory in that both models postulate that people evaluate gambles using a weighted average of the payoffs to the outcomes. In Kahneman and Tversky's model, however, the weights used are not the subjective probabilities of the outcomes but rather functions of the probabilities. They also argue, against expected utility theory, that the outcome value functions should treat gains and losses asymmetrically.

Let x and y be two distinct monetary outcomes where p is the probability of x and q is the probability of y. With probability $1 - p - q$, nothing happens or the payoff is 0. Kahneman and Tversky define prospects as strictly positive if $x, y > 0$ and $p + q = 1$, strictly negative if $x, y < 0$ and $p + q = 1$, and regular in all other cases. For a regular prospect, agents maximize

$$V(x, p; y, q) = \pi(p) v(x) + \pi(q) v(y)$$

where $v(x)$ and $v(y)$ are the values of each outcome and $\pi(p)$ and $\pi(q)$ are weights based on the outcome probabilities. They assume that $v(0) = 0$, $\pi(0) = 0$, and $\pi(1) = 1$. This function would be equivalent to a expected utility function if v were a Bernoulli function and $\pi(p) = p$ for all p.

For strictly positive or strictly negative prospects such as $x > y > 0$ and $x < y < 0$ where $p + q = 1$, agents maximize

$$V(x, p, y, q) = v(y) + \pi(p) [v(x) - v(y)].$$

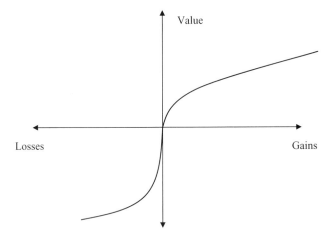

Figure 3.9. Prospect Theoretical Value Functions.

This functional form captures the idea that people evaluate such lotteries as a risk-free component $v(y)$ plus a risky component $v(x) - v(y)$.

A key assumption of Prospect Theory is that $v(\cdot)$ is asymmetric with respect to gains and losses. Kahneman and Tversky make three specific assumptions.

(1) The value function is defined in terms of deviations from a reference point (no gains or losses).
(2) The value function is concave for gains and convex for losses.
(3) The value function is steeper for losses than for gains.

Figure 3.9 illustrates a function satisfying these properties.

Additionally, Kahneman and Tversky make several assumptions about the form of the decision weights $\pi(p)$.

(1) π is an increasing function of p.
(2) $\pi(0) = 0$.
(3) $\pi(1) = 1$.
(4) For low values of p, $\pi(p) > p$.
(5) For low values of p, π is subadditive: that is, $\pi(rp) > r\pi(p)$ for $0 < r < 1$.
(6) For all p, π satisfies the property of subcertainty: that is, $\pi(p) + \pi(1-p) < 1$.
(7) For all $0 < p, q, r < 1$, π is subproportional: that is, $\pi(pq)/\pi(p) \leq \pi(pqr)/\pi(pr)$.

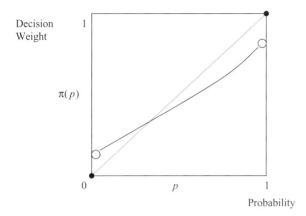

Figure 3.10. Decision Weights.

The first three assumptions are straightforward. The fourth is simply the idea that people overweigh small probabilities. Subadditivity, which helps resolve the Allais paradox, implies in conjunction with assumption 2 that p is convex for low values of p (see exercises 1 and 2). Subcertainty also helps resolve the Allais paradox. Recall that the modal choices require that $v(2400) > \pi(.33)v(2500) + \pi(.66)v(2400)$ and $\pi(.33)v(2500) > \pi(.34)v(2400)$. These two inequalities require that $1 > \pi(.66) + \pi(.34)$. Subproportionality accounts for many of the violations of the independence axiom because it implies that for a fixed ratio of probabilities, the ratio of decision weights is closer to unity when the probabilities are high.

A function satisfying these assumptions is plotted in Figure 3.10.

5. Time Preferences

Many dynamic models in this book require agents to trade off payoffs received now against those received in the future. It is natural to assume that agents value current utility more than future utility (if for no other reason, we could die tomorrow). We use the *discount factor* to model this intuition. Let $0 < \delta < 1$ be the weight that players place on utilities one period in the future relative to current utility. Such constant discounting implies that utilities two periods in the future are weighted by δ^2, and so on, such that utilities t periods in the future are discounted by δ^t.

5.1. Computing Payoff Streams. Often we model games with no determinate end point as infinite games where the number of periods goes to ∞. Clearly, in an infinite game we cannot simply add up the payoffs from each period in order to determine the utility from a sequence of actions. Any such sum of a constant stream of utilities is infinite. Fortunately, geometric discounting helps facilitate these calculations.

Consider the easiest case: an agent receives a payoff of $u_t = u$ for an infinite number of periods. There are two ways to calculate the value v^∞ of this stream of utilities.

Method 1: Note that one can write v^∞ as $u + \delta u + \delta^2 u + \cdots = u \sum_{t=0}^\infty \delta^t$. Because $0 < \delta < 1$, $\sum_{t=0}^\infty \delta^t$ is a convergent power series. It is a well-known result that $\sum_{t=0}^t \delta^t$ converges to $1/(1-\delta)$ as $t \to \infty$, so that $v^\infty = u/(1-\delta)$. We can easily derive the following facts about this important power series:

$$\sum_{t=0}^T \delta^t = \frac{1 - \delta^{T+1}}{1 - \delta}$$

$$\sum_{t=T}^\infty \delta^t = \frac{\delta^T}{1 - \delta}$$

$$\sum_{t=T}^S \delta^t = \frac{\delta^T - \delta^{S+1}}{1 - \delta}.$$

We can use these results to compute finite streams of utility as well. For example, the value of receiving u for T periods is $u \sum_{t=0}^T \delta^t = u\left(1 - \delta^{T+1}\right)/(1 - \delta)$.

Method 2: Another way to derive v^∞ is to use recursion. This approach also forms the basis of Bellman's (1957) principle of optimality. Because v^∞ is an infinite stream of utilities, we can write it as a one-period utility u plus the discounted value of an infinite stream of utility beginning one period hence. Therefore,

$$v^\infty = u + \delta v^\infty$$

so that $v^\infty = u/(1-\delta)$. We can compute finite streams by using this method as well. Again suppose that the agent receives payoff u for T periods, and we wish to compute v^T. We know that $v^T = v^\infty - \delta^{T+1} v^\infty$ so that $v^T = u/(1-\delta) - \delta^{T+1} u/(1-\delta) = u\left(1 - \delta^{T+1}\right)/(1-\delta)$.

Although the advantages of this method are small in this simple example, they are substantial in more complex settings. Assume that there are n states of the world $(s_1, \ldots, s_n)$. In each state, the agent receives u_j. We assume that the state evolves according to a *Markov process* such that the conditional probabilities of a state in period t depend only on the state in period $t - 1$. In other words, assume that for each i, j, t, $\Pr(S_t = s_i | S_{t-1} = s_j) = \pi_{ij}$.

Now suppose we want to compute the value v_j of the stream of utilities beginning from state j. Using recursion, it is easy to see that

$$v_j = u_j + \delta \sum_{i=1}^{n} \pi_{ij} v_i.$$

This creates a linear system of n equations and n unknowns (the v_is). Sometimes it is easier to solve such a system by replacing one of the equations with the requirement that $\sum_{i=1}^{n} \pi_{ij} = 1$ for all j.

Consider an easy example. Suppose we want to compute the long-term payoff to a political party that receives payoff u_1 per period for each period it is in office and gets a payoff of u_2 in periods in which it does not hold office. Suppose that there is an incumbent party effect so that in periods that it holds office, the party is reelected with probability $p > 1/2$ and remains in office (i.e., state 1). This also implies, however, that when it is out of office (state 2), it remains out of office in the next period with probability p. With probability $1 - p$, it transitions either from in office to out of office or vice versa. To compute the party's payoffs from each state, we can set up the relevant recursive equations. Note that there are $n = 2$ unknowns and the equations defining the system are $\pi_{11} = \pi_{22} = p, \pi_{12} = \pi_{21} = 1 - p$. In addition assume that $u_1 > u_2$. Consequently, the equations are

$$v_1 = u_1 + \delta(pv_1 + (1 - p)v_2)$$
$$v_2 = u_2 + \delta((1 - p)v_1 + pv_2).$$

Solving the two equations with two unknowns, we derive

$$v_1 = \frac{(1 - \delta p)u_1 + \delta(1 - p)u_2}{1 - 2\delta p + \delta^2(2p - 1)}$$
$$v_2 = \frac{\delta(1 - p)u_1 + (1 - \delta p)u_2}{1 - 2\delta p + \delta^2(2p - 1)}.$$

In these examples, the utility streams are exogenous – either constants or generated by a fixed probability distribution. This can be relaxed significantly. Suppose that the agent chooses a policy x_t from a state contingent choice set $X(s_t)$ to maximize the discounted value of the stream $u(x_t, s_t)$ where $s_t \in (s_1, \ldots, s_n)$ is the state of the world in time t. We may also allow the probability distribution of transitions from s_t to depend on x_t so let $\pi(s_{t+1}|x_t, s_t)$ be the probability of observing some state s_{t+1} after state s_t and choice x_t. We only consider stationary plans (i.e., those in which the prescription depends only on the state). Let $x(s)$ be a stationary plan specifying the action taken when the state is s.

We can then characterize the payoffs to implementing plan $x(s)$ in state s as

$$v(x(s), s) = u(x(s), s) + \delta \sum_{s'} v(x(s'), s)\pi(s'|x(s), s).$$

Assuming that we can solve for $v(x(s), s)$ for all plans, we can compute the optimal one as

$$v^*(s) = \sup_x v(x(s), s).$$

Bellman's principle of optimality is that

$$v^*(s) = \sup_{x \in X(s)} \left[u(x, s) + \delta \sum_{s'} v^*(s')\pi(s'|x, s) \right].$$

5.2. Hyperbolic Discounting. Although most models in game theory use constant geometric discounting, a growing literature in behavioral decision theory focuses on alternative specifications more consistent with experimental evidence.[8] The most widely studied alternative is hyperbolic discounting, which assumes that at time 0 agents discount the utility at time t by

$$h(t) = (1 + \alpha t)^{-\frac{\gamma}{\alpha}}$$

for $\gamma > 0$ and $\alpha > 0$. Unless α is close to 0, hyperbolic discounting weighs the future much more heavily than constant discounting does. It also implies that agents have a "time consistency" problem. The optimal plan for time t depends on how far time t is in the future.

---

[8] The reader should review optimization in the Mathematical Appendix before reading this section.

Suppose that an agent decides how to allocate \$1 of consumption over three periods $0, 1, 2$. Let $U(x) = \sqrt{x}$. Using constant discounting the optimal plan solves

$$\sqrt{x_0} + \delta\sqrt{x_1} + \delta^2\sqrt{x_2}$$
$$\text{such that } \sum x_t = 1.$$

The solution must satisfy $x_1 = \delta^2 x_0$ and $x_2 = \delta^4 x_0$. Substituting into the budget constraints, we find that

$$x_0 = \frac{1}{1 + \delta^2 + \delta^4}$$
$$x_1 = \frac{\delta^2}{1 + \delta^2 + \delta^4}$$
$$x_2 = \frac{\delta^4}{1 + \delta^2 + \delta^4}.$$

Now consider what happens if the agent reoptimizes after consuming $x_0 = 1/(1 + \delta^2 + \delta^4)$ in the first period. She again optimally chooses $x_2 = \delta^2 x_1$. Substituting this into the constraint $x_1 + x_2 = (\delta^2 + \delta^4)/(1 + \delta^2 + \delta^4)$, we get

$$x_1 = \frac{1}{1 + \delta^2} \cdot \frac{\delta^2 + \delta^4}{1 + \delta^2 + \delta^4} = \frac{\delta^2}{1 + \delta^2 + \delta^4}$$
$$x_2 = \frac{\delta^4}{1 + \delta^2 + \delta^4}.$$

Therefore, she wishes to continue with her optimal consumption plan by consuming exactly as much as in period 2 as she had originally forecast.

Now consider the same allocation problem when the agent uses hyperbolic discounting. To keep the algebra simple, let $\alpha = \gamma = 1$. Thus, the agent solves

$$\sqrt{x_0} + \frac{1}{2}\sqrt{x_1} + \frac{1}{3}\sqrt{x_2}$$
$$\text{such that } \sum x_t = 1$$

The first-order conditions for the optimum are $x_1 = (1/4)x_0$ and $x_2 = (1/9)x_0$. Therefore, the solution is

$$x_0 = \frac{36}{49}$$

$$x_1 = \frac{9}{49}$$

$$x_2 = \frac{4}{49}.$$

Again consider what happens if the agent re-optimizes after consuming x_0. Now the first-order condition is $x_2 = (1/4)x_1$. Substituting the constraint that $x_1 + x_2 = (13/49)$, we find that

$$x_1 = \frac{4}{5} \cdot \frac{13}{49} = \frac{52}{245} > \frac{9}{49}$$

$$x_2 = \frac{13}{245} < \frac{4}{49}.$$

The agent wishes to change her optimal plan and shift more consumption to period 1. The reason for this anomaly is that the relative weight of period 1 to period 2 consumption is higher in period 1 than it was in period 0.

Though hyperbolic discounting has been useful in explaining experimental anomalies and temporal patterns in consumption (e.g., retirees consume less than a constant discounting model would predict), there have been few applications in political science.[9]

6. Exercises

EXERCISE 3.1 *Smith is a member of the House of Representatives. She is trying to decide whether or not to run for the Senate. She believes that she has a 50 percent chance of winning her party's nomination and if she gets the nomination has a 40 percent chance of winning the seat. Suppose that her utility from the Senate seat is W whereas her utility of losing, returning home, and running her family used car lot is L. Her utility of keeping her House seat is H.*

---

[9] One conceptual obstacle is that utilities over infinite horizons may not be well defined. Suppose that an agent evaluates an infinite stream of constant utilities u. Evaluation requires that the series $\sum_{t=0}^{\infty} h(t)u$ converge. This, however, is not the case for a large set of parameters α and γ.

(1) Using a lottery tree, describe the lottery involved with running for the Senate.

(2) Compute the expected utility of running for the Senate.

(3) How low must H be relative to W and L before Smith decides to run for the Senate?

EXERCISE 3.2 *Prove Theorem 3.1.*

EXERCISE 3.3 *Compute the expected payoff of the following lottery. In each of five periods, the agent flips a coin and receives $1 for each consecutive period she obtains heads. In other words, if she receives heads x consecutive times, she receives $x.*

EXERCISE 3.4 *Suppose that instead of always revealing a goat, Monte Hall randomly selects a door to open and thus occasionally reveals the car. Clearly, a contestant should switch to the open door if the car is revealed, but should she switch to the closed door if a goat is revealed?*

EXERCISE 3.5 *A country is fighting a war. In each period, it costs $f > 0$ to fight a battle. The country wins each battle with probability π. The country wins the war and receives a payoff of $w > 0$ forever if it wins two consecutive battles. If it loses two consecutive battles, it loses and receives $l = 0$ forever. The country discounts future periods by δ.*

There are five states corresponding to the consecutive wins and losses in battle. Two of these are terminal states corresponding to victory or loss of the overall war. For each of the nonterminal states, compute the expected utility of continuing the war. Find a condition for f in terms of π, w, l for which the country chooses not to start the war. Find a condition for the country to surrender after losing one battle.

EXERCISE 3.6 *Prove that $\pi(p) > p$ and sub-additivity imply that the decision weight function π is convex for small values of p.*

EXERCISE 3.7 *Consider the following pairs of lotteries:*

*Lottery **a**: .45 chance of $6000, .55 chance of 0*
*Lottery **b**: .90 chance of $3000, .10 chance of 0*
*Lottery **c**: .001 chance of $6000, .999 chance of 0*
*Lottery **d**: .002 chance of $3000 and .998 chance of 0*

Which choices are predicted by Prospect Theory? Why?

EXERCISE 3.8 *Kahneman and Tversky find that **b** and **c** are the modal choices in the following experiment:*

Treatment 1: A person has been given $1000 and then offered

Lottery **a**: .5 chance of an additional $1000, .5 chance of 0
Lottery **b**: $500 for sure

Treatment 2: A person has been given $2000 and offered the choice of

Lottery **c**: .5 chance of losing $1000, .5 chance of 0
Lottery **d**: Loss of $500 for sure.

Is this behavior alone inconsistent with the expected utility framework?

EXERCISE 3.9 Show that

(1) $\sum_{t=0}^{\infty} \delta^t = \frac{1}{1-\delta}$.

(2) $\sum_{t=1}^{\infty} \delta^{t-1} = \sum_{t=0}^{\infty} \delta^t$.

(3) $\sum_{t=0}^{T} \delta^t = \frac{1-\delta^{T+1}}{1-\delta}$.

(4) $\sum_{t=T}^{\infty} \delta^t = \frac{\delta^T}{1-\delta}$.

(5) $\sum_{t=T}^{S} \delta^t = \frac{\delta^T - \delta^{S+1}}{1-\delta}$.

EXERCISE 3.10 Find the value of $\sum_{t=0}^{\infty} \delta^{2t}$.

EXERCISE 3.11 What is the value of the sequence of payoffs $(1, 2, 1, 2, 1, 2, 1, \ldots\ldots)$ when the discount rate $\delta = 2/3$ is used?

EXERCISE 3.12 Suppose that you toss a three-sided die for an infinite number of periods and receive $1 in each period that the die lands on face $1 and $0 in each period that the die lands on face 2 and 2 dollars in each period that the die lands on face 3. Assume that the die lands on face x with probability π_x and that these draws are independent. Assume that the die is fair and that discounting occurs at rate δ. What is the expected value of this sequence of lotteries? Suppose that the utility function for (dollars) is given by $u(x) = \ln(x)$. What is the certainty equivalent of this lottery?

EXERCISE 3.13 Repeat the last exercise under the assumption that the die is very special. It's realizations follow a Markov process with transition probabilities π_{ij} for $i, j \in \{1, 2, 3\}$. Let the discount rate be 3/4 and $\pi_{ii} = 2/3$, $\pi_{ij} = 1/6$ for $i \neq j$.

EXERCISE 3.14 Let $\{x_t\}_{t=1}^{\infty}$ denote a sequence of payoffs. Provide necessary conditions on this sequence such that the value $\sum_{t=0}^{\infty} x_t \delta^{t-1}$ is finite.

EXERCISE 3.15 *For what values of the parameters α, γ is $\sum_{t=1}^{\infty} h(t) = \sum_{t=1}^{\infty} (1 + \alpha t)^{-\gamma/\alpha}$ finite?*

EXERCISE 3.16 *What is the value of the sequence of payoffs $(1, 2, 1, 2, 1, 2, 1, \ldots)$ when the agent uses hyperbolic discounting with $h(t) = (1 + \alpha t)^{-\gamma/\alpha}$?*

4 Social Choice Theory

1. The Open Search

In the pages that follow we consider a scenario that many readers of this book may soon encounter in their professional lives (if they have not already): the "open" faculty search. Consider a fictional, yet realistic, political science department whose membership is spread evenly across five subfields: American (A), comparative (C), international relations (I), theory (T), and formal theory/methods (F). The fictional university is having a mediocre year financially so the dean gives the department authorization for only one additional hire. This dean, unwilling to alienate any of the department's various factions, does not specify in which field the department should search, but tells the department, "Because you study politics you should be able to settle this fairly." Those readers who have experienced a similar situation in their own departments should smile knowingly at the dean's folly.

Members of each subfield have homogeneous preferences over which field to hire. Indeed, each field has its own complete and transitive ordering over the fields. These rankings are given by Table 4.1.

Thus, Americanists find hiring an Americanist most desirable and hiring in international relations least desirable. So the department chair begins to decide how the department should decide. The first idea she entertains is having the department vote on the basis of *plurality rule*. Each member of the department is to cast a ballot for his favorite field and the one with the most votes wins. The chair quickly determines, however, that the election would generate a five-way tie so she abandons that idea. Next she considers *pairwise majority* voting. Under this procedure, each field is paired against each other field. If any field wins all of the pairwise comparisons, the department hires in that field. Confident that this is a fair way to decide, she implements this procedure in the next department meeting. The meeting begins with a vote between A and C. Field C wins with support from T and I. In the vote between C and I, I wins 3-2. In turn, T beats I. Whereas T survives votes against F and A, it loses to C. Consequently, each field is defeated in at least one pairwise vote. The chair's procedure failed to produce any resolution. The chair notes, however, that A loses in every pairwise vote and F loses to all fields except A. So at least she can conclude that neither an Americanist nor a formal theorist should be hired.

Table 4.1				
A	C	I	T	F
A	C	I	T	F
F	T	C	I	A
C	I	T	C	I
T	A	F	F	C
I	F	A	A	T

Frustrated, the chair decides that a scoring system such as the one used to rank college football teams might do the trick. Undeterred by previous failures, she proposes that each department member rank each field. A top ranking gives the field 5 points, a second ranking 4 points, and so on (this procedure is known as the Borda Count). If everyone voted according to his preferences, the chair calculated that the ranking would be C (17 points), I (16 points), T (15 points), F(14 points), and A(13 points).

When the vote occurs, the chair is taken aback by the results. The formal theorists, sensing the opportunity to be strategic, cast their ballots with I in the first position and C in the fifth position. This results in 18 points for I and only 16 for C, an outcome preferred by F. Infuriated by the duplicity, the Cs call for a revote. Their plan is to drop I to the fifth position on their ballots to ensure that C ties for the lead. The chair quickly realizes that in this revote, I would simply drop C to the bottom in retaliation; this might even lead to T's winning if they also cast their ballots strategically. She quickly adjourns the meeting. The next day she calls the dean to have the faculty line transferred to the economics department.

That such a collective choice problem ends in failure is not surprising. A fundamental result of social choice theory is that collective choice processes must either restrict the set of alternatives, or the set of possible preference profiles or violate some other desirable normative properties. As we discuss later, all reasonable mechanisms for making collective decisions are subject to strategic manipulation by agents such as that perpetrated by F in the Borda Count example.

2. Preference Aggregation Rules

This section provides the basic notation and ideas for the formal analysis of preference aggregation rules. The discussion is limited to the case of a finite set of agents $N = \{1, 2, \ldots, n\}$ ($n > 2$) who must choose an outcome from the set X.[1] Our goal is to understand how the preferences of the individual agents map into collective preferences. Agent i holds preference ordering R_i on X. As in Chapter 2, these preference orderings are complete, reflexive, and transitive. The set of all possible complete, reflexive, and transitive preference orderings is denoted by $\mathcal{R}$. We denote a list of preference orderings for all n agents as $\rho = \{R_1, R_2, \ldots, R_n\}$, which we call a preference profile. The set of profiles is therefore $\mathcal{R}^n$. The set $\mathcal{B}$ is the set of complete social orderings on X. An ordering in $\mathcal{B}$ need not be transitive.

DEFINITION 4.1 *A preference aggregation rule is a function* $f : \mathcal{R}^n \rightarrow \mathcal{B}$.

A preference aggregation rule is simply a procedure that takes the set of individual preference orderings and produces a social preference ordering. Subscripted R_i represents individual orderings, but we denote the social ordering as R. As an example, consider the pairwise-majority voting illustrated in the introduction to this chapter. We define the corresponding preference aggregation rule as $x R y$ if at least as many agents have the ordering $x R_i y$ as have $y R_i x$. Because a complete ordering can be produced for any set of preferences, this procedure satisfies the definition. Importantly, the definition does not restrict the outcomes of preference aggregation rules to be transitive. Indeed, in our fictional department, pairwise-majority voting produces the cyclic ordering $T\ P\ I\ P\ C\ P\ T$.

What properties do we want preference aggregation rules to satisfy? Perhaps the most important feature is the ability to generate a best outcome so that the agents can actually choose something. In other words, it is desirable for the social maximal set $M(R, X)$ to be nonempty for all preference profiles. We know from Chapter 2 that this occurs if R is acyclic or transitive.

DEFINITION 4.2 *A preference aggregation rule f is transitive if for every* $\rho \in \mathcal{R}^n$ *the social ordering attained by f is transitive.*

---

[1] Throughout this chapter, we focus only on models of complete information so that we can speak interchangeably of choosing actions, policies, or outcomes.

Second, the rule should be at least minimally democratic so that the preferences of a single agent or dictator do not completely determine the social ranking of the alternatives.

DEFINITION 4.3 *A preference aggregation rule* f *is nondictatorial if there does not exist an* $i \in N$ *such that for every* $\rho \in \mathcal{R}^n$ *and every* $x, y \in X$, $x P_i y$ *implies* $x P y$.

This condition is very strong. If it is violated, the "dictator" gets her way under every possible profile of preferences.

Next, social rankings that agents unanimously disagree with are also undesirable. If all agents prefer x to y, society's preferences should also reflect this ordering. This criterion, named in honor of the Italian economist Vilfredo Pareto, is often referred to as *Pareto efficiency* or *Pareto optimality*.

DEFINITION 4.4 *A preference aggregation rule* f *is weakly Paretian if* $x P_i y$ *for every* $i \in N$ *implies that* $x P y$ *for all* $x, y \in X$.

Finally, the social preferences ordering for any two outcomes should depend only on the individual preference orderings for those two outcomes. One of the reasons that the formal theorists were able to manipulate the outcome of the chair's counting procedure is that the social ranking between C and T depended on F's relative preferences for F, A, and I. From the perspective of a choice between C and T those preferences should be irrelevant. This property is known as the *independence of irrelevant alternatives (IIA)*.

DEFINITION 4.5 *A preference aggregation rule* f *is independent of irrelevant alternatives if* $x R y$ *if and only if* $x R' y$ *for any pair of policies* $x, y \in X$ *and any two profiles* $\rho, \rho' \in \mathcal{R}^n$ *satisfying the condition that for each* $i \in N$, $x R_i y$ *if and only if* $x R'_i y$.

These all seem to be reasonable properties and each can be justified easily on normative or practical grounds (though the case for IIA is weaker). Unfortunately, one of the most fundamental results in the social sciences proves that aggregation rules cannot satisfy all of these properties simultaneously. Arrow's Theorem (1951) says that the only aggregation function that produces transitive preferences, satisfies the Pareto principle, and is IIA is a dictatorship. In other words, the only way social preferences behave as individual preferences is if they are the individual preferences of a single person (the dictator).

We now state and prove Arrow's Theorem.

THEOREM 4.1 *If X is finite and has at least three alternatives, there is no preference aggregation rule $f : \mathcal{R}^n \to \mathcal{B}$ that is transitive, nondictatorial, weakly Paretian, and independent of irrelevant alternatives.*

An important, and often misunderstood, aspect of the result is that we are looking for aggregation rules that are defined for all possible profiles in $\mathcal{R}^n$. The result does not say that an IIA, weak Paretian, and nondictatorial rule results in an intransitive ordering for any profile $\rho \in \mathcal{R}^n$, just that transitivity is violated for some profile(s). Some authors state Arrow's Theorem with an additional condition known as unrestricted domain – all profiles in $\mathcal{R}^n$ are possible. We prefer just to be clear that a preference aggregation rule has as its domain $\mathcal{R}^n$. We need one more definition before proving Arrow's Theorem.

DEFINITION 4.6 *For a preference aggregation rule f, a set $W \subset N$ is semidecisive for x against y if $x P y$ for every $\rho \in \mathcal{R}^n$ in which $x P_i y$ for all $i \in W$ and $y P_j x$ for all $j \in W^c = N \backslash W$. A set W is decisive for x against y if $x P y$ for every $\rho \in \mathcal{R}^n$ in which $x P_i y$ for all $i \in W$. A set W is decisive if it is decisive for x against y for every $x, y \in X$.*

A convenient proof of Arrow's Theorem rests on first establishing a property about decisive sets when the rule satisfies some of the Arrovian conditions.

LEMMA 4.1 *If f is a transitive preference aggregation rule that is independent of irrelevant alternatives and weakly Paretian, $W \subset N$ is decisive if W is semidecisive for x against y for some $x, y \in X$.*

Proof Assume that $W \subset N$ is semidecisive for x against y and that $x P_i z$ for all $i \in W$ under the profile $\rho \in \mathcal{R}^n$. Consider another profile $\rho' \in \mathcal{R}^n$ with the following properties: (1) $x P_i' y P_i' z$ for $i \in W$; (2) $y P_j' x$ and $y P_j' z$ for all $z \notin \{x, y\}$ and $j \in W^c$; and (3) $x R_j z$ if and only if $x R_j' z$ for all $z \notin \{x, y\}$ and $j \in W^c$. So ρ and ρ' do not differ on individual orderings of x and z. Because W is semidecisive for x against y, $x P' y$. That f is weakly Paretian implies that $y P' z$, whereas the transitivity of f implies that $x P' z$. But because (1) preferences of W^c on x and z have not been specified in ρ' and (2) ρ and ρ' agree on x and z (i.e., $x R_j z$

if and only if xR'_jz), the assumption that f is IIA requires that xPz. Consequently, W **is decisive for** x **against** z. This, of course, implies that W is semidecisive for x against z. An analogous argument demonstrates that W **is decisive for** x **against** y. We now verify that W is decisive for y against z. Consider two profiles: $\rho^0 \in \mathcal{R}^n$ with yP_i^0z for all $i \in W$, and $\rho^+ \in \mathcal{R}^n$ with $yP_i^+xP_i^+z$ for all $i \in W$ and both zP_j^+x and yP_j^+x for all $j \in W^c$. Further, assume that yR_j^0z if and only if yR_j^+z for all $j \in W^c$. Because W is decisive for x against z, xP^+z. Further, yP^+x because f is weakly Paretian. Because f is transitive, yP^+z. Only the preferences of members of W have been specified on $\{y, z\}$ by ρ^+ and both ρ^0 and ρ^+ agree on y and z. Consequently, IIA implies yP^0z, so that W **is decisive for** y **against** z. This implies that W is semidecisive for y against z. Relabeling the first step and using this fact imply that W **is decisive for** y **against** x. Combining these conclusions leads to the claim that W is decisive. $\qquad\qquad\square$

Accordingly, if any group is semidecisive for some pairwise comparison then the group is decisive. For preference aggregation rules satisfying IIA and the weak Pareto criterion, a group that gets its way on one pairwise comparison gets it on all of them. We now complete the proof of Arrow's Theorem by showing that either a single agent is decisive or the entire collective is not decisive. The first finding violates the nondictatorial condition and the second violates the weak Paretian condition. Consequently, Arrow's conditions are logically incompatible.

Proof of Arrow's Theorem Assume that X is finite and contains at least three alternatives. To generate a contradiction, assume that a preference aggregation rule is transitive, nondictatorial, weakly Paretian, and independent of irrelevant alternatives. Given Lemma 4.1, for any set $W \subset N$ either W is decisive or there is no pair of alternatives $x, y \in X$ such that W is semidecisive for x against y. Consider two disjoint sets $A, B \subset N$ that are not semidecisive for any x and y (and thus not decisive). Let $C = N\backslash\{A \cup B\}$. Because $n > 2$ and no singleton set $\{i\}$ is decisive, three such sets A, B, C exist. Now consider the profile $\rho^- \in \mathcal{R}^n$ with $xP_i^-yP_i^-z$ for $i \in A$; $zP_j^-xP_j^-y$ for $j \in B$; and $yP_t^-zP_t^-x$ for $t \in C$. Because A and B are not semidecisive for any pairs, zR^-x and yR^-z. That f is transitive requires yR^-x. This implies that the set $A \cup B$ is not semidecisive for x against y, and the set $A \cup B$ is not decisive. Thus the union of two disjoint sets that are not decisive is not decisive. Because f is not dictatorial, no singleton set is decisive. This conclusion means that no union of agents is decisive. But this implies that N is not decisive. This contradicts the assumption that f is weakly Paretian. □

The introduction of this chapter provides some examples of the implications of Arrow's Theorem. As we have shown, pairwise majority voting is not transitive and the Borda Count does not satisfy IIA. An additional example is the unanimity rule defined as xPy if and only if xR_iy for all i and xP_iy for some i. Clearly, this rule satisfies the weak Pareto criterion and satisfies IIA because the rule chooses between x and y on the individuals preferences over x and y. But it is not transitive. To see this consider the individual preference orderings, as in Table 4.2.

Clearly, the unanimity rule implies xRy and yRz. Yet, the rule also implies zPx.

Table 4.2

1	2	3
y	z	z
z	y	x
x	x	y

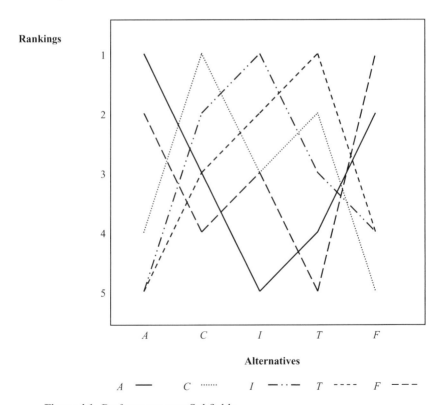

Rankings

Alternatives

A —   C ⋯⋯   I —··—   T ----   F ———

Figure 4.1. Preferences over Subfields.

Because the domain of a preference aggregation rule is the set of all possible preference profiles, Arrow's Theorem still allows for the possibility that there is a satisfactory way to aggregate preferences for a given profile. Thus, one response to Arrow's Theorem is to restrict the set of profiles and consider whether there are preference aggregation rules that satisfy the normative axioms on the restricted set.

One common restriction is *single-peakedness*. Intuitively, single-peakedness requires that there is some ordering of the outcomes so that each agent's preference ranking increases up to the most preferred outcome and then declines after that. Consider Figure 4.1, which plots the preference orderings of our fictional political science department. Given the ordering $ACITF$, only fields I and T have preferences with a single peak as their preference rankings increase up to their ideal outcome and decline afterward. The other fields have multiple-peaked preferences over the ordering $ACITF$. For example, field A has peaks at A and F. The motivated reader can verify that there is no way to order the outcomes so that all preferences have a single peak. Thus, the preference profile of our fictional department is not single-peaked. Consider the profile shown in Table 4.3, however.

Table 4.3				
A	C	I	T	F
A	C	I	T	F
F	T	C	C	A
I	I	A	I	I
C	A	F	A	C
T	F	T	F	T

Now if we order the outcomes $TCIAF$ (or $FAICT$) then all subfield preferences have a single peak at the outcome associated with their own field as illustrated in Figure 4.2. To foreshadow the next main result of this section, consider the outcome of pairwise-majority voting. Now I defeats all of the other alternatives. Furthermore, pairwise-majority voting produces the transitive strict preference order $IACFT$, identical to the preferences of I. Is it a coincidence that majority voting works well with our single-peaked preference profile? No, single-peakedness is a sufficient (though not necessary) condition for the transitivity of majority rule.

Stating and proving this result require a bit more notation. Let q be an ordering function that takes the set of outcomes and assigns each a unique rank. Formally, $q : X \to \{1, 2, \ldots, |X|\}$ is a one-to-one and onto function (or bijection).[2] Now we define single-peakedness.

---

[2] A function $q : X \to X$ is one-to-one if for every $y \in X$ the set $q^{-1}(y) = \{x \in X; q(x) = y\}$ is a singleton. The function is onto if for every $y \in X$ there is some $x \in X$ such that $q(x) = y$.

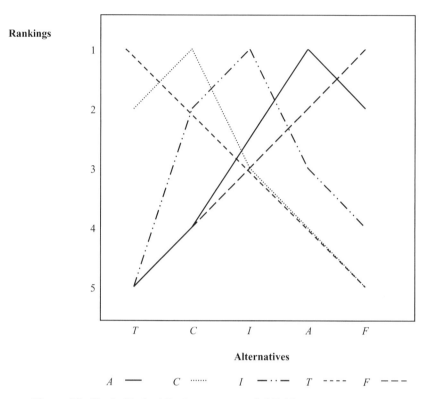

Figure 4.2. Single-Peaked Preferences over Subfields.

DEFINITION 4.7 *For a set N and a finite choice space X, a preference profile $\rho \in \mathcal{R}^n$ is single-peaked if there exists some bijection $q : X \rightarrow \{1, 2, \ldots, |X|\}$ such that for every $i \in N$ there is some $t_i \in X$ such that if $q(y) < q(t_i)$ then $t_i P_i y$ (and if $q(x) < q(y) < q(t_i)$ then $t_i P_i y P_i x$) and if $q(t_i) < q(b)$ then $t_i P_i b$ (and if $q(t_i) < q(b) < q(c)$ then $t_i P_i b P_i c$). The set of single-peaked profiles is denoted $\mathcal{S} \subset \mathcal{R}^n$.*

In this definition the policy t_i is interpreted as i's ideal policy as it is the unique element of $M(R_i, X)$. Agent i's preference ordering declines as $q(x)$ deviates from $q(t_i)$ both above and below.
We now formally state the theorem.

THEOREM 4.2 *Given $\rho \in \mathcal{S}$ majority rule is transitive, weakly Paretian, IIA, and nondictatorial.*

The proof is very straightforward. We begin by proving transitivity. Let x, y, and z be three alternatives where without loss of generality, we can define the single-peaked ordering (using definition 4.7) as $q(z) > q(y) > q(x)$. Let $P(x, y; \rho)$ be the set of agents who prefer x to y given profile ρ.

Single-peakedness puts restrictions on the preference orderings over x, y, and z. For example, suppose than an agent prefers x to y. With single-peakedness, such an agent can have only one preference order – $x P_i y P_i z$ – any other ordering has peaks at both x and z. Consequently, we know that she also prefers x to z. Thus, all agents who prefer x to y also prefer x to z so that $P(x, y; \rho) \subseteq P(x, z; \rho)$. We ask the reader to verify that single-peakedness generates all of the following conditions:

$$P(x, y; \rho) \subseteq P(x, z; \rho)$$
$$P(z, x; \rho) \subseteq P(y, x; \rho)$$
$$P(z, y; \rho) \subseteq P(z, x; \rho)$$
$$P(x, z; \rho) \subseteq P(y, z; \rho).$$

A property of majority rule is that a set of agents is decisive over a pair of alternatives if any of its subsets is decisive – if a group is a majority, all the groups to which its belongs are bigger and therefore must be majorities as well. Thus, the restrictions imposed by single-peakedness imply the following:

If $x P y$ then $x P z$.   (4.1)

If $z P x$ then $y P x$.   (4.2)

If $z P y$ then $z P x$.   (4.3)

If $x P z$ then $y P z$.   (4.4)

In order to establish transitivity, we need to show that none of the following six statements is contradicted. Either each of the following statements follows directly from one of the preceding conditions or its premise is contradicted.[3]

(1) If $x P y$ and $y P z$ then $x P z$. This follows from (4.1).
(2) If $x P z$ and $z P y$ then $x P y$. The premise is contradicted by (4.3).

---

[3] If a statement's premise (the "if" part) is invalid, then the statement is not contradicted.

(3) If yPx and xPz then yPz. This follows from (4.4).
(4) If yPz and zPx then yPx. This follows from (4.2).
(5) If zPx and xPy then zPy. The premise is contradicted by (4.2).
(6) If zPy and yPx then zPx. This follows from (4.3).

Having exhausted the possibilities, we establish that majority rule is transitive if preferences are single-peaked when the choice space has three policies. The extension is not challenging. We leave it to the reader to show that majority rule is weakly Paretian, IIA, and nondictatorial.

3. Collective Choice

Whereas it is useful to begin with the properties of aggregate preference orderings, ultimately we are interested in the set of policies that are maximal given a preference aggregation rule. Analogously to individual choices, we assume social choices are generated from the maximal set determined by the aggregate preference ordering. In the social choice setting, we refer to the set of maximal choices as the core.

DEFINITION 4.8 *Given X, $\rho \in \mathcal{R}^n$, and a preference aggregation rule f, the core is defined as $C_{f(\rho)}(X) = M(f(\rho), X)$.*

Applying Theorem 2.1 establishes that if X is finite and the collective preference is complete and transitive, the core is nonempty, and the social choice is well defined. Arrow's Theorem, however, indicates that transitivity of preference aggregation rules is not always satisfied. In such cases, the core may be empty.

When a majority-rule core exists, its outcomes are known as *Condorcet winners* after the Marquis de Condorcet, who was among the first to study the properties of voting procedures formally. Nevertheless, the result that the majority-rule core is nonempty with single-peaked preferences is generally attributed to Duncan Black.

THEOREM 4.3 *Let $n > 2$ (odd), $\rho \in \mathcal{S}$, and $f(\cdot)$ be pairwise-majority voting. Then $C_{f(\rho)}(X) = \{t_m : |j \in N\backslash m : q(t_j) \leq q(t_m)| = |k \in N\backslash m : q(t_k) \geq q(t_m)|\}$. Consequently, the core is the median voter's ideal point.*

The proof is similar to, but easier than, the proof of the transitivity of majority rule with single-peaked preferences. Let t_m be the median ideal point so that $n/2$ agents have ideal points such that $q(t_i) < q(t_m)$ and $n/2$ agents have ideal points such that $q(t_i) > q(t_m)$. Then we can define $P(t_m, x)$ as the set of agents that prefer t_m to x. If $q(x) < q(t_m)$, then single-peakedness implies that $P(t_m, x)$ must include the median agent and all agents for whom $q(t_i) > q(t_m)$. This set is a majority as it contains at least $(n+1)/2$ agents. Similarly, if $q(x) > q(t_m)$, $P(t_m, x)$ contains the median and all agents for whom $q(t_i) < q(t_m)$. Consequently, $t_m P x$ for all $x \neq t_m$ and is therefore the unique element of the maximal set.

This result indicates that if preferences are single-peaked, the majority-rule core is well defined. In such cases, submitting to the "will of the majority" might be a reasonable way to make collective choices.

The restriction to single-peaked preferences may not always be appropriate, however. For example, the set of policies may be multi-dimensional. In such cases, the generalization of single-peakedness is extraordinarily restrictive. Consider Figure 4.3, which shows ideal points for five voters in two dimensions. Each agent has circular indifference curves so that in any binary comparison, she prefers the alternative closest to her ideal point. These indifference curves correspond to Euclidean preferences. Point 5 is a majority-rule core point or the Condorcet winner as a majority prefers it to any other point in the policy space. To demonstrate this claim, we show that at least three voters block any other policy. First, consider a move to any policy in the region marked W. Obviously, voter 5 votes against any such move, as do voters 1 and 3. Thus, 5's ideal point is majority preferred to any

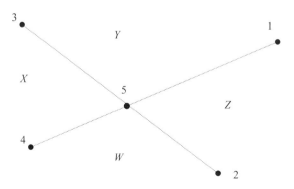

Figure 4.3. Condorcet Winner in Two Dimensions.

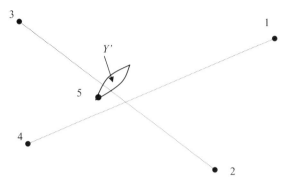

Figure 4.4. No Condorcet Winner.

policy in region *W*. Similarly, voters 1, 2, and 5 vote against moves to region *X*, voters 2, 4, and 5 vote against points in region *Y*, and 3, 4, and 5 vote against points in region *Z*.

Voter 5's ideal point is the core because voter 5 is the median voter over any two alternatives: if she prefers *x* to *y* at least two other voters do so as well. Because this must also be true for comparisons of the ideal points of other players, voter 5's ideal point must lie on the lines connecting opposing pairs of ideal points (2–3 and 1–4). This condition is closely related to the Plott (1967) conditions. We formalize the condition in the next section; for now it is sufficient to note that the condition is fragile. A slight deviation from the intersection of these lines as in Figure 4.4 destroys the majority core. First, the intersection cannot be a core point because voters 3, 4, and 5 prefer 5's ideal point to the intersection. Second, voter 5's ideal point cannot be a Condorcet winner because there is a set of points *Y'* that are preferred by 1, 2, and 3.

Given that the conditions for the existence (or more precisely the nonemptiness) of a majority rule core are so restrictive, an obvious question is whether majority rule can at least reduce the set of possible outcomes by eliminating some as undesirable. Recall in our introductory example the department chair felt that it was reasonable to conclude that the department should not hire in American or formal theory – both of those fields were defeated by the three other fields. Consequently, majority rule eliminates two options even though it created a cycle among the three top alternatives. In the example, *C*, *I*, and *T* represent a *top cycle set:* a set of alternatives that defeat all alternatives outside the set but over which the aggregation rule is

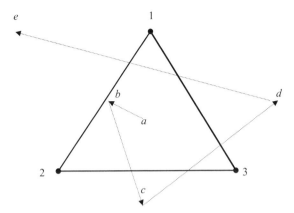

Figure 4.5. McKelvey's Theorem.

intransitive. Perhaps, although majority rule does not produce a core, it can produce a small top cycle set. Unfortunately, this optimism is also unwarranted. Richard McKelvey (1976) has shown that with sincere voting (given any pair of alternatives, each agent votes for the one she prefers) and Euclidean preferences the top cycle set is either the core or the entire set of alternatives. We treat McKelvey's result more formally in the next section, but its intuition is illustrated in the example of Figure 4.5. Here three voters have quadratic preferences, and there is an initial status quo policy a. To illustrate the result, it is sufficient to demonstrate that pairwise-majority voting can lead from point a to anywhere in the policy space. First, note that point b is majority preferred to a because voters 1 and 2 prefer it. Continuing, note that voters 2 and 3 prefer c to b, and voters 1 and 3 prefer d to c. At each subsequent stage of the agenda, the set of policies that are majority preferred to the current status quo is getting larger. This allows us to reach points farther and farther away from the voters' ideal points. Ultimately voters 1 and 2 prefer the very distant point e to d. From e, the agenda can return to a (the voters unanimously prefer a to e) or e can be leveraged to get to even more distant points.

This approach to preference aggregation is not well suited as a positive methodology because it does not offer clear empirical predictions. Some have interpreted McKelvey's result to predict political chaos: choices are unstable with observable cycles. This interpretation is naive; it attributes a positive prediction to a model that does not make any. A more reasonable interpretation is that the results demonstrate the importance of investigating the effects of the political institutions within which collective choices are made. The conclusion, therefore, is that a model that takes as primitives only preferences and a preference aggregation rule is often underspecified. The tools of noncooperative game theory developed in later chapters allow us to construct more empirically relevant models of collective choice.

3.1. Formal Analysis of the Plott Conditions and McKelvey's Theorem*. In this section, we present a formal analysis of Plott and McKelvey's results for majority rule and multidimensional preferences. The following analysis is based on the following social choice environment.

Condition 4.1 *Let $X \subset \mathbb{R}^d$ (d finite) be convex. Agents have strictly convex, continuous preferences on X.*

If X is compact, Theorem 2.3 and Theorem 2.4 imply that each agent has a unique ideal point y_i in X. Instead of assuming that X is compact, therefore, we assume that each agent has an ideal point. The assumption that preferences are strictly convex requires that the upper contour sets be strictly convex sets. If we further restrict the model to Euclidean preferences, $u_i(x) = -\|x - y_i\|$, we can specify exactly how utility changes as the policy alternatives are varied.

DEFINITION 4.9 *If preferences are Euclidean then for any $x \in X$ the gradient vector $\nabla u_i(x) = y_i - x$.*

The gradient vector is a directed vector or line segment pointing in the direction that agent i prefers policy to move from point x. For a general utility function, the gradient vector at x is simply the vector of partial derivatives evaluated at x.

DEFINITION 4.10 *Given a utility function $u : \mathbb{R}^d \to \mathbb{R}^1$ the gradient vector is $\nabla u_i(x) = (\partial u(x)/\partial x_1, \partial u(x)/\partial x_2, \ldots, \partial u(x)/\partial x_d)'$.*

The statement of Plott's result also uses the notion of a *pairing*. For a finite set A, a mapping $p : A \to A$ is a pairing if it is a bijection. This means that each i in A is paired with exactly one j in A. Now we can define Plott's conditions.

DEFINITION 4.11 *In the spatial model with Euclidean preferences the Plott conditions are satisfied at a policy $x \in X$ if there exists a pairing $p(\cdot)$ on the set $L = \{j \in N : y_j \neq x\}$ such that for every $i \in L$, $\nabla u_i(x) = -\lambda_i \nabla u_{p(i)}(x)$ for some $\lambda_i > 0$.*

If the Plott conditions are satisfied at x, each agent with an ideal point different from x can be paired with an agent so that each agent in the pair wants policy to move in the exact opposite direction. Because proponents of any change are paired with opponents, it is impossible to build a majority coalition to overturn x. The following result characterizes the relationship between the Plott conditions and the majority-rule core in the spatial model with Euclidean preferences.

THEOREM 4.4 *In the spatial model with Euclidean preferences and n odd the point x in the interior of X is in the core $C_{f(\rho)}(X)$ if and only if the Plott conditions are satisfied at x.*[4]

It is clear that the Plott conditions are not satisfied generally. Suppose the conditions are satisfied for some x. Then for all i, $y_i - x = -\lambda_i \left(y_{p(i)} - x\right)$. If we perturb $y_{p(i)}$ so that it lies on a different vector from the origin, this condition no longer holds at x. More precisely if $\mathbb{R}^{dn}$ is the space of possible ideal points of n agents with Euclidean preferences on the choice space $\mathbb{R}^d$ then the subset of $\mathbb{R}^{dn}$ for which the Plott conditions are satisfied at some $x \in \mathbb{R}^d$ is incredibly small. It contains no open sets and has an empty interior. If one randomly picked an arbitrary preference profile, the probability of selecting one that satisfies the Plott conditions for some point would be 0.

Although the set of profiles with a core point is very small, each profile with a core point is arbitrarily close to another profile with a core point. In the exercises, we ask the reader to show that if one perturbs a profile with a core point, the core point of the new profile (if it exists) is arbitrarily close to the old one.[5]

Even though the core is generally empty, is there some other subset of the policy space that possesses normatively desirable properties and is a reasonable prediction? One possibility is the top cycle set.

---

[4] A policy x is in the interior of X if there is an open ball $B(x, \varepsilon)$ that is contained in X. See the Mathematical Appendix for more on this concept.

[5] The assumption that preferences are Euclidean can be replaced by a differentiability condition to produce a more general result.

DEFINITION 4.12 *For a set X, a profile $\rho \in \mathcal{R}^n$, and a preference aggregation rule f, the top cycle set is $T_{f(\rho)} = \{x \in X : \forall y \in X\backslash x, \exists\{a_0, \ldots, a_t\} \subset X$ such that $a_0 = x, a_t = y$ for $t < \infty$ and $\forall z \leq t\ a_{z-1} P a_z\}$.*

The top cycle set is the set of points that can be reached from any other point via a finite chain of strict preferences. That is, if $x \in T_{f(\rho)}$ then for every $y \in X\backslash x$ we can select a finite number of policies $\{a_1, a_2, \ldots, a_t\}$ such that $x P a_1 P a_2 P \ldots P a_t P y$. The following result (proved by McKelvey) indicates that either the Plott conditions are satisfied or the top cycle set covers the policy space.

THEOREM 4.5 *In the spatial model either $C_{f(\rho)}(X)$ is nonempty or $T_{f(\rho)} = X$.*

The implications of the last two theorems are striking. In the spatial model with Euclidean preferences, any policy can be reached by any other policy in a finite chain of strict preferences unless the knife-edged Plott condition holds at some policy.

4. Manipulation of Choice Functions

The previous section illustrates that majority rule very often fails to provide sufficient guidance for making social choices. Even when a majority core exists, however, agents may not have incentives to reveal their preferences truthfully. As Gibbard (1973) and Sattherwaite (1975) have proved, all *reasonable* social choice functions including majority rule are susceptible to manipulation by strategic agents. Recall the attempt of the formal theorists to manipulate the Borda Count by misrepresenting their preferences over the fields. Similar manipulation is also possible in voting. Consider a voting agenda in which x is first paired against y and then against z. Suppose that by majority vote, $x P y$, $z P x$, and $y P z$. If all voters vote according to their actual preferences, x defeats y and loses to z. Voters who prefer x to y and y to z, however, have incentives to vote strategically for y (i.e., misrepresent their preferences over x and y) in the first round so that y might win round 1 and go on to defeat z.

Formalizing the Gibbard-Sattherwaite theorem requires additional notation and definitions.

DEFINITION 4.13 *The social decision function is an onto function $G : \mathcal{R}^n \to X$ that generates an outcome given a preference profile.*

A social decision function inputs a preference profile and generates an outcome. The requirement that G be "onto" suggests that every outcome is supported by some profile. Now we define manipulation.

DEFINITION 4.14 $G(\rho)$ *is manipulable at profile* ρ *if and only if for some* i *there exists an alternative profile* $\rho' = \{ R_1, \ldots, R_{i-1}, R_i', R_{i+1}, \ldots, R_n \}$ *such that* $G(\rho') P_i G(\rho)$. *G is nonmanipulable if it is not manipulable at any* ρ.

A social decision function is manipulable if a single agent can change the outcome to one she prefers by misreporting her preferences. In the definition, agent i changes the outcome from $G(\rho)$ to $G(\rho')$, one she prefers, by reporting preferences R_i' instead of R_i. The following is Gibbard and Sattherwaite's theorem:

THEOREM 4.6 *If there are more than three alternatives and G is non-manipulable, then there is a dictator (i.e., $G(\rho) P_i x$ for some i, all $x \in X \setminus G(\rho)$ and all $\rho \in \mathcal{R}^n$).*

An outline of the proof follows. Assume that G is nonmanipulable. Then we can construct a transitive and IIA preference ordering by applying G to all of X to get the most preferred outcome, and subsequently applying G to the remaining elements of X to get the second outcome, and so on. Because this ordering satisfies the weak Pareto criterion, Arrow's Theorem says there must be a dictator.

Now consider the details. Suppose that G is nonmanipulable. For step 1, let ρ be such that there exists a set B where $x P_i y$ for all i, all $x \in B$, and all $y \in X \setminus B$. Consequently, B is a set of alternatives that all agents prefer to all alternatives outside the set. The first claim is that the social decision is an element of this "best" set, $G(\rho) \in B$. Suppose that this were not true. Because G is onto, we can pick an alternative profile ρ' such that $G(\rho') \in B$. Then we can construct a series of alternatives:

$$y_0 = G(\rho)$$
$$y_1 = G(\rho | R_1') = G(R_1', R_2, \ldots, R_n)$$
$$y_i = G(\rho | R_1' \ldots, R_i') = G(R_1', \ldots, R_i', R_{i+1}, \ldots, R_n)$$
$$y_n = G(\rho').$$

Let k be the smallest integer such that $y_k \in B$. Because agent k prefers everything inside B to everything outside it, she generates a better outcome by reporting R'_k instead of R_k. So G is not nonmanipulable. It must be true that $G(\rho) \in B$.

The next step is to create an aggregation rule or social ranking over all policies given ρ. Let the highest-ranked element be $x_1 = G(\rho)$. We can then move x_1 to the bottom of everyone's preference ranking to create ρ_2. The second-ranked choice is $x_2 = G(\rho_2)$. From step 1, $x_2 \neq x_1$. We continue this process until we rank all of the alternatives.

It is easy to see that this preference ordering satisfies the weak Pareto criterion – at every stage the decision rule chooses an element of the "best" set for the constructed profile. Now we show that our aggregation rule is IIA. Suppose that it were not. Then there would be two profiles ρ and ρ' and two alternatives $x, y \in X$ such that $x R_i y$ if and only if $x R'_i y$ for all i but $x f(\rho) y$ and $y f(\rho') x$. Let $\rho(x, y)$ be the profile that agrees with ρ everywhere except that x and y are moved to the top of everyone's ordering. We claim that $G(\rho(x, y)) = x$. Suppose this statement were not true. Then let $\widehat{\rho}$ be the profile created by dropping alternatives to the bottom until $G(\widehat{\rho}) = x$. Consider a sequence $y_i = G(\rho(x, y)|\widehat{R}_1, \ldots, \widehat{R}_i)$ so that y_i is the social decision created by switching the first i agents to the new profile. Note that $y_n = G(\widehat{\rho}) = x$ and $y_0 = G(\rho(x, y)) = y$ because step 1 implies $G(\rho(x, y)) \in \{x, y\}$. As earlier, let k be the smallest integer such that $y_k \neq y$. If $y_k = x$ and $x P_k y$, G can be manipulated by switching from R_k to $\widehat{R}_k$. Alternatively, if $y P_k x$, a switch from $\widehat{R}_k$ to R_k manipulates G. If $y_k \neq x$, then consider the smallest $j > k$ such that $y_j \in \{x, y\}$. Using exactly the same logic as earlier, we can verify that agent j can manipulate G. So we contradict the assumption that G is nonmanipulable and establish $G(\rho(x, y)) = x$.

Now consider a sequence $z_i = G(\rho(x, y)|R'_1(x, y), \ldots, R'_i(x, y))$. The assumption of not IIA implies that $z_n = G(\rho'(x, y)) = y$ and $z_0 = G(\rho(x, y)) = x$. As earlier, there must be an agent who prefers y to x and can switch his stated preference from $R(x, y)$ to $R'(x, y)$ to change the outcome from x to y or an agent who prefers x to y who can switch from $R'(x, y)$ to $R(x, y)$ Thus, G is manipulable. This contradiction implies that the preference ordering must be IIA. From Arrow's Theorem, there must be a dictator for f and therefore a dictator for G.

Although the Gibbard-Sattherwaite Theorem is a negative result, it has important implications for the study of politics. Perhaps the most important is that strategic behavior is ubiquitous in politics: "strategy-proof" mechanisms often do not exist. Appropriately, the next chapter begins our study of strategic models of politics.

5. Exercises

EXERCISE 4.1 *Suppose players have the following preferences:*

1	*2*
a	*e*
b	*b*
c	*d*
d	*a*
e	*c*

(1)   What are the Borda counts for each of the alternatives?

(2)   How can player 1 do better by misrepresenting her preferences?

(3)   How can player 2 do better by misrepresenting his preferences?

(4)   Is there any combination of statements (not necessarily truthful) for which the two players would not have an incentive to change, ex post?

EXERCISE 4.2 *Prove the following proposition: Given $\rho \in S$ majority rule is transitive, weakly Paretian, IIA, and nondictatorial.*

EXERCISE 4.3 *(drawn from Austen-Smith and Banks 1999) A preference aggregation rule f satisfies citizen's sovereignty if for all $x, y \in X$ (where $x \neq y$) there exist $\rho \in \mathcal{R}^n$ such that $x P y$. A preference aggregation rule f is monotone if for all $x, y \in X$, and for all $\rho, \rho' \in \mathcal{R}^n$ the following is true: if (1) $x P_i y$ implies $x P_i' y$, and (2) $x R_i y$ implies $x R_i' y$, and (3) $x P y$ then it must be the case that $x P' y$. Prove that if f is weakly monotonic and satisfies citizen's sovereignty then f is weakly Paretian.*

EXERCISE 4.4 *Suppose there are three voters who are to decide on an alternative via pairwise-majority rule. If there are three alternatives, all preferences are strict, and each voter has a different preference ordering from the other two, what percentage of the possible combinations of preferences result in a Condorcet winner? (Note that if two agents share a common preference ordering, their most preferred must be a Condorcet winner. Why?)*

EXERCISE 4.5 *Assume that there are three voters with Euclidean preferences in two dimensions with ideal points at $(-1, 0)$, $(0, 1)$, and $(1, 0)$, respectively.*

(1)   Construct an agenda to get from (0, 0) to (2, 2).
(2)   Construct an agenda to get from (0, 0) to (5, 5).
(3)   Construct an agenda to get from (0, 0) to (−5, −5).
Try to keep these agendas as short as possible.

EXERCISE 4.6 *Show that if $\rho \in \mathbb{R}^{dn}$ is a profile of ideal points for which the Plott conditions are satisfied at some $x \in \mathbb{R}^d$ then for every $\varepsilon > 0$ there exists a profile $\rho^\varepsilon \in B(\rho, \varepsilon)$ for which the Plott conditions are not satisfied at any point for the profile ρ^ε.*

EXERCISE 4.7 *Show that if $\rho \in \mathbb{R}^{dn}$ (n odd) is a profile of ideal points for which the Plott conditions are satisfied at some $x \in \mathbb{R}^d$ then for every $\varepsilon > 0$ there exists a $\delta > 0$ such that if $\rho^\delta \in B(\rho, \delta)$ and the Plott conditions are satisfied for some point at the profile ρ^δ then the Plott conditions are satisfied for a point $x' \in B(x, \varepsilon)$ by the profile ρ^δ.*

5 Games in the Normal Form

At twelve and a half minutes into the broadcast, Detectives Logan and Briscoe arrest two murder suspects. District Attorney Adam Schiff instructs Assistant D.A. Jack McCoy to make the following offer to each separately:

- If you confess and provide evidence of first-degree murder by your accomplice, you will receive a 1 year sentence on a weapons charge provided that your accomplice does not confess. If she does confess as well, you both will get 8 years for murder II.
- If you hold out and your accomplice turns state's evidence, you will serve 25 to life for murder I. If she also holds out, you will serve 4 years for voluntary manslaughter.

Assuming each suspect loses one unit of utility for each year in prison, Table 5.1 shows the payoffs of each subject given all of the possible outcomes. The rows represent the actions of suspect 1 whereas the columns represent the actions of suspect 2. Each pair of numbers represents the payoffs for suspect 1 and suspect 2 for each combination, respectively.

The situation of the suspects is *strategic* because the outcome of any action by suspect 1 depends on the choices of suspect 2, and vice versa. What should the suspects do? Collectively, they prefer to hold out. If they both hold out, the total jail time is only eight years, far less than any other outcome. Unless, however, they reach a binding agreement, the individual incentives of the suspects undermine this outcome. Suppose that suspect 1 holds out. Suspect 2 then recognizes that she does better by confessing, reducing jail time from 4 years to 1. In fact, both suspects recognize that each does better by confessing regardless of the other's actions. Thus, they both confess, leading to a total of 16 years of jail. Individual rationality leads to socially inferior outcomes (where society refers to the suspects; the D.A. and the police presumably prefer this outcome).[1]

In this game, the well-known "Prisoner's Dilemma," we deduce the strategies of rational actors straightforwardly. In other strategic situations, however, the predictions are more subtle. Consider the "Terrorist Hunt." Two agencies, the FBI and the CIA, are responsible for investigating and apprehending terror suspects. There are two types of suspects: kingpins and operatives. Both agencies prefer the capture of kingpins to the capture of operatives, and both agencies prefer either of these outcomes to a failure to capture anyone. Capturing a kingpin, however, requires that the two agencies cooperate by dedicating resources to a joint effort. If one agency fails to cooperate, the other agency fails to capture any suspects. On the other hand, each agency captures an operative by conducting its own investigation. Table 5.2 illustrates the strategic situation of each agency in deciding whether to go after the kingpin or the operative.

Table 5.1. The Prisoner's Dilemma

1\2	*Hold Out*	*Confess*
Hold Out	−4, −4	−25, −1
Confess	−1, −25	−8, −8

The rows of this matrix represent the possible strategies of the FBI (*hunt kingpin* or *hunt operative*) whereas the columns represent those of the CIA. Both agencies earn a utility of 2 for capturing the kingpin, 1 for capturing the operative, and 0 for failing. We begin with the FBI's decision. Unlike in the Prisoner's Dilemma, the FBI's best choice depends on the choice of the CIA. If the CIA hunts the kingpin, the FBI gets 2 units of utility for cooperating instead of the 1 unit it receives for hunting the operative by itself. If the CIA strikes out on its own, however, the FBI gets 0 for hunting the kingpin. Consequently, the FBI's choice depends on what it believes the CIA does, and vice

Table 5.2. The Terrorist Hunt

FBI\CIA	*Kingpin*	*Operative*
Kingpin	2, 2	0, 1
Operative	1, 0	1, 1

---

[1] Not to leave the reader in limbo, here is a quick summary of the rest of the episode. The confessions are thrown out on a technicality by an Upper West Side judge. The episode ends with a pithy piece of wisdom by Schiff just as McCoy pours himself an eighteen year old Scotch.

versa. What is reasonable for each agency to believe? A key development in the study of strategic interaction is John Nash's characterization of rational equilibrium behavior. In Nash's formulation, each agency chooses strategies that are "best responses" to the strategies of the other agency. If both agencies choose this way, the outcome is a best response to a best response, and neither agency has an incentive to change its strategy. Because such a combination of strategies produces a stable behavioral prediction, it is called an equilibrium. In honor of Nash's (1950b) contribution, it is called a Nash equilibrium.

To ascertain whether a particular combination (or profile) of strategies is a Nash equilibrium, it suffices to check that neither agency can achieve a higher utility level by unilaterally deviating to another strategy. Is the outcome in which both agencies hunt the kingpin a Nash equilibrium? If the CIA hunts the kingpin, the best choice of the FBI is to hunt the kingpin. Similarly, the CIA's best response to the FBI's choice to hunt the kingpin is to hunt the kingpin also. Thus, both agencies' pursuing the kingpin is a Nash equilibrium. This is not the only Nash equilibrium of the game, however. If the CIA decides to hunt the operative, the best that the FBI can do is also to settle for the operative. Because the CIA also prefers to hunt the operative when the FBI hunts one, both agencies' pursuing an operative is also a Nash equilibrium.[2] Although Nash's solution does not lead to a unique prediction, it rules out some behavior. A situation in which one agency hunts the kingpin while the other tracks an operative is not a Nash equilibrium – the agency hunting the kingpin would get more utility if it switched to searching for an operative. Conversely, the agency hunting an operative also prefers to deviate from its strategy.

Although these examples are quite simple, Nash's equilibrium concept is a very powerful tool in analyzing behavior across a large class of games. Consequently, the remainder of this chapter (and most of this book, for that matter) extends and develops the Nash equilibrium concept.

1. The Normal Form

The first step in using game theory to model political phenomena is to decide how to represent the strategic situation. We begin with the

---

[2] Although we defer the discussion of such possibilities, there is also a third equilibrium where each agency pursues the kingpin with probability .5 and the operative with probability .5.

simplest representation: the *normal form* with complete and perfect information. This representation contains the following elements:

(1) *Agents:* Let N represent the set of agents. In referring to an arbitrary agent, we use the notation $i \in N$. The symbol $-i \in N$ (read "not agent i") refers to all agents other than agent i.

(2) *Pure Strategies:* A pure strategy is an agent's plan of action such as "confess" or "hunt an operative" in our motivating examples. In games with single interactions such as our examples, a strategy is simply an action. In a game with multiple interactions, however, a strategy specifies the action to be taken in each interaction as a function of what happened in previous stages. In the normal form representation, we specify the set of pure strategies for each player and denote them as S_i for each $i \in N$. We write an arbitrary strategy by agent i as $s_i \in S_i$. Listing all possible combinations of strategies generates the set of strategy *profiles* S. Formally, $S \equiv \times_{i \in N} S_i$. A profile is therefore a vector $s = (s_1, \ldots, s_i, \ldots, s_n) \in S$. The set $S_{-i} \equiv \times_{j \in N \setminus \{i\}} S_j$ contains the set of strategies for every player except i. An element of this set, s_{-i}, is the profile of strategies for players $N \setminus \{i\}$. To economize on notation, we often write s as (s_i, s_{-i}). In the following we extend the definition of strategies to allow agents to randomize over pure strategies.

(3) *Payoffs*: A normal form representation requires von Neumann-Morgenstern utility functions over lotteries on S. Agents have utility functions defined over the set of strategy profiles, $u_i(s) : S \to \mathbb{R}^1$. Sometimes the utility function for i is denoted $u_i(s_i, s_{-i})$. Following the development in Chapter 3, the functions $u_i(\cdot)$ are Bernoulli utility functions, and given any lottery over S the agent calculates her expected utility under the lottery. The normal form representation can also be used in situations in which the payoffs are interpreted as expected utilities. For example, the payoff of 2 associated with both agencies' playing kingpin could be interpreted as the expected utility from the lottery over catching bad guys that is associated with each agency choosing kingpin.

One interpretation of a normal form game is that in period 1 each player $i \in N$ chooses her strategy $s_i \in S_i$ and in period 2 each player i receives a payoff of $u_i(s)$. Recall that $s = (s_1, \ldots, s_n)$. Games with more periods, as we demonstrate later, can be reinterpreted as large normal form games.

Accordingly a normal form game is defined by the collection $\langle N, \{S_i, u(\cdot, \ldots, \cdot)\}_{i \in n}\rangle$. The shorthand $\langle N, S, u\rangle$ also represents a game where u without a subscript represents the vector of utility functions $(u_1(\cdot), \ldots, u_n(\cdot))$. Some simple, yet interesting games that involve only two players can be represented as matrices (as we have seen already).

To make these ideas concrete, we now describe our two motivating examples using the normal form. First consider the Prisoner's Dilemma. Clearly $N = \{$player 1, player 2$\}$, $S_1 = S_2 = \{hold\ out, confess\}$. The payoff functions are

$$u_i(s_i, s_{-i}) = \begin{cases} -8 \text{ if } s_i = s_{-i} = confess \\ -4 \text{ if } s_i = s_{-i} = hold\ out \\ -1 \text{ if } s_i = confess\ \&\ s_{-i} = hold\ out \\ -25 \text{ if } s_i = hold\ out\ \&\ s_{-i} = confess \end{cases}.$$

Similarly, we represent the Terrorist Hunt as $N = \{CIA, FBI\}$, $S_1 = S_2 = \{hunt\ kingpin,\ hunt\ operative\}$, and

$$u_i(s_i, s_{-i}) = \begin{cases} 2 \text{ if } s_i = s_{-i} = hunt\ kingpin \\ 1 \text{ if } s_i = s_{-i} = hunt\ operative \\ 1 \text{ if } s_i = hunt\ operative\ \&\ s_{-i} = hunt\ kingpin \\ 0 \text{ if } s_i = hunt\ kingpin\ \&\ s_{-i} = hunt\ operative \end{cases}.$$

We can represent both of these normal forms with matrices. For two-agent games and finite strategy spaces, the relationship between the normal form and a game matrix generalizes to the pattern shown in Table 5.3, where $N = \{1, 2\}$, $S_1 = \{s_{11}, \ldots, s_{1l}\}$, and $S_2 = \{s_{21}, \ldots, s_{2k}\}$.

Table 5.3. Generic Normal Form Game

1\2	s_{21}	s_{22}	$\cdots$	s_{2k}
s_{11}	$u(s_{11}, s_{21})$	$u(s_{11}, s_{22})$	$\cdots$	$u(s_{11}, s_{2k})$
s_{12}	$u(s_{11}, s_{21})$	$u(s_{12}, s_{22})$	$\cdots$	$u(s_{12}, s_{22})$
$\vdots$	$\vdots$	$\vdots$	$\ddots$	$\vdots$
s_{1l}	$u(s_{1l}, s_{21})$	$u(s_{1l}, s_{22})$	$\cdots$	$u(s_{1l}, s_{2k})$

Using a matrix to represent a normal form with more than two players is more difficult because we cannot show the strategy combinations in two dimensions. Sometimes, however, we can use a trick to put such games in matrix form. Suppose the Terrorist Hunt includes a third agency, the National Security Agency (NSA), whose strategy set is the same as that of the other two, $S_3 = \{hunt\ kingpin, hunt\ operative\}$. Now capturing the kingpin requires cooperation by at least two agencies, but each still can capture an operative on its own. The payoff function for the FBI is now

$$u_1(s_1, s_{-1}) = \begin{cases} 2 \text{ if } s_2 = kingpin \text{ or } s_3 = kingpin \\ 1 \text{ if } s_1 = operative \\ 0 \text{ if } s_2 = operative\ \&\ s_3 = operative \end{cases}.$$

Consider the pair of matrices shown in Tables 5.4 and 5.5.

Table 5.4 displays the payoff triples corresponding to the strategy combinations where the NSA hunts the kingpin, whereas the payoffs in Table 5.5 are those in which the NSA hunts the operative. In general three-player normal form games with finite strategy spaces can be represented by matrices of payoff triples corresponding to each possible strategy for player 1.[3]

Table 5.4 Game If NSA Hunts Kingpin

FBI\CIA	Kingpin	Operative
Kingpin	2, 2, 2	2, 1, 2
Operative	1, 2, 2	1, 1, 0

There is no uncertainty in any of the games considered thus far. In each game, players know the strategy sets and the payoffs, and they know that the other players know these elements, and they know that the other players know that they know, and they know that the other players know that they know that they know, and so on. This infinite loop is termed common knowledge. The normal form representation, however, can accommodate more complex situations when the agents do not know the

Table 5.5. Game If NSA Hunts Operative

FBI\CIA	Kingpin	Operative
Kingpin	2, 2, 1	0, 1, 1
Operative	1, 0, 1	1, 1, 1

---

[3] For games with more than three players, graphical representations are more difficult without moving pages and holograms.

Table 5.6. Terrorist Hunt with Uncertainty

FBI\CIA	Kingpin	Operative
Kingpin	$10 \times \frac{1}{5} + 0 \times \frac{4}{5}$, $10 \times \frac{1}{5} + 0 \times \frac{4}{5}$	$0, 6 \times \frac{1}{6} + 0 \times \frac{5}{6}$
Operative	$6 \times \frac{1}{6} + 0 \times \frac{5}{6}$, 0	$6 \times \frac{1}{6} + 0 \times \frac{5}{6}$, $6 \times \frac{1}{6} + 0 \times \frac{5}{6}$

payoffs associated with each strategy profile. Instead they know the expected utility associated with strategy profiles, and they know that they know this expected utility, and so forth. For example, consider a modified Terrorist Hunt model where the players believe that catching a terrorist is a bit unpredictable. Here both players have beliefs about the probability of catching a terrorist conditional on strategies. We can rationalize the original matrix with Table 5.6, where the payoffs are explicitly represented in expected utilities.

In Table 5.6, 10 is the utility payoff to catching a *kingpin* and $1/5$ is the probability of catching a *kingpin* if both agencies cooperate on a *kingpin* search. Alternatively 0 is the payoff to a failed *kingpin* search that occurs with probability $4/5$ when the agencies cooperate on a *kingpin* search. Although the overall payoffs are the same in this matrix and the earlier one, this representation explicitly shows how payoffs can depend both on strategies and on random events. In this example, however, all players have the same beliefs about the random variation. Consequently, this is a game of symmetric information. Of course, many strategic situations involves players' having different beliefs and information about the likelihood of outcomes. Our next chapter discusses these games of asymmetric information.

2. Solutions to Normal Form Games

One aim of a game theoretic model is to generate a prediction that one element of S will be chosen by the agents. A second goal is to rule out the elements of S that are inconsistent with rationality. In the Prisoner's Dilemma we argued that {*confess, confess*} is plausible and that {*kingpin, kingpin*} or {*operative, operative*} is likely outcome of the Terrorist Hunt. Now we develop the general principles behind these predictions.

2.1. Elimination of Dominated Strategies. The first principle of rational behavior is that agents should not choose a strategy if there exists an alternative strategy that raises her payoffs against all possible strategies of her opponent. Recall the Prisoner's Dilemma of Table 5.1. The premise of our solution is that player 1 never plays *hold out* because it provides strictly less utility than *confess* independently of the choice of player 2. The strategy *hold out* is therefore, *strictly dominated* for player 1 by *confess*. Similarly, *hold out* is strictly dominated for player 2 as well. The only strategy combination that does not contain strictly dominated strategies is {*confess, confess*}. A formal definition of strict dominance follows.

DEFINITION 5.1 *(Strict dominance in pure strategies) A strategy s_i is strictly dominated by s'_i for player i if and only if $u_i(s_i, s_{-i}) < u_i(s'_i, s_{-i})$ for all $s_{-i} \in S_{-i}$.*

In what follows, it is useful to focus on the strategy profiles in which strictly dominated strategies have been eliminated.

DEFINITION 5.2 *(Elimination by Strict Dominance in Pure Strategies) A strategy profile $s = (s_i, s_{-i})$ is consistent with elimination by strict dominance if s_i is not strictly dominated for any $i \in N$.*

Generally, unique solutions cannot be obtained by simply eliminating dominated strategies. Nevertheless, predictions often can be tightened by using the procedure iteratively. This involves eliminating the strictly dominated strategies from a strategy profile whose strictly dominated strategies were eliminated in previous iterations. To illustrate how this works, consider the game matrix in Table 5.7.

Table 5.7

1\2	Left	Middle	Right
Up	1, 0	1, 2	0, 1
Down	0, 3	0, 1	2, 0

In this game agent 1 has no strictly dominated strategies. For agent 2, *Right* is dominated by *Middle* because *Middle* generates 2 versus 1 against *Up* and 1 versus 0 against *Down*. If agent 1 recognizes that agent 2 will not choose *Right*, he perceives the game as in Table 5.8.

In this reduced form, *Down* is now dominated for agent 1 by *Up* (payoff of 1 versus 0 for any strategy by agent 2). Because agent 2 knows that agent 1 plays *Up*, she prefers *Middle*. Thus, {*Down*, *Middle*} is the unique solution consistent with iterated elimination of strictly dominated strategies. The following definition is a formal description of this process.

Table 5.8

1\2	Left	Middle
Up	1, 0	1, 2
Down	0, 3	0, 1

DEFINITION 5.3 *(Iterated elimination of strictly dominated strategies) For a normal form game* $\Gamma^0 = \langle N, S^0, u^0 \rangle$, *the following algorithm iteratively deletes strictly dominated strategies.*

In period t arbitrarily select a player $i^t \in N \backslash \{i^{t-1}\}$ *and remove from* S_i^{t-1} *each strategy that is strictly dominated in the game* Γ^{t-1}. *Call the set of strategies that survive* S_i^t. *Let* $S_j^t = S_j^{t-1}$ *for* $j \in N \backslash i^t$ *and let* u_z^t *be the restriction of* u_z^0 *to* S^t *for each* $z \in N$.

If at τ *there is no* $i^\tau \in N$ *having a strictly dominated strategy in the game* $\Gamma^{\tau-1}$ *then call the set* $S^{\tau-1}$ *the set of outcomes that survive iterative deletion of strictly dominated strategies.*

Regardless of the sequence of players, the same set of iteratively undominated strategies is reached. A behavioral justification for this process is that agents reason in the following manner.

I know that my opponents do not use strictly dominated strategies, and I know that my opponents know that I do not use strictly dominated strategies. Given this we are all really choosing from the smaller strategy space that survives the first *n* iterations. But I know that my opponents do not use a strategy that is strictly dominated in this game, and I know that my opponents know that I do not play a strategy that is strictly dominated in this new game, . . . , ad infinitum.

Although it is based on a much stronger premise, we can also use *weak* dominance to generate predictions. Weakly dominated strategies are those such that some alternative strategy produces at least as large a payoff against all opponents' strategy profiles and generates a strictly higher payoff against at least one profile.

DEFINITION 5.4 *(Weak dominance in pure strategies) A strategy* s_i *is weakly dominated by* s_i' *if and only if* $u_i(s_i, s_{-i}) \leq u_i(s_i', s_{-i})$ *for all* $s_{-i} \in S_{-i}$ *and* $u_i(s_i, s_{-i}) < u_i(s_i', s_{-i})$ *for at least one* $s_{-i} \in S_{-i}$.

The definition of *elimination by weak dominance* is analogous to that of elimination by strict dominance. An important application of elimination by weak dominance in political science occurs in majority-rule voting games. Consider n (an odd number) agents voting between two candidates D and R. Each agent gets a payoff of 1 if her preferred candidate wins and 0 otherwise. We define the strategy sets so that $s_i = 1$ is a vote for D and $s_i = 0$ is a vote for R. Because the choice is made by majority rule, the payoff for an agent who prefers D is

$$u_D = \begin{cases} 1 \text{ if } \sum s_i > \frac{(n+1)}{2} \\ 0 \text{ otherwise.} \end{cases}$$

and the payoff for an agent who prefers R is $1 - u_D$. It is easy to verify that no strategies are strictly dominated. Unless exactly $(n-1)/2$ agents choose $s_i = 1$ and exactly $(n-1)/2$ choose $s_i = 0$, an agent's utility does not depend on her individual vote. Consequently, under almost all strategy profiles, agents do not have strict preferences. Agent i, however, has strict preferences at profiles of S_{-i} that generate ties – she prefers voting for the candidate whose victory provides her the most utility. Thus, voting for the preferred candidate weakly dominates voting for the less preferred. It generates a strictly higher utility for one profile and the same utility at all other profiles. If we eliminate weakly dominated strategies, each agent votes for her preferred candidate and the candidate preferred by a majority wins.

Although solutions based on dominance are attractive, dominance often fails to eliminate any strategies. Neither version of the Terrorist Hunt contains dominated strategies (strict or weak). All strategy profiles are plausible if we consider only the criterion of dominance.

2.2. Nash Equilibrium. John Nash's fundamental contribution to game theory is the formulation of a solution for normal form games that can be applied broadly. Nash's solution involves selection of strategy profiles s^* such that agent i's strategy s_i^* is a "best response" to the strategies played by the other players s_{-i}^* for all $i \in N$. Consequently, one of the most important concepts in game theory is the best response correspondence.[4]

---

[4] For a discussion of correspondences, see the Mathematical Appendix.

DEFINITION 5.5 *The best response correspondence for agent* $i \in N$ *is a mapping* $b_i(s_{-i}) : S_{-i} \rightarrow\rightarrow S_i$ *defined as* $b_i(s_{-i}) = \{s_i \in S_i : u_i(s_i, s_{-i}) \geq u_i(s_i', s_{-i})$ *for every* $s_i' \in S_i\}$ *for every* $s_{-i} \in S_{-i}.$

The best response to an opponent's profile s_{-i} is simply the set of strategies that maximize an agent's utility when played against s_{-i}. So the best response correspondence simply assigns the set of best responses by agent i to each profile s_{-i}. Consider the best response correspondences from some of our examples. In the Prisoner's Dilemma, the best responses are:

$$b_1(confess) = \{confess\}$$
$$b_1(hold\ out) = \{confess\}$$
$$b_2(confess) = \{confess\}$$
$$b_2(hold\ out/) = \{confess\}.$$

Similarly, the best response correspondences for the two-agency version of Terrorist Hunt are

$$b_1(kingpin) = \{kingpin\}$$
$$b_1(operative) = \{operative\}$$
$$b_2(kingpin) = \{kingpin\}$$
$$b_2(operative) = \{operative\}.$$

In these examples, the best response is a single action, but in many cases it may be a set of strategies. Recall the majority-voting game. Unless the opposing agents' profile generates an exact tie, voting for either candidate represents a best response. Formally best response correspondence for agent i preferring candidate D is

$$b_i\left(s_{-i} : \sum_{j \in N\setminus\{i\}} s_j = \frac{n-1}{2}\right) = \{1\}$$

$$b_i\left(s_{-i} : \sum_{j \in N\setminus\{i\}} s_j \neq \frac{n-1}{2}\right) = \{0, 1\}.$$

A Nash equilibrium is simply a strategy profile in which every agent is playing an element of her set of best responses given the strategies of the other agents.

DEFINITION 5.6 *A Nash equilibrium (in pure strategies) to a normal form game is a strategy profile, s^*, satisfying*

$$s_i^* \in b_i(s_{-i}^*) \text{ for every } i \in N.$$

We can also state a definition of Nash equilibrium that is not based on the best response correspondence.

DEFINITION 5.7 *A Nash equilibrium (in pure strategies) of a normal form game is a strategy profile, s^*, satisfying*

$$u_i(s_i^*, s_{-i}^*) \geq u_i(s_i', s_{-i}^*) \text{ for every } s_i' \in S_i \text{ and every } i \in N.$$

The two definitions are equivalent. The concept of a Nash equilibrium is deceptively simple. It requires that agents correctly conjecture what the other players do and then play a best response to this conjecture. An alternative interpretation of Nash equilibrium, based on the second definition, is that no player has an incentive to change her strategy unilaterally from a Nash equilibrium profile.

We can apply these definitions to our examples.

(1) The Prisoner's Dilemma: The strategy {*confess*} is the sole element of the best response set for both agents against all outcomes. Consequently, the unique Nash equilibrium is {*confess, confess*}.

(2) The two-agency Terrorist Hunt: Because $b_i(kingpin) = \{kingpin\}$ for both agencies, {*kingpin, kingpin*} is a Nash equilibrium. Similarly, $b_i(operative) = \{operative\}$ suggests that {*operative, operative*} is also a Nash equilibrium.

(3) The three-agency Terrorist Hunt: Verify that the best response correspondence is

$$b_i(kingpin, kingpin) = \{kingpin\}$$
$$b_i(operative, kingpin) = \{kingpin\}$$
$$b_i(kingpin, operative) = \{kingpin\}$$
$$b_i(operative, operative) = \{operative\}.$$

From the first definition, $b_i(kingpin, kingpin) = \{kingpin\}$ implies that {*kingpin, kingpin, kingpin*} is a Nash equilibrium. The best response correspondence $b_i(operative, operative) =$

{*operative*} implies that {*operative, operative, operative*} is also a Nash equilibrium. But $b_i(operative, kingpin) = \{kingpin\}$ and $b_i(kingpin, kingpin) = \{kingpin\}$ imply that there are no Nash equilibria where just two agencies pursue the kingpin, even though cooperation of two agencies is sufficient to capture him.

(4) Majority-Voting Game: Almost any strategy profile is a Nash equilibrium. Consider any profile such that $\sum_{i \in N} s_i < (n-1)/2$ or $\sum_{i \in N} s_i > (n+1)/2$. For these profiles, $b_i(s) = \{0, 1\}$ for all i. Consequently, each such profile is a Nash equilibrium. Now consider $\sum_{i \in N} s_i \in \{(n-1)/2, (n+1)/2\}$. Suppose that $\sum_{i \in Ni} = (n+1)/2$. This profile is a Nash equilibrium if and only if all agents choosing $s_i = 1$ prefer D. If this were not true, there is some agent i that chooses $s_i = 1$ but prefers R. But because $\sum_{j N \setminus \{i\}} s_j = (n-1)/2$, $b_i(s_{-i}) = \{0\}$. Such a profile is not a Nash equilibrium. Similarly, if $\sum_{i \in N} s_i = (n-1)/2$, s is a Nash equilibrium if all agents choosing $s_i = 0$ prefer R. In summary, the set of Nash equilibria includes every profile except those in which one candidate wins by a bare majority and a voter who prefers the losing candidate votes for the winning candidate.

It is important to observe the similarities and differences between the set of Nash equilibria and the set profiles surviving iterated elimination of strictly dominated strategies. In one case, the Prisoner's Dilemma, the predictions are the same. In the various versions of the Terrorist Hunt, the set of Nash equilibria is smaller than the set of profiles surviving elimination of dominated strategies. In the case of majority-rule voting, the set of Nash equilibria is smaller than the set of strategies surviving strict dominance but much larger than the unique prediction of the elimination of weakly dominated strategies.

The following theorems establish the precise link between Nash equilibria and profiles surviving iterated elimination of strictly dominated strategies.

THEOREM 5.1 *If a strategy profile* $(s_1^*, \ldots, s_N^*)$ *is a Nash equilibrium, none of its strategies can be eliminated through iterated elimination of strictly dominated strategies.*

Proof Suppose the theorem is false. Let s_i^* be the first of the strategies in the equilibrium profile to be eliminated. Elimination requires that $u_i(s_i^*, s_{-i}) < u_i(s_i, s_{-i})$ for some s_i and for all s_{-i} that have not been eliminated. By assumption s_{-i}^* has not been eliminated so that we require $u_i(s_i^*, s_{-i}^*) < u_i(s_i, s_{-i}^*)$. This violates the assumption that $(s_1^*, \ldots, s_N^*)$ is a Nash equilibrium. $\square$

THEOREM 5.2 *If the strategy profile* $(s_1^*, \ldots, s_N^*)$ *is the unique survivor of iterated elimination of strictly dominated strategies it is the unique pure strategy Nash equilibrium.*

Proof Uniqueness follows from the previous theorem because any Nash equilibrium must survive iterated elimination. So we focus on showing that the remaining profile must be a Nash equilibrium. Suppose $(s_1^*, \ldots, s_N^*)$ is not a Nash equilibrium. Then there exists s_i' such that $u_i(s_i^*, s_{-i}^*) < u_i(s_i', s_{-i}^*)$ but s_i' must be eliminated by dominance. Let s_i be the strategy that eliminates s_i'. If $s_i = s_i^*$, there is an immediate contradiction. So assume that $s_i \neq s_i^*$. Then because s_i eliminates s_i', $u_i(s_i', s_{-i}^*) < u_i(s_i, s_{-i}^*)$. This process may continue no more than a finite number of times until we conclude that $u_i(s_i^*, s_{-i}^*) > u_i(s_i', s_{-i}^*)$. $\square$

In all of our examples, there is at least one Nash equilibrium. It is possible, however, that there are no strategy profiles satisfying the requirements of a Nash equilibrium. Consider the following game. There are two armies: one defending army (D) and an invader (I). The invading army decides whether to invade through the mountains M or to march through the plains P. In response to the threat, the defender decides whether to fortify its defenses in the mountains or in the plains. If the invader attacks an undefended area, it wins a payoff of 1. It loses 1 if it attacks a fortification, however. The defender gets 1 by correctly predicting the direction of the attack and loses 1 otherwise. We can represent this normal form game, known as a Colonel Blotto game, with the matrix in Table 5.9.

Table 5.9. Colonel Blotto

D\I	M	P
M	1, −1	−1, 1
P	−1, 1	1, −1

The best response correspondences are $b_D(M) = \{M\}$, $b_D(P) = \{P\}$, $b_I(M) = \{P\}$, and $b_I(P) = \{M\}$. The existence of Nash equilibrium requires that there is some strategy pair $\{s_D, s_I\}$ such that $b_I(s_D) = s_I$ and $b_D(s_I) = s_D$. The best response correspondences of this game do not satisfy these conditions. Given any pair of strategies, one agent has an incentive to choose a different one. Absent a Nash equilibrium (or any restrictions imposed by dominance), we lack a prediction for how this game is played.

In applications one generally defines a game and characterizes the set of Nash equilibria. In characterizing the equilibrium set, the two most important properties are existence and uniqueness. For applied researchers, a unique Nash equilibrium is desirable as there is little ambiguity about the empirical predictions. Accordingly, the case of multiple equilibria is less desirable as the model yields ambiguous predictions. The case of no equilibria is especially unsatisfactory as the model makes no predictions. We show later, however, that for games with finite numbers of strategies and actors, like the Colonel Blotto games, the opportunity for agents to randomize over strategies is sufficient for the existence of Nash equilibria.

3. Application: The Hotelling Model of Political Competition

The Hotelling (1929) model of political competition, as extended by Downs (1957), is one of the most widely applied games in political science. A small town must decide where to build a school. Its citizens live uniformly along a one-mile stretch of road and all want the school built as close to their home as possible. Thus, the voters' ideal locations are distributed uniformly over $[0, 1]$. The town holds an election in which two candidates compete for office by campaigning on promises about the school's location. The winning candidate builds the school at the promised location and receives a payoff of 1. The losing candidate gets -1. In the case of a tie, the election is decided by a coin toss, with each candidate winning with probability .5. To keep the discussion simple, the voters are not strategic agents in the game but always vote for the closest candidate.[5]

The candidate's strategy sets are $S_1 = S_2 = [0, 1]$. On the assumption that voters vote for the closest candidate, we compute the vote shares for both candidates for any strategy profile (s_1, s_2). Because the voters are distributed uniformly, the number of voters in any interval is equal to the width of that interval. So if $s_2 > s_1$, all voters to the left of $(s_1 + s_2)/2$ vote for candidate 1 and her vote share is $(s_1 + s_2)/2$. The remaining $1 - (s_1 + s_2)/2$ percentage of the voters support candidate 2. Conversely, if $s_1 > s_2$, candidate 2 receives a vote share of $(s_1 + s_2)/2$,

---

[5] It turns out that this assumption is innocuous; voting for the candidate who promises the preferred school is consistent with the appropriate notion of equilibrium in a larger game in which voters decide how to vote after hearing candidate locations.

and candidate 1 gets the rest. The candidate payoffs for any strategy profile are

$$u_1(s_1, s_2) = \begin{cases} 1 \text{ if } s_1 < s_2 \text{ and } \frac{s_1+s_2}{2} > .5 \text{ or if } s_1 > s_2 \text{ and } \frac{s_1+s_2}{2} < .5 \\ 0 \text{ if } s_1 = s_2 \\ -1 \text{ if } s_1 < s_2 \text{ and } \frac{s_1+s_2}{2} < .5 \text{ or if } s_1 > s_2 \text{ and } \frac{s_1+s_2}{2} > .5 \end{cases}$$

and

$$u_2(s_1, s_2) = -u_1(s_1, s_2).$$

The unique Nash equilibrium of this game is $s_1 = s_2 = .5$. To demonstrate, we begin by computing the best response correspondence of candidate 1. Suppose that $s_2 < .5$; then candidate 1 wins with certainty by choosing any platform that generates a vote share of .5 or more. Thus, $b_1(s_2) = (s_2, 1 - s_2)$. For $s_2 > .5$, similar calculations suggest that $b_1(s_2) = (1 - s_2, s_2)$. If $s_2 = .5$, candidate 1 generates a tie at best by also choosing .5 so that $b_1(.5) = .5$. Because candidate 2's situation is symmetric, her best response correspondence is

$$b_2(s_1) = (s_1, 1 - s_1) \quad \text{if } s_1 < .5$$
$$b_2(s_1) = (1 - s_1, s_1) \quad \text{if } s_1 > .5$$
$$b_2(s_1) = s_1 \quad \text{if } s_1 = .5.$$

That $s_1^* = s_2^* = .5$ is in fact a Nash equilibrium follows immediately because $b_1(.5) = .5$ and $b_2(.5) = .5$. The trick is to show that it is the only Nash equilibrium. Suppose to the contrary that $s_1^* = s_2^* \neq .5$. This cannot be a Nash equilibrium, however, because $b_1(s_2^*)$ does not include s_2^*. Now suppose $s_1^* < s_2^*$. Now $b_1(s_2^*) = (1 - s_2^*, s_2^*)$ whereas $b_2(s_1^*) = (s_1^*, 1 - s_1^*)$. Putting all of these conditions together, a Nash equilibrium requires that $1 - s_2^* < s_1^*$ and $s_2^* < 1 - s_1^*$. But these inequalities are contradictory because they require $s_2^* > 1 - s_1^*$ and $s_2^* < 1 - s_1^*$. The case of $s_1^* > s_2^*$ is analogous and so establishes the uniqueness of $s_1^* = s_2^* = .5$ as a Nash equilibrium.

A more intuitive proof of the claim follows from our second definition of Nash equilibrium (a strategy profile from which no agent has a strict preference to deviate). Clearly, no candidate wishes to defect from $s_1^* = s_2^* = .5$ as her payoff would fall from 0 to -1. Now consider another possible equilibrium (s_1^*, s_2^*). If one candidate wins in this equilibrium, the other candidate can move to .5 and at least generate a tie. Any equilibrium, therefore, must generate a tie. Furthermore, unless $s_1^* = s_2^* = .5$, either candidate can move to .5 and win for sure. The profile $s_1^* = s_2^* = .5$ is the only Nash equilibrium.

The same outcome is generated by applying elimination of weakly dominated strategies. Each candidate generates at least a tie by choosing .5. The tie occurs only if the opponent chooses .5 as well. Against this profile any other platform loses. Consequently $s_i = .5$ weakly dominates all other strategies.

3.1. Vote Maximizing Candidates. Instead of maximizing chances of winning, each candidate now maximizes his vote share. Thus, the new payoffs are

$$u_1(s_1, s_2) = \begin{cases} \frac{s_1+s_2}{2} \text{ if } s_1 < s_2 \\ .5 \text{ if } s_1 = s_2 \\ 1 - \frac{s_1+s_2}{2} \text{ if } s_1 > s_2 \end{cases}$$

and

$$u_2(s_1, s_2) = 1 - u_1(s_1, s_2).$$

The profile $s_1^* = s_2^* = .5$ is again the unique Nash equilibrium. Again, start with the best response correspondences. Suppose that $s_2 < .5$; candidate 1 prefers the smallest platform greater than s_2. Because the strategy sets are continuums, no such platform exists. Similarly, if $s_2 > .5$, candidate 1 would like to choose the smallest platform less than s_2, which does not exist either. Candidate 2 faces the same situation so that $b_i(s_{-i} \neq .5) = \emptyset$, the empty set. Now consider the best response to $s_2 = .5$. Candidate 1 gets .5 for proposing .5, generating the tie, and a strictly lower vote share for any other platform. Thus, .5 is the best response. Because candidate 2 faces the same incentives, $b_i(s_{-i} = .5) = .5$. Clearly $s_1^* = s_2^* = .5$ is a Nash equilibrium. Because the best response sets for any other strategy pair are empty, it is also the unique Nash equilibrium.

3.2. Ideological Candidates. Consider another version of the Hotelling model. In this version, the candidates are ideological because they care about which policy is implemented by the winning candidate. Candidate 1 wants the school to be as close to 0 as possible and her utility from the winning outcome x is $-x^2$. Similarly, candidate 2 wants the outcome to be as close to 1 as possible and has a utility function of $-(1-x)^2$. As earlier, the candidates choose platforms that they must implement if they win.[6] In a tied election, the voters flip a coin, and the winner implements her platform. Given the candidates' incentives to move policy to extreme positions, it might appear that the outcomes should no longer be located at the median voter. This is not the case, and we show again that $s_1^* = s_2^* = .5$ is the unique Nash equilibrium.

The payoff functions for each candidate are now

$$u_1(s_1, s_2) = \begin{cases} -s_1^2 \text{ if } s_1 < s_2 \text{ and } \frac{s_1+s_2}{2} > .5 \text{ or if } s_1 > s_2 \text{ and } \frac{s_1+s_2}{2} < .5 \\ -.5s_1^2 - .5s_2^2 \text{ if } s_1 = s_2 \text{ and } \frac{s_1+s_2}{2} = .5 \\ -s_2^2 \text{ if } s_1 < s_2 \text{ and } \frac{s_1+s_2}{2} < .5 \text{ or if } s_1 > s_2 \text{ and } \frac{s_1+s_2}{2} > .5 \end{cases}$$

and

$$u_2(s_1, s_2)$$
$$= \begin{cases} -(1-s_1)^2 \text{ if } s_1 < s_2 \text{ and } \frac{s_1+s_2}{2} > .5 \text{ or if } s_1 > s_2 \text{ and } \frac{s_1+s_2}{2} < .5 \\ -.5(1-s_1)^2 - .5(1-s_2)^2 \text{ if } s_1 = s_2 \text{ and } \frac{s_1+s_2}{2} = .5 \\ -(1-s_2)^2 \text{ if } s_1 < s_2 \text{ and } \frac{s_1+s_2}{2} < .5 \text{ or if } s_1 > s_2 \text{ and } \frac{s_1+s_2}{2} > .5 \end{cases}.$$

We begin with candidate 1's best response. If $s_2 < .5$, no proposal less than s_2 defeats s_2. So candidate 1's best response is to choose s_2 or a proposal that loses to s_2. This implies that $b_1(s_2 < .5) = [0, s_2] \cup (1 - s_2, 1]$. Alternatively, if $s_2 > .5$, candidate 1 wants to choose the smallest platform that defeats s_2. Just as in the last section, such a platform does not exist so that $b_1(s_2 > .5) = \emptyset$. Despite this, it is clear that for any policy s_1 that beats s_2 the choice of $s_2 > .5$ is suboptimal for candidate 2. Similar arguments suggest that $b_2(s_1 > .5) = [s_1, 1] \cup [0, 1 - s_1)$ and $b_2(s_1 < .5) = \emptyset$. Similarly, $s_1 < .5$ is suboptimal for whenever 2 chooses a policy that beats s_1. Last, consider the best response to $s_i = .5$. Any proposal by the other candidate loses for sure – generating a utility of $-.25$. Responding with a platform of .5 leads to a lottery over $s_1 = s_2 = .5$. This lottery has an expected value of $-.25$ for both candidates. Thus, the best response is $b_i(.5) = [0, 1]$.

---

[6] We ignore the problem that the candidates prefer to implement their own ideal points regardless of their electoral platform.

From these best response correspondences, it is easy to see that $s_1^* = s_2^* = .5$ is a Nash equilibrium because $.5 \in b_i (.5)$ for both candidates. Now we show uniqueness. Because $b_1 (s_2 > .5) = \emptyset$ and $b_2 (s_1 < .5) = \emptyset$, the only possible candidates for Nash equilibria are $s_1^* > .5 > s_2^*$. This inequality in conjunction with $b_1 (s_2 < .5) = [0, s_2] \cup (1 - s_2, 1]$ and $b_2 (s_1 > .5) = [s_1, 1] \cup [0, 1 - s_1)$ implies that $s_1^* > 1 - s_2^*$ and $s_2^* < 1 - s_1^*$. Because these last two inequalities cannot be simultaneously satisfied, $s_1^* = s_2^* = .5$ is the only possible Nash equilibrium.

3.3. Ideological Candidates with Uncertainty. The reason why even ideological candidates gravitate to the median voter is that no candidate can win without the median's support. But we now consider what happens when the candidates do not know which platform obtains that support.[7]

Now the policy-motivated candidates are uncertain about the location of the median voter. Instead of knowing that the voters are arranged uniformly on the unit interval, the candidates believe that the median voter's location is randomly drawn from the uniform distribution on $[0, 1]$. This model is an example of models developed by Wittman (1977) and Calvert (1985). Let $\Omega = [0, 1]$ denote the set of possible locations of the median voter. Because candidate preferences are common knowledge, all of the uncertainty in the game is captured by the probability distribution $F(\omega) = \omega$ on $[0, 1]$. Once we express the candidates' expected utility as a function of the candidate strategies, we can model this as a normal form game. Again candidate preferences over policy are quadratic so that $u_1(x) = -x^2$ and $u_2(x) = -(1 - x)^2$. For any two platforms, candidate 1 wins if the realization of the median voter is closer to s_1 than s_2. If $s_1 < s_2$ candidate 1 wins, therefore, if the median is less than $(s_1 + s_2)/2$. Because the median is uniformly distributed, candidate 1 wins with probability $(s_1 + s_2)/2$. We use this fact to express the expected utilities of the candidates as

$$
Eu_1(s_1, s_2) = \begin{cases} -s_1^2 \left(\frac{s_1+s_2}{2}\right) & -s_2^2(1 - \frac{s_1+s_2}{2}) \text{ if } s_1 < s_2 \\ -s_2^2 \left(\frac{s_1+s_2}{2}\right) & -s_1^2(1 - \frac{s_1+s_2}{2}) \text{ if } s_1 > s_2 \end{cases}
$$

---

[7] Students may want to review the material on optimization in the Mathematical Appendix before tackling this section.

and

$$Eu_2(s_1, s_2) = \begin{cases} -(1 - s_1)^2 \left(\frac{s_1 + s_2}{2}\right) - (1 - s_2)^2 (1 - \frac{s_1 + s_2}{2}) \text{ if } s_1 < s_2 \\ -(1 - s_2)^2 \left(\frac{s_1 + s_2}{2}\right) - (1 - s_1)^2 (1 - \frac{s_1 + s_2}{2}) \text{ if } s_1 > s_2 \end{cases}.$$

To construct a Nash equilibrium, suppose that candidate 1 knows that candidate 2 locates at $z \geq 1/2$. Then candidate 1 chooses $s_1 \in [0, z]$ to maximize

$$\max_{s_1} \left\{ -s_1^2 \left(\frac{s_1 + z}{2}\right) - z^2 \left(1 - \frac{s_1 + z}{2}\right) \right\}.$$

We can ignore the possibility of choosing $s_1 > z$ because this strategy is always dominated by $s_1 = z$.[8] To find the optimal choice of s_1, we can differentiate the objective function with respect to s_1 and set this derivative to 0. This first-order condition is

$$-\frac{3}{2} s_1^2 - z s_1 + \frac{z^2}{2} = 0.$$

Solving for s_1 yields two solutions, but only one lies in the appropriate range $[0, 1]$. This solution then generates the best response function

$$s_1(s_2) = \frac{s_2}{3}.$$

To ensure that this solution characterizes a local maximum (as opposed to a local minimum or saddle point), we check that the second derivative of the objective function is negative when evaluated at the solution. Differentiating the objective function with respect to s_1 and treating z as a constant yield the second-order condition that simplifies to $-2z$ and is negative for any value of $z \in (0, 1]$.

Similarly, treating s_1 as a fixed parameter $z \leq 1/2$ we can differentiate candidate 2's objective function

$$\max_{s_2} \left\{ -(1 - z)^2 \left[\frac{z + s_2}{2}\right] - (1 - s_2)^2 \left[1 - \frac{z + s_2}{2}\right] \right\}$$

[8] Indeed if candidate 1 chose $s_1 > z$, she would prefer candidate 2 to win.

to find an optimal $s_2 \in [z, 1]$. The solution is

$$s_2(s_1) = \frac{2}{3} + \frac{1}{3}s_1.$$

We leave verification of the second-order condition to the reader. A Nash equilibrium is then a strategy combination (s_1^*, s_2^*) that solves the following system of equations:

$$s_1^* = \frac{1}{3}s_2^*$$

$$s_2^* = \frac{2}{3} + \frac{1}{3}s_1^*.$$

The unique solution to this system is $s_1^* = 1/4$ and $s_2^* = 3/4$. With policy-motivated candidates and uncertainty about voter preferences, the two candidates choose divergent platforms. In the model with certainty moving from .5 leads to a certain electoral loss. Such a movement in the current model only results in a smaller probability of winning. Ideological candidates are generally willing to trade small losses in the probability of winning for policy platforms closer to their own ideal point. As a result, both candidates move their platforms away from the median in accord with their own preferences. Because both candidates behave this way, however, each still wins with a 50 percent probability.

4. Existence of Nash Equilibria

As demonstrated by the Colonel Blotto model, there is no guarantee that a Nash equilibrium in *pure strategies* exists. In this section, we explore conditions for the existence of Nash equilibria.

We begin with a set of sufficient conditions for the existence of equilibria in pure strategies. The first is a concavity condition on the utility functions.

DEFINITION 5.8 *A function* $f(x) : X \to \mathbb{R}^1$ *(where X is convex) is strictly quasi-concave if* $f(\lambda x + (1 - \lambda)y) > t$ *for $x \neq y \in X, \lambda \in (0, 1)$, and any $t \in \mathbb{R}^1$ such that $f(x) \geq t$ and $f(y) \geq t$.*

Alternatively, a function is strictly quasi-concave if its upper contour sets are convex. Because strictly convex preferences produce singleton maximal sets (see Chapter 1), a game with a convex strategy space S and utility functions $u_i(s_i, s_{-i})$ that are strictly quasi-concave in s_i for each $s_{-i} \in S_{-i}$ have best response correspondences that are functions (i.e., single-valued correspondences). In the next subsection we prove the following result.

THEOREM 5.3 *A Nash equilibrium to the normal form game $\langle N, S, u \rangle$ exists if the following conditions are satisfied.*

(1) S_i is a convex and compact subset of a Euclidean space for each $i \in N$.

(2) $u_i(s_i, s_{-i}) : S \to \mathbb{R}^1$ is a continuous function for each $i \in N$.

(3)   for every $i \in N$ and every $s'_{-i} \in S_{-i}$ the function $u_i(s_i, s'_{-i}) : S_i \to \mathbb{R}^1$ is strictly quasi-concave in S_i.

Although useful, this theorem is obviously restrictive in that many games do not satisfy its assumptions. The Colonel Blotto game, for example, does not satisfy condition 1 as its strategy set is not convex (a linear combination of M and P is not an available strategy). Even though unique Nash equilibria exist, the payoffs in many versions of the Hotelling game are not strictly quasi-concave as there are a number of regions in which the payoffs are "flat" in the candidate's platform choice (a losing platform is still a losing platform as it moves away from the median voter).

One solution for games with nonconvex strategy spaces is to allow agents to use *mixed strategies*. A mixed strategy, denoted by σ_i, is a randomization over a combination of pure strategies. The notation $\sigma_i(s_i)$ denotes the probability that agent i chooses strategy s_i. The set of mixed strategies for player i is the set of probability distributions over S_i and is denoted $\Delta_i = \Delta(S_i)$.

A game in mixed strategies is similar to a game in pure strategies with the exception that each agent chooses $\sigma_i \in \Delta_i$ rather than $s_i \in S_i$ and the players evaluate strategies by the expected utility of the lottery induced by σ_i. A formal definition of a game in mixed strategies follows.

DEFINITION 5.9 *For a normal form game $\Gamma = \langle N, S, u \rangle$, the mixed extension game is denoted $\Gamma^m = \langle N, \Delta, u^m \rangle$; the set of strategy profiles is denoted $\Delta_i = \Delta(S_i)$. An arbitrary strategy is denoted as $\sigma_i \in \Delta_i$ for all $i \in N$ and $\Delta = \times_{i \in N} \Delta_i$ and $\sigma_i(s_i)$ denotes the probability that σ_i assigns to pure strategy s_i. The expected utility function, $U_i(\sigma_i, \sigma_{-i}) : \Delta \to \mathbb{R}^1$,* *is defined as*

$$u_i(\sigma_i, \sigma_{-i}) = \sum_{s_{-i} \in S_{-i}} \sum_{s_i \in S_i} u_i(s_i, s_{-i})\sigma_i(s_i), \sigma_{-i}(s_{-i}) \text{ for all } i \in N.$$

Because the mixed extension of a normal form game is itself a normal form game, the definition of Nash equilibrium applies directly to mixed extensions.

To understand how agents use mixed strategies, recall the Colonel Blotto game. Each side now chooses lotteries over its strategies. Let $\sigma_1 = \sigma_1(M)$ be the probability that the defender protects the mountains and $\sigma_2 = \sigma_2(M)$ be the probability that the invader attacks the mountains. The expected utilities for each player for each action are given by the following equations.

$$u_1(M, \sigma_2) = \sigma_2 - (1 - \sigma_2) = 2\sigma_2 - 1$$
$$u_1(P, \sigma_2) = -\sigma_2 + (1 - \sigma_2) = 1 - 2\sigma_2$$
$$u_2(\sigma_1, M) = -\sigma_1 + (1 - \sigma_1) = 1 - 2\sigma_1$$
$$u_2(\sigma_1, P) = \sigma_1 - (1 - \sigma_1) = 2\sigma_1 - 1.$$

It is now straightforward to compute $b_1(\sigma_2)$ and $b_2(\sigma_1)$. The defender prefers to protect the mountains (e.g., $u_1(M, \sigma_2) > u_1(P, \sigma_2)$) when $\sigma_2 > 1/2$. The defender is indifferent if $\sigma_2 = 1/2$ and prefers to protect the plains if $\sigma_2 < 1/2$. Thus, the defender's best response to the invader's mixed strategy, σ_2, is

$$b_1(\sigma_2) = \begin{cases} M \text{ if } \sigma_2 > \frac{1}{2} \\ P \text{ if } \sigma_2 < \frac{1}{2}. \\ \{M, P\} \text{ if } \sigma_2 = \frac{1}{2} \end{cases}$$

Because $b_1(\sigma_2) = \{M, P\}$ when $\sigma_2 = 1/2$, any randomization over $\{M, P\}$ is also a best response. The invader's best response is generated the same way. Given that

$$u_2(\sigma_1, M) > u_2(\sigma_1, P) \text{ if } \sigma_1 < \frac{1}{2}$$

$$u_2(\sigma_1, M) < u_2(\sigma_1, P) \text{ if } \sigma_1 > \frac{1}{2}$$

$$u_2(\sigma_1, M) = u_2(\sigma_1, P) \text{ if } \sigma_1 = \frac{1}{2}$$

the invader's best response correspondence is

$$b_2(\sigma_1) = \begin{cases} M \text{ if } \sigma_1 < \frac{1}{2} \\ P \text{ if } \sigma_1 > \frac{1}{2} \\ \{M, P\} \text{ or } \sigma_2 \text{ if } \sigma_1 = \frac{1}{2} \end{cases}.$$

We saw earlier that there are no Nash equilibrium where one agent plays either of its pure strategies. So in constructing a Nash equilibrium, we need only check whether there exists a combination of σ_1 and σ_2 that satisfies Nash's criteria. The mixed strategy σ_1 is a best response by the defender only if $\sigma_2 = 1/2$, and σ_2 is a best response only if $\sigma_1 = 1/2$. Consequently, $\sigma_1 = 1/2$ and $\sigma_2 = 1/2$ is the unique Nash equilibrium in mixed strategies.

For a two-player, two-strategy game, plotting best response functions is often useful for finding mixed strategy equilibria. Consider Figure 5.1. The horizontal axis plots the defender's mixed strategy, which ranges from $\sigma_1 = 0$ (plains) to $\sigma_1 = 1$ (mountains). The vertical axis plots the invader's mixed strategy from $\sigma_2 = 0$ (plains) to $\sigma_2 = 1$ (mountains). The solid line represents the defender's best response to σ_2 and the dotted line represents the invader's best response to σ_1. The only intersection of these best response curves is at the Nash equilibrium $\sigma_1 = 1/2$ and $\sigma_2 = 1/2$.

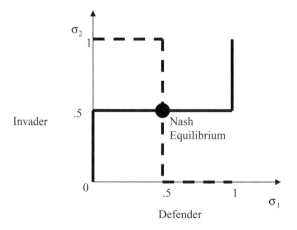

Figure 5.1. Mixed Strategy Nash Equilibrium to Colonel Blotto Game.

   Mixed strategy equilibria may also exist in games with pure strategy
equilibria. Consider the two-agency Terrorist Hunt game represented
in Table 5.2. Now let σ_1 and σ_2 be the probabilities that the FBI and
the CIA hunt the kingpin, respectively. The expected utilities of each
agency for each action follow:

$$u_1(kingpin, \sigma_2) = 2\sigma_2$$
$$u_1(operative, \sigma_2) = 1$$
$$u_2(\sigma_1, kingpin) = 2\sigma_1$$
$$u_2(\sigma_1, operative) = 1.$$

As before we compare these utilities to generate the best response
functions.

$$b_1(\sigma_2) = \begin{cases} \text{kingpin if } \sigma_2 > \frac{1}{2} \\ \text{operative if } \sigma_2 < \frac{1}{2} \\ \sigma_1 \in [0, 1] \text{ if } \sigma_2 = \frac{1}{2} \end{cases}$$

$$b_2(\sigma_1) = \begin{cases} \text{kingpin if } \sigma_1 > \frac{1}{2} \\ \text{operative if } \sigma_1 < \frac{1}{2} \\ \sigma_2 \in [0, 1] \text{ if } \sigma_1 = \frac{1}{2} \end{cases} .$$

Figure 5.2 plots these best response functions. Now there are three

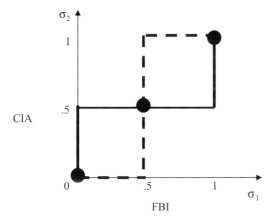

Figure 5.2. Mixed Strategy Nash Equilibria to Terrorist Hunt.

intersections of of the best responses: $\{0, 0\}$, $\{1, 1\}$, and $\{1/2, 1/2\}$. The first two correspond to the pure strategy equilibria computed earlier, but the third is an additional mixed strategy equilibrium.

A feature of mixed strategy equilibria is that the probability that an agent plays a particular strategy is not a function of her own preferences but those of her opponent. This feature arises because an agent plays mixed strategies only if she is indifferent among a set of pure strategies. Consequently, her opponent chooses his own mixed strategy to ensure that she is indifferent. It is, therefore, the preferences of the opponent that determine the mixing probabilities. Occasionally, this fact leads to counterintuitive predictions. For example, suppose we modify the Terrorist Hunt so that the CIA receives a much higher payoff than the FBI for capturing the kingpin. The new payoffs follow in Table 5.10.

A naive prediction, based on simple decision theory, is that because the CIA receives a higher payoff from the kingpin in the new game it is increasingly likely to hunt him. This prediction is wrong. The best response functions are now

$$
b_1(\sigma_2) = \begin{cases} \textit{kingpin} \text{ if } \sigma_2 > \frac{1}{2} \\ \textit{operative} \text{ if } \sigma_2 < \frac{1}{2} \\ \sigma_1 \in [0, 1] \text{ if } \sigma_2 = \frac{1}{2} \end{cases}
$$

$$
b_2(\sigma_1) = \begin{cases} \textit{kingpin} \text{ if } \sigma_1 > \frac{1}{4} \\ \textit{operative} \text{ if } \sigma_1 < \frac{1}{4}. \\ \sigma_2 \in [0, 1] \text{ if } \sigma_1 = \frac{1}{4} \end{cases}
$$

We plot these responses in Figure 5.3. The mixed strategy equilibrium is now $\{1/4, 1/2\}$. The change in the CIA's preferences did not lead it to hunt the kingpin with a higher probability – it still hunts him $1/2$ of the time. Alternatively, the change actually *decreases* the likelihood that the FBI hunts the kingpin. Somewhat perversely, the probability that the kingpin is caught in the mixed strategy equilibrium declines. The logic behind this result is not difficult to grasp. In the mixed strategy equilibrium, the

Table 5.10. Modified Terrorist Hunt

FBI\CIA	Kingpin	Operative
Kingpin	2, 4	0, 1
Operative	1, 0	1, 1

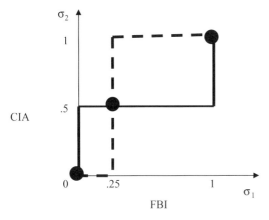

Figure 5.3. Mixed Strategy Nash Equilibrium to Terrorist Hunt (Modified Payoffs).

CIA chooses σ_2 to make the FBI indifferent between hunting the kingpin and the operative. Because the FBI's preferences do not change, σ_2 does not change. Because the FBI chooses σ_1 to make the CIA indifferent, an increased utility for the kingpin means that the FBI must lower the probability of searching for the kingpin to maintain this indifference.

Although mixed strategy equilibria have these undesirable properties, they are guaranteed to exist in games with finite strategy sets. This is the result of Nash's famous theorem.

THEOREM 5.4 *(Nash) Given a normal form game $\Gamma = \langle N, S, u \rangle$ in which S is finite, the mixed extension $\Gamma^m = \langle N, \Delta, u^m \rangle$ has at least one Nash equilibrium. In other words every finite game has a mixed strategy Nash equilibrium.*

The proof of this theorem utilizes some advanced mathematics so we relegate it to a later advanced section. That is to say, all readers should know the result, but for a first reading the details of the proof may be skipped.

5. Dominance and Mixed Strategies

We can extend the definition of dominance to include mixed strategies.

DEFINITION 5.10 *A pure strategy* $s_i \in S$ *is strictly dominated if there exists a* $\sigma'_i \in \Delta(S_i)$ *such that*

$$u_i(\sigma'_i, s_{-i}) > u_i(s_i, s_{-i}) \text{ for every } s_{-i} \in S_{-i}.$$

The strategy s_i *is weakly dominated if there is a* σ'_i *for which the inequality holds weakly for every* $s_{-i} \in S_{-i}$ *and strictly for some* $s'_{-i} \in S_{-i}$.[9]

Table 5.11

1\2	L	M	R
U	3, 1	4, 2	1, 4
D	2, 4	1, 2	3, 1

This extension is straightforward. Now we ask whether a strategy is dominated by a mixed strategy. The following example shows that this extended definition is much stronger than dominance in pure strategies as some strategies are dominated by mixed strategies that are not dominated by pure strategies.[10] Consider the game in Table 5.11.

Neither player has any strategies that are dominated by pure strategies. But consider a mixed strategy by player 2 of $\sigma_2(L) = 1/2$ and $\sigma_2(R) = 1/2$. This mixture has an expected value of 2.5 when played against both U and D – a higher utility than player 2's pure strategy of M. Thus, the mixture strictly dominates M.

The following theorem establishes an important relationship between mixed strategy Nash equilibria and iterated elimination of strategies that are strictly dominated by mixed strategies.

THEOREM 5.5 *Let* $\Gamma^m = \langle N, \Delta, u^m \rangle$ *be a finite normal form game with a mixed strategy Nash equilibrium* σ^*. *If the strategy* s_i *is played with positive probability under* σ^*_i *then it survives iterated deletion of strategies that are strictly dominated by mixed strategies.*

We leave the proof as an exercise. This theorem is quite useful in computing mixed strategy equilibria. Instead of computing best responses to lotteries over all strategies, we need only compute best responses for mixtures of the strategies that survive iterated dominance.

---

[9] Recall that $u_i(\sigma'_i, s_{-i}) = \sum_{s'_i \in S_i} u_i(s'_i, s_{-i})\sigma_i(s_i)$.

[10] Obviously, the converse cannot be true as any strategy dominated by a pure strategy is dominated by a mixed strategy placing probability 1 on the dominating strategy.

6. Calculating Nash Equilibria

Although we can specify sufficient conditions for the existence of Nash equilibria, computing the equilibria of a game is often more art than science. In fact, games like chess are known to have Nash equilibria despite the fact that the actual equilibrium strategies have never been calculated. Nevertheless, there are a few tricks and algorithms that can facilitate computation.

6.1. Pure Strategy Nash Equilibria in Finite Games. We now outline a process for checking whether a given strategy profile is an equilibrium. For a finite game, one way to characterize all of the pure strategy Nash equilibria is to test whether each profile $s' \in S$ is a Nash equilibrium. One begins with a profile $s' = (s'_1, \ldots, s'_n)$ and asks the following sequence of questions:

(1) If one holds $s'_2, \ldots, s'_n$ fixed, is there a strategy s''_1 such that $u_1(s''_1, s'_{-1}) > u_1(s'_1, s'_{-1})$? If so, s' is not a Nash equilibrium. If not, continue.

(2) If one holds $s'_1, s'_3, \ldots, s'_n$ fixed, is there a strategy s''_2 such that $u_2(s''_2, s'_{-2}) > u_2(s'_2, s'_{-2})$? If so, s' is not a Nash equilibrium. If not, continue.

$\vdots$

(i) If one holds $s'_1, \ldots, s'_{i-1}, s'_{i+1} \ldots, s'_n$ fixed, is there a strategy s''_i such that $u_i(s''_i, s'_{-i}) > u_i(s'_i, s'_{-i})$? If so s' is not a Nash equilibrium. If not continue.

$\vdots$

(n) If one holds $s'_1, \ldots, s'_{n-1}$ fixed, is there a strategy s''_n for which $u_n(s''_n, s'_{-n}) > u_n(s'_n, s'_{-n})$? If so s' is not a Nash equilibrium. If not s' is a Nash equilibrium.

This algorithm is then repeated for each profile in S.

In two-player finite games – those representable by matrices – the algorithm is particularly straightforward. Start with a matrix entry and verify whether there is an entry in the same column that makes the row player better off. If so, the original profile is not a Nash equilibrium. If not, repeat the exercise interchanging row and column. Consider the example in Table 5.12.

Table 5.12

1\2	l	c	r
t	5, 4	2, 3	6, 2
m	2, 5	3, 6	5, 5
b	5, 2	0, 3	7, 4

Consider a conjecture that (t, l) is a pure strategy Nash equilibrium. Given $s_2 = l$, player 1 chooses between $u_1(t, l) = 5$, $u_1(m, l) = 2$ and $u_1(b, l) = 5$. Accordingly $b_1(l) = \{t, b\}$. Given $s_1 = t$ player 2 chooses between utilities of 4, 3, and 2 so $b_2(t) = \{l\}$. Accordingly (t, l) is a Nash equilibrium. Because $b_2(l)$ has a single element, (t, l) is the only pure strategy Nash equilibrium involving play of t. Recall that $b_1(l) = \{t, b\}$ so (m, l) is not a Nash equilibrium as player 1 would deviate to either t or b if she conjectures that player 2 selects l. Next we conjecture that (m, c) is a Nash equilibrium. Because $b_1(c) = \{m\}$ and $b_2(m) = \{c\}$, our conjecture is correct. Given that $r \notin b_2(m)$, the only pure strategy Nash equilibrium that m is played is (m, c). A conjecture that (b, l) is a Nash equilibrium is refuted by $b_2(b) = \{r\}$. Similarly a conjecture that (b, c) is a Nash equilibrium is inconsistent with $b_1(c) = \{m\}$. Finally, a conjecture that (b, r) is a Nash equilibrium is correct because neither player can gain from deviating. Through this tedious process, we conclude that the set of pure strategy Nash equilibria is $\{(t, l), (m, c), (b, r)\}$.

6.2. Pure Strategy Nash Equilibria in Games with Continuous Strategy Spaces. Unless the strategy space is finite, the algorithm discussed earlier does not work.[11] Sometimes, however, we can use the techniques of optimization to compute equilibria. If the utility functions $u_i(s)$ are twice differentiable, calculus may be used to characterize the best response correspondences. Because a best response to s_{-i} is the maximizer of $u(s_i, s_{-i})$ over S_i, a sufficient condition for $s_i \in b_i(s_{-i})$ is that $\partial u_i(s_i, s_{-i})/\partial s_i = 0$ and $\partial^2 u_i(s_i, s_{-i})/\partial s_i^2 < 0$. The first of these conditions is the first-order condition (FOC) whereas the second is the second-order condition (SOC).[12] If the FOC and SOC hold, the solutions to $\partial u_i(s_i, s_{-i})/\partial s_i = 0$ provide each of the best response correspondences. Further, if $u_i(s)$ is strictly concave, the solution satisfying the FOC and SOC is unique and the best responses are functions. In

---

[11] The reader may want to review the discussion of optimization in the Mathematical Appendix before reading this section.

[12] If S_i has more than one dimension, the term $\partial u_i(s_i, s_{-i})/\partial s_i$ is a vector where each coordinate is the partial derivative with respect to one coordinate of s_i. The quantity 0 denotes the vector of 0s. The second-order condition is the requirement that the matrix of second derivatives be negative definite.

such a case, every solution to the system

$$s_1^* = b_1(s_{-1}^*)$$
$$\cdot$$
$$s_i^* = b_i(s_{-i}^*)$$
$$\cdot$$
$$s_n^* = b_n(s_{-n}^*)$$

is a Nash equilibrium. Often this procedure is unnecessarily cumbersome – it requires solving both for each best response function and the system of equations. Generally it is more convenient to solve the system of first-order conditions directly:

$$\frac{\partial u_1(s_1, s_{-1})}{\partial s_1} = 0$$
$$\cdot$$
$$\frac{\partial u_i(s_i, s_{-i})}{\partial s_i} = 0$$
$$\cdot$$
$$\frac{\partial u_n(s_n, s_{-n})}{\partial s_n} = 0.$$

To guarantee that the solution is a Nash equilibrium, one must check the second-order conditions for each agent at the solution.

If either system of equations has multiple solutions, there is more than one equilibrium in pure strategies. The absence of a solution, however, does not imply that there are no pure strategy Nash equilibria. The FOCs and SOCs are sufficient, but not necessary conditions, and there are many games for which the best responses do not satisfy them. These situations arise for a variety of reasons. If the payoffs against s_{-i} are not quasi-concave or if they are monotonically increasing or decreasing over S_i, agent i's best response is at the boundary of S_i. Such best responses, known as "corner solutions," typically violate the first-order conditions. The FOC approach also fails if the payoff functions are discontinuous in s_{-i}; at the discontinuities, we cannot compute the first- or second-order conditions.

7. Application: Interest Group Contributions

Two interest groups $N = \{1, 2\}$ seek to influence a government policy. Both groups know the final policy is a function of how much campaign support they give to the government. Group 1's most preferred policy is 0 and group 2's most preferred policy is 1. The government favors the policy $1/2$ but may be influenced by the campaign contributions. Each group chooses to contribute an amount $s_i \in [0, 1]$, and the final policy is $x(s_1, s_2) = 1/2 - s_1 + s_2$. The groups make their choices simultaneously, and the government keeps all of the contributions to buy advertisements for the next election.[13] The interest groups each have utility functions over their contribution and the final policy of the form

$$u_1(s_1, s_2) = -(x(s_1, s_2))^2 - s_1$$
$$u_2(s_1, s_2) = -(1 - x(s_1, s_2))^2 - s_2.$$

If we substitute the policy function into the utility functions we obtain

$$u_1(s_1, s_2) = -\left(\frac{1}{2} - s_1 + s_2\right)^2 - s_1$$
$$u_2(s_1, s_2) = -\left(1 - \left(\frac{1}{2} - s_1 + s_2\right)\right)^2 - s_2.$$

Differentiation generates the first-order conditions

$$FOC_1 : 2\left(\frac{1}{2} - s_1 + s_2\right) - 1 = 0$$
$$FOC_2 : 2\left(1 - \left(\frac{1}{2} - s_1 + s_2\right)\right) - 1 = 0.$$

Solving FOC_1 for s_1 as a function of s_2 yields the best response

$$b_1(s_2) = s_2.$$

From FOC_2 we obtain

$$b_2(s_1) = s_1.$$

Clearly, the Nash equilibria are not unique. Any pair of contributions such that $s_1 = s_2$ is a Nash equilibrium. We write the set of pure strategy

---

[13] This game is closely related to the all-pay auction from economics. We return to auctions later in the book.

Nash equilibria to this game as

$$\{(s_1, s_2) \in [0, 1]^2 : s_1 = s_2\}.$$

This result has a straightforward interpretation. Any pair of equivalent contributions is a Nash equilibrium and in all of these equilibria the policy outcome is $1/2$. No contributor wants to deviate unilaterally because the marginal gain of an additional unit of contribution (in terms of pulling policy in the desired direction) is exactly offset by the marginal cost of losing another unit of resources. As in the Prisoner's Dilemma, the Nash equilibria of this game are inefficient. That is, the contributors would rather commit to not giving any money to the government. But because no such commitment is possible, there are equilibria with positive contributions.

8. Application: International Externalities

Two countries must decide how much to invest in pollution abatement. Their strategies are levels of investment $s_1 > 0$ and $s_2 > 0$. Each country pays a cost $c(s_i) = k_i s_i$. Let $k_1 < k_2$ so that country 1 abates a given amount of pollution at a lower cost than country 2. The total amount of pollution affects citizens of both countries so that the utility of abatement is based on the total investment, $u_i(s_1, s_2) = \sqrt{s_1 + s_2}$. The payoff for each country depends on the utility and costs of abatement and is given by

$$\sqrt{s_1 + s_2} - k_i s_i.$$

From these payoffs, it is straightforward to generate the FOC conditions:

$$\frac{1}{2}(s_1 + s_2)^{-\frac{1}{2}} - k_1 = 0$$

$$\frac{1}{2}(s_1 + s_2)^{-\frac{1}{2}} - k_2 = 0.$$

The SOCs for both countries, $-1/4 (s_1 + s_2)^{-3/2} < 0$, are satisfied.

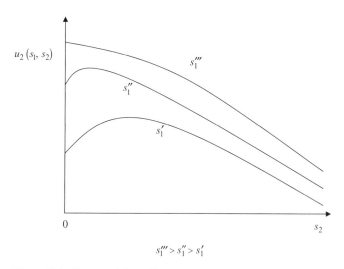

Figure 5.4. Country 2 Payoffs as a Function of Country 1's Investment.

There is no solution to the system of FOCs because $k_1 < k_2$. Suppose that $s_1 > (2k_2)^{-2}$; the left-hand side of country 2's FOC is always negative. This implies that country 2's payoff is always decreasing in its investment. Figure 5.4, where country 2's payoffs are plotted as a function of country 1's investment, shows this graphically for values of $s_{-1}''' > (2k_2)^{-2}$. Because investments are nonnegative, country 2's best response to this level of country 1 investment is 0. Similarly, if $s_2 > (2k_1)^{-2}$, country 1's best response is 0 investment. These "corner solutions" are part of each country's best response functions, and we cannot use the FOC approach.

It is easy, however, to see the solution graphically. In Figure 5.5 we plot the best response functions for both countries. The vertical axis represents both country 2's strategy and its best response to country 1. Similarly, the horizontal axis represents country 1's strategy and best response. The dotted line represents country 2's best response function. It declines in s_1 until $s_1 > (2k_2)^{-2}$, where it is 0. The solid line is the country 1's best response, which also declines to 0 at $s_2 = (2k_1)^{-2}$. Clearly, the only intersection of the best responses is $s_1 = (2k_1)^{-2}$ and $s_2 = 0$.

If $k_2 < k_1$ so that country 2 is the low-cost country, it is easy to check that the Nash equilibrium strategies would be $s_1 = 0$ and $s_2 = (2k_2)^{-2}$. The unique Nash equilibrium of this game is one where the high-cost country free-rides completely on the low-cost country. The low-cost

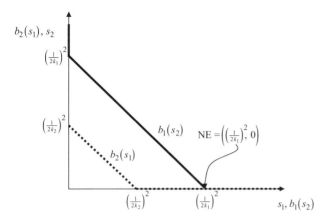

Figure 5.5. Best Response Functions for Externality Game.

country base is its optimal investment on the knowledge that the high-cost county is investing nothing.

9. Computing Equilibria with Constrained Optimization

When a game has best response functions that map onto the boundary of the strategy space, the techniques of constrained maximization such as Kuhn-Tucker programming can be used to compute necessary conditions for Nash equilibria.[14] To illustrate, reconsider the externality game. Now we explicitly impose the constraints $s_1 \geq 0$ and $s_2 \geq 0$. We incorporate these constraints into the optimization problem with Lagrange multipliers λ_1 and λ_2. Now agent i chooses s_i to maximize

$$\sqrt{s_1 + s_2} - k_i s_i + \lambda_i s_i.$$

The necessary conditions for a Nash equilibrium are the first-order conditions

$$\frac{1}{2}(s_1 + s_2)^{-\frac{1}{2}} - k_1 + \lambda_1 = 0$$

$$\frac{1}{2}(s_1 + s_2)^{-\frac{1}{2}} - k_2 + \lambda_2 = 0$$

---

[14] Readers may wish to review the section on constrained optimization in the Mathematical Appendix.

along with the "slackness" conditions

$$\lambda_1 s_1 = 0$$
$$\lambda_2 s_2 = 0$$

and the constraints

$$\lambda_i \geq 0 \text{ for all } i$$
$$s_i \geq 0 \text{ for all } i.$$

A Nash equilibrium is a solution to the four equations that satisfies the constraints. The first two equations imply that $\lambda_i = k_i - (1/2)(s_1 + s_2)^{-\frac{1}{2}}$. We can use this result to rewrite the slackness conditions as

$$s_1 \left[k_1 - \frac{1}{2}(s_1 + s_2)^{-\frac{1}{2}} \right] = 0$$
$$s_2 \left[k_2 - \frac{1}{2}(s_1 + s_2)^{-\frac{1}{2}} \right] = 0$$

and the constraints on λ as

$$k_1 \geq \frac{1}{2}(s_1 + s_2)^{-\frac{1}{2}}$$
$$k_2 \geq \frac{1}{2}(s_1 + s_2)^{-\frac{1}{2}}.$$

As before, we see that there is no solution where both countries make positive investments. Such a solution requires the bracketed terms of each FOC to be 0 – an impossibility. The profile $s_1 = s_2 = 0$ is also not an equilibrium, because the condition that $k_i \geq (1/2)(s_1 + s_2)$ is violated. Further, suppose that $s_1 = 0$ and $s_2 > 0$. The second first-order condition implies that $k_2 = (1/2)(s_1 + s_2) k$, a result that violates the nonnegativity constraints on λ_1. Consequently, the only possible Nash equilibrium involves $s_1 > 0$ and $s_2 = 0$. The first FOC implies that $s_1^* = (2k_1)^{-2}$. This is exactly the result we derived in the last section.

10. Proving the Existence of Nash Equilibria**

We now provide a rigorous proof of Nash's Theorem. First we present some related mathematical concepts. The most important of these is the idea of a *fixed point*. Intuitively, a fixed point of a function (or correspondence) is a point in the domain that maps into itself in the range. Formally, for a correspondence $c : A \rightrightarrows A$, a fixed point $x^* \in A$ is a point such that $x^* \in c(x^*)$. If $c(\cdot)$ is a function, a fixed point is a point x^* such that $x^* = c(x^*)$. Because a Nash equilibrium is a strategy profile s^* such that $s_i^* \in b_i(s_{-i}^*)$ for every $i \in N$, it is a fixed point of the the the best response correspondence

$$b(s) = (b_1(s_{-1}), \ldots, b_i(s_{-i}), \ldots, b_n(s_{-n})).$$

Proving the existence of a Nash equilibrium, therefore, is simply a matter of determining whether or not a fixed point exists for the best response correspondence. Fortunately, a body of mathematics is dedicated to determining sufficient conditions for the existence of fixed points. A specification of such conditions is a *fixed point theorem*. If the properties of a game's best response correspondence match the conditions for a fixed point theorem, a Nash equilibrium exists.

A number of conditions are useful in establishing the existence of a fixed point. The first is that the correspondence is convex valued.

DEFINITION 5.11 *A correspondence* $c : A \rightrightarrows A$ *is convex valued if* $c(a)$ *is a convex subset of* A *for every* $a \in A$.

A correspondence $c(\cdot)$ is convex valued if for each $x \in X$ the point $\lambda y + (1 - \lambda)z \in c(x)$ whenever $y, z \in c(x)$ and $\lambda \in [0, 1]$.

Another useful definition is the upper inverse of a set. For a set B, the upper inverse is the set of points in the domain that the correspondence maps into subsets of B.

DEFINITION 5.12 *For a correspondence* $c : A \rightrightarrows A$, *the upper inverse of a set* $B \subseteq A$ *is* $c^+(B) = \{x \in A : c(x) \subset B\}$.

Upper inverse sets play an important role in defining a notion of continuity for correspondences, *upper hemicontinuity*.

DEFINITION 5.13 *A correspondence* $c : A \rightarrow\rightarrow A$ *is upper hemicontinuous if the upper inverse set* $c^+(O)$ *is open for every open set* $O \subseteq A$.

Definition 5.13 is often hard to verify. The existence of a closed graph is easier to check.

DEFINITION 5.14 *A correspondence* $c : A \rightarrow\rightarrow A$ *has a closed graph if for any two sequences* $x^n \rightarrow x \in A$ *and* $y^n \rightarrow y \in A$ *with* $x^n \in A$ *and* $y^n \in c(x^n)$ *for every n we have* $y \in c(x)$.

The following theorem (we leave its proof as an exercise) establishes that correspondences with closed graphs are upper hemicontinuous.

THEOREM 5.6 *If* A *is compact a correspondence* $c : A \rightarrow\rightarrow A$ *is upper hemicontinuous if it has a closed graph.*

The intuition behind the closed-graph condition is not difficult. Suppose that there are two sequences of points in A, x^n and y^n, such that $y^n \in c(x^n)$ for each n and that these sequences converge to x and y in A, respectively. If c has a closed graph, it must be the case that $y \in c(x)$. Also for a correspondence with a closed graph, the set $\{(x, y) \in A^2 : y \in c(x)\}$ is closed in the space A^2. For a more complete treatment of these concepts see Border (1989).

Recall that if a correspondence $c : A \rightarrow\rightarrow A$ is single valued for every $a \in A$, it is a function. If a single-valued correspondence is upper hemicontinuous then it is a continuous function.

To establish Theorem 5.3, we use Brouwer's fixed point theorem.

THEOREM 5.7 *(Brouwer) Suppose* $A \subset \mathbb{R}^d$ *is a compact and convex set. If* $f : A \rightarrow A$ *is a continuous function then* $f(\cdot)$ *has a fixed point in* A.

To establish Theorem 5.4, we use Kakutani's fixed point theorem.

THEOREM 5.8 *(Kakutani) Suppose that* $A \subset \mathbb{R}^d$ *is a compact and convex set with* $c : A \rightarrow\rightarrow A$ *a correspondence satisfying the conditions*

(1) $c(x)$ *is nonempty for every* $x \in A$
(2) $c(\cdot)$ *is convex valued*
(3) $c(\cdot)$ *is upper hemicontinuous*
     then $c(\cdot)$ *has a fixed point in* A.

Various proofs of these results appear in Border (1989). To establish the existence of Nash equilibria, we show that in the case of Theorem 5.7 $b(s)$ is a continuous function and in the case of Theorem 5.8 $b(s)$ is a correspondence that satisfies the conditions 1–3. A result useful in demonstrating that $b(s)$ is nonempty and upper hemicontinuous is due to Berge (1997).

THEOREM 5.9 *(Berge's Theorem of the Maximum) Let* $X \subset \mathbb{R}^d$, $M \subset \mathbb{R}^z$ *be compact and convex sets. Let the function* $f(x, m) : X \times M \to R^1$ *be continuous in x and m. The correspondence* $c : M \to\to X$ *defined as*

$$c(m) = \arg\max_{x \in X}\{f(x, m)\}$$

is nonempty for every $m \in M$ *and upper hemicontinuous.*

That $c(\cdot)$ defined in Theorem 5.9 is upper hemicontinuous has the following interpretation: let the vector m be a parameter vector of the optimization problem. If we consider a sequence of parameter vectors m^n converging to m, then $x \in c(m)$ for any selection of optimal policies $x^n \in c(m^n)$ that converge to x.

We now prove Theorem 5.3.

Proof of Theorem 5.3 Assume that S_i is a convex subset of $\mathbb{R}^d$ for each $i \in N$ and for each $i \in N$. Let $u_i(s) : S \to \mathbb{R}^1$ be continuous and strictly quasi-concave in s_i for each $s'_{-i} \in S_{-i}$. From Theorem 5.9, the correspondence $b_i(s_{-i}) : S_{-i} \to\to S$ defined by

$$b_i(s_{-i}) = \arg\max_{s_i \in S_i}\{u_i(s_i, s_{-i})\}$$

is nonempty for each $s_{-i} \in S_{-i}$ and upper hemicontinuous. Because strictly quasi-concave utility functions can be represented by strictly convex preferences orders, Theorem 2.4 implies that $b_i(s_{-i})$ is a singleton for every $s_{-i} \in S_{-i}$. That a single-valued upper hemicontinuous correspondence is a continuous function (see Exercise 5.15) implies that $b_i(s_{-i})$ is a continuous function from S_{-i} into S_i for each $i \in N$. We now construct the function

$$b(s) : S \to S$$

by defining $b(s_1, \ldots, s_n) = (b_1(s_{-1}), \ldots, b_n(s_{-n}))$. The vector s_{-i} is a continuous function of s (a projection) and we can form the composite function $\widetilde{b}_i(s) = b_i(s_{-i}(s))$. The function $b(s)$ is, therefore, continuous because (1) $b_i(\cdot)$ is continuous, (2) the composition of continuous functions $\widetilde{b}_i(s)$ is continuous, and (3) the product of continuous functions $(\widetilde{b}_1(s), \ldots, \widetilde{b}_n(s))$ is continuous. Brouwer's fixed point theorem implies this mapping has a fixed point, $s^* = b(s^*)$. Consequently, $b_i(s_{-i}^*) = s_i^*$ for every $i \in N$ so that s^* is a Nash equilibrium. $\square$

The proof of Theorem 5.4 is similar. It establishes that in any mixed extension of a finite game, the best response correspondence satisfies the conditions of Kakutani's fixed point theorem.

Proof of Theorem 5.4 For normal form game Γ, let S_i be finite for each $i \in N$. Thus, in the mixed extension Γ^m Δ_i is a compact and convex subset of a finite-dimensional Euclidean space. From definition 5.9 we know that $u(\sigma_i, \sigma_{-i})$ is linear and therefore continuous in σ. Let $b_i(\sigma_{-i}) : \Delta_{-i} \to\to \Delta_i$ be defined as

$$b_i(\sigma_{-i}) = \arg \max_{\sigma_i \in \Delta_i} \left\{ u(\sigma_i, \sigma_{-i}) \right\}.$$

Theorem 5.9 implies that $b_i(\sigma_{-i})$ is nonempty for every $\sigma_{-i} \in \Delta_{-i}$ and upper hemicontinuous. Because $u(\sigma_i, \sigma_{-i})$ is linear for any σ_{-i}, if $u(\sigma_i', \sigma_{-i}) = u(\sigma_i'', \sigma_{-i})$ then $u(\lambda \sigma_i' + (1 - \lambda)\sigma_i'', \sigma_{-i}) = u(\sigma_i', \sigma_{-i})$ for any $\lambda \in (0, 1)$. Thus, $b_i(\sigma_{-i})$ is convex valued. These results establish that the correspondence

$$b(\sigma) : \Delta \to \Delta$$

defined as $b(\sigma_1, \ldots, \sigma_n) = (b_1(\sigma_{-1}), \ldots, b_n(\sigma_{-n}))$ satisfies the requirements of Kakutani's fixed point theorem. So there is a mixed strategy profile satisfying the condition $\sigma^* \in b(\sigma^*)$. Such a profile is a Nash equilibrium to Γ^m and a mixed strategy Nash equilibrium to Γ. $\square$

11. Comparative Statics

One feature of game theoretic models that makes them particularly useful for applied research is that they generate explanations for how exogenous features of political problems affect endogenous features. These relationships are called comparative statics.[15] We begin with a simple example. Consider a model of electoral campaigns in which candidates compete for office by simultaneously selecting expenditure levels for political advertisements. There are two candidates, called 1 and 2. Each candidate $i \in \{1, 2\}$ selects a nonnegative real-valued spending level $s_i \in \mathbb{R}_+$. The cost of s_i is incurred by i regardless of who wins the election. By $c_i(s_i)$ denote the cost to candidate i from spending level s_i. The value of winning the election is normalized to 1 and the value of not winning the election is 0. Let $p(s_1, s_2)$ denote the probability that candidate 1 wins, given the spending levels s_1, s_2. The payoffs to the candidates are thus

$$u_1(s_1, s_2) = p(s_1, s_2) - c_1(s_1)$$
$$u_2(s_1, s_2) = 1 - p(s_1, s_2) - c_2(s_2).$$

First, assume that $c_i(s_i) = ks_i^2$ and $p(s_1, s_2) = (\max\{0, \min\{1, 1/2 + \beta(s_1 - s_2)\}\})$ where k and β are strictly positive parameters. To focus the analysis on interior solutions we assume that $\beta^2 < 2k$. Differentiating yields the first-order conditions for an equilibrium with values of s_1^*, s_2^* that satisfy the condition that $p(s_1^*, s_2^*) \in (0, 1)$. The first-order conditions are

$$\beta = 2ks_1$$
$$\beta = 2ks_2.$$

Rearranging yields the equilibrium solutions

$$s_1^* = \frac{\beta}{2k}$$
$$s_2^* = \frac{\beta}{2k}.$$

To emphasize the relationship between parameters and equilibrium behavior we can write $s_i^*(\beta, k) = \beta/(2k)$. To see how this solution varies

---

[15] Readers unfamiliar or rusty with calculus should consult the review of calculus in the the Mathematical Appendix before continuing.

with the exogenous parameters we differentiate and attain

$$\frac{\partial s_i^*(\beta, k)}{\partial \beta} = \frac{1}{2k}$$

$$\frac{\partial s_i^*(\beta, k)}{\partial k} = -\frac{\beta}{2k^2}.$$

So the equilibrium advertisement levels are increasing in the marginal productivity of ads and decreasing in the marginal cost of ads. In this example the first-order conditions yield best response functions that do not depend on the other player's choice variable; in general this is not the case. Given this, the comparative statics exercise is very easy. In general, however, first-order conditions implicitly characterize the individual best response correspondences and then an equilibrium is a fixed point of the best response correspondence. In principle we might not be comfortable making strong assumptions about the functional forms of $p(\cdot, \cdot)$ and $c(\cdot)$. How could we learn about the comparative statics of equilibria to this game when the functional forms are not specified? Similarly how do we proceed if we chose functional forms that do not allow a closed form solution for s_i^* as an explicit function of parameters? The implicit function theorem provides a framework for answering these types of questions. In a more general advertising game we can let $p(s_1, s_2; \beta)$ denote the probability of victory for candidate 1 as a function of the choice variables and a parameter. Similarly let $c_1(s_1; k_1)$ and $c_2(s_2; k_2)$ denote the costs as functions of the choice variables and parameters k_1 and k_2. It is common to use a semicolon to separate endogenous variables from exogenous ones. The preceding example is a special case of this class of models. The first-order conditions are

$$\frac{\partial p(s_1, s_2; \beta)}{\partial s_1} - \frac{\partial c_1(s_1; k_1)}{\partial s_1} = 0 \qquad (5.1)$$

$$\frac{\partial p(s_1, s_2; \beta)}{\partial s_1} + \frac{\partial c_2(s_2; k_2)}{\partial s_2} = 0.$$

To avoid some technical issues we, first, assume that the system 5.1 yields best responses that are single valued; thus we assume that best response functions exist.[16] Before considering equilibria, we can analyze how the best responses vary with the exogenous parameters and

---

[16] The reader is now in a position to provide sufficient conditions on the primitive functions for this assumption to hold. Review the results associated with Theorem 5.3.

the other player's strategy – treated for the moment as exogenous. The implicit function theorem states that as long as a certain condition is satisfied we can use differential calculus to characterize how candidate 1's optimal choice varies in response to small changes in the values of s_2, β, or k_1. A general statement of the theorem appears in the Mathematical Appendix. In the context of this problem the application is as follows. Let $b_1(\cdot; \cdot, \cdot, \cdot)$ mapping $(s_2; \beta, k_1, k_2)$ into s_1 denote the best response for player 1. Assume that at the parameter vector (s_2, β, k_1, k_2) the functions $p(\cdot, \cdot; \cdot)$, $c_1(\cdot; \cdot)$, and $c_2(\cdot; \cdot)$ are continuously differentiable and that $\partial^2 p(s_1, s_2; \beta)/(\partial s_1 \partial s_1) \neq \partial^2 c_1(s_1; k_1)/(\partial s_1 \partial s_1)$ when $s_1 = b_1(s_2; \beta, k_1)$. The implicit function theorem says that on a neighborhood of the vector (s_2, β, k_1) the function b_1 is differentiable and has the following partial first derivatives

$$\frac{\partial s_1}{\partial s_2} = -\frac{\frac{\partial^2 p(s_1, s_2; \beta)}{\partial s_1 \partial s_2}}{\frac{\partial^2 p(s_1, s_2; \beta)}{\partial s_1 \partial s_1} - \frac{\partial^2 c_1(s_1; k_1)}{\partial s_1 \partial s_1}}$$

$$\frac{\partial s_1}{\partial \beta} = -\frac{\frac{\partial^2 p(s_1, s_2; \beta)}{\partial s_1 \partial \beta}}{\frac{\partial^2 p(s_1, s_2; \beta)}{\partial s_1 \partial s_1} - \frac{\partial^2 c_1(s_1; k_1)}{\partial s_1 \partial s_1}}$$

$$\frac{\partial s_1}{\partial k_1} = \frac{\frac{\partial^2 c_1(s_1; k_1)}{\partial s_1 \partial k_1}}{\frac{\partial^2 p(s_1, s_2; \beta)}{\partial s_1 \partial s_1} - \frac{\partial^2 c_1(s_1; k_1)}{\partial s_1 \partial s_1}}.$$

The requirement that $\partial^2 p(s_1, s_2; \beta)/(\partial s_1 \partial s_1) \neq \partial^2 c(s_1; k_1)/(\partial s_1 \partial s_1)$ when $s_1 = b_1(s_2; \beta, k_1)$ ensures that the denominators are not equal to 0. The implicit function theorem allows us to characterize how parameters affect the first-order conditions. We leave it as an exercise to derive the relevant comparative statics for $b_2(\cdot; \cdot, \cdot, \cdot)$. Relaxing the assumption that the first-order conditions yield unique best responses is not difficult. As long as $\partial^2 p(s_1, s_2; \beta)/(\partial s_1 \partial s_1) \neq \partial^2 c(s_1; k_1)/(\partial s_1 \partial s_1)$ a solution to the first-order condition is locally unique; in a neighborhood of any FOC solution no other solution exists. Thus, the comparative statics characterize local changes at each element of the best response correspondence.

An important caveat is warranted. The preceding analysis characterizes how the best response varies across parameter values; it does not express how equilibrium behavior varies. The next section addresses this issue.

11.1. Equilibrium Effects*. An equilibrium pair s_1^*, s_2^* solves system 5.1.[17] To see how changes in the parameters (β, k_1, k_2) affect an equilibrium, we apply the implicit function theorem to the system of equations. In the last section we only applied the implicit function theorem to each best response. To analyze the equilibrium comparative statics, it is necessary to use the tools of matrix algebra. The Jacobian matrix is given by

$$\begin{bmatrix} \frac{\partial^2 p(s_1,s_2;\beta)}{\partial s_1 \partial s_1} - \frac{\partial^2 c_1(s_1;k_1)}{\partial s_1 \partial s_1} & \frac{\partial^2 p(s_1,s_2;\beta)}{\partial s_1 \partial s_2} \\ \frac{\partial^2 p(s_1,s_2;\beta)}{\partial s_2 \partial s_1} & \frac{\partial^2 p(s_1,s_2;\beta)}{\partial s_2 \partial s_2} - \frac{\partial^2 c_2(s_2;k_2)}{\partial s_2 \partial s_2} \end{bmatrix}.$$

The analog to the condition that $\partial^2 p(s_1, s_2; \beta)/(\partial s_1 \partial s_1) \neq \partial^2 c(s_1; k_1)/(\partial s_1 \partial s_1)$ is that the determinant of this matrix is nonsingular (i.e., its determinant is not equal to 0).[18] Consider continuously differentiable functions $p(\cdot, \cdot; \cdot), c_1(\cdot; \cdot), c_2(\cdot; \cdot)$ and assume that at the parameter vector (β, k_1, k_2) the vector s_1^*, s_2^* is a solution to system 5.1. Further assume that at this solution the Jacobian is nonsingular. The implicit function theorem states that there exists a neighborhood of the vector (β, k_1, k_2), B, and a neighborhood of the solution s_1^*, s_2^*, A, upon which solutions to system 5.1 are given by a differentiable function of the parameters $s : B \to A$ and the first derivatives of this function are given by

$$\begin{bmatrix} \frac{\partial s_1}{\partial \beta} \\ \frac{\partial s_2}{\partial \beta} \end{bmatrix} = - \begin{bmatrix} \frac{\partial^2 p(s_1,s_2;\beta)}{\partial s_1 \partial s_1} - \frac{\partial^2 c_1(s_1;k_1)}{\partial s_1 \partial s_1} & \frac{\partial^2 p(s_1,s_2;\beta)}{\partial s_1 \partial s_2} \\ \frac{\partial^2 p(s_1,s_2;\beta)}{\partial s_2 \partial s_1} & \frac{\partial^2 p(s_1,s_2;\beta)}{\partial s_2 \partial s_2} - \frac{\partial^2 c_2(s_2;k_2)}{\partial s_2 \partial s_2} \end{bmatrix}^{-1} \begin{bmatrix} \frac{\partial^2 p(s_1,s_2;\beta)}{\partial s_1 \partial \beta} \\ \frac{\partial^2 p(s_1,s_2;\beta)}{\partial s_2 \partial \beta} \end{bmatrix}$$

$$\begin{bmatrix} \frac{\partial s_1}{\partial k_1} \\ \frac{\partial s_2}{\partial k_1} \end{bmatrix} = \begin{bmatrix} \frac{\partial^2 p(s_1,s_2;\beta)}{\partial s_1 \partial s_1} - \frac{\partial^2 c_1(s_1;k_1)}{\partial s_1 \partial s_1} & \frac{\partial^2 p(s_1,s_2;\beta)}{\partial s_1 \partial s_2} \\ \frac{\partial^2 p(s_1,s_2;\beta)}{\partial s_2 \partial s_1} & \frac{\partial^2 p(s_1,s_2;\beta)}{\partial s_2 \partial s_2} - \frac{\partial^2 c_2(s_2;k_2)}{\partial s_2 \partial s_2} \end{bmatrix}^{-1} \begin{bmatrix} \frac{\partial c_1(s_1;k_1)}{\partial s_1 \partial k_1} \\ 0 \end{bmatrix}$$

$$\begin{bmatrix} \frac{\partial s_1}{\partial k_2} \\ \frac{\partial s_2}{\partial k_2} \end{bmatrix} = - \begin{bmatrix} \frac{\partial^2 p(s_1,s_2;\beta)}{\partial s_1 \partial s_1} - \frac{\partial^2 c_1(s_1;k_1)}{\partial s_1 \partial s_1} & \frac{\partial^2 p(s_1,s_2;\beta)}{\partial s_1 \partial s_2} \\ \frac{\partial^2 p(s_1,s_2;\beta)}{\partial s_2 \partial s_1} & \frac{\partial^2 p(s_1,s_2;\beta)}{\partial s_2 \partial s_2} - \frac{\partial^2 c_2(s_2;k_2)}{\partial s_2 \partial s_2} \end{bmatrix}^{-1} \begin{bmatrix} 0 \\ \frac{\partial c_2(s_2;k_2)}{\partial s_2 \partial k_2} \end{bmatrix}.$$

---

[17] This section utilizes concepts from linear algebra and multidimensional differential calculus.

[18] This matrix is a 2 by 2 matrix. For a 2 by 2 matrix, $\begin{bmatrix} a & b \\ c & d \end{bmatrix}$ the determinant is given by $\det = ad - cb$. In the 2 by 2 case the inverse is given by $1/\det \begin{bmatrix} d & -a \\ -b & a \end{bmatrix}$. For larger matrices the calculations are quite tedious.

A few comments are in order. First, the fact that $\partial s_1/\partial k_2$ can be nonzero indicates the relevance of equilibrium effects. Recall that k_2 does not affect the best response for candidate 1. A change in k_2 can move the best response $b_2(\cdot;\cdot,\cdot)$; a change in this best response can change the equilibrium solution for s_1. Second, determining the sign of the comparative statics can be tedious, especially for problems with higher-dimensional strategy spaces. Third, multiple solutions to the first-order conditions create some difficulties. When dealing with best response correspondences, comparative statics can be ambiguous. Each equilibrium for which the Jacobian is nonsingular has a convenient property, however. It is locally isolated: on a neighborhood of the equilibrium there are no other equilibria. Moreover, for small enough changes in the parameters, any new equilibrium is also locally isolated. A problem that analysts confront when there are multiple equilibria is that for a fixed parameter vector, $\partial s_i/\partial\beta$ may have opposite signs in two different equilibria. In the following two sections we present results for games in which this problem can be addressed straightforwardly.

11.2. Strategic Complementarity. Again, suppose that candidates 1 and 2 run for office by choosing spending levels $s_i > 0$. For simplicity assume that the opportunity cost of this spending is $c_i(s_i) = c_i s_i$ where $c_i > 0$. The probability that 1 wins, $p(s_1, s_2)$, is increasing in s_1 and decreasing in s_2. In formulating a model of campaigns, we confront an important question. Do the primitives of the problem result in a setting in which candidate 1's best response is increasing or decreasing in candidate 2's spending? It seems natural that candidate 1 would select higher levels of s_1 in response to higher levels of s_2, and vice versa. If this is the case, the two choice variables are *strategic complements*. Games with strategic complementarity are known as *supermodular*. Such games are particularly amenable to equilibrium and comparative static analysis. In this section we sketch the intuition behind the analysis of such games by using an example, we leave the technical details for the subsequent section.

Kahn and Kenney's (1999) study of Senate elections posits that competitiveness is an important factor in determining how much media coverage campaign activities generate. Competitiveness shapes the way that voters respond to campaigns while campaigns influence the competitiveness of a race. Absent a competitive election, the media and voters tune out, and the marginal value of campaign advertisements is low. On the other hand, when competitiveness is high,

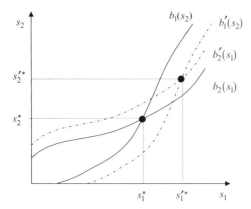

Figure 5.6. Strategic Complementarity.

campaign messages have large effects. Kahn and Kenney's theory portrays the media as a mechanism that determines competitiveness as a function of campaigning. Consistent with this interpretation, higher levels of campaigning are likely to result in more competitiveness. In highly competitive races advertising and spending are more influential. This feedback loop suggests that candidate advertising levels are strategic complements. Consequently, both of the best responses are strictly increasing functions of the other candidate's strategy. In Figure 5.6, we depict the best responses for a game of this form with a unique equilibrium point, (s_1^*, s_2^*).

Whereas pictures with multiple equilibria could be drawn, it is not difficult to see that the equilibria would be completely ordered such that if (s_1^*, s_2^*) and (s_1^{**}, s_2^{**}) are two Nash equilibria and $s_1^* > s_1^{**}$ then $s_2^* > s_2^{**}$ (and if $s_2^* > s_2^{**}$ then $s_1^* > s_1^{**}$). To see that this must be true, try drawing a counterexample while maintaining the assumption that the best responses are strictly increasing.

We can take Kahn and Kenney's hypothesis about competitiveness further. Suppose at the beginning of a campaign, there is an exogenous level of competitiveness. Sources of variation in competitiveness might include the importance of the office, the media environment, and the attentiveness of the voters. Consider two electoral environments where one is more competitive than the other. For a fixed level of s_i, we would expect that $b_{-i}(s_i)$ is higher in the more competitive race. In Figure 5.6, $b_i'(s_{-i})$ denotes the best responses for the more competitive election while $b_i(s_{-i})$ represents those of the less competitive one. The figure demonstrates that equilibrium campaign spending of the more competitive race, $(s_1'^*, s_2'^*)$, is higher than equilibrium spending in the less competitive race, (s_1^*, s_2^*). We conclude therefore that competitiveness generates more campaign spending.

This comparative static result is generated by nothing more than the assumption of strategic complementarity. As long as both best responses are increasing, a common upward shift in the best responses leads to a higher intersection point. It is easy to see, however, that the effect of competitiveness is ambiguous if one of the players has a downward sloping best response. As long as candidate spending levels are strategic complements, the result does not hinge on any assumptions about functional forms or player preferences. The need for the continuous and differentiable best response functions required for use of the implicit function theorem is obviated.

The trick, of course, is to determine model primitives that are consistent with complementarity. In the following technical section, we present the underlying theory of supermodular games and present some sufficiency conditions for the existence of equilibria exhibiting *monotone* comparative statics.

11.3. Supermodularity and Monotone Comparative Statics*. Nash's Theorem relies on continuous best response correspondences and compact strategy sets so that Kakutani's fixed point theorem establishes the existence of equilibria. Unfortunately, these requirements often necessitate strong assumptions about the primitives of the model. A different fixed point theorem, however, establishes existence of Nash equilibria if the best responses satisfy monotonicity conditions like the ones discussed in the previous section. As an analytical bonus, the comparative statics analysis of the equilibrium set is immediate when the best responses satisfy these conditions. Analyses of such equilibria are much simpler and more straightforward than those based on the implicit function theorem. In this section, we summarize several results for supermodular games. The payoff is the ability to prove the existence of equilibria with discontinuous best response correspondences and the availability of direct comparative static results.

The concepts of this section can be developed on the basis of monotonicity for any partial ordering. To keep matters concrete, however, we consider only the natural partial ordering $\geq$ on sets contained in $\mathbb{R}^n$. Some important definitions follow. For any two numbers $x, y \subset \mathbb{R}^1$, the *join* is $x \vee y = \max\{x, y\}$ and the *meet* is $x \wedge y = \min\{x, y\}$. These definitions are extended to vectors element by element. Consequently, for any two vectors in x, y in $\mathbb{R}^n$, $x \vee y = (\max\{x_1, y_1\}, \ldots, \max\{x_n, y_n\})$ and $x \wedge y = (\min\{x_1, y_1\}, \ldots, \min\{x_n, y_n\})$. A set that contains all of the joins and meets of its elements is called a *lattice*.

DEFINITION 5.15 *A set A is a lattice if $x \vee y \in A$ and $x \wedge y \in A$ for each $x, y \in A$*

The intervals and the products of intervals are lattices, but sets like $\{x \in \mathbb{R}^3 : x_1 + x_2 + x_3 \leq 1\}$ – the simplex – are not lattices.[19] Intuitively, squares (products of intervals) are lattices but triangles are not.[20] In this section we are interested in single-agent or multiagent decision theoretic problems defined by a set of choice variables X and a set of exogenous parameters P. Both of these sets are lattices. The agents' objective function depends on both types of variables, $f(x, p) : X \times P \to \mathbb{R}^1$.

DEFINITION 5.16 *The function $f(\cdot, \cdot) : X \times P \to \mathbb{R}^1$ is supermodular in (x, p) if $f(z) + f(z') \leq f(z \vee z') + f(z \wedge z')$ for all $z, z' \in X \times P$.*

Although verification of this condition is often difficult, a more intuitive condition, *increasing differences*, is often easily verified.

DEFINITION 5.17 *The function $f(\cdot, \cdot) : X \times P \to \mathbb{R}^1$ has increasing differences in (x, p) if $f(x', p') - f(x, p') \geq f(x', p) - f(x, p)$ for all $p \leq p'$ and $x \leq x'$.*

For a function with increasing differences the marginal effect of changes in x is increasing in p. In other words, increasing difference formalizes the idea of complementarity. Increasing differences is often easier to interpret in terms of the substance of models than is supermodularity. Therefore it is convenient that increasing differences is equivalent to supermodularity.

---

[19] See Topkis (1998) for a dicusssion of translations that convert nonlattices into lattices.
[20] Although we do not consider examples where the sets are discrete or other nonconvex sets, the definition of a lattice and subsequent results can be readily applied to nonconvex sets.

THEOREM 5.10 *(Topkis) The function* $f(\cdot, \cdot) : X \times P \to \mathbb{R}^1$ *has increasing differences in* (x, p) *if and only if it is supermodular in* (x, p).

In the case of a twice-differentiable function $f(\cdot, \cdot) : X \times P \to \mathbb{R}^1$, supermodularity (and increasing differences) is equivalent to $\partial^2 f/(\partial z_1 \partial z_2) \geq 0$ for any coordinates z_1 and z_2 of X or P or both.

The tractability of supermodular models is further facilitated because supermodularity is preserved under several types of mathematical operations.

THEOREM 5.11 *Let X be a lattice. The following statements are true.*

(1) *If $f(x)$ is supermodular on X and $\alpha > 0$ then $\alpha f(x)$ is supermodular on X.*

(2) *If $f(x)$ and $g(x)$ are supermodular on X then $f(x) + g(x)$ is supermodular on X.*

(3) *If $f_t(x)$ is a sequence of supermodular functions on X for $t = 1, 2, \ldots$, and $f(x) = \lim_{k \to \theta} f_k(x)$ for each $x \in X$ then $f(x)$ is supermodular in X.*

(4) *If $F(\omega)$ is a distribution function on a set Ω and $g(x, \omega)$ is supermodular on X for each $\omega \in \Omega$ then $f(x) = \int_\Omega g(x, \omega) dF(\omega)$ is supermodular on X.*

Now we consider the implications of supermodularity for the simple case of an individual optimization problem. Most importantly, supermodularity implies that the optimal solution has monotone comparative statics: each element of $\arg\max_{x \in X} f(x, p)$ is an increasing function of p.

THEOREM 5.12 *(Topkis) If* $f(\cdot, \cdot) : X \times P \to \mathbb{R}^1$ *is supermodular in* (x, p) *and* $g(p) = \arg\max_{x \in X} f(x, p)$ *then each component of $g(p)$ is increasing in p on every subset $B \subset P$ of parameters for which $g(p)$ is nonempty.*

The theorem does not establish that an optimal solution exists. Recall that Theorem 2.3 establishes the nonemptiness of the maximal set for lower continuous orderings on compact sets. Lower continuity of preferences corresponds to what is called upper semicontinuity of objective functions.

DEFINITION 5.18 *A function* $f(x) : X \to \mathbb{R}^1$ *is upper semicontinuous at* $x_0 \in X$ *if for all* $\varepsilon > f(x_0)$ *there is some* $\delta > 0$ *such that for all* $x \in B(x_0, \delta)$ *(an open ball around* x_0 *with radius* δ*)* $\varepsilon \geq f(x)$. *A function is upper semicontinuous on* X *if it is upper semicontinuous at every* $x_0 \in X$.

Upper semicontinuity at x_0 requires that $\liminf_{x \to x_0} f(x) \leq f(x_0)$. Using the result of exercise 5.21, Theorem 2.3, and a restatement of Topkis's result lead to the following conclusion.

THEOREM 5.13 *If* $f(\cdot, \cdot) : X \times P \to \mathbb{R}^1$ *is supermodular in* (x, p) *and upper semicontinuous in* x *for each* p *then* $g(p) = \arg\max_{x \in X} f(x, p)$ *is nonempty for every* $p \in P$ *and each component of* $g(p)$ *is increasing in* p.

In the proof of Theorem 5.4, we highlighted properties of objective functions that generated the properties of the best responses required to apply a specific fixed point theorem. Analogously, Tarsky's fixed point theorem allows us to use monotonicity of best responses to establish existence of Nash equilibria. Theorem 5.13 thus leads to the conclusion that a game with supermodular and upper semicontinuous utility functions has at least one Nash equilibrium. We now present Tarsky's theorem.

THEOREM 5.14 *(Tarsky) If* $f(x)$ *is an increasing function from a compact lattice* X *into itself then there exists at least one fixed point* x^* *such that* $f(x^*) = x^*$.

In Figure 5.7 we demonstrate the case in which X is one-dimensional. As long as the function $f(x)$ is increasing, the presence of discontinuities does not enable us to skip all of the crossings of $f(x)$ and the dotted 45° line. Just as Kakutani's theorem generalized Brouwer's to the case of correspondences, Zhou (1994) represents a generalization of Tarsky to the case of correspondences. We do not present this result because it requires much additional notation. Instead we present directly the result for supermodular games.

DEFINITION 5.19 *A regular supermodular game is a normal form game* $\langle N, \{S_i, u(\cdot, \ldots, \cdot)\}_{i \in n}\rangle$ *in which* S_i *is a compact lattice for each* $i \in N$ *and* $u(\cdot, \ldots, \cdot)$ *is supermodular and upper semicontinuous for each* $i \in N$.

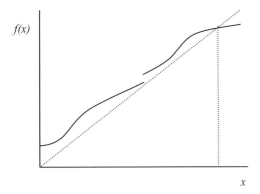

Figure 5.7. Tarsky's Fixed Point Theorem.

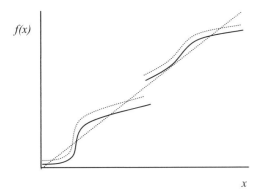

Figure 5.8. Comparative Statics of Extreme Fixed Points.

The main result for regular supermodular games can now be stated.

THEOREM 5.15 *A regular supermodular game has at least one pure strategy Nash equilibrium, and the set of such equilibria is a lattice with a smallest and biggest equilibrium profile.*

Why do we care about the existence of a smallest and largest equilibrium? The second important result for supermodular games deals with comparative statics of the smallest and largest equilibria. To motivate this result we return to the case of a function $f(x)$ on $\mathbb{R}^1$.

Figure 5.8 depicts an increasing function with four fixed points $f(x) = x$. The dotted curve $f'(x)$ represents the result of shifting $f(x)$

up. The largest and smallest fixed points shift to the right (get larger) when the function is shifted up. In contrast some fixed points move the other way. The smallest and biggest fixed points are generally the result of the function's crossing the $45°$ line from above and behave the same way. This intuition forms the basis for the following comparative static result.

THEOREM 5.16 *In a regular supermodular game the smallest and largest equilibrium profiles are increasing in p.*

Figure 5.8 suggests that other equilibria can behave differently. Echenique (2002) shows that in games with complementaries any equilibrium without the comparative statics of the biggest and smallest equilibria is unstable. In other words there are clear reasons to select equilibria that exhibit monotone comparative statics.

Returning to Kahn and Kenney's competitiveness hypothesis, suppose that candidate 1 maximizes $p(s_1, s_2, c) - c_1 s_1$ and candidate 2 maximizes $1 - p(s_1, s_2, \gamma) - c_2 s_2$ where $p(s_1, s_2, \gamma)$ depends on an exogenous level of competitiveness $\gamma \in \mathbb{R}^1$. If campaign spending influences competitiveness and voters pay closer attention in more competitive races, the incremental effect of s_1 on $p(s_1, s_2, \gamma)$ is higher when s_2 or γ is higher. A symmetric argument applies for the incremental effect of s_2. Accordingly, the assumption that payoffs are supermodular is consistent with Kahn and Kenney's claim. Assuming compactness of the choice sets and upper semicontinuity of $p(s_1, s_2, \gamma)$ in s_1 and $-p(s_1, s_2, \gamma)$ in s_2 allows us to conclude (from Theorems 5.16 and 5.17) that equilibria exist. Moreover, s_i is increasing in γ in the biggest and smallest equilibria. This is a strong conclusion; it is robust to the particular specification of $p(\cdot, \cdot, \cdot)$. The power of monotone comparative statics is that it enables analysts to identify the minimal structure generating a particular prediction.[21]

12. Refining Nash Equilibria

In the majority-rule voting game of Section 2.2, any profile in which no single voter is pivotal is a Nash equilibrium. We justify ignoring

---

[21] For a thorough review of results for supermodular games and monotone comparative statics see Topkis (1998). A focused summary of results and applications to political science appear in Ashworth and Bueno de Mesquita (2006).

these equilibria because they involve weakly dominated strategies. The elimination of weakly dominated strategies, however, is not the only way that we can justify *refining* the set of Nash equilibria in this game. Instead of assuming that every agent plays her best response with probability 1, suppose that each player *trembles* with some small probability and plays another strategy. To keep matters very simple, consider a three-player version of the game in which two voters prefer D and one prefers R. Formally, each player is constrained to play each pure strategy with at least probability ε that is assumed to be a small positive number less than $1/2$.[22] This assumption captures the idea that mistakes ensure that all strategies are played with at least a minimal probability.

Clearly maximizing the probability that their preferred candidate wins is a best response. This goal is identical to minimizing the probability that the least desired candidate wins. So we need only compute the probability that each candidate wins under various combinations of strategies. The probabilities of a R victory are as follows:

$$\Pr\left(R|3\text{ attempted votes for }R\right) = (1 - \varepsilon)^3 + 3(1 - \varepsilon)^2\varepsilon$$

$$\Pr\left(R|2\text{ attempted votes for }R\right) = (1 - \varepsilon)^3 + (1 - \varepsilon)^2\varepsilon + 2(1 - \varepsilon)\varepsilon^2$$

$$\Pr\left(R|1\text{ attempted votes for }R\right) = \varepsilon^2(1 - \varepsilon) + 2(1 - \varepsilon)^2\varepsilon + \varepsilon^3$$

$$\Pr\left(R|0\text{ attempted votes for }R\right) = \varepsilon^3 + 3\varepsilon^2(1 - \varepsilon).$$

One can verify that $\varepsilon < 1/2$ implies the probability that a Republican wins is strictly increasing in the number of intended votes.

First, consider the "bad" equilibrium of the original game where R wins unanimously. Does this outcome survive in the presence of trembles (i.e., does each voter vote R with the maximal probability $1 - \varepsilon$)? Clearly, the R voter maximizes the probability of an R victory by voting R with probability $1 - \varepsilon$. Consider the choice of a D voter. She can conform with the equilibrium by intending to vote R, in which case R wins with probability $(1 - \varepsilon)^3 + 3(1 - \varepsilon)^2\varepsilon$. Conversely, she can defect by intending to vote for D. In this case R wins with probability $(1 - \varepsilon)^3 + (1 - \varepsilon)^2\varepsilon + 2(1 - \varepsilon)\varepsilon^2$. This defection reduces the probability that R wins by $2(1 - \varepsilon)^2\varepsilon - 2(1 - \varepsilon)\varepsilon^2 > 0$. Thus, the D voter

---

[22] The idea that voters might not vote for the candidate whom they intended to support has taken on renewed substantive importance since the 2000 U.S. presidential election.

prefers the defection. It is easy to show that the equilibrium that corresponds to all voters' choosing D also does not survive trembles.

This idea of refining the set of equilibria by focusing on equilibria that are robust to small mistakes by the agents is due to Reinhardt Selten (1965), who named such equilibria *perfect*. A formal definition of perfect equilibria follows:

DEFINITION 5.20 *For a fixed $\varepsilon > 0$ an "ε-constrained" equilibrium is a totally mixed strategy profile σ^ε such that for each player i, σ_i^ε solves $max_{\sigma_i} u_i(\sigma_i, \sigma_{-i}^\varepsilon)$ subject to $\sigma_i(s_i) \geq \varepsilon$ for each s_i. A perfect equilibrium is the limit of some sequence of ε-constrained equilibrium as ε goes to 0.*

It is easy to see how unanimous voting equilibria fail to meet this definition. In the ε-constrained equilibria, all players vote for their least preferred candidate with probability ε. Consequently, the limit of these equilibria are strategy profiles that place 0 probability on voting for the less preferred candidate. Indeed, the only perfect equilibrium is the one where all voters vote for their favorite candidate.

Perfect equilibria have a number of desirable properties. First, all perfect equilibria are Nash equilibria of the game without the ε constraints. Thus, the set of perfect equilibria is a proper subset of the set of Nash equilibria. Second, using arguments similar to ones used to establish the existence of Nash equilibria, finite game normal form games have at least one perfect equilibrium.[23]

13. Application: Private Provision of Public Goods

Since the publication of Mancur Olson's *The Logic of Collective Action* in 1965, the conditions under which individually rational agents willingly incur private costs to contribute to the public good have been a central question in political science. In this section, we present one such model based on the work of Palfrey and Rosenthal (1984).

A group of n agents decide whether to make private contributions to the provision of a public good. Provision requires the contribution of at least one agent. If the good is provided, each agent obtains a gain of one unit of utility. Any contributor pays a cost $c < 1$. The strategy set

---

[23] The proof follows from the fact that the ε-constrained mixed strategy space is compact, convex, and nonempty. Of course after establishing the existence of an ε-constrained equilibrium, one must show it converges to a Nash equilibrium.

for each agent is {*contribute, don't contribute*}. We define *contribute* as $s_i = 1$ and *don't contribute* as $s_i = 0$. Because we also consider mixed strategy equilibria, let σ_i be the probability that agent i contributes. The payoff for each agent is $1 - c$ if she contributes, 1 if she does not contribute but some other agent does, and 0 otherwise. Consequently, the model captures the incentive to free-ride. Each agent prefers someone else to contribute so that she may capture the gains without incurring the costs.

First, we consider the set of pure strategy equilibria. It is easy to verify that for each agent i there is a pure strategy Nash equilibrium where $s_i = 1$ and $s_{-i} = 0$. In each of these equilibria, agent i receives $1 - c$, and all other agents receive a utility of 1. Clearly, agent i does not defect because failing to contribute lowers her payoff to 0. Similarly, no other agent defects to contributing because defection lowers his payoff from 1 to $1 - c$. Now we check that no other combination of strategies is a pure strategy Nash equilibrium. First, consider $s_i = 0$ for all i. In this case, any agent does better by contributing so this profile cannot be an equilibrium. Next consider a strategy combination where more than one agent contributes. Clearly, any contributor increases her utility by unilaterally withholding the contribution – the good is provided by a contribution from another agent.

The implications of these equilibria are quite different from those of Olson's decision theoretic analysis. In particular, Olson's analysis predicts that free-riding leads to inefficient levels of public goods provision. In the Palfrey-Rosenthal game, however, all of the pure strategy equilibria are Pareto efficient – the public good is provided by the minimal required contributions. Nevertheless, there are reasons to doubt that the pure strategy equilibria are valid descriptions of how this game is actually played. First, because there are so many Nash equilibria, how do the agents coordinate on one of them? Second, each of the pure strategy Nash equilibria involves ex ante identical agents' playing different strategies. An equilibrium where identical agents play identical strategies seems more plausible. Consequently, we consider symmetric mixed strategy equilibria where $\sigma_i = \sigma$ for all i. This restriction is consistent with our criticism of the asymmetry inherent in the pure strategy Nash equilibria.

Recall that agent i only plays a mixed strategy if she is indifferent among the pure strategies in the support of the mixture. Thus, agent i is willing to play $0 < \sigma_i < 1$ when $n - 1$ players each contribute with probability σ if and only if u_i (*contribute*, σ) $= u_i$ (*not contribute*, σ).

Because the probability that at least one other agent contributes is $1 - (1 - \sigma)^{n-1}$, the indifference condition is

$$1 - c = 1 - (1 - \sigma)^{n-1}.$$

From this condition, we solve for the equilibrium value of the contribution probability $\sigma = 1 - c^{1/(n-1)}$. This equilibrium is more consistent with Olson's prediction. As n gets large, σ goes to 0. If c goes to 0, however, σ goes to 1.

13.1. Multiple Contributions. Now we consider an extension of this model in which the public good is provided if at least k of the n agents contribute. Because more than one contribution is necessary for provision, abstaining by all n agents is now a Nash equilibrium. From this profile a single contributor gains nothing from contributing and loses c. There are, however, many pure strategy equilibria in which exactly k agents make contributions. Clearly, in such an equilibrium, noncontributors have no incentive to defect (i.e., make a contribution); it costs c without changing the probability of obtaining the public good. Conversely, any contributor who defects prevents the provision of the good. Because saving the contribution cost is less valuable than losing the public good, such a defection is not desirable. In summary, there is an equilibrium corresponding to contributions by every possible combination of k agents. From a basic result in combinatorics, there are exactly $\binom{n}{k}$ distinct Nash equilibria where k contributions are made.[24]

These pure strategy equilibria are even less compelling than the pure strategy equilibria of the one-contribution game. Again we compute the symmetric mixed strategy equilibria for this game and let σ denote the probability that an individual contributes. Given that the players $N \backslash \{i\}$ each randomize, let x_{-i} be the random variable representing the number of contributions made by agents other than i. The payoff to agent i from contributing is

$$\Pr(x_{-i} < k - 1) \cdot 0 + \Pr(x_{-i} \geq k - 1) \cdot 1 - c$$

---

[24] The notation $\binom{n}{k} \equiv n!/(k!\,(n-k)!)$, known as the binomial coefficient, represents the number of combinations of k elements drawn from n objects.

whereas the payoff from abstaining is

$$\Pr\left(x_{-i} < k\right) \cdot 0 + \Pr\left(x_{-i} \geq k\right) \cdot 1.$$

As before, the mixed strategy equilibrium requires indifference between contributing and abstaining. Equating these payoffs and doing a bit of algebra, the necessary condition for choosing a mixed strategy is

$$\Pr\left(x_{-i} = k - 1\right) = c.$$

This condition has a nice intuitive interpretation. Contributing only has a positive benefit if exactly $k - 1$ other agents contribute. Thus, the payoff from the contributing to the public good is discounted by the probability that a contribution is pivotal. Because agents are mixing, this expected benefit must be equated to the contribution costs c.

Because all agents independently play the same mixed strategy, we can compute the exact value of $\Pr\left(x_{-i} = k - 1\right)$: it equals the probability of obtaining exactly $k - 1$ successes in $n - 1$ trials with a success probability of σ. A standard result of probability theory is that

$$\Pr\left(x_{-i} = k - 1\right) = \binom{n-1}{k-1} \sigma^{k-1} \left(1 - \sigma\right)^{n-k}.$$

Computing the symmetric, mixed strategy equilibrium involves finding the values of σ that solve

$$\binom{n-1}{k-1} \sigma^{k-1} \left(1 - \sigma\right)^{n-k} = c.$$

This condition simplifies to

$$\sigma^{k-1} \left(1 - \sigma\right)^{n-k} = \frac{(k-1)! \, (n-k)!}{(n-1)!} c.$$

Before characterizing the solution set, it is worthwhile to look at a couple of examples. First, suppose that $n = 5$ and $k = 3$. Then the equilibrium condition reduces to $\sigma^2 \left(1 - \sigma\right)^2 = c/6$. The solid lines of Figure 5.9 represent the left and right sides of the condition. As long as c is sufficiently low, there are two solutions to the equation, $\sigma_L^* < 1/2 < \sigma_H^*$. Each represents a distinct mixed strategy equilibrium. The comparative statics depends on whether an equilibrium is the low

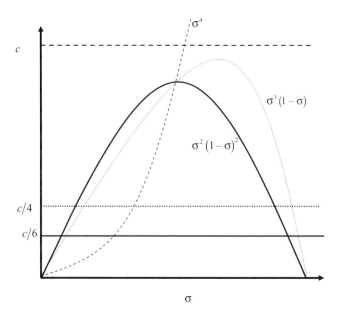

Figure 5.9. Equilibria to Palfrey-Rosenthal Contribution Game.

solution or the high solution. It is easy to see how the equilibrium mixtures change as a function of c. The effect of increasing c is to raise σ_L^* and lower σ_H^*.

In Figure 5.9 we also plot the conditions for $k = 4$ and $k = 5$: $\sigma^3 (1 - \sigma) = (1/4)c$, and $\sigma^4 = c$, respectively. The case of $k = 4$ is similar to that of $k = 3$: it also has two mixed strategy equilibria. Note that $\sigma^3 (1 - \sigma) > \sigma^2 (1 - \sigma)^2$ if $\sigma > 1/2$. This effect plus $(1/4)c > (1/6)c$ implies that σ_H^* increases in k. Because $\sigma^3 (1 - \sigma) < \sigma^2 (1 - \sigma)^2$ if $\sigma < 1/2$, σ_L^* also increases in k. For the case of $k = 5$, that σ^4 increases monotonically for $0 \leq \sigma \leq 1$ implies that there is one mixed strategy equilibrium. It has a higher contribution probability than σ_L^* does when $k = 4$ and also increases in c.

Many of the implications of the examples generalize. First, regardless of n and k, there can be at most two mixed strategy equilibria. To see this, let $c(\sigma)$ be the level of costs that supports σ as the equilibrium mixing strategy or

$$c (\sigma) = \binom{n - 1}{k - 1} \sigma^{k-1} (1 - \sigma)^{n-k}.$$

Differentiating with respect to σ, we find that

$$c'(\sigma) = \binom{n-1}{k-1} [(k-1)(1-\sigma) - (n-k)\sigma]\sigma^{k-2}(1-\sigma)^{n-k-1}$$

It is easy to see that if $k < n$ the function $c(\sigma)$ is single peaked (increasing to the left of a global maxima and decreasing to the right of the maxima) because

$$c' \gtreqless 0 \text{ if } \sigma \lesseqgtr \frac{k-1}{n-1}.$$

If $1 < k < n$ and c is less than the value $c((k-1)/(n-1)) \equiv c_{\max}$, there are two symmetric mixed strategy equilibria. But if $c > c_{\max}$, there are none.[25] If $k = n$ or $k = 1$, there is one symmetric mixed strategy equilibrium so long as $c < 1$.

For the high-contribution equilibria where $\sigma_H^* > (k-1)/(n-1)$, contribution probabilities decrease in c and n and increase in k. For the low-contribution equilibria where $\sigma_L^* < (k-1)/(n-1)$, the contribution probabilities increase in c and n. For low-contribution equilibria where $\sigma_L^* < (k-1)/n$, contributions are falling in k, but they increase in k for equilibria where $\sigma_L^* \in \left(\frac{k-1}{n}, \frac{k-1}{n-1}\right)$.[26] As in the case of $k = 1$, contribution probabilities go to 0 as n gets very large.[27]

14. Exercises

EXERCISE 5.1 *Verify that the two definitions of Nash equilibrium are equivalent. Hint: First show that if a strategy profile satisfies the first definition then it must satisfy the second. Then show that if it satisfies the second it must satisfy the first.*

EXERCISE 5.2 *Show that the Prisoner's Dilemma has no Nash equilibria in which players use nonpure strategies.*

---

[25] Of course in the unlikely event that $c = c_{\max}$, there is a single symmetric mixed strategy equilibrium.

[26] Some derivations useful in proving these claims appear in the appendix to Palfrey and Rosenthal (1988).

[27] The proof of this last statement is closely related to the law of large numbers. Because $c(\sigma)$ is the probability function of the binomial distribution, it goes to zero everywhere except $(k-1)/(n-1)$ as n gets large. Thus, σ_L^* and σ_H^* must converge to $(k-1)/(n-1)$, which itself is converging to 0.

EXERCISE 5.3 *Consider the normal form game*

1\2	a	b	c	d
w	1, 2	1, 3	2, 1	5, 1
x	4, 2	2, 4	3, 4	4, 3
y	3, 2	2, 3	4, 5	2, 2
z	3, 2	1, 2	2, 2	1, 4

EXERCISE 5.4

(1) *What strategies survive iterative deletion of strictly dominated strategies (check for dominance by mixed strategies)?*

(2) *What are the pure strategy Nash equilibria?*

(3) *What are the mixed strategy Nash equilibria?*

EXERCISE 5.5 *Find the mixed strategy Nash equilibria of the following game:*

1\2	L	R
T	2, 1	0, 2
B	1, 3	3, 0

EXERCISE 5.6 *Consider the normal form game*

1\2	a	c	c	d
u	2, 0	3, 1	4, 0	6, 1
m	3, 4	4, 2	6, 3	4, 1
d	4, 4	3, 3	5, 6	6, 2

EXERCISE 5.7

(1) *Are any strategies weakly dominated?*

(2) *What strategies survive iterated deletion of strictly dominated strategies (check for dominance by mixed strategies)?*

(3) *Find the mixed and/or pure strategy Nash equilibria.*

EXERCISE 5.8 *Consider a three-member legislature that operates under majority rule. There are a status quo y and an alternative x. A lobbyist L_1 wants to have x enacted and a lobbyist L_2 wants to have y retained. Each lobbyist can "bribe" a legislator to vote for his preferred policy. For simplicity assume that only bribes of exactly p can be made (with $p > 0$ a fixed number). If a legislator receives a bribe from only L_1 she votes for x; if she receives a bribe from only L_2 she votes for y. If a legislator receives a bribe from both lobbyists or no lobbyists she votes for y. The preferences of the two lobbyists are given by the utility functions*

$$U_{L_1}(x) = u^* - pB_{L_1}$$
$$U_{L_1}(y) = -pB_{L_1}$$
$$U_{L_2}(x) = -pB_{L_2}$$
$$U_{L_2}(y) = u^* - pB_{L_2}$$

where B_{L_1} is the number of legislators L_1 bribes (either 0, 1, 2, or 3), and B_{L_2} is the number of legislators L_2 bribes (either 0, 1, 2, or 3). Assume that $u^* \geq 3p$. A pure strategy for each lobbyist indicates which legislators (if any) she bribes. For example, $(b, 0, b)$ indicates that bribes were made to legislators 1 and 3 but not 2. A mixed strategy is then a probability distribution (lottery) over the eight possible pure strategies.

(1) *Characterize the Nash equilibria (mixed or pure) of this game. Hint: First delete strictly dominated strategies.*
(2) *What is the probability that x will be enacted in equilibrium? How does this probability respond to changes in the parameters p and u^*?*

EXERCISE 5.9 *Consider two candidates a and b competing for office. Let the policy space consist of the three points $\{-1, 0, 1\}$ and assume that voters have symmetric tent-shaped utility functions. Moreover, assume that the candidates do not know the location of the median voter. Suppose their beliefs are that she is located at -1 with probability $\pi < 1/2$, located at 1 with probability π, and located at 0 with probability $1 - 2\pi$. Suppose that candidate a is better than b. (She has a distinguished service record, is more attractive, or is from a popular party.) This quality difference is small, though, so if a and b locate equidistantly from the median voter (or a is closer to the median voter) then a wins, but if b is closer to the median voter then b wins. Analyze the normal form game where* *candidates simultaneously select a policy position in the policy space* $\{-1, 0, 1\}$.

(1)   Are there any pure strategy Nash equilibria? If so, characterize them.

(2)   Are there any mixed strategy Nash equilibria? If so, characterize them.

EXERCISE 5.10 *Consider a modification of the Downsian/Hotelling model in which candidates have policy preferences and the median voter's ideal point is uniformly distributed on* $[0, 1]$. *Now assume that one candidate's ideal point is distributed uniformly on* $[0, 1/3]$ *and the other candidate's ideal point is distributed uniformly on* $[1/2, 1]$. *Characterize the Nash equilibria.*

EXERCISE 5.11 *In the each of Hotelling models, show that there are no equilibria in pure strategies if there are three parties. What is the Nash equilibrium with four parties if parties maximize vote share?*

EXERCISE 5.12 *Prove Theorem 5.5.*

EXERCISE 5.13 *Characterize the pure strategy Nash equilibria to the International Externality game when* $k_1 = k_2$.

EXERCISE 5.14(*) *Prove Theorem 5.6.*

EXERCISE 5.15(*) *Show that an upper hemicontinuous correspondence that is single valued is a continuous function.*

EXERCISE 5.16 *Assume that* s_1^* *solves the first-order condition* $\beta - 2ks_1 = 0$. *Use the implicit function theorem to find* $\partial s_1^*/\partial\beta$ *and* $\partial s_1^*/\partial k$.

EXERCISE 5.17 *Find the derivatives of* $b_2(\cdot, :, \cdot)$ *from system 5.1.*

EXERCISE 5.18 *Find the second- (and cross-) partial derivatives of the best responses from system 5.1.*

EXERCISE 5.19 *Verify that if* $f(\cdot, \cdot)$ *has increasing differences in* (x, p) *then for all* $p \leq p'$ *and* $x \leq x'$ $f(x, p') - f(x, p) \geq f(x', p') - f(x', p)$.

EXERCISE 5.20(*) *Prove parts a–c of Theorem 5.11.*

EXERCISE 5.21(*) *Assume that* X *is a compact subset of* $\mathbb{R}^n$ *and* R *is a lower continuous partial order on* X. *Show that if* $u(x)$ *is a utility function that represents* R *on* X *then* $u(\cdot)$ *is upper semicontinuous on* X.

Now show that if $u(x)$ is upper semicontinuous on X then any preference relation that it represents is lower continuous.

EXERCISE 5.22(*) *Show that every finite game has at least one perfect equilibrium.*

EXERCISE 5.23 *For the Palfrey-Rosenthal contribution game, construct an asymmetric Nash equilibrium where l agents contribute ($\sigma_i = 1$), m agents do not contribute ($\sigma_i = 0$), and $n - m - l$ agents choose a mixed strategy $\sigma_i = q \in (0, 1)$. Show that if $l > 0$ or $m > 0$, q^* is unique.*

EXERCISE 5.24 *Consider an extension of the Palfrey-Rosenthal model where contributions are refunded if the public good is not provided (i.e., fewer than k contributions are made). Characterize the pure strategy and mixed strategy equilibria of this game.*

6 Bayesian Games in the Normal Form

The normal form games of the previous chapter assume that agents have complete information or, if there is uncertainty, the same beliefs. But this assumption is often unreasonable. Candidates for office may know more about their policy preferences than voters; interest groups may know more about the relationship between policies and outcomes than legislators; a nation may know more than its rivals about its own military capacity. In many settings ignoring asymmetric information misses many important strategic incentives. Recall the Terrorist Hunt game, which is reproduced in Table 6.1.

The CIA knows that the FBI prefers arresting operatives to making no arrests. The FBI knows that the CIA knows this fact, and so on. The game changes in important ways, however, if the CIA is uncertain whether the FBI prefers arresting operatives to not arresting anyone. Perhaps the FBI feels that the homeland security benefits of capturing the operative do not exceed the costs. If the CIA believed this were the case, it would perceive the game as that in Table 6.2.

The CIA could even believe that the FBI might have yet another preference ordering valuing operatives over kingpins. Perhaps operatives usually fold under pressure, providing lots of information, whereas kingpins remain silent. In this case, the CIA might believe that the game is Table 6.3.

If the CIA is unsure how the FBI evaluates the outcomes, the CIA's calculation of which strategy to play is more complicated. In the original game the pure strategy Nash equilibria are (*kingpin*, *kingpin*) and (*operative*, *operative*). But if the CIA thinks that the FBI is playing one of the modified games, it is less clear which strategy the CIA

prefers. It is not clear how to compute a Nash equilibrium or eliminate dominated strategies. Even if
the modeler knows the FBI's payoffs
and can determine which strategies
are best responses or are dominated
for the FBI, these solution concepts
require that the CIA also have a clear understanding of the FBI's
payoffs.

Table 6.1. The Terrorist Hunt

FBI\CIA	Kingpin	Operative
Kingpin	2, 2	0, 1
Operative	1, 0	1, 1

In this section we develop the tools necessary to analyze models in
which agents do not know the payoffs of the other players. This feature is called *incomplete information*. The standard practice (originated
by Harsanyi 1967–1968) is to convert
such a game into one where a fictional
player (usually called Nature) moves
first, drawing the utility functions of
the agents from a probability distribution. The agents know this probability distribution but do not observe
Nature's draw. Typically, agents observe some aspects of the draw such

Table 6.2. Modified Hunt 1

FBI'\CIA	Kingpin	Operative
Kingpin	2, 2	0, 1
Operative	0, 0	0, 1

as their own payoffs. Following Nature's move, agents simultaneously
select their actions. This modified game form is one of complete but *imperfect information*. As applied to the modified Terrorist Hunt, Nature
randomly selects the preferences (or type) of the FBI from a known
probability distribution. The FBI knows its type and chooses an action. When it chooses its action, the CIA does not know the FBI's
type but knows the likelihood of each
type. Specifying strategies for the CIA
is somewhat complicated. In evaluat-
ing its own strategies, the CIA must
form a conjecture about the strategy
played by each of the three possible
FBI types. Given such a conjecture, the
CIA can compare the expected util-

Table 6.3. Modified Hunt 2

FBI''\CIA	Kingpin	Operative
Kingpin	1, 2	0, 1
Operative	2, 0	2, 1

ity of choosing *kingpin* or *operative*. Conversely, given a conjecture
about the CIA's strategy, each of the possible FBI types chooses a
best response. In essence Harsanyi's maneuver translates a model
in which the CIA does not know the preferences of the FBI to a
new game in which the CIA is playing one of three possible FBI

players drawn from a known distribution. In this translated game, each player type (e.g., three FBI types and the CIA) chooses a strategy.

A comment is in order about the role of common knowledge in games of incomplete information. As indicated at the beginning of this chapter, games of complete information assume that all elements of the game – players, strategies, and payoffs – are known to all players and all players know this, and so on. Games of incomplete information also maintain the common knowledge assumption: all players know the probability distribution that Nature uses in selecting player types. Moreover, all players know how much information about Nature's draw is revealed to the other players. All players know that all players know these details, and so on.

1. Formal Definitions

We now modify the basic normal form structure, Γ, to account for imperfect information about player types.[1] To Γ, we add player types, additional state variables, and lotteries over these random variables.

(1) Types: For each player $i \in N$, there is a finite set Θ_i of possible types. Player i's type is $\theta_i \in \Theta_i$, and the profile of n types is $\theta \in \Theta = \times_{i \in N} \Theta_i$. By θ_{-i} and Θ_{-i} we denote a profile and the set of such profiles of types for all players other than i. In the first example of this section, the CIA's type set is a singleton, and the FBI's contains three elements.

(2) Random state variables: Γ may contain an additional random state variable $\omega \in \Omega$ where Ω is finite.[2]

(3) Nature's randomization: At the beginning of the game, Nature selects the vector of player types $\theta = (\theta_1, \ldots, \theta_n) \in \Theta = \prod_{i \in N} \Theta_i$ and $\omega \in \Omega$ from a joint probability distribution where

---

[1] Some readers may want to review probability theory in the Mathematical Appendix before proceeding.

[2] Strictly speaking, the random state ω does not need to be included in our definition of a Bayesian game. We could define expected utilities over payoffs that depend on just θ and assume that agents maximize these expected utilities. By explicitly including the state vector, we define utilities over θ and ω. Just as in the previous chapter we showed that normal form games allow for random payoffs, these two constructions are equivalent. We make the random state explicit to clarify the two ways that uncertainty can enter the game (uncertainty about what others know, θ, and persistent uncertainty about how actions affect payoffs, ω).

each pair (θ, ω) occurs with probability $p(\theta, \omega)$. The function $p(\theta_{-i}, \omega \mid \theta_i)$ is the conditional probability of θ_{-i}, ω given θ_i.

(4) Strategies: Each player selects an action s_i from the strategy set S_i.

(5) Expected utilities: For each possible strategy profile s, type θ, and state ω, agent i's utility function is $u_i(s_i, s_{-i}, \theta, \omega)$. Given type θ_i, agent i's conditional expected utility from strategy profile s is

$$EU_i(s; \theta_i) = \sum_{\theta_{-i} \in \Theta_{-i}} \sum_{\omega \in \Omega} p(\theta_{-i}, \omega \mid \theta_i) u_i(s, \theta_i, \theta_{-i}, \omega).$$

Accordingly a normal form Bayesian game is the collection $\langle N, \Omega, \{S_i, \Theta_i, u(\cdot, \ldots, \cdot)\}_{i \in n}, p(\cdot, \cdot) \rangle$, which we can abbreviate as $\langle N, \Omega, S, \Theta, u, p \rangle$. Just as normal form games can be defined with infinite strategy spaces, Bayesian games can be defined with infinite type and action spaces.[3] We provide several such examples later.

In a Bayesian game, strategy profiles must include a strategy for each player type. Accordingly a strategy for player i is a function $\phi_i(\theta_i) : \Theta_i \to S_i$ that selects a strategy $s_i \in S_i$ for each possible type $\theta_i \in \Theta_i$. In the uncertainty version of Terrorist Hunt, the FBI's types are designated as $\Theta_{FBI} = \{standard, pro\text{-}kingpin, pro\text{-}operative\}$. An example of a strategy for the FBI is $\phi_{FBI}(standard) = kingpin$, $\phi_{FBI}(pro\text{-}kingpin) = kingpin$, $\phi_{FBI}(pro\text{-}operative) = operative$.

In a Bayesian normal form game the analog of Nash equilibria is Bayesian Nash equilibria. Because strategies are now functions of types, evaluation of best responses is somewhat complicated. Thus, it is easiest to define Bayesian Nash equilibria by generalizing the second definition of Nash equilibria.

DEFINITION 6.1 *For a normal form Bayesian game $\langle N, \Omega, S, \Theta, u, p \rangle$, a Bayesian Nash equilibrium is a profile of strategies, $(\phi_1^*(\cdot), \ldots, \phi_n^*(\cdot))$ such that*

$$EU_i(\phi_i^*(\theta_i), \phi_{-i}^*(\cdot); \theta_i) \geq EU_i(s_i', \phi_{-i}^*(\cdot); \theta_i) \tag{6.1}$$

for every $i \in N$, for every $s_i' \in S_i$, and for every $\theta_i \in \Theta_i$.

---

[3] If the type and action spaces are nonfinite, the mathematics involved in characterizing equilibria is more complicated.

Thus, in a Bayesian Nash equilibrium, each player type chooses a strategy that maximizes her expected utility given the strategies of all the other player types and the probability distribution over the types.

We now solve for a Bayesian Nash equilibrium to the multiple-type Terrorist Hunt. For simplicity, assume that each of the three FBI types is equally probable. Suppose that the FBI strategy is $\phi_{FBI}(standard) = kingpin$, $\phi_{FBI}(pro\text{-}kingpin) = kingpin$, $\phi_{FBI}(pro\text{-}operative) = operative$. In this game the CIA has only one possible type, and there is no uncertainty other than that over FBI types. So we suppress ω. Given the strategy of the FBI types, the expected utilities of the CIA are

$$EU_{CIA}(kingpin, \phi_{FBI}(\cdot)) = \frac{2}{3}2 + \frac{1}{3}0 = \frac{4}{3}$$

$$EU_{CIA}(operative, \phi_{FBI}(\cdot)) = \frac{2}{3}0 + \frac{1}{3}1 = \frac{1}{3}.$$

Thus, the CIA's best response to $\phi_{FBI}(\cdot)$ is to select *kingpin*. Now we must verify whether any of the FBI types wishes to deviate. For the standard-type FBI matching the CIA is a best response. Thus, $\phi_{FBI}(standard) = kingpin$ is a best response. For the pro-*kingpin* type selecting kingpin when the CIA selects *kingpin* results in the highest possible payoff (2) so that no desirable deviation exists. Finally, for the pro-*operative* FBI, selecting *operative* when the CIA selects *kingpin* results in utility of 2 whereas a deviation to *kingpin* results in utility 1. No profitable deviation exists for this type, either. Consequently, these strategies characterize a Bayesian Nash equilibrium.

2. Application: Trade Restrictions

Two nations contemplate restrictive trade policies. Let $N = \{1, 2\}$ and suppose that each country has two possible types $\Theta_i = \{u, b\}$. A type u country wishes to limit its imports from the other country *u*nilaterally, and a type b country wishes to pursue a *b*ilateral policy of limiting trade only if the other country does so. The country types are independently drawn, and type u occurs with probability $p \in (0, 1)$. The strategy space for each country is $S = \{l, f\}$ where l denotes enacting an import limit and f denotes a free-trade policy. The payoffs for country i are

$$u_i(s_i, s_{-i}; \theta_i) = \begin{cases} 3 \text{ if } s_i = l, s_{-i} = f \text{ and } \theta_i = u \\ 2 \text{ if } s_i = f, s_{-i} = f \text{ and } \theta_i = u \\ 1 \text{ if } s_i = l, s_{-i} = l \text{ and } \theta_i = u \\ 0 \text{ if } s_i = f, s_{-i} = l \text{ and } \theta_i = u \\ 3 \text{ if } s_i = f, s_{-i} = f \text{ and } \theta_i = b \\ 2 \text{ if } s_i = l, s_{-i} = f \text{ and } \theta_i = b \\ 1 \text{ if } s_i = l, s_{-i} = l \text{ and } \theta_i = b \\ 0 \text{ if } s_i = f, s_{-i} = l \text{ and } \theta_i = b \end{cases}.$$

A strategy in this game is a mapping $s_i(\theta_i) : \{u, b\} \to \{l, f\}$. A key feature of this game is that a u-type country always receives a higher payoff from l independently of the actions of the other country. If it is common knowledge that both countries are type u, the game is a Prisoner's Dilemma; each country has a dominant strategy to choose l. Alternatively, if it is common knowledge that both countries are type b, there are two pure strategy Nash equilibria, (f, f) and (l, l).

To compute Bayesian Nash equilibria, we begin with conjectures about equilibrium strategies and check to see whether they satisfy the equilibrium requirements. Because a type u country has a dominant strategy of selecting l, every equilibrium involves $s_i(u) = l$. Thus, the only possible symmetric pure strategy equilibria are $(s_i(u), s_i(b)) = (l, l)$ and $(s_i(u), s_i(b)) = (l, f)$. Thus, we first investigate the possibility that $s_i(u) = l$ and $s_i(b) = f$ for both $i = 1, 2$. If country 2 uses this strategy, then $s_2 = l$ with probability p and $s_2 = f$ with probability $(1 - p)$. Thus, country 1's expected utilities are

$$Eu_1(s_1, \theta_1 = u) = \begin{cases} p + (1 - p)3 \text{ if } s_1 = l \\ 2(1 - p) \text{ if } s_1 = f \end{cases}$$

$$Eu_1(s_1, \theta_1 = b) = \begin{cases} 2(1 - p) + p \text{ if } s_1 = l \\ 3(1 - p) \text{ if } s_1 = f \end{cases}$$

for types u and b, respectively. Is the conjectured strategy a best response? The strategy $s_i(u) = l$ is a best response because type u has a dominant strategy to erect trade barriers. Alternatively, $s_i(b) = f$ is a best response if $3(1 - p) \geq 2(1 - p) + p$. This condition holds so long as $p \leq 1/2$. Because the calculations for country 2 are identical, the profile $s_i(u) = l$ and $s_i(b) = f$ is a Bayesian Nash equilibrium for $p \leq 1/2$.

Now we check to see whether and when $s_i(b) = l$ for both countries is a best response. If country 2 uses the strategy $s_2(\theta_2) = l$ regardless of θ_2 then country 1 with type b has the expected utility function

$$Eu_1(s_1, \theta_1 = b) = \begin{cases} 1 \text{ if } s_1 = l \\ 0 \text{ if } s_1 = f \end{cases}.$$

Independently of the value of p, the strategy combination $s_i(b) = l, s_i(u) = l$ for both countries is a Bayesian Nash equilibrium. So there is always a Bayesian Nash equilibrium in which bilateral limits (l, l) occur. Moreover, if $p \leq 1/2$ there is a second equilibrium with $s_i(u) = l$ and $s_i(b) = f$. In this equilibrium free trade occurs if both countries are type b. This outcome occurs with an ex ante probability of $(1 - p)^2$. So bilateral free trade policies emerge when each country is a bilateral type and believes that its opponent is likely to be a bilateral type.

3. Application: Jury Voting

Suppose that three jurors $N = \{1, 2, 3\}$ are responsible for deciding whether to *c*onvict or *a*cquit a defendant.[4] Collectively they choose an outcome $x \in \{c, a\}$. The jurors simultaneously cast ballots $v_i \in S_i = \{c, a\}$, and the outcome is chosen by majority rule. Each juror is uncertain whether or not the defendant is guilty, G, or innocent, I. So the set of state variables is $\Omega = \{G, I\}$. Each juror assigns prior probability $\pi > 1/2$ to state G. If the defendant is guilty, the jurors receive 1 unit of utility from convicting and 0 from acquitting. Alternatively, if the defendant is innocent, the jurors receive 1 unit from acquitting and 0 from convicting.

Absent any additional information, each juror receives an expected utility of π from a guilty verdict and $1 - \pi$ from an acquittal. Because $\pi > 1/2$, the Nash equilibrium that survives the elimination of weakly dominated strategies is the one where each juror votes guilty.

Now, before voting, each juror receives a private signal about the defendant's guilt $\theta_i \in \{0, 1\}$. The signal is informative so that a juror is more likely to receive the signal $\theta_i = 1$ when the defendant is guilty

---

[4] This is a simple example of the jury model developed by Austen-Smith and Banks (1996).

than when the defendant is innocent. To keep matters simple, the probability of receiving a guilty signal ($\theta_i = 1$) when the defendant is guilty is the same as that of receiving the innocent signal ($\theta_i = 0$) when the defendant is innocent. Formally, let $\Pr(\theta_i = 1 \mid \omega = G) = \Pr(\theta_i = 0 \mid \omega = I) = p > 1/2$ so that $\Pr(\theta_i = 0 \mid \omega = G) = \Pr(\theta_i = 0 \mid \omega = I) = 1 - p$.

After receiving her signal, voter i selects her vote $v(\theta_i)$ to maximize the probability of a correct decision – conviction of the guilty and acquittal of the innocent. Suppose that each voter uses the *sincere* strategy, $v_i(1) = c$ and $v_i(0) = a$. The sincere strategy calls for a vote to convict upon receipt of a guilty signal and a vote to acquit upon a notguilty signal. Sincere strategies constitute a Bayesian Nash equilibrium only if voter 1 is willing to use this strategy when she believes that voters 2 and 3 also use it. Given these conjectures, the expected utility of voting to convict is

$$\Pr(\theta_2 = 1 \text{ and } \theta_3 = 0 \text{ and } \omega = G \mid \theta_1) +$$
$$\Pr(\theta_3 = 1 \text{ and } \theta_2 = 0 \text{ and } \omega = G \mid \theta_1) +$$
$$\Pr(\theta_2 = 1 \text{ and } \theta_2 = 1 \text{ and } \omega = G \mid \theta_1) +$$
$$\Pr(\theta_2 = 0 \text{ and } \theta_2 = 0 \text{ and } \omega = I \mid \theta_1).$$

The expected utility of voting to acquit is

$$\Pr(\theta_2 = 1 \text{ and } \theta_3 = 0 \text{ and } \omega = I \mid \theta_1) +$$
$$\Pr(\theta_3 = 1 \text{ and } \theta_2 = 0 \text{ and } \omega = I \mid \theta_1) +$$
$$\Pr(\theta_2 = 0 \text{ and } \theta_2 = 0 \text{ and } \omega = I \mid \theta_1) +$$
$$\Pr(\theta_2 = 1 \text{ and } \theta_2 = 1 \text{ and } \omega = G \mid \theta_1).$$

The last two terms of each sum are the same. Consequently, these terms cancel out when comparing the utilities. Accordingly, voting to convict is a best response if and only if

$$\Pr(\theta_2 = 1 \text{ and } \theta_3 = 0 \text{ and } \omega = G \mid \theta_1)$$
$$+ \Pr(\theta_3 = 1 \text{ and } \theta_2 = 0 \text{ and } \omega = G \mid \theta_1)$$
$$\geq \Pr(\theta_2 = 1 \text{ and } \theta_3 = 0 \text{ and } \omega = I \mid \theta_1)$$
$$+ \Pr(\theta_3 = 1 \text{ and } \theta_2 = 0 \text{ and } \omega = I \mid \theta_1).$$

Because these expressions depend on the conditional probabilities of observing combinations of the state variable and the signals of the other jurors, juror 1 uses Bayes' rule to evaluate each term. Suppose that juror 1 receives $\theta_1 = 1$. In this case, Bayes' rule yields

$$\Pr(\theta_2 = 1 \text{ and } \theta_3 = 0 \text{ and } \omega = G \mid \theta_1 = 1)$$
$$= \Pr(\theta_3 = 1 \text{ and } \theta_2 = 0 \text{ and } \omega = G \mid \theta_1 = 1)$$
$$= \frac{\pi p^2 (1 - p)}{\pi p + (1 - \pi)(1 - p)}$$

and

$$\Pr(\theta_2 = 1 \text{ and } \theta_3 = 0 \text{ and } \omega = I \mid \theta_1 = 1)$$
$$= \Pr(\theta_3 = 1 \text{ and } \theta_2 = 0 \text{ and } \omega = I \mid \theta_1 = 1)$$
$$= \frac{(1 - \pi) p (1 - p)^2}{\pi p + (1 - \pi)(1 - p)}.$$

Thus, $v_i(1) = c$ is optimal for juror 1 if

$$2 \frac{\pi p^2 (1 - p)}{\pi p + (1 - \pi)(1 - p)} \geq 2 \frac{(1 - \pi) p (1 - p)^2}{\pi p + (1 - \pi)(1 - p)}.$$

After simplifying and rearranging, this inequality becomes

$$\frac{\pi p^2 (1 - p)}{\pi p^2 (1 - p) + (1 - \pi) p (1 - p)^2} \geq \frac{1}{2}.$$

The left-hand side is simply the conditional probability of guilt given two signals of $\theta = 1$ and one signal of $\theta = 0$. In other words, agent 1 wants to vote to convict if she believes that the defendant is more likely to be guilty than innocent, conditional, on her signal and the belief that she is pivotal. Similarly, the requirement for a vote of innocence conditional on a signal of 0 is

$$\frac{\pi p (1 - p)^2}{\pi p (1 - p)^2 + (1 - \pi) p^2 (1 - p)} \leq \frac{1}{2}.$$

To summarize, in any Bayesian equilibrium in which voting corresponds to the private signals, the following statements must be true (1) conditional on the supposition that i is pivotal and observes $\theta_i = 1$, the posterior probability of guilt is greater than $1/2$ (2) conditional on the supposition that i is pivotal and observes $\theta_i = 0$, the posterior probability of guilt is less than $1/2$.

Austen-Smith and Banks (1996) show that in many cases the sincere strategy is inconsistent with equilibrium behavior. It is easy to find parameters π and p for which one of the necessary conditions does not hold. There are alternative strategies jurors might choose. Jurors can randomize for some signals, vote the same way regardless of their signal, or use different strategies than other jurors use. Fedderson and Pessendorfer (1998) consider the properties of equilibria of this game when one varies the voting rule and number of jurors.

4. Application: Jury Voting with a Continuum of Signals

Instead of receiving a binary signal, each juror now receives a signal $\theta_i \in [0, 1]$ where θ_i is drawn from a conditional distribution $F(\theta_i|\omega)$. This distribution function is associated with a differentiable density function $f(\theta_i|\omega)$ that satisfies the *monotone likelihood ratio* condition.[5]

DEFINITION 6.2 *A conditional density function satisfies the strict monotone likelihood ratio condition (SMLR) if $f(\theta_i \mid G)/f(\theta_i \mid I)$ is a strictly monotone function of θ_i on $[0, 1]$.*

To see why this assumption is important, note that Bayes' rule implies that

$$\Pr(G|\theta_i) = \frac{f(\theta_i \mid G)\pi}{f(\theta_i \mid G)\pi + f(\theta_i \mid I)(1 - \pi)}$$
$$= \frac{\frac{f(\theta_i|G)}{f(\theta_i|I)}\pi}{\frac{f(\theta_i|G)}{f(\theta_i|I)}\pi + (1 - \pi)}.$$

Accordingly, $\Pr(G|\theta_i)$ is increasing in θ_i if and only if $f(\theta_i \mid G)/f(\theta_i \mid I)$ is increasing in θ_i. Thus, the SMLR condition implies that higher signals correspond to higher posterior probabilities that $\omega = G$.

To keep matters simple, we focus exclusively on symmetric strategies where voters who receive the same signal choose the same strategy. A symmetric strategy profile is, therefore, a mapping $v_i(\theta_i) : [0, 1] \to \{c, a\}$. As in the binary signal case, Bayesian Nash equilibrium strategies are those that are optimal when each agent acts conditionally on her private information and the conjecture that she

[5] Duggan and Martinelli (2001) and Meirowitz (2002) pursue this extension.

is pivotal. An agent votes to convict if she thinks the probability of guilt is no less than $1/2$ and she votes to acquit if she thinks the probability of guilt is no more than $1/2$. Because higher signals are better indicators of guilt, a natural conjecture is that the strategy must be weakly increasing. For low values of θ_i an acquittal vote is cast and for high values of θ_i a conviction vote is cast. A monotone strategy of this form can be characterized by a cut point $\widehat{\theta} \in [0, 1]$. Assume that agents $i \in N\backslash i$ use the monotone strategy

$$v_i(\theta_i) = \begin{cases} c \text{ if } \theta_i \geq \widehat{\theta} \\ a \text{ if } \theta_i < \widehat{\theta} \end{cases}.$$

If all players other than i use this cut point strategy, the posterior probability of $\{\omega = G\}$ given signal θ_i and the event that i is pivotal is given by

$$\Pr(G \mid piv, \theta_i; \widehat{\theta}) =$$

$$\frac{\pi f_G \widehat{F}_G^{\,n-q-1} \left[1 - \widehat{F}_G\right]^{q-1}}{\pi f_G \widehat{F}_G^{\,n-q-1} \left[1 - \widehat{F}_G\right]^{q-1} + (1 - \pi) f_I \widehat{F}_I^{\,n-q-1} \left[1 - \widehat{F}_I\right]^{q-1}} \quad (6.2)$$

where $f_\omega = f(\theta_i \mid \omega)$ and $\widehat{F}_\omega = F(\widehat{\theta} \mid \omega)$. We leave the derivation of this expression as an exercise. This probability is a function of the parameter $\widehat{\theta}$. In this model the existence of a symmetric equilibrium in which voters use a cut point hinges on finding a value of $\widehat{\theta}$ such that

$$\Pr(G \mid piv, \widehat{\theta}; \widehat{\theta}) = \frac{1}{2}$$

and demonstrating that $\Pr(G \mid piv, \theta_i; \widehat{\theta}) \leq 1/2$ if $\theta_i < \widehat{\theta}$ and $\Pr(G \mid piv, \theta_i; \widehat{\theta}) \geq 1/2$ if $\theta_i > \widehat{\theta}$. Although analysis of examples is cumbersome, it is easy to derive conditions on the primitives of the game to ensure that such a $\widehat{\theta} \in (0, 1)$ exists. First, $\Pr(G \mid piv, \theta_i; \widehat{\theta}) \geq 1/2$ if and only if

$$\frac{\pi f(\theta_i \mid G) F(\widehat{\theta} \mid G)^{n-q-1} \left[1 - F(\widehat{\theta} \mid G)\right]^{q-1}}{(1 - \pi) f(\theta_i \mid I) F(\widehat{\theta} \mid I)^{n-q-1} \left[1 - F(\widehat{\theta} \mid I)\right]^{q-1}} =$$

$$\frac{f(\theta_i \mid G)}{f(\theta_i \mid I)} \frac{\pi F(\widehat{\theta} \mid G)^{n-q-1} \left[1 - F(\widehat{\theta} \mid G)\right]^{q-1}}{(1 - \pi) F(\widehat{\theta} \mid I)^{n-q-1} \left[1 - F(\widehat{\theta} \mid I)\right]^{q-1}} \geq 1.$$

The strict monotone likelihood ratio condition then implies that if $\Pr(G \mid piv, \widehat{\theta}; \widehat{\theta}) = 1/2$ then $\theta_i < \widehat{\theta}$ implies $\Pr(G \mid piv, \theta_i; \widehat{\theta}) \leq 1/2$ and $\theta_i > \widehat{\theta}$ implies $\Pr(G \mid piv, \theta_i; \widehat{\theta}) \geq 1/2$. If $\Pr(G \mid piv, 0; 0) \leq 1/2 \leq \Pr(G \mid piv, 1; 1)$ then the intermediate value theorem implies that such a cut point exists because the function $\Pr(G \mid piv, \cdot; \cdot)$ is continuous. For a large class of games these boundary conditions are satisfied.

In the simple binary type model, equilibria where everyone uses the same rule and voting is determined by private information may not exist. This type of equilibrium generally exists in the continuum model, however. In the case of unanimity rule, the choice of models is consequential for the conclusions about its desirability. Using the binary model, Fedderson and Pesendorfer (1998) show that the unanimity rule is a uniquely bad way to aggregate information for large populations because in equilibrium voters condition on the assumption that everyone else is voting to convict. In the continuum model, Meirowitz (2002) shows that the unanimity rule often turns out to be as good as the other voting rules.

5. Application: Public Goods and Incomplete Information

In this section, we present a version of the Palfrey-Rosenthal contribution game in which potential contributors are uncertain about the contribution costs of other players. To keep the model as close as possible to the one analyzed in Chapter 4, every agent receives a utility of 1 if at least k agents contribute and 0 otherwise. Agent i pays a cost c_i to contribute, but now c_i is distributed uniformly on $[0, 1]$. Each agent learns her own cost but remains uncertain about the other players' costs.

5.1. The Case of $k = 1$. First, we consider the case where a single contribution is necessary and sufficient for the provision of the good. Because $c_i \leq 1$ for all i, there are always n Bayesian Nash equilibria corresponding to agent i's contributing with certainty. As before, however, we concentrate on symmetric equilibrium where all player types with the same cost play the same strategy. We, therefore, focus on equilibria in cut point strategies. In such equilibria, agent i contributes if and only if $c_i < \widehat{c}_n$ where $\widehat{c}_n$ is an equilibrium cut point for the game with n players.[6] If all of agent i's opponents choose this cut

---

[6] All equilibria involve cut point strategies. Given any strategy by $-i$, let p_{-i} be the probability that at least one other player contributes. Given, p_{-i}, player i's expected

point strategy, her utility from contributing is $1 - c_i$. If she does not contribute, she receives 1 if there is at least one contributor and 0 otherwise. Because c is distributed uniformly on $[0, 1]$, other contributors contribute with probability $\widehat{c}$ so that the probability of no other contributions is $[1 - \widehat{c}_n]^{n-1}$. Thus, agent i's utility from not contributing is $1 - [1 - \widehat{c}_n]^{n-1}$. Accordingly, agent i contributes so long as

$$[1 - \widehat{c}_n]^{n-1} \geq c_i.$$

Because an agent with cost $\widehat{c}_n$ must be indifferent over her choices, a Bayesian Nash equilibrium requires

$$[1 - \widehat{c}_n]^{n-1} = \widehat{c}_n.$$

The cut point $\widehat{c}_n$ is declining in n. Suppose this were not true so that $\widehat{c}_{n+1} \geq \widehat{c}_n$. The cut point conditions imply that $[1 - \widehat{c}_{n+1}]^n \geq [1 - \widehat{c}_n]^{n-1}$. But because $\widehat{c}_n$ and $\widehat{c}_{n+1}$ are between 0 and 1, this statement requires that $\widehat{c}_n > \widehat{c}_{n+1}$ – a contradiction. Because $\widehat{c}_n$ is declining in n the probability that any agent contributes goes to 0 as the group expands. It is also the case that the probability that no agents contribute $[1 - \widehat{c}_n]^n$ also converges to 0. So in this model, although the probability that any particular agent contributes vanishes as n gets large, the probability of provision, $1 - [1 - \widehat{c}_n]^n$, converges to 1.

5.2. The Case of $k > 1$. Now multiple contributions are required for the provision of the good. Again we assume that agents use cut point strategies and contribute only if $c_i \leq \widehat{c}_n$. Let x_{-i} be the realized number of contributions from agents other than i. From arguments identical to those of the last chapter, we know that agent i's net utility from contributing is

$$\Pr(x_{-i} = k - 1) - c_i.$$

Because each agent contributes with an ex ante probability of $\widehat{c}_n$,

$$\Pr(x_{-i} = k - 1) = \binom{n-1}{k-1} \widehat{c}_n^{k-1} (1 - \widehat{c}_n)^{n-k}.$$

---

utility from contributing is $1 - c_i$, and her expected utility from not contributing is p_{-i}. Accordingly, player i's best response is to contribute if $c_i < 1 - p_{-i}$ and not to contribute if $c_i > 1 - p_{-i}$. This best response is a cut point strategy.

Because agent i must be indifferent if her cost is $c_i = \widehat{c}_n$, we again generate an implicit solution for $\widehat{c}_n$:

$$\binom{n-1}{k-1} \widehat{c}_n^{k-1} (1 - \widehat{c}_n)^{n-k} = \widehat{c}.$$

This solution is very similar to that of the mixed strategy equilibrium with complete information. The main difference is that $\widehat{c}_n$ plays the role of σ^*. Thus, many of the implications of our previous analysis carry over.

To reduce notation let

$$\Pi(\widehat{c}_n) = \binom{n-1}{k-1} \widehat{c}_n^{k-2} (1 - \widehat{c}_n)^{n-k},$$

so that our equilibrium condition is $\Pi(\widehat{c}_n) = 1$. Differentiating $\Pi(\widehat{c}_n)$ yields

$$\frac{\partial \Pi(\widehat{c}_n)}{\partial \widehat{c}_n} = \binom{n-1}{k-1} \left[(k-2)\widehat{c}_n^{k-3}(1 - \widehat{c}_n)^{n-k} - \widehat{c}_n^{k-2}(n-k)(1 - \widehat{c}_n)^{n-k-1} \right].$$

This term has the same sign as $-(\widehat{c}_n n - k - 2\widehat{c}_n + 2)$. This implies that

$$\Pi' \gtreqless 0 \text{ if } \widehat{c}_n \lesseqgtr \frac{k-2}{n-2}.$$

Thus, so long as $2 < k < n$, $\Pi(\widehat{c}_n)$ increases to a unique maximum at $\widehat{c}_n = (k-2)/(n-2)$ and then decreases for $\widehat{c}_n > (k-2)/(n-2)$. At $\widehat{c}_n \in \{0, 1\}$, $\Pi(\widehat{c}_n) = 0$. These features of $\Pi(\widehat{c}_n)$ suggest that if $2 < k < n$ and $\max \Pi > 1$, there are two equilibrium cut points $\widehat{c}_H$ and $\widehat{c}_L$. If $\max \Pi < 1$, there are no symmetric equilibria with cut points in $(0, 1)$.[7]

As before, it is easy to demonstrate that the cut point equilibria disappear as n gets very large. Rewriting the equilibrium condition yields

$$\binom{n-1}{k-1} \widehat{c}_n^{k-1} (1 - \widehat{c}_n)^{n-k} = \widehat{c}_n.$$

[7] In the unlikely event that $\max \Pi = 1$, there is a unique cut point equilibrium.

For any $\widehat{c}_n$ the left-hand side,

$$P(n, \widehat{c}_n) = \binom{n-1}{k-1} \widehat{c}_n^{k-1} (1 - \widehat{c}_n)^{n-k},$$

is the probability of $k-1$ successes from $n-1$ trials with probability of success given by $\widehat{c}_n$. A useful fact about this probability function is that $P(n, \widehat{c}_n)$ converges to 0 as n goes to infinity unless $\widehat{c}_n$ converges to the expected proportion of successes $(k-1)/(n-1)$.[8] If $\widehat{c}_n$ does not converge to $(k-1)/(n-1)$ and $P(n, \widehat{c}_n)$ converges to 0, the equilibrium condition requires that $\widehat{c}_n$ converge to 0. Alternative if $\widehat{c}_n$ converges to $(k-1)/(n-1)$, it must also converge to 0 because $(k-1)/(n-1)$ converges to 0.

We leave it to the reader to verify that the effects of n and k on $\widehat{c}_H$ and $\widehat{c}_L$ are essentially the same as the effects of n and k on σ_L^* and σ_H^* in the symmetric mixed strategy equilibrium of the previous chapter.

6. Application: Uncertainty About Candidate Preferences

Recall the Hotelling model of candidate competition with policy-motivated candidates and uncertainty about the location of the median voter. Now in addition to uncertainty about the location of the median voter, candidates have private information about their own policy preferences. Candidate 1 has an ideal point $\theta_1 \in \{0, 1/2\}$ and candidate 2 has an ideal point $\theta_2 \in \{1/2, 1\}$. Consequently, candidate i's utility of policy location x is $u(x) = -(\theta_i - x)^2$. For simplicity, all types are drawn with equal probability, and the candidates' types are independent. As before the median voter's ideal point is randomly drawn from a uniform distribution over $[0, 1]$. A strategy for candidate 1 is a mapping $s_1(\theta_1) : \{0, 1/2\} \to [0, 1/2]$, and a strategy for candidate 2 is a mapping $s_2(\theta_2) : \{1/2, 1\} \to [1/2, 1]$. For simplicity, we ignore the possibility that a candidate chooses a strategy outside the interval of its possible types. We begin by conjecturing that candidate 2 uses the strategy $s_2(1/2) = a$ and $s_2(1) = b$. In considering the optimal location for candidate 1 with type $\theta_1 = 1/2$, it is easy to see that any location $s_1 < 1/2$ is dominated by the location $1/2$. This is true because for fixed

---

[8] This result is closely related to the law of large numbers. This law implies that the limiting distribution of the sample mean places positive weight only on the expected value of the random variable.

a and b the location $1/2$ is more likely to win than a location of $s_1 < 1/2$. Moreover, conditional on winning a location of $s_1 < 1/2$ is less desirable than a location of $1/2$ to candidate 1 with type $\theta_1 = 1/2$. Accordingly, we know that $s_1(1/2) = 1/2$ and $s_2(1/2) = 1/2$ strictly dominate all other platforms.

The best response for candidate 1 of type $\theta_1 = 0$ solves

$$\max_{s_1}\left\{ -s_1^2 \left(\frac{s_1 + \frac{1}{2}}{4} + \frac{s_1 + b}{4} \right) - \frac{(\frac{1}{2})^2}{2}\left(1 - \frac{s_1 + \frac{1}{2}}{2}\right) - \frac{b^2}{2}\left(1 - \frac{s_1 + b}{4}\right) \right\}.$$

Differentiating with respect to s_1 and setting this term equal to 0 yield the first-order condition

$$\frac{1}{8}b^2 - \frac{1}{2}bs_1 - \frac{1}{4}s_1 - \frac{3}{2}s_1^2 + \frac{1}{16} = 0.$$

In the appropriate range of $[0, \frac{1}{2}]$, the solution is

$$s_1(0; b) = \frac{1}{12}\sqrt{4b + 16b^2 + 7} - \frac{1}{6}b - \frac{1}{12}.$$

Candidate 2's problem is the mirror image of candidate 1's. This means that we can find the equilibrium values of $s_2(1) = b$ and $s_1(0) = 1 - b$ that solve the relevant first-order conditions by solving for b that satisfies the equality

$$1 - b = \frac{1}{12}\sqrt{4b + 16b^2 + 7} - \frac{1}{6}b - \frac{1}{12}.$$

The solution is $b = 11/7 - \sqrt{106}/14 \simeq 0.836$. Thus, the Bayesian Nash equilibrium is $s_1(0) = 0.164$, $s_1(1/2) = 1/2$, $s_2(1/2) = 1/2$, $s_2(1) = 0.836$. It is interesting to compare the platforms of $\theta_1 = 0$ and $\theta_2 = 1$ types with the outcomes of the game where candidate ideal points are known to be 0 and 1. One might expect the platforms to be more convergent because each candidate believes that she might be campaigning against a moderate candidate. This intuition is incomplete. Because they are policy-motivated, candidates prefer to lose to moderate opponents rather than to extreme opponents. This condition dampens the incentives for extreme candidates to moderate. Indeed, we observe platforms in the candidate uncertainty game that are even more divergent than those when candidate preferences are known.

7. Application: Campaigns, Contests, and Auctions

In the models of campaigns reviewed so far candidates' are restricted to choosing policies on a continuum. Such a restriction, however, neglects many of the strategic choices available in real campaigns. In this section, we consider an alternative based on economic models of *contests*. In these models, candidates choose levels of costly effort. The more effort a candidate exerts the greater the likelihood that she wins. One example of this approach focuses on the role of money in campaigns. Consider a set $N = \{1, \ldots, n\}$ of candidates running for office. Candidates compete by raising money and spending it on advertisements. Let $a_i \in R_+^1$ denote the level of advertising by candidate i. Given $a = (a_1, \ldots, a_n)$, the winner is determined by $p(a) : \mathbb{R}_+^n \to N$ where p is a weakly increasing function. One example is the mapping $p(a) = \arg\max_{i \in N} a_i$ that awards the office to the candidate advertising the most.[9] Candidate i's utility depends on the identity of the winner; the level of advertising a_i; and the candidate's value of winning office $\theta_i \in [0, 1]$. Each candidate's value of winning office is private information that is independently drawn from a uniform distribution on $[0, 1]$. Specifically, candidate i's utility takes the form $u_i(a) = \theta_i 1_{\{p(a)=i\}} - a_i$ where $1_{\{p(a)=i\}}$ is an indicator function that takes the value 1 if $p(a) = i$ and 0 otherwise. All candidates simultaneously selects their level of a_i and then the payoffs are realized.[10] A Bayesian Nash equilibrium is a function for each candidate that maps $\theta_i \in [0, 1]$ into $a_i \in \mathbb{R}_+^n$. Again we focus on symmetric equilibria where any two candidates with the same type select the same levels of advertising.

Directly solving for continuous strategy functions is often quite difficult. Therefore, we use a trick. We assume that the strategy function has a specific functional form. Then we solve for any free parameters and verify that the solution constitutes an equilibrium. Here we conjecture that players $j \neq i$ use a strategy of the form, $a_j(\theta_j) = b\theta_j^c$, where b and c are parameters to be determined. If players $2, \ldots, n$ use the conjectured strategy, and candidate 1 selects a_1 then the probability that 1 wins is $\Pr\{\max_{j \neq i} b\theta_j^c < a_1\}$. This probability is

$$
\Pr\left\{ \max_{j \neq i} \theta_j < \left(\frac{a_1}{b}\right)^{\frac{1}{c}} \right\} = \left(\frac{a_1}{b}\right)^{\frac{n-1}{c}}.
$$

---

[9] An alternative interpretation of this model is to treat a_i as the level of effort or time that the candidate spends running for office.

[10] This model is also equivalent to a first-price all-pay auction with independent types.

Accordingly, the expected utility to player 1 with type θ_1 from action a_1 is

$$\left(\frac{a_1}{b}\right)^{\frac{n-1}{c}} \theta_1 - a_1.$$

Differentiating with respect to a_1 yields the first-order condition

$$\theta_1 \frac{n-1}{cb} \left(\frac{a_1}{b}\right)^{\frac{n-1-c}{c}} = 1,$$

and solving for a_1 yields

$$a_1 = b \left(\frac{cb}{(n-1)\theta_1}\right)^{\frac{c}{n-1-c}}. \tag{6.3}$$

Note we began by conjecturing that players $j = 2, \ldots, n$ use a strategy of the form $a_j(\theta_j) = b\theta_j^c$ and have found that player 1's best response is to use a strategy of exactly that form. Consequently, an equilibrium can then be found by solving for values of b and c such that

$$b\theta_1^c = b \left(\frac{cb}{(n-1)\theta_1}\right)^{\frac{c}{n-1-c}}.$$

The solution is $b = (n-1)/n$ and $c = n$. Substituting it into the right-hand side of equation 6.3 and simplifying yield

$$a_1 = \frac{n-1}{n}\theta_1^n.$$

This result confirms that $b = (n-1)/n$ and $c = n$ correspond to an equilibrium. Thus, a symmetric Bayesian Nash equilibrium is for each candidate to select

$$a_i(\theta_i) = \frac{n-1}{n}\theta_i^n.$$

Several implications follow. First, in equilibrium, candidate advertising is positively related to the candidate's valuation of office. Second, the connection between advertising and the value of office depends on the number of candidates. Differentiating yields

$$\frac{\partial a_i(\theta_i)}{\partial \theta_i} = \theta_i^{n-1}(n-1)$$

$$\frac{\partial^2 a_i(\theta_i)}{\partial \theta_i \partial n} = \theta_i^{n-1}(n \ln \theta_i - \ln \theta_i + 1).$$

The cross-partial derivative is negative (because $\ln(\theta_i) < 0$ for $\theta_i \in (0, 1)$). So as the number of candidates increases equilibrium strategies become flatter. Similarly, as n gets large, the upper bound of candidate advertising converges to 0 (i.e., $a_i(1)$ goes to 0 as n gets large). This finding reflects the fact that when many candidates are in the race, the probability that a particular candidate has the highest value of θ tends to 0; a candidate is not willing to exert much effort in a contest she is unlikely to win.[11]

The relationship between this model and other auctions can easily be seen. In this game, a candidate suffers disutility a_i regardless of whether or not she wins. An alternative model might involve all agents' announcing promises to pay if they win. Another example of this form would involve interest groups' promising contributions to a committee chairman if their preferred nominee is confirmed. In our later chapter on mechanism design we consider many such auctions.

8. Existence of Bayesian Nash Equilibria

Can we guarantee that a Bayesian Nash equilibrium exists? Bayesian normal form games are generally special cases of normal form games: all player types simultaneously select a strategy and the payoffs are defined as the agents' expected utility over strategy profiles. Consequently, the existence requirements are very much like those for Nash equilibrium. We can apply our previous results to establish the existence of Bayesian Nash equilibria in mixed strategies for games with finite type and action spaces.

Consider a Bayesian game $\langle N, S, \Theta, u, p \rangle$ where N, S, Θ are all finite sets. Thus, without loss of generality we denote types in the following manner: $\Theta_i = \{\theta_i^1, \ldots, \theta_i^{k_i}\}$. We define a new normal form

---

[11] An analog to this finding is the claim that in the popular parlor game of Texas Hold'em players should become more aggressive as the number of players at the table decreases. Any particular hand is more likely to be the best hand when the number of other hands is smaller.

game Γ' as follows: Let $N' = \{\theta_1^1, \ldots, \theta_1^{k_1}, \theta_2^1, \ldots, \theta_n^{k_n}\}$. In this normal form game all agents with subscript i have strategy space $S_i' = S_i$. Let $\Theta_{-i} = \times_{j=N\backslash i}\Theta_j$ denote the set of possible type profiles for the agents $N\backslash i$ in the original Bayesian game. Given a strategy profile $s^+ = (s_1^1, \ldots, s_i^j, \ldots, s_n^{k_n}) \in \times_{i=1}^n S_i'$ to the game Γ' we can identify this strategy with one in Γ by letting $s_i^+(\theta_i = \theta_i^j) = s_i^j$. The utility to agent θ_i^j is then defined by using the notion of expected utility from the original Bayesian game,

$$v_i^j(s^+) = EU_i(s_i^+(\theta_i), s_{-i}^+(\cdot); \theta_i^j).$$

The new finite normal form game $\Gamma' = \langle N', S', v \rangle$ is well defined, leading to the existence result.

PROPOSITION 6.1 *Given the Bayesian game $\langle N, S, \Theta, u, p \rangle$ with N, S, Θ all finite sets, a Bayesian Nash equilibrium exists in mixed strategies.*

Proof Given Nash's Theorem (Theorem 5.4), the finite game $\langle N', S', v \rangle$ has a Nash equilibrium in mixed strategies. Let σ_i^j denote the lottery over S_i that such a mixed strategy equilibrium specifies. Because the profile σ satisfies the condition for a Nash equilibrium, the strategy in which $\phi_i(\theta_i) = s'$ with probability $\sigma_i^j(s')$ satisfies the condition 6.1. $\qquad\square$

9. Exercises

EXERCISE 6.1 *Consider the jury voting game where $p = 3/4$ and $\pi = 2/3$. Characterize the set of Bayesian Nash equilibria to the game. Now instead of using of majority rule, a version of unanimity rule is used – if all agents vote to convict, the defendant is convicted, if at least one agent votes to acquit, the defendant is acquitted. Characterize the Bayesian Nash equilibria to this game (again assuming that $p = 3/4$ and $\pi = 2/3$).*

EXERCISE 6.2 *Consider the Jury Voting game with a continuum of types. Prove equation 6.2.*

EXERCISE 6.3 *Consider a version of the Palfrey-Rosenthal model where k contributions are required for the provision of the public good. Now* *contributions are refunded if there are fewer than k. How does this modification affect the value of the cut point $\hat{c}$? Now suppose that contributions in excess of k are returned randomly to the agents. What happens?*

EXERCISE 6.4 *Consider a version of the Palfrey-Rosenthal model where k contributions are required for the provision of the public good. Conduct a comparative statics analysis of the effects of changes in n and k on the endogenous values $\hat{c}_H$ and $\hat{c}_L$.*

EXERCISE 6.5 *Consider the candidate location game with private information about candidate preferences. Suppose that the location of the median voter were known to be 3/4. Characterize the Bayesian Nash equilibria.*

7 Extensive Form Games

Because all players choose their strategies simultaneously, normal form representations of games are static. Many applications in political science, however, involve players choosing strategies sequentially. Although it is possible to model these situations as games in the normal form, it is often easier and more satisfying to use the *extensive* form, which treats time explicitly.

To motivate the extensive form, consider the following application. *A* is a colony controlled by *B*. Country *B* generates revenue from control of *A*'s oil fields and from direct taxes on *A*'s residents.

In the first stage, *A* decides whether to *R*evolt or *C*onsent to the status quo. If *A* revolts, *B* decides whether to *G*rant independence or to *S*uppress the revolution. If *B* suppresses, the situation escalates into a war. In the event of war, *A* wins with probability *p*. At stake is control of the lucrative oil field, which generates a payoff of 4 to the side that controls it.

Starting a revolution costs *A* one unit if *B* does not suppress. Suppression by *B* costs each side 6 units. If *A* does not revolt, *B* can continue to *T*ax *A*'s residents at 2 units or it can *E*liminate these taxes. Table 7.1 gives the payoffs from each of the possible outcomes. *A*'s payoff is listed first.

If we modeled this game in the normal form, we would ignore that *B* knows *A*'s choice when *B* makes its decision. A better way of representing this game is by using a game tree as in Figure 7.1. A game tree consists of *nodes* representing all previous decisions. Alternatively, the nodes represent the *histories* of play. There is an initial node at the beginning of the game. At each node there are *branches* representing the actions available to the player who chooses at that node. Each of these branches leads to the nodes of the next stage. The end of the game is

Table 7.1. Revolution Game

If A does not revolt and B eliminates the tax, $(0, 4)$
If A does not revolt and B continues the tax, $(-2, 6)$
If A revolts and B grants independence, $(3, 0)$
If A revolts and B suppresses $(4p - 6 - 2(1 - p), 6(1 - p) - 6)$

represented by terminal nodes that specify the payoffs for each player of the game.

Colony A makes its decision at the initial node, from which there are two branches corresponding to R and C. Following a decision to revolt, B chooses between G or S. Following a decision by A of C, B chooses between T and E. At each of the four terminal nodes, the corresponding payoffs are denoted.

Just as a matrix is used to represent a normal form game, the game tree is a representation of the extensive form. The elements of the extensive game follow.

(1) The set of agents N.

(2) A set of histories H. The elements of H correspond to nodes of the game tree. H^T is the set of terminal histories. By convention, the initial node is represented as $H^0 = \emptyset$, the empty set.

(3) A mapping $p(h) : H \backslash H^T \to N$ assigns to each nonterminal history h an agent who must make a decision at h.

(4) For each h a set of actions $A(h)$ that $p(h)$ may take after history h. These may involve randomizations over actions.

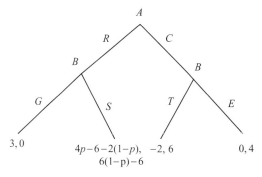

Figure 7.1. Revolution Game.

(5) Information sets $I \subseteq H \backslash H^T$ that form a partition of the set of histories. If $h \in I$, $p(h)$ is uncertain whether she is at node h or some other node $h' \in I$. If h and h' are in the same information set, then $p(h) = p(h')$. In the preceding game, each player knows the history when it is called upon to play so that each information set contains a single element. When all information sets are singletons, the game is said to have *complete and perfect* information (or simply perfect information). Later we relax this assumption so that players do not observe all actions preceding their moves. Consequently, some information sets may contain multiple elements. These are games of *complete but imperfect* information (or simply imperfect information). We require that histories satisfy certain conditions to ensure that they constitute well-behaved trees.[1]

(6) Payoffs U that are a list of Bernoulli utility functions $u_i(h) :$ $H^T \to \mathbb{R}^1$ for each $i \in N$.

In summary, a finite extensive from game Γ^E is a collection $\langle N, H, p(\cdot), U \rangle$. In the extensive form, a strategy is a complete plan of action. Therefore, it specifies for each player a feasible action in every history that the player might be called upon to act. A formal definition of a strategy follows.

DEFINITION 7.1 *For an extensive form game Γ^E, a strategy profile for player $i \in N$ is a mapping $s_i(h) : H_i \to A(h)$ where $s_i(h) = s_i(h')$ if h and h' are in the same information set and H_i is the set of histories $h \in H$ for which $p(h) = i$. A strategy profile is a mapping $s(h) : H \backslash H^T \to A(h)$ with $S(h) = S_i(h)$ if $h \in H_i$.*

Using this definition, we can specify the strategy sets for both players in our revolution example. Because A moves only at the initial node, its strategy set is simply $\{R, C\}$. For B, a strategy must specify an action at each information set. So its strategy set is $\{G$ and T, G and E, S and

---

[1] Specifically, the set of nodes uses the weak order *precedes*. We write $a \to b$ if node a precedes node b. Recall that weak orders are transitive, so that in our extensive form games there are no cycles. In addition, to avoid the case where multiple nodes lead to a single node, we assume that if $h \to h'$ and $h'' \to h'$ then either $h \to h'$ or $h' \to h$. Finally, there exists exactly one node (called the initial node) H^0 for which $H^0 \to h$ for every $h \in H$, and at any terminal history $h \in H^T$ it is the case that there are no histories h' with $h \to h'$.

Table 7.2. Escalation Game in Normal Form

B \ A	R	C
G and T	0, 3	6, −2
G and E	0, 3	4, 0
S and T	$4p − 6 − 2(1 − p)$, $6(1 − p) − 6$	6, −2
S and E	$4p − 6 − 2(1 − p)$, $6(1 − p) − 6$	4, 0

T, S and E} where "G and T" means grant independence following R and T following C.

Now that we have specified the strategies, it is easy to see that we can represent this game in the normal form, see Table 7.2.

From this representation, it is easy to verify that there are three Nash equilibria. The first two are the strategy profiles $(R, G$ and $T)$ and $(R, G$ and $E)$. Each of these predicts that A revolts and B grants independence. The third Nash equilibrium is the profile $(C, S$ and $T)$. It predicts that the threat that B escalates deters a revolt by A.

This example shows some of the limitations of the Nash equilibrium concept in dynamic games. In particular, the predictions of the second and third equilibria are somewhat implausible. Consider the second equilibrium. This equilibrium calls for B to eliminate the taxes after a decision by A to consent to B's rule. B, however, has no incentive to decrease taxes at this information set. In other words, Nash equilibria allow for behavior that is not rational at histories that are "off the equilibrium path." In the case of equilibrium 2, this problem seems small as it produces identical behavior to that produced by equilibrium 1, in which all behavior is rational at all information sets. Consider the third equilibrium, however. Suppose that A defects from the conjectured equilibrium by revolting. Following the deviation, B is clearly better off choosing G for any value of p. Thus, B's threat to suppress is not credible because it would never be rational to do so. This peaceful outcome is supported by expected behavior that is not *sequentially rational* because it does not maximize the agent's utility at every information set.

In the next couple of sections, we discuss refinements of Nash equilibria appropriate for dynamic games that eliminate strategies that are not sequentially rational.

1. Backward Induction

The most common way of solving dynamic games of perfect information is through backward induction. In this procedure, the last player to act at each node chooses the action that maximizes her utility. The second to last player then chooses his actions optimally, knowing that the last player chooses optimal actions at each node. This process continues until each player has chosen optimally under the assumption that all future players make optimal choices.

It is easy to apply backward induction in the revolution game. First, we require that B make optimal choices at each node. At the R node, B clearly gets more utility from granting independence. At the C node, B maximizes its utility with continued taxation. Given the expectation that B makes rational choices, A choose to revolt. Thus, the solution from backward induction is $(R, G$ and $T) -$ the Nash equilibrium that does not involve sequentially irrational behavior.

This procedure is straightforward, but cumbersome to formalize. So we focus on some examples.

1.1. Example: The Centipede Game. Figure 7.2 presents a game tree used extensively in experimental economics – the Centipede game. Two players take turns choosing between Down and Left. The choice of D ends the game, but L continues it until stage 5. One of the reasons experimentalists find this game interesting is that a naive player 1 may attempt to continue to play L in order to get the large payoff of 6 at stage 5. Such a strategy, however, is not sequentially rational and does not survive backward induction. We begin the analysis at stage 5 where player 1 clearly chooses D. Backing up to stage 4, player 2 knows that player 1 plays D in the last stage, leaving her a payoff of 4 instead of the 5 she can obtain from playing D. Backing up one more stage, player 1 knows that L generates 2 while D guarantees 3. Thus, he chooses D. Clearly, if we continue this process back to the first stage, we see that

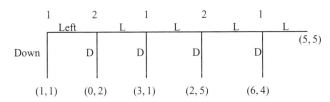

Figure 7.2. The Centipede Game.

in fact player 1 rationally chooses D. Indeed, the only strategy profile that survives backward induction is $\{D, D, D, D, D\}$.

1.2. Example: Sequential Bargaining. The application of bargaining models is increasingly important in political game theory. Indeed, we dedicate an entire chapter to it later in the book. Here we consider one of the simplest versions of these models. There are two players, 1 and 2, who bargain over the allocation of \$1. In the first period, player 1 proposes a division of the dollar in which she keeps x_1 and offers $x_2 = 1 - x_1$ to player 2. If player 2 accepts this proposal, the dollar is divided accordingly, and the game ends. Alternatively if player 2 rejects the offer, the value of the dollar decreases to δ where $1 > \delta > 0$. This assumption captures the impatience of the players – they prefer to settle sooner than later. In round 2, player 2 makes an offer where she keeps x_2 and gives $x_1 = \delta - x_2$ to player 1. If player 1 accepts, the remaining δ is divided accordingly. If she rejects, however, the dollar disappears and both players receive 0. For simplicity, the payoffs to each player are $u_i(x_i) = x_i$.

There are lots of Nash equilibria to this game. In fact any allocation can be supported with Nash equilibrium strategies. Consider the following strategy combination:

Player 1: Propose $x_2 = z$. If the offer is rejected, reject any offer in round 2.

Player 2: Accept in round 1 if $x_2 \geq z$; reject otherwise and then propose $x_2 = \delta$ in round 2.

Clearly, for a fixed $z \leq 1$, the best response of player 1 is to propose $x_2 = z$ in round 1. Otherwise, player 1 receives 0. Similarly, player 2's best response is to accept z. These strategies, however, are not sequentially rational. It is not rational for player 1 to reject all second-period proposals. He should accept any proposal that gives him at least 0, his payoff from rejection. Thus, in round 2 player 2 can propose to keep nearly the entire δ. Consequently player 1 needs to offer player 2 at least as much as player 2 gets from her second-period proposal. The following strategy is consistent with backward induction.

Player 1: Propose $x_2 = \delta$. If the offer is rejected, accept any offer in round 2.

Player 2: Accept in round 1 if $x_2 \geq \delta$; reject otherwise. Propose $x_2 = \delta$ in round 2.

Clearly in period 2 accepting 0 is no worse for player 1 than rejecting the offer. Therefore, the optimal proposal for player 2 is $x_2 = \delta$. Backing up to period 1, it is clear that player 1 must offer player 2 at least δ to prevent her rejecting it. The equilibrium offers in period 1 are, therefore, $x_1 = 1 - \delta$ and $x_2 = \delta$.

2. Dynamic Games of Complete but Imperfect Information

In the models considered so far, the player who moves at each history recalls all of the previous moves and, therefore, can infer from which node she is moving. In other words, each information set contains a single element. Now we consider models in which information sets contain multiple histories. Games of this form are said to have *imperfect information*. Such a situation occurs when some moves either are not observed or are taken simultaneously.

Consider a simple game between a bureaucrat B and a politician P where some actions are not observable. The bureaucrat chooses a regulatory enforcement level from $\{H, L\}$ representing high and low, respectively. High enforcement costs $c > 0$ to B, but low enforcement is costless. To keep matters simple, B gets no utility from enforcement. Therefore, it receives $-c$ for choosing H and 0 for choosing L. The politician, however, prefers H to L. Her utility function is $u_P(H) = 1$ and $u_P(L) = 0$. P cannot observe B's enforcement level unless it chooses to conduct oversight at a cost $1 > k > 0$. If B is found to have chosen lax enforcement, it suffers a penalty f and is forced to choose H.

At the point she decides whether to conduct oversight, P does not know whether the history is H or L. The extensive form given in Figure 7.3 uses dotted lines connecting H and L to show that they are in the same information set.

Because P does not observe B's action, she must play the same action at each node. A strategy for B is simply a choice at the first node so we can write this game in the normal form in Table 7.3.

Table 7.3. Oversight Game		
$B \backslash P$	*Oversight*	*No Oversight*
H	$-c, 1 - k$	$-c, 1$
L	$-f - c, 1 - k$	$0, 0$

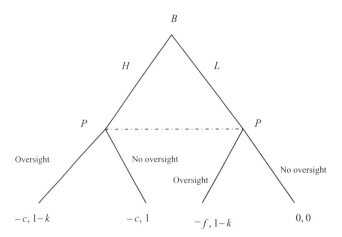

Figure 7.3. Regulatory Enforcement Game.

There are no pure strategy Nash equilibria in this game. If B chooses H, P's best response is not to conduct oversight, but the best response to no oversight is low enforcement, leading P to prefer oversight. The mixed strategy equilibrium of this game involves B's choosing the high enforcement level with probability $1 - k$ and P's conducting oversight with probability c/f.

This example suggests that games with sequential moves unobserved by the second player are identical to games with simultaneous moves. We return to a familiar example to illustrate exactly how the extensive form accommodates simultaneous action. Consider the Prisoner's Dilemma where two crooks have to decide whether or not to confess. We can model this game in extensive form by letting player 1 move first and then putting both *confess* and *don't confess* in the same information set for player 2 as we have in Figure 7.4.

Finally to show the flexibility of the extensive form, consider the following game with three stages in Figure 7.5. Each player has three available moves: *Left, Middle, Right*. If player 1 plays L, the move is observed by all. But if player 1 plays R or M, player 2 does not observe 1's action. Player 2 therefore has two information sets $\{L\}, \{M, R\}$. Player 3 also does not perfectly observe the actions of players 1 and 2 and has four information sets, $\{LL, LM\}, \{LR\}, \{ML, MM, RL, RM\}$, and $\{MR, RR\}$.

The difficulty with games of imperfect information is that we can no longer easily apply backward induction because players do not always know which history has been reached. One solution to this problem

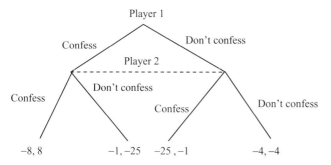

Figure 7.4. Prisoner's Dilemma in Extensive Form.

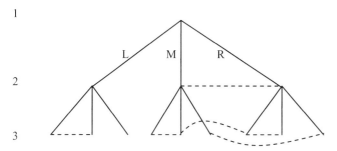

Figure 7.5. Complex Information Sets. In stage 1, player 1 has one information set that is a singleton. In stage 2, player 2 has two information sets. In stage 3, player 3 has four information sets.

hinges on the observation that sometimes parts of an extensive form game can be conceptualized as distinct games. A notion of sequential rationality then requires that all the players play Nash equilibrium strategies in each of these smaller games. These games within a game are known as *subgames*. A subgame is a subset of an extensive form that satisfies the following criteria.

(1) It begins at a node that is in a singleton information set. In other words, at the initial or first node of any subgame the player who moves knows exactly which node she is at.
(2) It includes all nodes following this initial node and no others.
(3) It does not cut any information sets. If histories h and h' are in the same information set, they are part of the same subgames.

The example in Figure 7.5 has three subgames: the original game, a subgame following L, and a subgame following the history LR. Strategy profiles that constitute Nash equilibrium behavior in all of the subgames are known as *subgame perfect Nash equilibria*, sometimes denoted by the acronym SPNE. In defining a *SPNE* it is convenient to use the idea of a restricted strategy profile. Given a strategy profile $s(\cdot)$ and a subgame with histories H', the restriction of $s(\cdot)$ to the subgame is the mapping s' that has as its domain H' and satisfies the condition $s'(h) = s(h)$ for every $h \in H'$.

DEFINITION 7.2 *Given an extensive form game Γ^E, a strategy profile $s(\cdot)$ is a subgame perfect Nash equilibrium (SPNE) if in every subgame to Γ^E the restricted strategy profile $s(\cdot)$ to the subgame is a Nash equilibrium of the subgame.*

An important result establishes the existence of SPNE for finite games.

THEOREM 7.1 *Every finite extensive form game has a SPNE. Moreover, if no player is indifferent between any two terminal histories then the SPNE is unique.*

As an example, consider a problem of sequential voting by three players $N = \{1, 2, 3\}$. Suppose that the choices x, y, z are to be voted using the following agenda: first choose between x and y under simple majority rule, then vote the winner against z by majority rule. The winner of this last vote is enacted. At each stage of voting ballots are cast simultaneously. Figure 7.6 (pp. 182–183) depicts the game.

Players have the following preferences over the enacted policy $x P_1 y P_1 z$; $y P_2 z P_2 x$; $z P_3 x P_3 y$. If we apply the criterion of subgame perfection and require that strategies are weakly undominated, players 2 and 3 vote for z against x in the final stage. Alternatively, players 1 and 2 vote for y against z.

Accordingly, when agents vote over x and y in the first period, they understand that the real choice is between the *sophisticated equivalents*, z and y.[2] Accordingly players 1 and 2 vote for y over x. Although player 1 prefers x to y, she casts a strategic vote for y over x because

[2] Richard McKelvey and Richard Niemi (1978) coined the term *sophisticated equivalents* in the study of strategic voting in agendas.

she realizes that a vote for x is really a vote for z, an unappealing outcome.

If voters use weakly dominated strategies, the set of SPNEs can be quite large. Recall that any unanimous vote is a Nash equilibrium in any of the subgames at the second stage of the agenda. Thus, a large number of SPNEs can be constructed by specifying different Nash equilibrium strategies for each second-stage subgame.

As a second example of SPNE, consider a model similar to one used by Weingast (1997) to explain the development of the rule of law. This game consists of a ruler R who chooses whether or not to expropriate wealth x from one of two social groups, A or B. After observing which group is expropriated, A and B decide simultaneously whether or not to challenge him. Each incurs cost c from challenging. If both challenge, the attempted expropriation fails and each receives a benefit b. A successful challenge also costs the ruler k. If one or zero groups challenge, the expropriation succeeds. The extensive form is shown in Figure 7.7 (p. 183).

We begin our analysis by computing the Nash equilibria of the subgame following the decision to expropriate from A. From the perspective of agents A and B, the normal form for this subgame is Table 7.4.

There are two pure strategy Nash equilibria to this subgame: one where both groups challenge and one where neither group challenges. There is also a mixed strategy equilibrium, but we ignore it to keep the example simple. Because the subgame following an attempted expropriation of B is symmetric, there are the same two pure strategy equilibria.

Now consider the first stage of the game where R anticipates that some Nash equilibrium is played in each of the subgames of the second stage. If he anticipates that both groups challenge in both subgames, R's best response is not to expropriate. If a group challenges in one of the subgames but not in the other, R expropriates from the group that

Table 7.4. Expropriation Subgame

$B \backslash A$	Challenge	Don't Challenge
Challenge	b, b	$-c, -x$
Don't Challenge	$0, -x - c$	$0, -x$

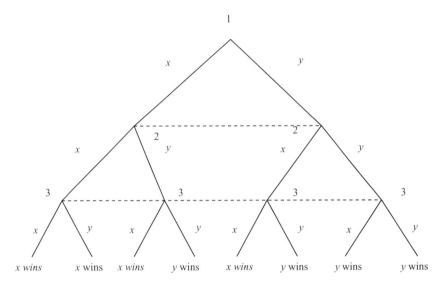

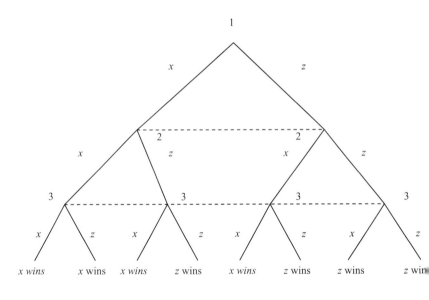

X Wins Subgame

Figure 7.6. Sequential Voting Game.

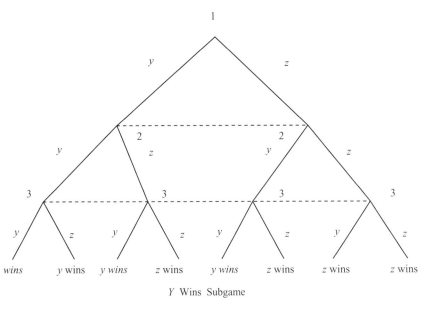

Figure 7.6. (*Continued*)

does not challenge. If there is no challenge in either subgame, the ruler expropriates from either group. Consequently, there are five SPNEs in pure strategies. Weingast argues that the key to establishing the rule of law is that A and B coordinate on the Nash equilibrium where both groups challenge any attempted expropriation by the ruler.

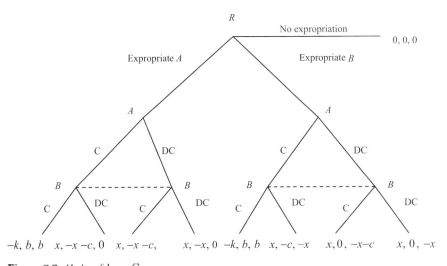

Figure 7.7. Rule of Law Game.

The solution via backward induction is a special case of SPNE. In a game of perfect information all information sets are singletons so that each node begins a new subgame of the extensive form. Optimization at every node constitutes a Nash equilibrium of all subgames. Therefore, any solution using backward induction is a SPNE.

3. The Single-Deviation Principle

Subgame perfection in finite games has a very useful property. In checking whether a strategy profile $s(\cdot)$ is subgame perfect, it is sufficient to verify that no player has an incentive to deviate at any single information set. We need not be concerned with defections from multiple information sets. This property is called the single-deviation principle. The intuition behind the result is as follows. If a profitable deviation involves changes at multiple histories, just making one of the last deviations is profitable in the subgame that starts at that history. Accordingly, if a strategy profile is not subgame perfect, there may be lots of deviations that are desirable. At least one of them involves a deviation in a single period.

As an exercise, we ask for a direct proof for a single-agent extensive form game. We now provide the result and proof for general finite games. One way to provide a formal statement of the principle is to define a single-stage deviation. Let H denote the set of nonterminal histories in an extensive form game and let h' denote an element of H. Given the strategy $s(\cdot)$ the strategy $s^{h'}(\cdot)$ involves a single deviation if $s(h) = s^{h'}(h)$ for all $h \in H \backslash \{h'\}$.

THEOREM 7.2 *(Single-Deviation Principle) Given a finite extensive form game with nonterminal histories H, the strategy profile $s(\cdot)$ is a subgame perfect Nash equilibrium if and only if for each $h' \in H$ the payoff to $p(h')$ from $s(\cdot)$ is at least as good as the payoff to $p(h')$ from the single-deviation $s^{h'}(\cdot)$.*

Proof Because every SPNE is a Nash equilibrium, no agent has a unilateral incentive to change her strategy. Thus, for each $h' \in H$ the payoff to $p(h')$ from $s(\cdot)$ is at least as good as the payoff to $p(h')$ from $s^{h'}(\cdot)$. This implies that in any SPNE no single-stage deviations are desirable. To establish the sufficiency of the single-deviation principle, assume there is a strategy profile $s(\cdot)$ that is not a SPNE, but that no profitable single deviations exist. Because $s(\cdot)$ is not a SPNE, there exists a subgame for which the restriction of $s(\cdot)$ is not a Nash equilibrium. Let H' denote one of the smallest collections of histories that form such a subgame. Because the game is finite such a collection exists. Let $h^1 \in H'$ denote the initial node of this subgame and let $i = p(h^1)$ denote the player who moves at h^1. By construction there is a profitable deviation from the restriction of $s(\cdot)$ to this subgame for player i who starts with a deviation at history h^1. Because we have assumed that no single deviation is desirable, there must be a nonterminal history, h^2, following h^1 for which deviating at h^1 and h^2 yields a higher payoff for i than the equilibrium. But this implies that in the subgame starting at h^2 player i has a profitable deviation. This contradicts the fact that H' is one of the smallest collections of histories for which the restriction to $s(\cdot)$ is not a Nash equilibrium.   □

The single-deviation principle also applies to nonfinite games as long as a continuity assumption is satisfied. We defer this discussion until the chapter on repeated games.

4. A Digression on Subgame Perfection and Perfect Equilibria

Although subgame perfection is generally used to solve extensive form games, it is closely related to the idea of *perfection* discussed in Chapter 5. Recall that a strategy profile is *perfect* if it is the limit of a sequence of mixed strategy profiles that form best responses when agents are constrained to play completely mixed strategies. We demonstrate the connection between perfection and subgame perfection by returning to the normal form representation of the revolution game. Consider the Nash equilibrium profile (C, S and T). Suppose each side must assign at least probability ε to each of its pure strategies. This captures the idea that agents may make mistakes in implementing their preferred strategies.

We now show that S and T cannot be B's best response when agent A plays both of her strategies with at least probability ε. If A chooses R with probability ε, B's expected utility of S and T is $\varepsilon(4p - 6 - 2(1 - p)) + (1 - \varepsilon)6$, but the expected utility of G and T is $(1 - \varepsilon)6$. Because $4p - 6 - 2(1 - p) < 0$, B wants to play G and T with the highest possible probability. As a result (C, S and T) cannot be the limit as ε converges to 0 of completely mixed Nash equilibria. Thus, it fails the requirements of SPNE and is not a perfect equilibrium in the normal form. We leave as exercises for the reader the argument that only (R, G and T) is a perfect equilibrium.

Although all subgame perfect Nash equilibria are perfect, there are perfect equilibria that are not subgame perfect. This problem arises because extensive form games represented in the normal form often generate correlation in the trembles when the same player moves more than once in the extensive form. One approach is to relabel the players so that no player moves at more than one information set. This approach yields what is sometimes called the *agent form*. In this representation the sets of perfect and subgame perfect equilibria coincide. This argument is left as an exercise for the motivated student.

5. Application: Agenda Control

5.1. The Romer-Rosenthal Model. In many localities in the United States, local school budgets must be approved by the voters. Generally, only the school board can place the budget on a referendum ballot. Consequently, the board has monopoly agenda control over proposals for school spending. Romer and Rosenthal (1978) were the first to develop a model of this form of agenda control.

We reproduce the Romer-Rosenthal model here. Let spending be denoted by $s \in [0, \infty)$ and let q denote the status quo level of spending. The school board wants to maximize the amount of spending so that the board's utility function $u_B(s)$ is strictly increasing in s. In the first stage of the game, the board makes a proposal of s. Once this referendum is on the ballot, citizens (an odd number) vote whether to approve it by majority rule. We assume that all voters turn out so that available strategies are $\{Y, N\}$. If a majority chooses Y, then s becomes the new level of spending. If a majority chooses N, then the reversion (or status quo) spending level, q, is adopted. Voters have single-peaked and symmetric preferences over school spending represented by the utility functions $u_i(s)$. Let v_i be the ideal point of voter i. As in Chapter 2, such preferences take the form $u_i(s) = h(-|s - v_i|)$, where $h(\cdot)$ is a strictly increasing function.

We are interested in identifying a subgame perfect equilibrium. Because the last stage of the game is a majority-rule voting game, there are Nash equilibria of the last stage that support accepting or rejecting any s. Consequently, we assume voters do not use weakly dominated strategies in any voting subgames. Given any proposal s, each voter votes Y if $u_i(s) \geq u_i(q)$. Single-peakedness implies that if the median voter prefers s to q then the proposal passes under weakly undominated voting. Similarly, if the median voter prefers q to s then the proposal fails under weakly undominated voting.

Given the equilibria of the voting subgames, the school board's best response is to choose the largest s that is acceptable to the median voter. Let v_m be the ideal point of the median voter. Given v_m and q, we can compute which policies the median prefers to q. Such policies, s, satisfy the condition $u_m(s) \geq u_m(q)$. Because h is an increasing function, this inequality requires that

$$|s - v_m| \leq |q - v_m|.$$

Therefore, if $q < v_m$, this inequality holds for $s \in [q, 2v_m - q]$. Conversely, if $q > v_m$, a successful proposal requires $s \in [2v_m - q, q]$. Thus, the highest obtainable budget is the maximum of $2v_m - q$ and q. Because the board wants to maximize s, it chooses $\max\{q, 2v_m - q\}$. Figure 7.8 plots the equilibrium value of s^* as a function of v_m and q.

This simple model produces some clear predictions about the relationships among voter preferences, statutory reversions, and policy

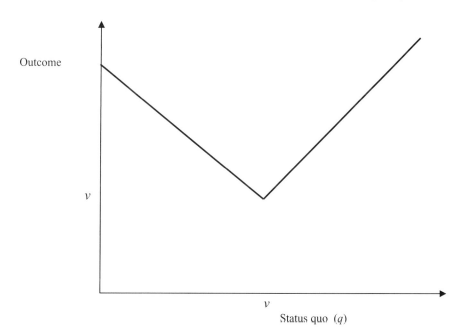

Figure 7.8. Equilibrium Policies from Romer-Rosenthal Game.

outcomes. First, the board uses its agenda control to generate higher spending outcomes when the statutory reversion is low and the median voter prefers to spend more than the reversion amount. Because the voter's threat to reject large spending proposals is not credible when the reversion is bad, the board is able to extract more spending. A second important implication is that although spending outcomes are responsive to changes in voter preferences (at least when $q < v_m$), spending grows twice as fast as the median voter's preferred spending level.

5.2. The Presidential Veto. In the United States and many other presidential systems, the executive has veto power over legislative enactments. Presidency scholars often use a version of the Romer-Rosenthal model to explore how the veto enhances the executive's influence over legislation.

To keep matters as simple as possible, we model the legislature as a single actor L with single-peaked symmetric preferences on a single dimension. Its ideal point is l. Consequently, the legislature's utility function is $u_l(x) = h(-|x - l|)$ for policy outcomes $x \in \mathbb{R}$ where $h(\cdot)$ is a strictly increasing function. Similarly, the president has ideal point p and utility function $u_p(x) = h(-|x - p|)$.

The game form is very simple. In the first stage, L proposes a bill b to change the status quo policy q. Subsequently, the president P decides either to accept b or to veto the bill. A veto results in the status quo q. For now we ignore the legislature's ability to override vetoes.

We solve this game by backward induction. In the last stage, the president's best response is to accept any bill for which $u_p(b) \geq u_p(q)$ or $-|b - p| \geq -|q - p|$. Thus, if $p > q$, she accepts any $b \in [q, 2p - q]$. Alternatively, if $p < q$, she accepts $b \in [2p - q, q]$. Let $P(q)$ denote the set of bills that the president accepts over the status quo. Now we back up to the legislature's decision node. Because the legislature knows which policies are acceptable, it chooses its most preferred policy from $P(q)$. If $l \in P(q)$, then clearly $b^* = l$. If c is below $\min P(q)$, then $b^* = \min P(q)$. If $l > \max P(q)$, then $b^* = \max P(q)$.

Suppose that $l > p$. Then, given our derivations of $P(q)$, the equilibrium policy outcome is

$$
b^* = \begin{cases} 2p - q \text{ if } p > q \text{ and } l > 2p - q \\ l \text{ if } p > q \text{ and } l < 2p - q \\ l \text{ if } l < q \\ q \text{ if } l > q > p \end{cases}.
$$

If $p > l$, the equilibrium outcomes are

$$b^* = \begin{cases} 2p - q \text{ if } p < q \text{ and } l < 2p - q \\ l \text{ if } p < q \text{ and } l > 2p - q \\ l \text{ if } l > q \\ q \text{ if } p > q > l \end{cases}.$$

Figure 7.9 plots the equilibrium outcomes as a function of l, p, and q. The comparative statics results are quite similar to those of the original Romer-Rosenthal model. In particular, the legislature does better when the status quo is far from the president's ideal point. Another important implication is that the influence conferred by the veto is not large. In all of the cases where the veto has an impact (i.e., $b^* \neq l$), the president is indifferent between the equilibrium proposal and the status quo. Finally, because the model is one of perfect information, the legislator perfectly predicts the president's behavior and no vetoes occur in equilibrium. Although vetoes are not observed on the path, the possibility of a veto is consequential. In later chapters, we consider models where vetoes occur as part of equilibrium strategies.

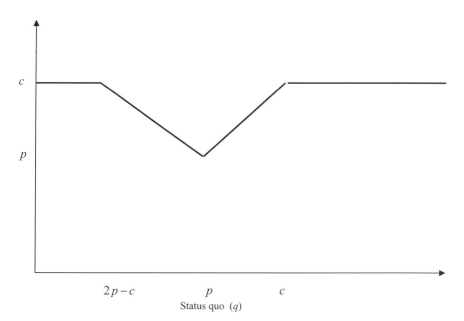

Figure 7.9. Equilibrium Outcomes from Veto Bargaining.

5.3. The Veto Override. Instead of assuming that q is the outcome following any veto, we consider a model where the legislature can override the veto with a supermajority. The legislature has n (odd) members and $k > (n+1)/2$ votes are required to override the executive veto. Each legislator has single-peaked preferences with utility functions of the form $u_i(x) = h(-|x - l_i|)$, and the ideal points l_i are ordered such that $l_i > l_j$ if and only if $i > j$. Motivated by a model in which legislative proposals are made according to an open rule agenda process, we assume that the legislative proposer is the median legislator with ideal point $m \equiv l_{(n+1)/2}$. We also limit consideration to equilibria in which voting is weakly undominated in all subgames.

Given these assumptions, a successful override requires that $u_k(b) \geq u_k(q)$ and $u_{n-k-1}(b) \geq u_{n-k-1}(q)$. To see that this is true, consider the case where $u_k(b) \geq u_k(q)$ and $u_{n-k-1}(b) < u_{n-k-1}(q)$. Because preferences are single peaked, there is some $i \in [n-k-1, k]$ such that $u_i(b) < u_i(q)$ for all legislators with ideal points lower that l_i. Therefore, the number of legislators who support the override must be strictly less than k. The logic of the other possibility is similar. Because their support is necessary and sufficient, legislators $n-k-1$ and k are commonly referred to as the *override pivots*.

Because an override is only necessary in case of a presidential veto, only one of the override pivots is strategically relevant. Consider a vetoed bill with $u_p(b) < u_p(q)$ and $u_m(b) > u_m(q)$. If $p < m$, single peakedness and $l_k > m$ imply that $u_k(b) > u_k(q)$. Thus, the override depends solely on $n-k-1$'s preferences. Similarly, if $p > m$, single peakedness and $l_{n-k-1} < m$ imply that $u_{n-k-1}(b) > u_{n-k-1}(q)$. The implication is that only the preferences of the pivot that lies on the same side of the median as the president matters for a successful override.

We have established the necessity for the proposer to attract the support of either the president or the override pivot on his side of the median. Now consider how the proposer chooses her optimal proposal. First suppose that $l_{n-k-1} < p < m$. Appealing again to single peakedness, we know that any bill that l_{n-k-1} and m prefer to q is also preferred to q by p. Thus, the proposer does not require the support of l_{n-k-1}. A similar argument establishes that when $p < l_{n-k-1} < m$, the proposer need only attract $n-k-1$'s support. The corresponding cases where $p > m$ are symmetric so that the proposer need only attract the closer of the president and the override pivot on the president's side of the median.

Thus, the pivotal actor's ideal point is $v = \max\{l_{n-k-1}, p\}$ if $p < m$ and $v = \max\{l_k, p\}$ otherwise. The SPNE proposal is given by

$$b^* = \begin{cases} 2v - q \text{ if } v > q \text{ and } m > 2v - q \\ m \text{ if } v > q \text{ and } m < 2v - q \\ m \text{ if } m < q \\ q \text{ if } m > q > v \end{cases}$$

if $v > m$, and

$$b^* = \begin{cases} 2p - q \text{ if } p < q \text{ and } m < 2p - q \\ m \text{ if } p < q \text{ and } m > 2p - q \\ m \text{ if } m > q \\ q \text{ if } m > q > p \end{cases}$$

otherwise. Figure 7.10 illustrates the equilibrium outcomes for different values of k. Not surprisingly, when the number of

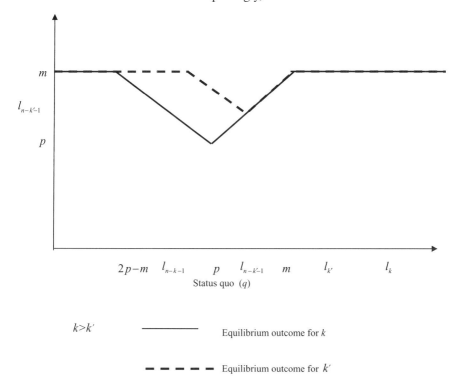

Figure 7.10. The Effects of Veto Overrides.

votes needed to override goes down, the effect of veto power is diminished.

6. Application: A Model of Power Transitions

Powell (1999) models how dramatic shifts of power in the international system lead to violent conflict. Suppose that there are two countries A and B. Country A is making a claim against a region controlled by B. The total value of the region is normalized to $1 per period. We focus on a two-period version of this game where each country values the outcome of each period equally.

First consider country B's options. It can appease A in the first period by offering it a share of the region's output $0 \leq x_1 \leq 1$, or it can attempt to settle the dispute militarily by attacking A. If B chooses to attack and wins the war, A drops its claim and the game ends. If B loses the war, A takes undisputed control of the region and the game ends. In the event of a war in the first period, the victor gets a stream of output equal to $1 in each of the two periods and the loser gets a stream of $0 in each of the two periods. Both the winner and loser each pay the cost c from fighting in a war. If country B makes an offer then country A's available choices are either to accept x_1 or to refuse it and go to war. If country B initiates a war, A has no choice but to fight. If a war did not occur in the first period, country B has the same choices open to her in the second period: offering a share of the output $0 \leq x_2 \leq 1$ or going to war. If a second-period offer is made, country A can either accept it or go to war. If a war occurs in the second period, the victor receives $1 and the loser receives $0. Again fighting the second-period war costs both sides c.

An important feature of the model is that over time country A's military capability is increasing relative to B's. In the first period A wins a war with probability p_1 whereas in the second period A wins with probability $p_2 > p_1$. To keep matters interesting, we assume that $p_2 > c > p_1$.

With respect to the incidence of violent conflict, there are two types of equilibria: one in which B appeases A in both periods and one in which B attacks A in the first period.

First, suppose that $2c > p_2 \quad 2p_1$. In the SPNE, B gives $p_2 - c$ to country A in the second period and $\max\{0, 2p_1 - p_2\}$ in the first period. Because this is a game of perfect information, we verify that these strategies are part of a SPNE using backward induction. In the second period, A's expected utility of fighting is $p_2 - c$ so B must offer A at least this much to prevent a conflict. This concession leaves B with a payoff of $1 - p_2 + c$. Because B's expected utility of fighting is $1 - p_2 - c$, it strictly prefers appeasing. The optimal action for B to take in the second period is to offer $x_2^* = p_2 - c$. Now consider period 1. A receives \$1 in each period if it wins a war and \$0 if it loses. Therefore, the expected utility of fighting is $2p_1 - c$. To appease A, B must choose x_1 so that $x_1 + p_2 - c \geq 2p_1 - c$. This inequality is equivalent to $x_1 \geq 2p_1 - p_2$. Because B rationally offers the minimal amount, her equilibrium proposal is $x_1^* = \max\{0, 2p_1 - p_2\}$. Now we need only check to see that B prefers to pay $x_1^* + x_2^*$. B's expected utility of war is $2(1 - p_1) - c$ so it prefers the payment if and only if $1 - x_1^* + 1 - x_2^* \geq 2(1 - p_1) - c$. This condition is equivalent to $2 - x_1^* - p_2 + c \geq 2(1 - p_1) - c$ or $2c \geq p_2 - 2p_1 + x_1^*$. This condition is satisfied if $2c > p_2 - 2p_1$.

Now suppose that this condition does not hold so that $p_2 - 2p_1 > 2c$. Because $c > 0$, this requires that $x_1^* = 0$. Thus, B prefers fighting to making the payments because $p_2 - 2p_1 + x_1^* > 2c$. Thus, when the condition fails, the SPNE predicts that B attacks A in the first period.

The necessary condition for a peaceful resolution only fails when p_2 is much greater than p_1 so that A is much weaker in the first stage than it is in the second stage. Thus, B prefers to attack when A is weak to avoid making large concessions when A becomes more powerful. If the distribution of power is stable (as in the case of $p_1 = p_2$), there is no war in equilibrium.

7. Application: A Model of Transitions to Democracy

Acemoglu and Robinson (2005) develop a number of models designed to explore the conditions under which authoritarian polities adopt democratic institutions. We sketch their framework by considering one of their models.

Suppose that there are two types of agents: rich and poor. Let $\lambda > 1/2$ be the proportion of citizens who are poor so that $1 - \lambda$ is the proportion of rich citizens. Rich citizens each receive income y^r and poor citizens have income y^p. The average income in the society is $\overline{y} = \lambda y^p + (1 - \lambda)y^r$. Clearly, $y^r > \overline{y} > y^p$. An important parameter in Acemoglu and Robinson's analysis is θ, which represents the share of income held by the poor. This term is implicitly defined by the identities

$$y^p = \frac{\theta \overline{y}}{\lambda} \text{ and } y^r = \frac{(1-\theta)\overline{y}}{1-\lambda}.$$

Thus, an increase in θ represents a decrease in inequality.

The primary policy instrument in this political economy is a linear tax and transfer scheme whereby the government sets a proportional tax rate τ and then transfers the tax revenue back to the citizens in a lump sum. Because the agents differ in their incomes, they have different preferences over tax rates. Given a tax rate τ, the per capita tax levy is $\tau \overline{y}$. As a simple way of capturing the distortionary effects of income taxation, Acemoglu and Robinson assume that actual revenues are less than the levy because of transaction costs in the collection of taxes. Formally, the transaction cost of levying $\tau \overline{y}$ is given by $C(\tau)\overline{y}$, where $C(\tau)$ is convex and increasing. To keep matters simple and generate a closed form solution, we set $C(\tau) = \frac{1}{2}\tau^2$. After deducting this deadweight loss, the amount of money available for transfers is given by $T = (\tau - C(\tau))\overline{y}$ and the after-tax and transfer income of an agent of type $i \in \{r, p\}$ is

$$V^i(\tau) = (1-\tau)\, y^i + \left(\tau - \frac{1}{2}\tau^2\right)\overline{y}.$$

Now we consider the preferred tax rates of rich and poor voters. Differentiating the after-tax income with respect to the tax rate and setting the derivative equal to 0 yield the first-order condition for the optimal tax rate choice by poor voters,

$$\overline{y} - y^p - \tau \overline{y} = 0.$$

After substituting the identity $y^p = (\theta \overline{y})/\lambda$, the poor's most preferred tax rate is found to be

$$\tau^p = \frac{\lambda - \theta}{\lambda}.$$

Because the poor have lower incomes than the rich, their income share is lower than their share in the population so that $\lambda > \theta$. Thus, $0 < \tau^p < 1$. Also note that τ^p is decreasing in θ so that the poor's preferred tax rate is increasing in inequality.

Now we consider the preferences of the rich. The necessary first-order condition for an interior optimal tax rate is

$$\overline{y} - y^r - \tau \overline{y} = 0.$$

This condition can only be satisfied at an infeasible negative tax rate. Thus, the rich's most preferred feasible tax rate is $\tau^r = 0$.

In Acemoglu and Robinson's model, there is a political shock in each period that determines the consequences of overthrowing the regime and replacing it by a dictatorship of the left. When the shock is S, $1 - \mu^S$ of the economy's income is destroyed where $S = H$, L and $\mu^H > \mu^L$. Thus, in state H the costs of overthrowing the regime are low compared to those in state L. During a revolution the income of the rich is confiscated and evenly divided among the poor. Thus in state S the payoff to the poor following a revolution is

$$V^p\left(R, \mu^S\right) = \frac{\mu^S \overline{y}}{\lambda}.$$

For simplicity, they assume that following the revolution the rich get no income so that $V^r\left(R, \mu^S\right) = 0$.

To characterize the outcome of Acemoglu and Robinson's model, we consider the extent to which revolution is a threat. We say that the revolution constraint binds in state S if the poor prefer revolution to an authoritarian outcome at the rich's ideal tax rate of 0. This is true if $V^p\left(R, \mu^S\right) > V^p(0)$. After substituting the preceding expressions we see that this constraint binds when $\mu^S > \theta$.

Given this specification of the economy and the costs of revolution, we turn to one of Acemoglu and Robinson's extensive form games, illustrated in Figure 7.11. To simplify the figure, we show only the extensive form following the realization of the state S.

First, the state, H or L, is revealed. Then the rich move first and decide whether to move to a democracy D or to maintain control in an authoritarian system N. If the rich choose N, they also choose a tax rate $\widehat{\tau}$.

After the rich choose, the poor decide whether to initiate a revolution R or to accept the rich's decision (NR). If they revolt, the payoffs are $V^p\left(R, \mu^S\right) = (\mu^S \overline{y})/\lambda$ and $V^r\left(R, \mu^S\right) = 0$. If they do not revolt against D, the tax rate is chosen by majority rule. Because the median voter is poor, the equilibrium tax rate is τ^p and the payoffs to D are $V^p(\tau^p)$ and $V^r(\tau^p)$. By comparing the payoffs of R and D, it is easy to establish

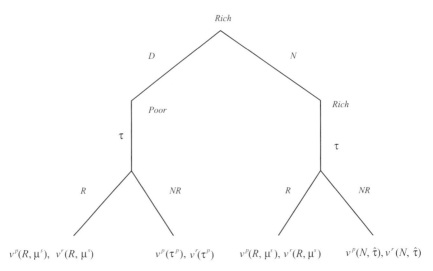

Figure 7.11. The Democratization Game.

that in state S the poor prefer to revolt rather than accept democracy if and only if $\mu^S > \theta + \tau^P (\lambda - \theta) - 1/2\tau^{P2}\lambda$. This condition simplifies to $\mu^S > \theta + (\lambda - \theta)^2 / (2\lambda)$.

Now suppose the rich choose N and the poor prefer not to revolt. Acemoglu and Robinson assume that the rich may not be able to commit to maintaining $\hat{\tau} > 0$ after the revolutionary threat has passed. To model this commitment problem, they assume that with probability p the rich maintain the tax rate $\hat{\tau}$ but with probability $1 - p$ they have the opportunity to renege and choose $\tau^r = 0$. Given the rich's initial choice of tax rate and the possibility of reneging, the utilities from N are

$$V^P (N, \hat{\tau}) = (1 - p) y^P + p \left[(1 - \tau) y^P + \left(\tau - \frac{1}{2}\tau^2 \right) \bar{y} \right]$$

$$= y^P + p \left[\tau (\bar{y} - y^P) - \frac{1}{2}\tau^2 \bar{y} \right]$$

and

$$V^r (N, \hat{\tau}) = (1 - p) y^r + p \left[(1 - \imath) y^r + \left(\imath - \frac{1}{2}\tau^2 \right) \bar{y} \right]$$

$$= y^r + p \left[\tau (\bar{y} - y^r) - \frac{1}{2}\tau^2 \bar{y} \right].$$

Given these payoffs, it is easy to see that the poor prefer to revolt against N if $\mu^S > \theta + p\left[\hat{\tau}(\lambda - \theta) - \frac{1}{2}\hat{\tau}^2\lambda\right]$.

In order to reduce the number of cases, Acemoglu and Robinson assume $\mu^L < \theta$ so that the poor never revolt in state L. This leaves us with three cases:

(1) Suppose that $\mu^H < \theta$. Then the revolution constraint does not bind in either case. Thus, the unique SPNE consists of N, a tax rate of 0, and no revolution.

(2) Suppose that $\mu^H > \theta + (\lambda - \theta)^2/(2\lambda)$. Then even democracy does not deter the poor from revolting, so a revolution occurs.

(3) Suppose that $\theta + (\lambda - \theta)^2/(2\lambda) > \mu^H > \theta$. In this case, it may be possible for the rich to prevent a revolution by accommodating the poor with a tax rate $\hat{\tau}$. From the preceding we know that doing so requires that the rich set the tax rate so that

$$p < \frac{\mu^H - \theta}{\hat{\tau}(\lambda - \theta) - \frac{1}{2}\hat{\tau}^2\lambda}.$$

If $p < (\mu^H - \theta)/(\tau^p(\lambda - \theta) - 1/2\tau^{p2}\lambda) = 2\lambda(\mu^H - \theta)/(\lambda - \theta)^2$, however, the rich prefer D rather than setting of the tax rate higher than τ^p. Thus, there is a critical value of $p^* = 2\lambda(\mu^H - \theta)/(\lambda - \theta)^2$ such that democracy is the outcome if $p^* > p$. Thus, when the rich have difficulty committing to a high tax rate, they can prevent revolution by transitioning to democracy.

To generate some predictions about when democratic transitions are likely to occur, we can examine how p^* is affected by changes in the parameters. Not surprisingly, p^* is increasing in μ^H, suggesting that when the costs of revolution are low, the rich are more likely to support democratization. Second, p^* and the likelihood of democracy are decreasing in θ. This is true because greater inequality makes revolution a more attractive option for the poor. In turn, the rich have to make more concessions to prevent it. If committing to these concessions is sufficiently difficult, a democratic transition occurs.

8. Application: A Model of Coalition Formation

One of the earliest applications of political game theory is the study of coalition formation (Riker 1962). The earliest models were developed within the cooperative game theoretic and social choice traditions, but there have been a number of recent applications using noncooperative bargaining models.

In this section, we examine a model of coalition governments developed by Austen-Smith and Banks (1988). There are three parties α, β, and γ, who have known policy positions p_α, p_β, and p_γ on a single dimensional policy space $P \subset \mathbb{R}$ where $p_\alpha > p_\beta > p_\gamma$. Let $w = \{\omega_\alpha, \omega_\beta, \omega_\gamma\}$ be the vector of vote shares for the parties in the last election. All vote shares are less than $1/2$ so that the government must be a coalition. To simplify matters, these vote shares are exogenous parameters, whereas Austen-Smith and Banks derive them endogenously from a model of voting. If $C \subset \Omega = \{\alpha, \beta, \gamma\}$ is a coalition of parties, the vote share of coalition C is given by

$$\omega_C = \sum_{k \in C} \omega_k.$$

Coalition C is a winning coalition if $\omega_C > 1/2$; under the assumption that all vote shares are less than $1/2$ any coalition with at least two parties is a winning coalition.

The three parties bargain over the formation of a new government. In doing so, they choose a policy $y \in P$ and allocate a fixed set of portfolios G. As in Austen-Smith and Banks, we assume that G is infinitely divisible and that the allocations $\mathbf{g} = \{g_\alpha, g_\beta, g_\gamma\}$ satisfy $\sum_{k \in C} g_k = G$.

Each party has separable utility functions with quadratic payoffs over policy and additive linear payoffs over portfolios. Therefore, the payoff to party k from policy y and allocation $\mathbf{g}$ is given by

$$-(y - p_k)^2 + g_k.$$

The protocol for bargaining is as follows. First, the party with the largest vote share, say k, is selected as formateur and chooses a coalition. The formatuer then proposes a policy y_k and an allocation $\mathbf{g}_k$. If its coalition partners accept, y_k and g_k are implemented and the game ends. If one of the coalition partners vetoes, however, the second largest party becomes the formatuer, selects a coalition and proposes y_l and $\mathbf{g}_l$. If this is defeated, the smallest party becomes the formatuer. If the smallest party is unsuccessful, a caretaker government takes office and maintains a status quo policy p_q and chooses $g_c = \{0, 0, 0\}$.

We solve this game via backward induction. At each proposal stage, $j \in \{\alpha, \beta, \gamma, c\}$, let v_i^j be the utility of party i, for $i \in \{\alpha, \beta, \gamma\}$. The payoffs to party i from a caretaker government are $v_k^c = -(p_q - p_k)^2$. To simplify, we assume that $v_k^c < -(p_j - p_k)^2$ for all j and k so that any party k prefers party j's ideal point and a 0 share of the portfolios to a caretaker government. Formally, this requires that $p_q \notin [2p_\gamma - p_\alpha, 2p_\alpha - p_\gamma]$.

First, consider vote shares such that $\omega_\alpha > \omega_\beta > \omega_\gamma$. In the third stage party γ is the formateur. By assumption, all parties prefer $y_\gamma = p_\gamma$ and $\mathbf{g}_\gamma = (0, 0, G)$ to the caretaker government so this must be party γ's optimal choice.

In stage 2, party β makes the proposal. The utilities of defeating any proposal by party β and moving to party γ's proposal stage are $v_\gamma^\gamma = G$ and $v_\alpha^\gamma = -(p_\gamma - p_\alpha)^2$. Because γ receives the highest possible utility from voting against β's offer, β must make an offer to party α. Because α prefers $y_\beta = p_\beta$ and $\mathbf{g}_\beta = (0, G, 0)$ to a government formed by γ, α accepts β's ideal point and requires no portfolios.

In the first stage of the game α makes a proposal. The utilities from defeating party α's proposal and moving to party β's proposal stage are $v_\beta^\beta = G$ and $v_\gamma^\beta = -(p_\beta - p_\gamma)^2$. Clearly, α has nothing to offer β and tries to form a coalition with γ. Thus, α chooses y_α and g_γ to maximize $-(y_\alpha - p_\alpha)^2 + G - g_\gamma$ subject to $-(y_\alpha - p_\gamma)^2 + g_\gamma \geq -(p_\beta - p_\gamma)^2$ and $G \geq g_\gamma \geq 0$.[3] There are three cases depending on whether or not the corner solutions $g_\gamma^* = G$ or $g_\gamma^* = 0$ are valid.

(1) If $p_\alpha - p_\beta \geq p_\beta - p_\gamma$ and $G \geq \frac{1}{4}(p_\alpha - p_\gamma)^2 - (p_\beta - p_\gamma)^2$, $y_\alpha^* = (p_\alpha + p_\gamma)/2$ and $g_\gamma^* = \frac{1}{4}(p_\alpha - p_\gamma)^2 - (p_\beta - p_\gamma)^2$.

(2) If $p_\alpha - p_\beta \geq p_\beta - p_\gamma$ and $G < \frac{1}{4}(p_\alpha - p_\gamma)^2 - (p_\beta - p_\gamma)^2$, $y_\alpha^* = p_\gamma + \sqrt{G + (p_\beta - p_\gamma)^2}$ and $g_\gamma^* = G$.

(3) If $p_\alpha - p_\beta < p_\beta - p_\gamma$, $y_\alpha^* = p_\beta$ and $g_\gamma^* = 0$.

In the first two cases, the distance from α's ideal point and p_β is greater than the distance from p_β to γ's ideal point. Thus, party α is willing to give up portfolios and offers a compromise policy. When G is sufficiently large, α offers the compromise policy $y_\alpha^* = (p_\alpha + p_\gamma)/2$, reflecting an optimal trade-off in its policy goals and its desire to hold portfolios. When G is small, however, α is willing to give up all of the

[3] A review of constrained optimization is contained in the Mathematical Appendix.

portfolios in order to move policy in the direction of its ideal point. Finally, in the last case, α is sufficiently well off under p_β compared to γ that α is unwilling to compensate γ for moving policy toward its ideal point. An interesting feature of this outcome is that the coalition is a *nonconnected* one of the extreme parties. This finding contrasts with arguments stressing that policy-motivated parties form coalitions with ideological allies (Axelrod 1970).

Now consider the case where $\omega_\beta > \omega_\alpha > \omega_\gamma$. Once again γ chooses $y_\gamma^* = p_\gamma$ and $\mathbf{g}_\gamma = (0, 0, G)$ in the last period. Now consider α's choice in the second period. Clearly, it has nothing to offer γ and therefore tries to build a coalition with β. Thus, α chooses y_α and g_β to maximize $-(y_\alpha - p_\alpha)^2 + G - g_\beta$ subject to $-(y_\alpha - p_\beta)^2 + g_\beta \geq -(p_\beta - p_\gamma)^2$ and $G \geq g_\beta \geq 0$. The solution has four distinct cases.

(1) If $(p_\alpha + p_\beta)/2 \geq 2p_\beta - p_\gamma$ and $G \geq \frac{1}{4}(p_\alpha - p_\beta)^2 - (p_\beta - p_\gamma)^2$,
$y_\alpha^* = (p_\alpha + p_\beta)/2$ and $g_\beta^* = \frac{1}{4}(p_\alpha - p_\beta)^2 - (p_\beta - p_\gamma)^2$.
(2) If $(p_\alpha + p_\beta)/2 \geq 2p_\beta - p_\gamma$ and $G < 1/4(p_\alpha - p_\beta)^2 - (p_\beta - p_\gamma)^2$,
$y_\alpha^* = p_\beta + \sqrt{G + (p_\beta - p_\gamma)^2}$ and $g_\beta^* = G$.
(3) If $p_\alpha > 2p_\beta - p_\gamma > (p_\alpha + p_\beta)/2$, $y_\alpha^* = 2p_\beta - p_\gamma$ and $g_\beta^* = 0$.
(4) If $p_\alpha < 2p_\beta - p_\gamma$, $y_\alpha^* = p_\alpha$ and $g_\beta^* = 0$.

In the last two cases, the bargaining between α and β is analogous to the Romer-Rosenthal setter game over policies with a reversion of p_γ. In cases 1 and 2, party α makes portfolio concessions to move policy further than the Romer-Rosenthal inflection point of $2p_\beta - p_\gamma$.

Despite the complexity of these cases, the important point to note is that $y_\alpha^* > p_\beta$ and $g_\alpha^* = 0$ is predicted. Thus, when party β makes its offer in the first period, it knows that party γ accepts $y_\beta^* = p_\beta$ and $g_\gamma^* = 0$. Thus, the subgame perfect Nash equilibrium outcomes are $y^* = p_\beta$ and $\mathbf{g}^* = (0, G, 0)$. This case generates a connected coalition that implements the ideal point of the median party.

We leave proofs for the remaining cases as exercises. Table 7.5 summarizes the outcomes for all cases.

A key point of the Austen-Smith and Banks model is that composition of the government and the policies it implements are driven by the voting weights that determine the sequence of proposals. Because these weights are determined by voting behavior, the key to making predictions is an understanding of how voters behave in anticipation

Table 7.5. Outcomes of Austen-Smith and Banks's Model		
Case	Governing Coalition	Policy
$\omega_\alpha > \omega_\beta > \omega_\gamma$	α and γ	$\frac{p_\alpha + p_\gamma}{2}$
$\omega_\beta > \omega_\alpha > \omega_\gamma$	β and γ	p_β
$\omega_\beta > \omega_\gamma > \omega_\alpha$	β and α	p_β
$\omega_\alpha > \omega_\gamma > \omega_\beta$	α and β	$\frac{p_\alpha + p_\beta}{2}$
$\omega_\gamma > \omega_\alpha > \omega_\beta$	γ and β	$\frac{p_\gamma + p_\beta}{2}$
$\omega_\gamma > \omega_\beta > \omega_\alpha$	γ and α	$\frac{p_\alpha + p_\gamma}{2}$

of the parliamentary bargaining. We refer the reader to the original for an analysis of the voting game.

9. Exercises

EXERCISE 7.1 *Represent the Centipede game as a normal form game. Characterize the set of Nash equilibra to this game.*

EXERCISE 7.2 *Prove that the strategy profile (R, G and T) is the only perfect equilibrium in the revolution game depicted in Table 7.2.*

EXERCISE 7.3 *Diane is collecting money for the Center for the Study of Democratic Politics coffee fund. She needs to collect $2 from at least three faculty members to operate the fund for the month. No member can contribute more that $2 and Diane cannot exclude non-contributors from drinking coffee. Each center member has an estimated $10 benefit from coffee service. If less than $6 is contributed, Diane keeps the money and no coffee is provided. If more than $6 is contributed, Diane provides the coffee and pockets the difference.*

(1) *Diane decides to ask the faculty members in the following order: Arnold, Bartels, Lewis, Prior, and Romer. Each faculty member can observe past contribution choices. What are the set of Nash equilibria to this game? What is the unique Nash equilibrium that survives backward induction?*

(2) *Now modify the game somewhat so that Lewis, Prior, and Romer do not know whether or not Arnold and Bartels contributed.*

Further, suppose that Lewis, Prior, and Romer must decide simultaneously. Draw a game tree for this game in extensive form.
Pay particular attention to the information sets. What are the subgame perfect equilibria to this game? Does Diane do better or
worse in this game?

(3) Now let Diane choose the information structure of the game (i.e.,
she can choose which contribution decisions are revealed at which
stage). Suppose she wants to maximize the amount of money she
keeps and does not care about coffee consumption. Which game
should she choose?

EXERCISE 7.4 *Consider the sequential bargaining problem. Show that
the strategy*

*Player 1: Propose $x_2 = \delta$. If the offer is rejected, accept any offer in
round 2.*
*Player 2: Accept in round 1 if $x_2 \geq \delta$; reject otherwise and then propose
$x_2 = \delta$ in round 2.*

*is the unique subgame perfect Nash equilibrium. Hint: Start by showing
that a strategy by player 1 that accepts any period 2 offer only if it gives her
at least $\varepsilon > 0$ cannot involve a Nash equilibrium in subgames following
a failed first-period offer.*

EXERCISE 7.5 *Consider a bargaining problem with two players. Suppose
player 1 makes an offer (x_1^1, x_2^1) to player 2 where x_j^i denotes the amount
that player j would get if the offer made by player i were accepted. In
period 1 player 1 proposes a split of \$1 (i.e., the proposals sum to 1 and
are nonnegative). Player 2 then accepts or rejects. If she accepts then
the split is consumed. If she rejects then player 2 makes an offer to split
$\delta < 1$ (so the proposals sum to δ and are nonnegative). Player 1 then
decides to accept or reject the offer. If player 1 accepts, player 2's split
is consumed. If it is rejected, however, each player consumes $\delta/2$. Both
players want to maximize their own consumption. Find the subgame
perfect Nash equilibrium of this game.*

EXERCISE 7.6 *This exercise is based on Groseclose (1999). There are
N legislators with policy preferences $u_i(x)$ for $x \in \mathbb{R}$. They vote over a
bill x_B and the status quo x_0 where $x_B > x_0$. So let $\alpha_i = u_i(x_B) - u_i(x_0)$,
the degree of preference for x_B over x_0 for legislator i. Each legislator's
policy payoff for voting for the bill is α_i whether or not the bill passes.
There are two vote buyers, L and R, with net preference parameters α_L*

and α_R, respectively. Vote buyer L wants to defeat x_B so that $\alpha_L < 0$ while R wants to pass it as $\alpha_R > 0$. Consider the following model. R moves first and offers z_i^R to each legislator who agrees to vote for the bill. L moves second and offers z_i^L to each legislator in exchange for voting against x_B. Thus, the payoff for voting in favor of x_B is $\alpha_i + z_i^R$ whereas the payoff for voting against is $-\alpha_i + z_i^L$.

(1) Let $N = 5$ and $\alpha_i = -3 + i$ for $i = 1, \dots, 5$. Characterize the subgame perfect Nash equilibrium to this game for arbitrary levels of α_L and α_R.

(2) Can the winning coalition be larger than a bare majority?

EXERCISE 7.7 Consider a one-player game in which player 1 selects A or B. If she chooses A then she selects between C and D. If she chooses B then she selects between E and F. Let the payoffs from each path be as follows: $u(A, C) = u_1, u(A, D) = u_2, u(B, E) = u_3, u(B, F) = u_4$. For arbitrary values of u_1, u_2, u_3, u_4 provide a direct proof that the single-deviation principle applies to this game. Specifically show that if a strategy is not subgame perfect then a profitable single deviation exists.

EXERCISE 7.8 (*) Consider an extensive form game in which each player moves at exactly one information set (the mapping $p(\cdot)$ is a bijection). Moreover, assume that each information set is a singleton. Show that in any such game the set of subgame perfect Nash equilibria coincides with the set of Nash equilibria that are perfect in the normal form.

EXERCISE 7.9 Derive the policy outcome and governing coalitions for the remaining cases of the Austen-Smith and Banks (1988) model.

8 Dynamic Games of Incomplete Information

In Chapter 6, we learned that uncertainty about the preferences of other players fundamentally alters the strategic situation in static normal form games. In dynamic, multistage games uncertainty leads to even more interesting strategic possibilities. Reconsider the revolution game depicted in Figure 7.1. The unique subgame perfect equilibrium involves a revolt by the colony and the grant of independence, $(R, (G, T))$. Now consider the game depicted in Figure 8.1. In contrast with the game of Figure 7.1, nation B incurs no cost from using force to suppress a revolution.

Now the unique subgame perfect equilibrium is $(C, (S, T))$. This chapter addresses the following question: How should nation A behave if it is not sure which figure accurately describes the game?

We now consider games in which players face uncertainty about preferences of other players. Games of this form involve *incomplete information*. As in Chapter 6, we model such uncertainty using the Harsanyi maneuver. Uncertainty about the payoffs of other players is modeled as a game in which players are uncertain about which node of the game they are located on. This trick involves the use of a fictitious player – Nature – who randomly selects players' types from a known probability distribution. Not all players, however, observe the realization of Nature's draw. To model a situation in which player i does not know player j's preferences, we assume that Nature chooses player j's payoffs (type) prior to agent i's decision, and we model player i as facing an information set with multiple nodes because she does not observe the choice by Nature. This trick converts games of incomplete information – agents do not know the game – to games of imperfect

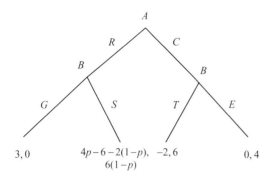

Figure 8.1. Modified Revolution Game.

information – agents know the game but not exactly where they are in the game.[1]

To make these issues more concrete, consider a model of conflict between two nations. Country A first chooses whether or not to initiate a conflict. If no conflict is initiated, the game ends. On the other hand, if A initiates conflict then nation B decides whether to acquiesce or escalate. Suppose that the payoffs from this interaction can be given by either Table 8.1 or Table 8.2.

Table 8.1. Game I

If A does not initiate (0, 0)

If A initiates and B acquiesces (4, −4)

If A initiates and B escalates (−8, −8)

Table 8.2. Game II

If A does not initiate (0, 0)

If A initiates and B acquiesces (4, −4)

If A initiates and B escalates (−8, −3)

---

[1] Games of incomplete information problematize notions of equilibrium. But as Mertens and Zamir (1985) have shown, subject to some very technical conditions, any description of incomplete information can be characterized as a Bayesian game.

Suppose that game I is played with probability p and game II is played with probability $1 - p$. Several distinct information structures are possible.

(1) Suppose neither country observes Nature's move as in Figure 8.2. Then we say that information is imperfect but symmetric in that both players find themselves in the same situation. This game is easy to analyze because we need only compute country B's expected utility of escalation and modify the game accordingly. Because B's expected utility of escalation is $-p8 - 3(1 - p) = -3 - 5p$, it prefers escalation whenever $p < 1/5$. Thus, if $p < 1/5$, the outcome is {*Do Not Initiate, Escalate*}; otherwise it is {*Initiate, Acquiesce*}.

(2) Suppose that only B observes Nature's move as in Figure 8.3. This information structure implies that A is uncertain of B's choice. Because B escalates only in game II, A's expected utility from initiating is $4p - (1 - p)8 = -8 + 12p$. Thus, A prefers initiating only if $p > 2/3$.

(3) Suppose that only A observes Nature's move as in Figure 8.4. This game has asymmetric information. The strategic situation is altered dramatically. Whereas B does not know Nature's choice, it knows that A knows it. Thus, A must consider what information her choices provide about Nature's draw. To illustrate that these informational incentives affect behavior, consider a natural way of playing the game where A initiates in game I, but not

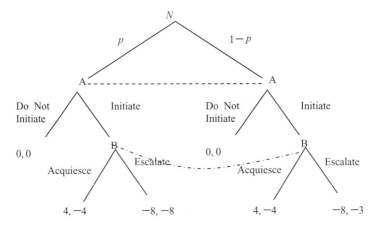

Figure 8.2. Information Structure I.

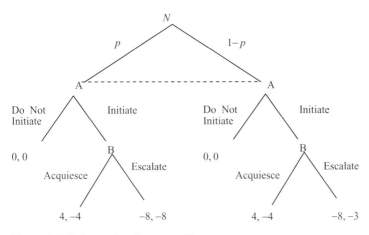

Figure 8.3. Information Structure II.

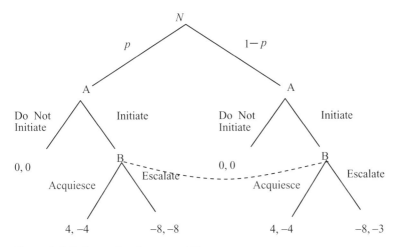

Figure 8.4. Information Structure III.

in game II. If *A* plays these strategies, *B* infers from *A*'s initiation that they are playing game I and acquiesces. If *B* responds in this way, however, *A* has a strong incentive to defect by initiating even in game II.

In this chapter, we focus on the strategic use of information in dynamic settings. Incomplete information raises a number of important issues.

- *Strategic Use of Information*: Does any of the players have a strategic advantage based on the way information is allocated? In many games, informed players have important advantages. But sometimes the uninformed player is advantaged – ignorance can be bliss!
- *Learning*: Can the uninformed players get more information from observing the actions of the informed players? How do these possibilities affect the strategies of the informed players?
- *Signaling*: Can the informed players credibly communicate information about the game to the uninformed players? Can informed players mislead uninformed players?

1. Perfect Bayesian Equilibria

Although subgame perfection rules out some unreasonable Nash equilibria, many extensive form games with imperfectly observed actions require a stronger equilibrium concept. Consider the extensive form game depicted in Figure 8.5. It models the incentives for a naval fleet action prior to the invention of radar. Player 1 chooses whether to deploy military capability secretly to attack an island. She chooses to send a small fleet of ships (S), to send a big fleet of ships (B), or not to deploy any ships, ND. Player 2 only observes whether there was a deployment. Lookouts, relying only on telescopes, can see the ships approaching but cannot determine how many there are. If there is no deployment player 2 keeps the island, and the payoffs are $(0, 5)$. If there is a deployment, player 2 decides whether to respond to the attack (R). If there is no response (NR) player 1 wins the island. If there

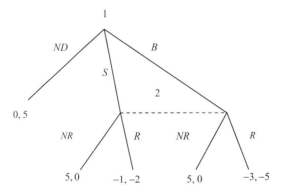

Figure 8.5. Naval Deployment Game.

is a response, player 2 wins the island, but the casualties for player 2 are much higher under S than under B. The casualties for player 1 are higher under B than under S.

There are three Nash equilibria to this game. The first is (ND, R) where player 1 does not deploy, but if she did, player 2 would respond. The second Nash equilibrium is (B, NR) – player 1 deploys a big line of ships, and player 2 does not respond. The profile (S, NR) is also an equilibrium.

There is something odd about the first Nash equilibrium. Regardless of whether B or S is played, player 2 is better off playing NR. Should not player 1 recognize this and send the ships? In the last chapter, we used subgame perfection to eliminate similar problems, but subgame perfection fails in this case. Because this game has no proper subgames, (NS, R) is also a subgame perfect Nash equilibrium.

The argument that this profile is unreasonable is predicated on the notion that player 1 should anticipate a rational response from player 2 at player 2's information set. The goal is to incorporate this type of *sequential rationality* into an equilibrium concept. This is accomplished by requiring that agents form *beliefs* about the history reached at each information set and select best responses given these beliefs. These equilibria are called perfect Bayesian equilibria (or PBE).

Returning to the example, no belief about the history of play at player 2's information set justifies the selection of R as a best response. Player 2 believes that either S or B has been played and that ships have been deployed. In either case, she is better off choosing NR.

This example is rather trivial, so now consider a more interesting example. Suppose that player 1 wins the island only if she selects B.

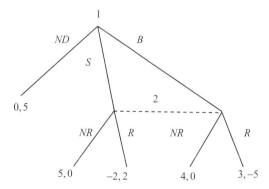

Figure 8.6. Naval Deployment Game II.

Moreover, player 2 prefers to defend the island if player 1 has selected S. Figure 8.6 represents the relevant payoffs.

In this version, whether R or NR is sequentially rational depends on what beliefs player 2 assigns to the two possible histories in her information set. If she believes that S was played then R is sequentially rational. Conversely if she believes that B was played then NR is sequentially rational. What should she believe? Clearly, her beliefs are based on expectations about what player 1 does. But player 1's choice depends on what she expects player 2 to believe. A few definitions help us close this loop.

1.1. Formal Definitions. Recall that an information set may be a singleton or a set containing multiple histories. In extensive form games a player is asked to choose an action at each information set I_j. Because $p(h) = p(h')$ if h and h' are in the same information set, it is unambiguous to write $p(I_J)$ if I_J is an information set. Given a list of information sets, we can define beliefs.

DEFINITION 8.1 *In an extensive form game with imperfectly observed actions, a belief on information set I_j is a probability distribution on I_j. A belief profile is a mapping from the set of histories into the unit interval, $b : H \to [0, 1]$, such that for every history I_j, $b(\cdot)$ is a belief on I_j. For every I_j, $\sum_{h \in I_j} b(h) = 1$ if I_j is finite and $\int_{h \in I_j} db(h) = 1$ if I_j is infinite.*

So in the preceding examples, a belief on player 2's information set is a probability distribution over $\{S, B\}$. A *belief profile* describes a complete list of beliefs for all information sets. Because only one player makes a decision at each information set (the mapping $p(\cdot)$ is a function), there is no ambiguity about whose beliefs are relevant on each portion of the belief profile. If player i is called to make a choice at information set I_j then the portion of the belief profile that describes the belief at information set I_j describes player i's belief on I_j at the time that i chooses.

We now define a condition on strategies known as *sequential rationality*. Loosely speaking, sequential rationality requires that all strategies are optimal at each information set given a specific belief profile. To formalize this idea, let $p(I_j)$ denote the player and $s(I_j)$ denote the action specified at information set I_j. These terms are equivalent to $p(h)$ and $s(h)$ when $h \in I_j$. For a fixed strategy profile, $s(\cdot)$, denote the expected utility of player $p(I_j)$ associated with choice a at history h by $Eu_{p(h)}(a, h, s(\cdot))$. This is an expected utility because other players may play mixed strategies. If player $p(I_j)$ assigns probability $b(h)$ to history $h \in I_j$ (conditional upon being at the information set I_j), the expected utility of taking action a at information set I_j is

$$Eu_{p(I_j)}(a, I_j, s(\cdot), b(\cdot)) = \sum_{h \in I_j} b(h) \, Eu_{p(h)}(a, h, s(\cdot)).$$

A strategy profile is sequentially rational for a given belief profile if it specifies optimal actions at each information set. Optimality requires that players evaluate the desirability of action a using $Eu_{p(I_j)}(a, I_j, s(\cdot), b(\cdot))$.[2]

DEFINITION 8.2 *Given an extensive form game with imperfectly observed actions and belief $b(\cdot)$ on each information set, the strategy profile $s(\cdot)$ is sequentially rational at information set I_j if*

$$Eu_{p(I_j)}(s(I_j), I_j, s(\cdot), b(\cdot)) \geq Eu_{p(I_j)}(s', I_j, s(\cdot), b(\cdot))$$

for all available actions s'. If the strategy profile is sequentially rational at every information set, then it is sequentially rational.

Returning to the example in Figure 8.6, if the beliefs assign a probability close to 1 on S then R is sequentially rational at the information set. Similarly, if player 2 believes B is sufficiently likely then NR is a sequentially rational response.

Defining perfect Bayesian equilibrium formally requires an additional condition on beliefs. *Weak consistency* of beliefs requires that, whenever possible, agents use Bayes' rule to formulate their beliefs at I_j.[3] In order to compute the probability of history h conditional on reaching information set I_j, we require the probability of reaching this information set. Of course, the probability of reaching I_j depends on the strategy profile. Let $\Pr(I_j|s(\cdot))$ denote the probability that I_j is reached conditional on the strategy profile $s(\cdot)$. If h is an

---

[2] If there is an infinite set of possible histories, the summation is replaced with integration.

[3] Recall that Bayes' rule generates the probability that event A occurs conditional on the occurrence of event B. This conditional probability is given by $\Pr(A \mid B) = \Pr(A \,\&\, B)/\Pr(B)$.

element of I_j, the probability that h and I_j are both reached under strategy $s(\cdot)$ is simply the probability that h is reached. We denote this probability as $\Pr(h|s(\cdot))$ and conclude that $\Pr(I_j \& h|s(\cdot)) = \Pr(h|s(\cdot))$. Therefore, Bayes' rule implies that the probability of reaching history $h \in I_j$ conditional on reaching information set I_j under strategy profile $s(\cdot)$ is

$$\Pr(h \mid I_j, s(\cdot)) = \frac{\Pr(h|\, s(\cdot))}{\Pr(I_j|\, s(\cdot))}.$$

DEFINITION 8.3 *Given an extensive form game with imperfectly observed actions and a strategy profile $s(\cdot)$, the beliefs $b(\cdot)$ are weakly consistent relative to strategy $s(\cdot)$ if $b(h) = \Pr(h \mid I_j, s(\cdot))$ whenever $\Pr(I_j \mid s(\cdot)) > 0$.*

Combining weak consistency of beliefs and sequential rationality of strategies yields the perfect Bayesian equilibrium concept.

DEFINITION 8.4 *Given an extensive form game with imperfectly observed actions, a perfect Bayesian equilibrium (PBE) is a pair $(s(\cdot), b(\cdot))$ such that: (1) the strategy profile $s(\cdot)$ is sequentially rational relative to the belief $b(\cdot)$, and (2) the belief $b(\cdot)$ is weakly consistent relative to the strategy profile $s(\cdot)$.*

If I_j is not reached under $s(\cdot)$ then $\Pr(I_j|\, s(\cdot)) = 0$, and Bayes' rule is undefined. Weak consistency places no requirements on beliefs at these "out of equilibrium" information sets. This ambiguity is sometimes problematic; it implies that there may be many different perfect Bayesian equilibria based on different specifications of beliefs at unreached information sets.[4]

---

[4] A caution about terminology is in order. Some scholars use the term *consistency* for what we call weak consistency; they then use the same label to describe a stronger concept that applies to sequential equilibria. We prefer to use two distinct terms for these conditions and to defer defining the stronger notion until later in this chapter. Also, some authors add several additional off-the-path conditions to the definition of perfect Bayesian equilibrium. Informally these conditions require that the (1) actions of agent i do not cause anyone else to update his beliefs about the type of agent j if agent i does not have additional information about agent j's type, and (2) players form beliefs that are consistent with a common joint distribution on the types. In games with two players these additional requirements are irrelevant; with more than two players they often matter. Few applications in political science require these additional

Returning to the game in Figure 8.5, we now characterize PBE. Clearly the Nash equilibrium (ND, R) is not a PBE. For any beliefs about whether player 1 chooses S or B, NR is the unique sequentially rational response. Given that player 2 chooses NR, player 1's optimal choice is to play either S or B. Now if player 1 chooses B then weakly consistent beliefs assign probability 1 to player 2's moving at history B. Thus, one PBE is (B, NR), $\Pr(B \mid \tilde{}ND) = 1$ where $\Pr(B \mid \tilde{}ND)$ is the posterior probability of B given that player 1 did not choose ND. Similarly there exists a PBE where (S, NR) and $\Pr(B \mid \tilde{}ND) = 0$.

Now consider the game in Figure 8.6. If player 2 believes that $\Pr(B \mid \tilde{}ND) = 1$, NR is the best response. On the other hand, if player 2 believes that $\Pr(B \mid \tilde{}ND) = 0$ then R is the best response. One candidate PBE is (ND, R) and $\Pr(B \mid \tilde{}ND) = 0$. Because weak consistency does not impose any constraints on beliefs when player 1 plays ND, the belief $\Pr(B \mid \tilde{}ND) = 0$ is weakly consistent relative to the strategy ND. But the strategy profile (ND, R) is not sequentially rational; player 1 prefers to play B rather than ND when she conjectures that player 2 plays R. It is also clear that ND cannot be a best response to NR.

Now suppose there is a pure strategy PBE in which ND is not played. If B is played and beliefs are weakly consistent, the only sequentially rational strategy by player 2 involves NR. But if player 1 conjectures that player 2 is playing NR she wants to play S. So B cannot be part of a pure strategy PBE profile. On the other hand, if player 1 chooses S, weakly consistent beliefs assign probability 1 to player 2's moving at history S. Thus, the only sequentially rational action involves playing R. But if player 1 conjectures that player 2 is playing R then she wants to play B. Thus, there is no pure strategy PBE in which S is played. Consequently, there are no pure strategy PBEs.

There are, however, mixed strategy PBEs. Suppose that player 1 plays B with probability q and S with probability $(1 - q)$. Player 2 plays R with probability z and NR with probability $(1 - z)$. Weak consistency of beliefs requires that $\Pr(B \mid \tilde{}ND) = q$. A mixed strategy equilibrium requires that player 2 be indifferent between R and NR following $\tilde{}ND$ so that $q(-5) + (1 - q)2 = 0$ or $q = 2/7$. Similarly, player 1 must be indifferent between B and S so that $(1 - z)5 + z(-2) = (1 - z)4 + z3$

conditions. For this reason, as well as a preference for using sequential equilibria when our definition of PBE is insufficient, we do not present the alternative definition of PBE. Interested readers should consult Chapter 8 of Fudenberg and Tirole (1991).

or $z = 1/6$. Accordingly, the strategy profile in which player 1 chooses S with probability 5/7 and B with probability 2/7 and player 2 chooses R with probability 1/6 and NR with probability 5/6 following $\tilde{} ND$ is supportable as a PBE given the beliefs $\Pr(B \mid \tilde{} ND) = 2/7$.

2. Signaling Games

An important class of games of imperfect information involve interaction between a more informed agent, the *sender*, and a less informed agent, the *receiver*. When the sender moves first the game is called a signaling game. These games take their name from the possibility that the sender's action conveys information about her type to the receiver. We focus on the simplest possible signaling game to demonstrate the incentives agents face and to emphasize the various types of equilibria that might exist.

Let Nature draw a type $\theta \in \{a, b\}$ for player 1. Player 1 observes her type and chooses a *message* $m \in \{a, b\}$. Player 2 observes the message but does not observe player 1's type. Following the message,

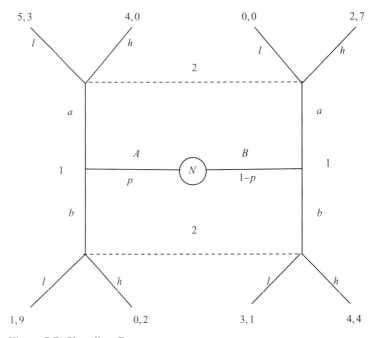

Figure 8.7. Signaling Game.

player 2 chooses a *policy* $p \in \{a, b\}$. The payoffs to each player from a type action pair are denoted $u_i(p, \theta)$. Figure 8.7 depicts the game form.

In this game player 2 faces information sets with multiple histories. These sets are represented by the dotted lines. When player 2 selects a policy, she knows player 1's message, but she does not know the state selected by Nature.

This game is most interesting if $u_2(p, \theta) > u_2(p', \theta)$ and $u_2(p', \theta') > u_2(p, \theta')$ for $p \neq p'$ and $\theta \neq \theta'$. Informally, this condition implies that player 2 wants to know θ before selecting p. This condition is satisfied in the case of opposed preferences. Suppose that θ affects the desirability of each policy to each agent: player 1 wants to match θ and p while player 2 wants the pair to be unmatched ($\theta \neq p$). To be even more concrete, suppose a legislature (agent 2) is choosing between the status quo, a, and a new policy, b. It is uncertain about the consequences of the new policy. The legislature wants to select a policy that results in an outcome to the right of the status quo. An informed expert (agent 1) gives unverifiable testimony before Congress about whether b results in an outcome to the right or to the left of the status quo. The expert does not share the legislature's preferences; she prefers a policy that results in an outcome to the left of a. Let $\theta = a$ denote information that b results in an outcome to the right of a and $\theta = b$ denote information that b results in an outcome to the left of a. Thus, θ is a signal about which policy the legislature actually prefers.

In this game player 1's action is *cheap talk* because agent 2 cannot verify the accuracy of 1's speech, and there is no cost to lying. The assumption that player 1 (the legislature) wants to match p and θ while player 2 (the expert) does not results in the following ordering of payoffs.

$$u_1(b, a) < u_1(a, a)$$
$$u_1(a, b) < u_1(b, b)$$
$$u_2(b, a) > u_2(a, a)$$
$$u_2(a, b) > u_2(b, b).$$

To specify a model of imperfect information, we further specify prior beliefs over the state θ. Suppose that $\theta = a$ with probability $\pi > 1/2$.

The natural first question is whether there is a PBE in which player 1, the sender, reveals her private information to the receiver. This specification requires that she use one of the following strategies:

$$m(\theta) = \begin{cases} a \text{ if } \theta = a \\ b \text{ if } \theta = b \end{cases}$$

or

$$m(\theta) = \begin{cases} b \text{ if } \theta = a \\ a \text{ if } \theta = b \end{cases} .$$

We begin by focusing on the first message strategy. Strategies of this form are called *fully revealing* because if the receiver knows the strategy and observes the message she can infer the private information. The first strategy is also called *truthful*. If player 1 uses the truthful strategy profile, weak consistency of beliefs requires that

$$b(\theta = a \mid m = a) = \frac{\pi \cdot 1}{\pi \cdot 1 + (1 - \pi) \cdot 0} = 1$$

and

$$b(\theta = a \mid m = b) = \frac{\pi \cdot 0}{\pi \cdot 0 + (1 - \pi) \cdot 1} = 0.$$

Given these beliefs sequential rationality requires that agent 2 select policy according to the following mapping:

$$p(m) = \begin{cases} b \text{ if } m = a \\ a \text{ if } m = b \end{cases} .$$

In verifying that we have characterized a PBE, the last point to check is whether the specified $m(\cdot)$ strategy is sequentially rational. The critical question is whether it represents a best response to the policy mapping $p(\cdot)$. Because $u_1(b, a) < u_1(a, a)$ and $u_1(a, b) < u_1(b, b)$, if player 1 observes that $\theta = a$ she prefers to deviate from the postulated strategy and announce $m = b$, resulting in outcome a. Similarly if player 1 observes $\theta = b$, she gains by deviating and announcing $m = a$. There is, consequently, no PBE in which the truthful message strategy $m(\theta) = \theta$ is employed. We leave for an exercise the demonstration that there cannot be a PBE in which the second fully revealing message strategy is used. The message strategies defined previously are called *separating* because in any PBE in which they are used by the sender, the receiver learns θ.

Although the game does not possess a separating equilibrium, it may have other PBEs. Suppose that the sender sends the same message (say a) regardless of θ. Thus $m(\theta) = a$. Given this message strategy, the receiver learns nothing from observing m. In this case weak consistency of beliefs requires that

$$b(\theta = a \mid m = a) = \frac{\pi \cdot 1}{\pi \cdot 1 + (1 - \pi) \cdot 1} = \pi.$$

What beliefs should the receiver form following an $m = b$? This question is tricky. When we try to use Bayes' rule we get

$$b(\theta = a \mid m = b) = \frac{\pi \cdot 0}{\pi \cdot 0 + (1 - \pi) \cdot 0} = \frac{0}{0}.$$

Because $0/0$ is not a number, Bayes' rule is not well defined. In expressing the posterior beliefs, we conditioned on a history that occurs with 0 probability in the given strategy profile. The definition of weak consistency only requires that beliefs obey Bayes' rule when the denominator is greater than 0. Because weak consistency imposes no constraints on this belief, we are free to specify this posterior in any manner that helps us construct equilibria. Let us say that $b(\theta = a \mid m = b) = \pi$. Given this specification of beliefs, the question of what receiver strategy is sequentially rational requires simply comparing expected utilities. Policy a is more desirable if

$$\pi u_2(a, a) + (1 - \pi)u_2(a, b) \geq \pi u_2(b, a) + (1 - \pi)u_2(b, b).$$

Otherwise policy b is more desirable. Accordingly, if

$$\pi \geq \frac{u_2(b, b) - u_2(a, b)}{u_2(a, a) - u_2(a, b) - u_2(b, a) + u_2(b, b)} \tag{8.1}$$

then given these beliefs sequential rationality of p is satisfied by $p(m) = b$. If the inequality in equation 8.1 is reversed then sequential rationality of p is satisfied with $p(m) = a$. Finally, we must check that the message strategy is sequentially rational given the policy function. This step is trivial. Because the policy function is constant in m, any message function is a best response. Accordingly, we have found an equilibrium of the signaling game. Such an equilibrium is known as a *pooling* equilibrium.

What we assume about $b(\theta = a \mid m = b)$ is important. Let π be sufficiently high that the receiver's best response is b. Now suppose that we set $b(\theta = a \mid m = b) = 0$. Here sequential rationality requires that $p(b) = a$. Thus, sequential rationality implies that when we change the off-the-path beliefs the off-the-path policy action changes.

Can we construct an equilibrium based on these new beliefs that uses the pooling message function $m(\theta) = a$? Suppose the sender observes $\theta = a$. In the conjectured equilibrium she sends the message a. The receiver learns nothing from the message and selects b because $\theta = a$ is more likely (π is high). But now, if our sender deviates from this conjectured strategy and sends the message b, the receiver's response is to select policy a. If this conjectured strategy and belief profile is a PBE, the sender cannot have an incentive to deviate in this way. If $\theta = a$, however, the sender prefers to deviate in order to elicit $p = a$ rather than to adhere to the conjectured equilibrium and elicit $p = b$. Although the pooling message function was supportable as a PBE for some weakly consistent beliefs, it is not supportable as a PBE for all such beliefs. The off-the-path beliefs matter; they generate the incentives for on-the-path behavior.

Another way of constructing pooling equilibria in this game is to use mixed strategies by the sender. Suppose now that regardless of her type the sender sends message a with fixed probability $\sigma \in (0, 1)$. Bayes' rule yields

$$b(\theta = a \mid m = a) = b(\theta = a \mid m = b) = \pi.$$

As before characterizing sequentially rational strategies for the receiver hinges on π. In this pooling equilibrium with mixed messages Bayes' rule pins down the beliefs at every observable information set; no information sets are off the equilibrium path.

In applications, scholars often assume that the type, message, and policy spaces are larger. Additionally, many models consider multiple senders and receivers. Despite the complexity introduced by these generalizations, the same concepts apply. Equilibrium analysis hinges on characterizing beliefs that are weakly consistent given strategies and checking that agents do not have incentives to deviate. In addition to separating and pooling equilibria, more general models may also have partially separating or partially pooling equilibria.[5]

DEFINITION 8.5 *In a general signaling game with multiple senders and one receiver in which each sender has a type space Θ_i, message space M_i, and the receiver has prior beliefs $\pi(\cdot)$ on $\Theta = \times_i \Theta_i$ the following definitions apply: In a separating equilibrium the receiver's posterior beliefs are concentrated at the true state on the equilibrium path. In a pooling equilibrium the posteriors correspond to the priors on the equilibrium path. In a partially separating equilibrium neither of the preceding conditions is true.*

3. Application: Entry Deterrence in Elections

One of the more intriguing puzzles in the study of campaign finance is the question of why incumbent politicians exert so much effort to raise more campaign money than seems necessary to finance their campaigns. A standard explanation is that because fund-raising success signals the incumbent's electoral strength, incumbents raise these sums to deter entry by potential challengers. Epstein and Zemsky (1995) develop a formal model of this argument. Suppose a challenger must decide whether to run against an incumbent, but that the challenger wishes to run only if the incumbent is politically *W*eak. If the incumbent is *S*trong, the challenger prefers to sit out the race. Conventional wisdom suggests that the incumbent may want to signal to the challenger her political strength by raising a large amount of campaign monies. If this *war chest* convinces the challenger that the incumbent is strong, he is deterred from entering.

To capture this intuition in a model, let p be the prior probability that the challenger (C) assigns to the incumbent's (I) being strong (S). Conversely, $1 - p$ is the probability that the incumbent is weak (W). For simplicity, both C and I receive 1 unit of utility from elected office. Let the probability that C wins against W be π_w and the probability that C wins against S be π_s. Naturally, $\pi_w > \pi_s$. Let k be C's cost of

---

[5] Those who see the glass half-empty will probably prefer the term *partially pooling*. Others will find *partially separating* more in line with their philosophy of life. We choose to randomize in our usage of the terms.

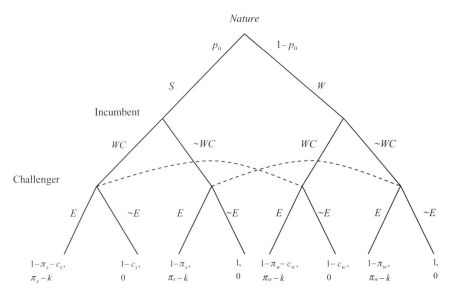

Figure 8.8. Campaign War Chest Game.

running. So that the model is interesting, we assume that $\pi_w > k > \pi_s$ because if $k > \pi_w$, C never enters, and if $k < \pi_s$ he always enters.

The key assumption of the model is that S and W incur different costs when raising a war chest. Politically strong incumbents raise money much more easily than weaker ones. To keep matters simple, we focus on whether or not the incumbent builds a war chest; we do not allow the incumbent to choose various size war chests.[6] Thus, the incumbent's strategy set is $S_I = \{WC, \,^\sim WC\}$ where WC is the decision to build a war chest and $^\sim WC$ is the decision to forgo one. By $s_I \in S_I$ we denote the strategy chosen by I. Types W and S must pay c_w and c_s, respectively, to build a war chest where $c_s < c_w$. The probability that the incumbent wins depends only on his type. The war chest has no direct effect on the election, but as we shall see it may have an indirect effect. After observing whether I builds a war chest, C decides whether to enter the race E or sit it out $^\sim E$. Figure 8.8 provides the extensive form of this game.[7]

Consider the last stage of the game. Sequential rationality requires that C enter only if the expected utility of entering is greater

---

[6] This assumption is relaxed in Epstein and Zemsky's (1995) original model.

[7] We can also present the game in Figure 8.8 in a manner similar to that in Figure 8.7. We depict both approaches to familiarize readers with different graphical presentations.

than or equal to k. Consequently, entry requires that $\pi_s \Pr\{S|s_I\} + \pi_w \Pr\{W|s_I\} \geq k$.

In the first period, W and S choose whether to build war chests. There are three possible types of equilibria:

(1) *Separating*: S and W choose different strategies.
(2) *Pooling*: S and W choose identical strategies.
(3) *Semipooling*: S and W choose different mixed strategies.

3.1. Separating Equilibria. First we consider a separating equilibrium in which the strong incumbent builds a war chest, and the weak incumbent does not. Given this strategy profile, the challenger learns the incumbent's type in equilibrium. Because $\pi_w > k > \pi_s$, she enters only if the incumbent does not build a war chest.

PROPOSITION 8.1 *If $c_s \leq \pi_s$ and $c_w \geq \pi_w$, the following strategies and beliefs constitute a perfect Bayesian equilibrium:* $s_I(S) = WC$, $s_I(W) = \tilde{}WC$, $s_C(\tilde{}WC) = E$, $s_C(WC) = \tilde{}E$, $\Pr\{S|WC\} = 1$, *and* $\Pr\{S|\tilde{}WC\} = 0$.

Given these strategies, Bayes' rule suggests that C's equilibrium beliefs are $\Pr\{S|WC\} = 1$ and $\Pr\{W|\tilde{}WC\} = 1$. Because $\pi_w > k > \pi_s$, C's strategy – enter only in the absence of a war chest – is a best response. Now, we check that the incumbent's strategy is a best response. Incumbent type S derives utility $1 - c_s$ from WC. Because $c_s \leq \pi_s$, this quantity is greater than her utility from $\tilde{}WC$, $1 - \pi_s$. For incumbent type W the payoff of building a war chest is $1 - c_w$, whereas the utility for not building a war chest is $1 - \pi_w$. So $\tilde{}WC$ is a best response given that $c_w \geq \pi_w$.

Why are $c_s \leq \pi_s$ and $c_w \geq \pi_w$ required to support a separating equilibrium? For a war chest to signal strength credibly, the cost of building a war chest must be considerably higher for the weak incumbent. If this were not the case, weak incumbents also would build war chests, and the deterrence of C would no longer be sequentially rational. And of course, if war chests do not deter challenges, neither type seeks to build them. Consequently there would be no separating PBE.

There are no equilibria in which the signal is reversed (i.e., weak incumbents build war chests and strong incumbents do not).

PROPOSITION 8.2 *If $c_s \leq \pi_s$ and $c_w \geq \pi_w$, the strategies $s_I(S) = \tilde{}WC$ and $s_I(W) - WC$ cannot be part of a perfect Bayesian equilibrium.*

To verify this proposition, note that C's best response to these strategies is to enter if and only if WC. Then S receives a utility of 1 for $\tilde{W}C$ and $1 - \pi_s - c_s$ for WC. So S's strategy is a best response. Consider W's best response, however. She receives $1 - \pi_w - c_w$ for WC and 1 for $\tilde{W}C$. Clearly, $s_1(W) = WC$ is not a best response.

The reason that no such separating equilibrium exists can be understood in terms of *incentive compatibility*. We say that a message mapping where θ types announce m and θ' types announce m' is incentive compatible for types θ and θ' if and only if $EU(m|\theta) \geq EU(m'|\theta)$ and $EU(m'|\theta') \geq EU(m|\theta')$. In other words, each type must weakly prefer its own message to that of the other type. In a separating equilibrium the message strategies must satisfy incentive compatibility.

Note that for the reversed signals to be an equilibrium, the incentive compatibility requirements are

$$EU(\tilde{W}C|S) \geq EU(WC|S)$$
$$EU(WC|W) \geq EU(\tilde{W}C|W).$$

Adding these inequalities and moving things around generate the requirement that

$$EU(\tilde{W}C|S) - EU(\tilde{W}C|W) > EU(WC|S) - EU(WC|W).$$

In terms of the model, therefore, we require

$$\Pr\{E|\tilde{W}C\}\,(\pi_w - \pi_s) > \Pr\{E|WC\}\,(\pi_w - \pi_s) + c_w - c_s.$$

Because $c_w > c_s$ and $\pi_w > \pi_s$, incentive compatibility requires that $\Pr\{E|\tilde{W}C\} > \Pr\{E|WC\}$. Given C's beliefs, however, this cannot be a best response. Therefore, reversing the signal is not possible in a PBE. Incentive compatibility plays a central role in the models of mechanism design in Chapter 11.

3.2. Pooling Equilibria. Now, we consider pooling equilibria where both types of incumbents choose the same strategy. Generally, the easiest way to construct such equilibria is to specify the most unfavorable beliefs about the sender's type in the event that an out-of-equilibrium message is delivered. In this model, such a specification requires that C believe that the incumbent is weak following an out-of-equilibrium action. If these *pessimistic* beliefs support a strategy profile, then that profile constitutes a PBE. A number of slightly less pessimistic beliefs also may support that profile as a PBE. It is a good practice to compute the full set of beliefs that support each PBE.

In the first pooling equilibrium, neither type of incumbent builds a war chest and the challenger does not enter on the equilibrium path.

PROPOSITION 8.3 *Suppose that $p \geq (k - \pi_w)/(\pi_s - \pi_w)$. The following strategies and beliefs are a perfect Bayesian equilibrium:* $s_I(W) = s_I(S) = \tilde{}WC$, $s_C(WC) = E$, $s_C(\tilde{}WC) = \tilde{}E$, $\Pr\{S|\tilde{}WC\} = p$, *and* $\Pr\{S|WC\} \leq (\pi_w - k)/(\pi_w - \pi_s)$.

Because W and S play the same strategy, Bayes' rule implies that $\Pr\{S|\tilde{}WC\} = p$. So C's utility from entering when there is no war chest is

$$\pi_s p + \pi_w(1 - p) - k = \pi_w - (\pi_w - \pi_s)p - k.$$

Consequently, after observing $\tilde{}WC$, C enters only if $p \leq (k - \pi_w)/(\pi_s - \pi_w)$. Given the assumption $p \leq (k - \pi_w)/(\pi_s - \pi_w)$, $s_C(\tilde{}WC) = \tilde{}E$ is sequentially rational. What should C believe and do if he observes WC? PBE is silent about what to do at off-the-equilibrium-path histories. To generate this specific PBE, we assign any belief satisfying the condition $\Pr\{S|WC\} \leq (\pi_w - k)/(\pi_w - \pi_s)$. Such beliefs and sequential rationality imply that C enters if he observes WC. Now consider the strategies of S and W. They both get 1 for forgoing a war chest and $1 - \pi_s - c_s$ and $1 - \pi_w - c_w$, respectively, for building one. Thus, the strategies are best responses.

Another pooling equilibrium, identical on the path to the first, can be supported with different off-the-path beliefs and strategies.

PROPOSITION 8.4 *Suppose that $p \geq (k - \pi_w)/(\pi_s - \pi_w)$. The following strategies and beliefs are a perfect Bayesian equilibrium:* $s_I(W) = s_I(S) = \tilde{}WC$, $s_C(WC) = s_C(\tilde{}WC) = \tilde{}E$, $\Pr\{S|\tilde{}WC\} = p$, *and* $\Pr\{S|WC\} \geq (\pi_w - k)/(\pi_w - \pi_s)$.

Here C's best response given the beliefs on the equilibrium path is to stay out of the race. Suppose instead that the incumbent defects and builds a war chest. In this equilibrium, C believes that it is relatively

likely that the incumbent is strong at the out-of-equilibrium information set. So C still chooses $\tilde{}E$. Because C always stays out, it is optimal
for neither incumbent to build a war chest.

There are also pooling equilibria where weak incumbents mimic
strong ones by building a war chest. The war chest deters C.

PROPOSITION 8.5 *Suppose that* $p \geq (k - \pi_w)/(\pi_s - \pi_w)$, $c_s \leq \pi_s$, *and*
$c_w \leq \pi_w$. *The following strategies and beliefs are a perfect Bayesian
equilibrium:* $s_I(W) = s_I(S) = WC$, $s_C(\tilde{}WC) = E$, $s_C(WC) = \tilde{}E$,
$\Pr\{S|WC\} = p$, *and* $\Pr\{S|\tilde{}WC\} \leq (k - \pi_w)/(\pi_s - \pi_w)$.

Clearly, given the equilibrium beliefs, C's deterrence by a war chest
is a best response. Alternatively, if C observes $\tilde{}WC$, she assigns a probability of incumbent type S sufficiently low that she chooses E. Now
consider incumbent type S. She gets $1 - c_s$ in equilibrium and $1 - \pi_s$
by defecting. Consequently, type S chooses WC so long as $c_s \leq \pi_s$. Incumbent type W gets $1 - c_w$ in equilibrium and $1 - \pi_w$ from defecting.
So WC is W's best response if $c_w \leq \pi_w$.

Finally, another set of pooling equilibria involve no war chests and
challenger entry.

PROPOSITION 8.6 *Suppose that* $p \leq (k - \pi_w)/(\pi_s - \pi_w)$. *The following strategies and beliefs are a perfect Bayesian equilibrium:* $s_I(W) =
s_I(S) = \tilde{}WC$, $s_C(WC) = S_C(\tilde{}WC) = E$, $\Pr\{S|\tilde{}WC\} = p$, *and* $\Pr\{S|WC\}$
$\leq (k - \pi_w)/(\pi_s - \pi_w)$.

Here C's strategy of entering is a best response because regardless of
the incumbent's action, C thinks it unlikely that the incumbent is S. On
the equilibrium path, Bayes' rule implies that $\Pr\{S|\tilde{}WC\} = p$. Off the
equilibrium path, we assign $\Pr\{S|WC\} \leq (\pi_w - k)/(\pi_w - \pi_s)$. Because
C always enters, a war chest by either type of incumbent wastes resources. Thus, neither type of incumbent has an incentive to build one.

Although many paths of play can be supported as pooling equilibria,
not all can be.

PROPOSITION 8.7 *There is no equilibrium where* $s_I(W) = s_I(S) = WC$
and $s_C(WC) = s_C(\tilde{}WC) = E$.

Both types prefer defecting to $\tilde{}WC$; it does not change C's behavior
but it avoids the cost of building a war chest.

To summarize, there are two types of pooling equilibria to this game: equilibria where both incumbents build war chests and equilibria where neither does. Both reveal the same amount of information to the challenger – none – but they differ in the costs incurred by the incumbent. Every player prefers (at least weakly) the PBE where both types play ~WC to the one where they both play WC. Thus, the former type of equilibria are *efficient* PBE and the latter are *inefficient* ones. Importantly, there is nothing intrinsic to the concept of PBE that allows us to predict which equilibria are more likely to be played. As discussed later, however, various criteria for refining the set of PBE have been formulated. Often these refinements select the efficient PBE.

3.3. Partial Pooling. The remaining possibility is that incumbent types select different mixed strategies. There are a couple of reasons for exploring this possibility. First of all, if such equilibria exist, a full characterization of the set of PBEs requires analysis of the partial pooling equilibria. Second, authors sometimes characterize the most informative equilibrium (i.e., the one in which the receiver's posteriors are closest to the true distribution of types). In many cases, semipooling equilibria exist for parameter values for which there are no separating equilibria. In these cases, the most informative equilibrium is partial pooling.

We present only one of the partial pooling equilibria and leave other possibilities to the reader as an exercise. In this equilibrium, the type S incumbent always builds a war chest. The type W incumbent builds one with probability q. If a war chest is built, C enters with probability r.

PROPOSITION 8.8 *Let $\pi_w \geq c_w$ and $p \geq (k - \pi_w)/(\pi_s - \pi_w)$. Then the strategies $s_I(S) = WC$, $s_I(W) = \{WC$ with prob $q\}$, $s_C(\tilde{}WC) = E$, $s_C(WC) = \{E$ with probability $r\}$ is a perfect Bayesian equilibrium.*

Clearly, Bayes' rule implies that $\Pr\{S|\tilde{}WC\} = 0$ and thus entry following ~WC is a best response. When WC is observed, Bayes' rule is more complicated:

$$\Pr(S \mid WC) = \frac{\Pr(WC \mid S)\Pr(S)}{\Pr(WC \mid S)\Pr(S) + \Pr(WC \mid W)\Pr(W)}$$

$$= \frac{p}{p + q(1 - p)}.$$

Because C plays a mixed strategy following WC, he must be indifferent between entering or not entering. This requires that

$$\pi_s \Pr\{S|WC\} + \pi_w \Pr\{W|WC\} = k.$$

Substitution yields

$$\frac{\pi_s p}{p + q(1 - p)} + \frac{\pi_w q(1 - p)}{p + q(1 - p)} = k.$$

Solving for q, we find that the indifference condition is satisfied at

$$q^* = \frac{p(k - \pi_s)}{(1 - p)(\pi_w - k)}.$$

Because we require that $q^* \leq 1$, $p \geq (k - \pi_w)/(\pi_s - \pi_w)$ is a necessary condition for this partial pooling equilibrium. Similarly r must satisfy an indifference condition; a challenger of type W must be indifferent between building WC and not doing so. If W chooses $\tilde{}WC$, she gets $1 - \pi_w$. A choice of WC yields the payoff $r(1 - \pi_w) + (1 - r) - c_w$. So the indifference condition requires that

$$r^* = \frac{\pi_w - c_w}{\pi_w}.$$

The requirement that $r^* \geq 0$ generates the condition $\pi_w > c_w$. Given these mixed strategies, we need only check that an incumbent of type S prefers WC. If she plays $\tilde{}WC$ she gets $1 - \pi_s$ whereas in equilibrium she receives $r(1 - \pi_s) + (1 - r) - c_s$. Thus, $EU_S(WC) - EU_S(\tilde{}WC) = \pi_s(1 - r) - c_s = (\pi_s c_w)/(\pi_w) - c_s$. This difference is positive because $\pi_s > \pi_w$ and $c_w > c_s$.

This partial pooling equilibrium exists when $c_w/\pi_w < 1$ and $p \geq (k - \pi_w)/(\pi_s - \pi_w)$. From the earlier discussion we know that the separating equilibrium exists only if $c_w/\pi_w \geq 1$. A separating equilibrium and this partial pooling equilibrium cannot both exist. So long as $p \geq (k - \pi_w)/(\pi_s - \pi_w)$, however, the partial pooling equilibrium exists when the separating equilibrium does not.

4. Application: Information and Legislative Organization

One of the longest-standing debates about legislative politics focuses on the role of standing committees. Some scholars focus on their role in stabilizing majority rule (Shepsle 1979), maintaining distributive coalitions (Shepsle and Weingast 1987; Weingast and Marshall 1988), and promoting the interests of the majority party (Cox and McCubbins 1994). Gilligan and Krehbiel (1987), however, develop a model where committees contribute policy-specific expertise to legislative deliberations. Their model is related to the signaling games described previously.

In their model policymakers do not always know the exact link between policy choices and policy outcomes. For example, legislators may not know how a specific agricultural policy affects farmers' incomes because they lack the expertise about how factors such as weather and foreign competition affect farm prices. Because legislators value such information, they desire institutional arrangements that facilitate its gathering and transmission. Gilligan and Krehbiel argue that a committee system with limited parliamentary rights helps solve such informational problems.

To capture the distinction between policy choices and outcomes, Gilligan and Krehbiel assume that the policy outcome, x, is an additive function of policy p and a random variable ω or $x = p + \omega$. The model has two players: the floor F and the committee C. In our simplified version of the model, C knows ω with certainty but F's prior beliefs are that

$$\omega = \begin{cases} \theta \text{ with prob .5} \\ -\theta \text{ with prob .5} \end{cases}.$$

Each player has quadratic spatial preferences over a single dimension: F has an ideal point of $f = 0$ and C has an ideal point of $c > 0$. Thus, the payoffs are $u_F(x) = -x^2$ and $u_C(x) = -(c - x)^2$, respectively. Because F does not know ω, his utility from policy p is

$$.5u_F(p + \theta) + .5u_F(p - \theta) = -.5[p^2 + 2p\theta + \theta^2] - .5[p^2 - 2p\theta + \theta^2]$$
$$= -p^2 - \theta^2.$$

Thus, F's utility has two components. The first is $-p^2$, reflecting the difference between his ideal point and the expected policy. The second is $-\theta^2$, reflecting the variance in the policy shock ω.[8] Because the variance of the shock enters F's utility function as a cost, F is risk averse; he is willing to "pay" to obtain information about ω. Our concern is whether F wishes to grant extraparliamentary rights to C to provide it with the incentive to specialize – learn the realization of ω – and then reveal the information. Formally, F chooses the procedures or rules under which legislation can be considered. To simplify, we assume that F chooses between the following two rules:

(1) Open rule: The committee reports a bill and the floor may freely amend it.
(2) Closed rule: The floor must vote up or down on C's proposal against the status quo policy, $SQ = 0$.

The closed rule represents more extensive parliamentary rights for C; she can make a take-it-or-leave-it offer to F. To solve this as a game of incomplete information, we must specify strategies of both types of committees $(-\theta, \theta)$, the floor's beliefs following any proposal, and the floor's best response given these beliefs. Following Gilligan and Krehbiel, we characterize the most informative equilibrium. Consequently, we focus on whether or not a separating equilibrium exists.[9]

4.1. Open Rule. Under the open rule, the committee must worry about whether the information it provides can be used to "roll" it on the floor. Suppose that the committee revealed all of its information by proposing its ideal policy for each outcome: the committee chooses p^c so that $x = c$ or $p^c = c - \omega$. Because there are distinct proposals for each state of the world, these proposal strategies fully reveal all information to the floor. Under an open rule, therefore, the floor amends the bill until $x = 0$ or $p^f = -\omega$. The expected utilities in this equilibrium are $u_F = 0$ and $u_C = -c^2$. Because we want to determine whether or not a separating equilibria exists, we specify beliefs unfavorable to C following an

---

[8] With quadratic preferences, expected utility can be decomposed into two parts: the utility at the expected value of the random variable and the variance of the random variable. Some authors refer to this result as the *mean-variance* property of quadratic preferences.

[9] The reader who is paying attention should respond, "Aha! but haven't you warned us that informative semipooling equilibria can sometime exist when separating equilibria do not!" The attentive reader should consult exercise 8.7 and verify for herself that this is not one of those cases.

Table 8.3. Possible Defections

Defection	Conditions	Utility
$p^c = c + \theta$	if $\omega = \theta$ and $c > \theta$	$-(c - 2\theta)^2$
$p^c \notin \{c + \theta, c - \theta\}$	if $\omega = \theta$ and $c < \theta$	$-c^2$
$p^c \neq c + \theta$	if $\omega = -\theta$	$-(c + 2\theta)^2$

out-of-equilibrium proposal. Thus, we assume that F treats any other bill as if it were reported by the "high" type, $\omega = \theta$. The sequentially rational strategy following such a deviation is therefore $p^f = -\theta$. Given F's best responses, we can verify that only three outcomes can occur, $-2\theta, 0, 2\theta$. The outcome -2θ results from an out-of-equilibrium proposal when $\omega = -\theta$, outcome 0 results from $p^c = c - \theta$ when $\omega = -\theta$ or $p^c = c + \theta$ when $\omega = -\theta$ or any out-of-equilibrium proposal when $\omega = \theta$, and outcome 2θ results from $p^c = c + \theta$ when $\omega = \theta$.

Is separation a best response given these responses by F? If C defects by proposing $p^c = c + \theta$ when $\omega = \theta$, F passes $p^f = \theta$. Because the resulting outcome is 2θ, C's utility from defecting is $-(c - 2\theta)^2$. Alternatively, by proposing $p^c = c - \theta$ when $\omega = -\theta$, the policy is $p^f = -\theta$, leading to $x = -2\theta$ and $u_c = -(c + 2\theta)^2$. Finally, consider $p^c \notin \{c + \theta, c - \theta\}$. Because all of these proposals generate $p^f = -\theta$, $u_c(\theta) = -c^2$ and $u_c(-\theta) = -(c + 2\theta)^2$.

Because $c > 0$ and $\theta > 0$, the most attractive defections are those in Table 8.3.

The low type C does not defect because $-c^2 > -(c + 2\theta)^2$. Similarly, if $c < \theta$, the high type does not defect; her equilibrium utility is the same as that of her most profitable defection. When $c > \theta$ and $\omega = \theta$, however, the high type prefers $-(c - 2\theta)^2$ to her equilibrium payoff. Therefore, the separating equilibrium does not exist if $c > \theta$. Absent a separating equilibrium, the only equilibrium is an uninformative pooling equilibrium where both types use the same mixed strategy across the set of proposals.

When the committee is an *outlier* (i.e., $c > \theta$), no information is revealed.

4.2. Closed Rule. Under the open rule, information cannot be revealed by the outlier committee because the floor uses this information to roll the committee and move policy to the floor median. Under the closed rule, however, the committee cannot be rolled. The floor must accept or reject the proposal in favor of the status quo. Suppose there is a separating equilibrium in which F learns the value of ω. The utility to the floor from the status quo is $-\omega^2$ and for any proposal p it is $-(p+\omega)^2$. This implies that F accepts any proposal in the interval between 0 and -2ω. Thus, when $\omega = \theta$, the largest policy F accepts is 0. This results in an outcome of θ. When $\omega = -\theta$, the largest policy F accepts is 2θ. This also results in an outcome of θ.

So the committee can guarantee an outcome as high as θ by proposing $p^c = 0$ when $\omega = \theta$ and $p^c = 2\theta$ otherwise. If $c < \theta$, an outcome of c can be guaranteed by proposing $p^c = c - \theta$ when $\omega = \theta$ and $p^c = c + \theta$.

To complete the specification of the perfect Bayesian equilibrium, we must specify F's behavior and beliefs following out-of-equilibrium proposals from C. To support all possible separating equilibria, it is sufficient to have F accept any proposal such that $-2\theta \le p^c \le 0$ and vote down proposals $p^c > 0$. This strategy is a best response to the beliefs $\Pr\{\omega = \theta | p^c\} = 1$ following an out-of-equilibrium proposal.

Now we check that C prefers its equilibrium strategy to any defection. When $c < \theta$, C gets its ideal point so she cannot do better by defecting. Thus, a separating equilibrium exists, just as it did for the open rule. So we need only focus on the case where $c > \theta$. First suppose that $\omega = -\theta$. Here C gets $-(c-\theta)^2$ for $p^c = 2\theta$ and $-(c+\theta)^2$ for any other bill. C does not defect in this case. Now suppose that $\omega = \theta$. Now C receives $-(c-\theta)^2$ for $p^c = 0$, $-(c-3\theta)^2$ for $p^c = 2\theta$, and $-(c-\theta)^2$ for any other bill. Thus, so long as $c < 2\theta$, C weakly prefers her equilibrium proposal $p^c = 0$. If $c > 2\theta$, the committee defects. In this case, the only equilibria are uninformative; both types of committee use the same mixed strategy over all proposals and the floor rejects all proposals except $p^c = 0$.

The closed rule can sustain a separating equilibrium in cases where the open rule cannot (i.e., $2\theta \ge c > \theta$). The model predicts, therefore, that restrictive rules can encourage greater information transmission from the committee to the floor.

4.3. Committee Specialization. In the Gilligan- Krehbiel model restrictive rules generate more information transmission from informed committees than do open rules. We now turn to an analysis of whether a commitment to restrictive rules by the floor can induce the committee to specialize in the first place. So now the game takes the following form:

(1) F chooses whether the committee reports the bill under open rule or closed rule.
(2) C decides whether to specialize by paying a cost k to learn ω.
(3) C proposes p^c.
(4) F observes the specialization decision and the proposal p^c and selects a policy. Under closed rule, F votes p^c up or down against SQ. Under open rule, F chooses p^f.

If the committee does not specialize, F decides on the basis of its prior beliefs. Therefore, under the closed rule, she vetoes any proposal other than $p^c = 0$. Under the open rule, F passes $p^f = 0$. Thus, non-specialization results in a policy of $p = 0$ for both rules.

Now consider the committee's specialization decision under the open rule. If the committee specializes when $c \leq \theta$, C and F play the open rule separating equilibrium, resulting in an overall payoff of $-c^2 - k$ for the committee. If the committee does not specialize, its expected utility from $p = 0$ is $-c^2 - \theta^2$. So the committee specializes if $k \leq \theta^2$. If $c > \theta$ and the committee specializes, the committee and floor play the pooling equilibrium leading to $p = 0$ and an overall committee payoff of $-c^2 - \theta^2 - k$. Thus, the committee obviously does not specialize under these circumstances.

Now consider the closed rule. If $c \leq \theta$, the separating equilibrium generates an outcome of c so that the committee's utility of specializing is $-k$. Similarly, if $c > \theta$, the utility of specializing is $-(c - \theta)^2 - k$. In both cases, non-specialization leads to a payoff of $-c^2 - \theta^2$. Comparing these utilities, it pays for the committee to specialize when $k \leq 2\theta c$ and $c > \theta$ or when $k < c^2 + \theta^2$ and $c \leq \theta$. Because both of these critical values for k are higher than θ^2, the committee often specializes under the closed rule when it would not specialize under the open rule.

4.4. Implications. Gilligan and Krehbiel draw several implications about institutional design by computing the floor's utility under the different rules. The floor's expected payoffs under the open rule are

$$E[u_F] = 0 \qquad \text{if } c \leq \theta \text{ and } k \leq \theta^2$$
$$E[u_F] = \quad \theta^2 \quad \text{otherwise}$$

while the payoffs under the closed rule are

$$E[u_F] = -c^2 \quad \text{if } c \le \theta \text{ and } k \le c^2 + \theta^2$$
$$E[u_F] = -\theta^2 \quad \text{otherwise.}$$

A few implications are worth noting. First, F is always better off when C's ideal point is close to the floor's ideal. This is the basis of Krehbiel's (1991) argument that majoritarian legislatures should appoint committees that are representative of the preferences of the chamber. He contrasts this implication with that of the distributive theory of legislatures that predicts committees composed of high demanders for the policies in the committee's jurisdiction.

Second, the model makes predictions about when F prefers a closed rule. Specifically, F chooses a closed rule when $c \le \theta$ and $\theta^2 \le k \le c^2 + \theta^2$. Thus, committees with preferences similar to those the chamber median and committees with intermediate specialization costs are most likely to receive closed rules.

5. Application: Informational Lobbying

The literature on interest group politics has generated a striking empirical regularity: interest groups almost always lobby their friends. Because these friends are likely to vote with the interest group anyway, this observation has often been interpreted to mean that lobbying activities are not a consequential part of the policy process.

Austen-Smith and Wright (1992, 1994), however, develop a model where groups do lobby their friends. Nonetheless in equilibrium these efforts are important. The main premise is that interest groups have private information about the consequences of a legislative decision. The legislators are relatively uninformed. In the model, lobbying consists of a group's making a speech to the legislator. Because lobbying is assumed to be costly, groups choose whether or not to lobby the legislator. The main result of their papers is that groups often lobby friendly legislators to counteract the lobbying efforts of opposing groups.

Before analyzing the full model, we begin with a model with only one interest group and one legislator. The legislator must choose between two policies A and B. But she is uncertain as to which policy she prefers. Assume that there are two states $s \in \{A, B\}$. The legislator prefers policy A in state A and policy B in state B. To keep matters simple, we assume that $u_L(A) = 1$ in state A and $u_L(A) = -1$ in state B; $u_L(B) = 0$ in both states. The prior probability is that $s = A$ with probability $p < 1/2$. Thus, in the absence of any additional information provided by lobbying, the legislator chooses B.

Interest group G_A prefers A to B. Its utility function is $u_{G_A}(A) = 1$ and $u_{G_A}(B) = -1$ in both states. If G_A decides to lobby, it pays cost $c > 0$ to learn the true state with certainty. Its ex ante beliefs are the same as the legislator's prior. Once informed, the group sends one of two messages $m = A$ or B where the messages are to be interpreted literally.

After observing message m, L can attempt to verify the group's information by *auditing* the message. In doing so, L incurs cost κ. If the message is found to be incorrect (i.e., $m \neq s$), the group is penalized by an amount δ.

Now consider the group's possible lobbying strategies. First, suppose G_A always reports A independent of s. Then the message is uninformative, and L always selects B if she does not audit. L chooses the optimal outcome following an audit. Because the utility of an audit is $1 - \kappa$, it is easy to show that L's best response to an "always A" strategy involves auditing if and only if $p > \kappa$.

Because an "always A" lobbying strategy does not affect the outcome, G_A prefers not to lobby at all rather than to employ it. Therefore, successful lobbying requires that G_A tell the truth at least some of the time. Suppose G_A tells the truth all of the time. Then L always follows such advice and never chooses to audit. This gives G_A the incentive to report A even when $s = B$. Because G_A has an incentive to deviate, this cannot be an equilibrium.

Thus, any perfect Bayesian equilibrium to this game has to be partial pooling. Consider an equilibrium where G_A reports A when $s = A$ and reports A with probability μ when $s = B$. Given this strategy, following a message of A, L uses Bayes' rule to update her belief that $s = A$ to

$$\widehat{p} = \frac{p}{p + \mu(1 - p)}.$$

In such an equilibrium, L must be indifferent between voting for A and auditing. The expected utility of voting A is $\widehat{p} - (1 - \widehat{p}) = 2\widehat{p} - 1$ whereas the expected utility of auditing is $\widehat{p} - \kappa$. Thus, μ must satisfy

$$\frac{p}{p + \mu(1 - p)} = 1 - \kappa.$$

Solving for μ yields

$$\mu = \frac{\kappa p}{(1 - p)(1 - \kappa)}.$$

To close the model, L chooses a probability of auditing α so that G_A is indifferent between lying and truth telling when $s = B$. If G_A is truthful, it gets -1. If G_A lies, it gets $-\alpha(\delta + 1) + (1 - \alpha)$. The value of α that equates these two expected utilities is $\alpha = 1/(\delta + 2)$.

Given these lobbying and auditing strategies, we compute G_A's expected utility to determine whether or not it chooses to become informed and lobby. Because L always chooses B in the absence of lobbying, the group's utility from not lobbying is -1. If it does lobby, the group gets A for sure when $s = A$ and an expected utility of -1 when $s = B$. Thus, the ex ante expected payoff from lobbying is $2p - 1 - c$, and the group lobbies if and only if $p > c/2$.

Finally, we must check that the mixed strategy probabilities are actually probabilities. In order for $0 \le \mu \le 1$ we need $1 - p > \kappa > 0$; it cannot be too costly for the legislator to audit. If it is too costly, the legislator does not audit and guarantees that the group has an incentive to lie. If the group always lies, however, lobbying is ineffective and the group chooses not to become informed.

Now consider the model with two groups. Group G_B's preferences are the opposite of G_A's; $u_{G_B}(B) = 1$ and $u_{G_B}(A) = -1$. It also learns the true state by paying a cost c. In the first period both groups simultaneously decide whether to lobby. If a group chooses to lobby it pays the cost c to become informed. In the second period the group(s) that chose to lobby learn the other player's choice and select their message. If both groups lobby then the messages, m_A and m_B, are sent simultaneously.

Because L chooses B in the absence of lobbying, there is no equilibrium where G_B lobbies and G_A does not. If G_B lobbies alone, it incurs cost c without altering the outcome. Austen-Smith and Wright interpret this result as implying that groups only lobby "friendly" legislators to counteract the lobbying of other groups.

Because the outcome of G_A lobbying alone is outlined previously, we focus only on the outcome when both groups lobby. Consider the following equilibrium. Both groups send truthful messages. When $m_A = m_B = s$, the legislator believes that the true state is s. If $m_A \ne m_B$, L audits the message and chooses her optimal policy. For auditing to

be a best response to out-of-equilibrium messages, we assume that
$\Pr(s = A | m_A \neq m_B) \geq \kappa$.

Now we verify that G_A does not deviate and choose an untruthful
message. Clearly, it has no incentive to choose $m_A = B$ when $s = A$.
So consider whether it chooses $m_A = A$ when $s = B$. Because this
message leads to an audit, it results in a policy of B and a penalty
of δ for a total payoff of $-1 - \delta$. Because telling the truth leads to a
payoff of -1, G_A has no incentive to deviate.

Turning to G_B's decision, we need to check that it does not choose
$m_B = B$ if $s = A$. As before, such a message leads to an audit and a
penalty for G_B. Thus, it does not defect.

It remains only to characterize conditions under which both groups
prefer to lobby. Because lobbying by both groups leads to the full
information outcome, the equilibrium utilities of G_A and G_B are $2p -
1 - c$ and $1 - 2p - c$, respectively. G_B's utility from having G_A lobby
alone is

$$-p + (1 - p) \left[\mu (2\alpha - 1) + (1 - \mu) \right] = 1 - 2p - \left[\frac{\kappa p}{(1 - \kappa)} \frac{2\delta + 2}{\delta + 2} \right].$$

This value is less than $1 - 2p - c$ if

$$p > \frac{1 - \kappa}{\kappa} \frac{\delta + 2}{2\delta + 2} c.$$

As argued earlier, if B alone lobbies, it provides no information, and
policy B is chosen. This gives G_A a utility of -1. G_A participates as
long as $2p - 1 - c \geq -1$. This condition reduces to $p \geq c/2$, the same
condition observed earlier. Thus G_A's decision to lobby is independent
of G_B.

Thus, we characterize the equilibrium lobbying decisions of both
groups as follows. If $p < c/2$, neither group lobbies. If

$$\frac{1 - \kappa}{\kappa} \frac{\delta + 2}{2\delta + 2} c > p > \frac{c}{2},$$

only G_A lobbies. If

$$p > \frac{1 - \kappa}{\kappa} \frac{\delta + 2}{2\delta + 2} c,$$

both groups lobby.

Austen-Smith and Wright attribute the following hypotheses to this perfect Bayesian equilibrium:

- Ceterus paribus, when a legislator is lobbied by groups from just one side of an issue, the only groups that lobby are those opposed to the legislator's ex ante position.
- The decision of a group to lobby an "unfriendly" legislator's is independent of the lobbying decisions of opposing groups.
- Conditional on a "friendly" legislator's being lobbied by an opposing group, a group's decision to lobby that legislator is purely counteractive.

6. Refinements of Perfect Bayesian Equilibrium*

6.1. Sequential Equilibria. Several of our examples demonstrate that weak consistency lives up to its name. Often, it does not impose strong enough constraints on off-the-path beliefs. In fact, a PBE need not even be subgame perfect, a fact demonstrated by the example in Figure 8.9.

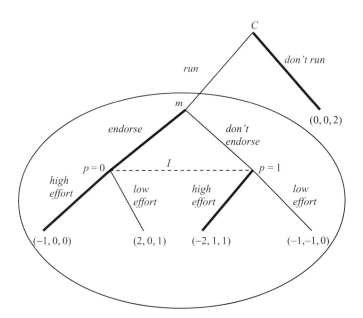

Figure 8.9. Electoral Endorsement Game.

In this extensive form game, C is a potential candidate for office and must decide whether or not to run. After this decision, the local newspaper decides whether or not to endorse C. After the endorsement decision is made but before observing it, the incumbent I decides how much campaign effort to exert.[10] The payoffs reflect C's preference to enter only if he is endorsed and the incumbent chooses low effort, the media's preference to endorse C only if the incumbent chooses low effort, and the incumbent's preference to exert effort only when C is not endorsed.

In Figure 8.9, the shaded branches denote a strategy profile and the numbers $p = 0$ and $p = 1$ denote beliefs. It is not difficult to see that the figure depicts a PBE. Given the belief that "not endorse" occurs with probability 1, the incumbent optimally selects high effort. Moreover, given the expectation that endorsement and high effort follow a decision to run, the optimal decision for C is not to run for office. Given this strategy profile, the incumbent's information set is not reached, and weak consistency does not restrict beliefs. Despite the fact that this is a PBE, the specified strategy profile is not subgame perfect. To see this, consider the circled subgame that starts with m's decision. Given that m chooses endorse, high effort is not a best response. The problem in this game is that there are nontrivial information sets for some strategy profiles several moves away from the equilibrium path.

In a reasonably defined equilibrium, I's beliefs about m's decision (conditional on reaching this information set) ought to be somehow consistent with player m's strategy. Accordingly, we might conjecture that (1) if C runs then either m endorses and I exerts low effort, or (2) m does not endorse and I exerts high effort, or (3) both m and I randomize. Combining sequential rationality and a stronger notion of consistency can prevent this pathology.

In this section we limit ourselves to finite games and present several stronger equilibrium concepts. All of the concepts defined involve sequential rationality as defined in Definition 8.2. Where these concepts differ is in the restrictions imposed on beliefs.

First we need a bit of notation. Given a finite extensive form game, a mixed strategy profile $\sigma(\cdot)$ is a mapping that determines a lottery over available actions at each information set. For a finite game such

---

[10] We can also interpret the endorsement and effort decisions as occurring simultaneously.

a strategy profile can be written as a vector $(\sigma(1, 1), \ldots, \sigma(a, I) \ldots)$ with generic coordinate $\sigma(a, I)$ denoting the probability that action a is played at information set I. A strategy profile is a *completely mixed profile* if it selects every action at every information set with positive probability. A pure strategy is then a vector containing only 0s and 1s. A sequence of mixed strategies $\{\sigma(\cdot)^n\}_{n=1}^{\infty}$ is said to converge to a mixed strategy $\sigma(\cdot)$ if for each $I, a,$ $\sigma(a, I)^n$ converges to $\sigma(a, I)$. The notion of sequential equilibrium replaces weak consistency with a stronger condition.

DEFINITION 8.6 *Given a finite extensive form game with imperfectly observed actions, a sequential equilibrium (SE) is a pair $(\sigma(\cdot), b(\cdot))$ such that (1) the strategy profile $\sigma(\cdot)$ is sequentially rational relative to the belief $b(\cdot)$, and (2) there exists some sequence of completely mixed strategies $\{\sigma(\cdot)^n\}_{n=1}^{\infty}$ and beliefs $\{b(\cdot)^n\}_{n=1}^{\infty}$ that converge to $\sigma(\cdot), b(\cdot),$ respectively, and satisfy the condition that for some $n', b(\cdot)^n$ is weakly consistent relative to the strategy profile $\sigma(\cdot)^n$ if $n > n'$.*

To demonstrate how this concept refines our notion of PBE, we first return to the game in Figure 8.9. Consider any sequence of completely mixed profiles $\{\sigma(\cdot)^n\}_{n=1}^{\infty}$ satisfying the condition that in $\sigma(\cdot)^n$ every pure strategy is played with at least probability ε_n. Let $\varepsilon_n \to 0$ as $n \to \infty$. If this sequence of mixed strategies converges to the PBE in Figure 8.9, $\sigma^n(endorse, run)$ must be a mixed best response to $\sigma^n(run) = \varepsilon_n$ and σ^n (high effort, run)$= 1 - \varepsilon_n$. The media's expected utility from *endorse* is therefore ε_n, but its payoff from *not endorse* is $1 - 2\varepsilon_n$. Therefore, as ε_n converges to 0, there must be some n' such that for all $n > n', m$ prefers to choose $\sigma^n(endorse, run) = \varepsilon_n \to 0$. Because this is not true of the equilibrium in Figure 8.9, it is not the limit of completely mixed equilibria and is not a sequential equilibrium.

Sequential equilibria also place restrictions on beliefs. Weak consistency requires that the beliefs about the media's decision correspond to the strategy, $b^n(endorse) = \sigma^n(endorse, run)$. Accordingly for a sequence of completely mixed strategies that converges to a profile playing *not run* and *endorse if run* with probability 1, $b(\cdot)^n$ must converge to beliefs that put probability 1 on *endorse*. Therefore, there are no sequences of completely mixed strategies and weakly consistent beliefs that converge to the strategies and beliefs depicted in Figure 8.9. In fact, it can be shown that every sequential equilibrium involves strategies that are subgame perfect. The proof of this result is left as an exercise.

Although sequential equilibrium is an improvement over PBE, in many applications the two concepts have equivalent equilibrium sets. For example, in the classic signaling games considered earlier the concepts coincide. Fudenberg and Tirole (1991) have proved the following equivalence result.

PROPOSITION 8.9 *(Fudenberg and Tirole 1991) If a finite extensive form game has only two periods or every player has at most two types then the set of PBE and set of SE coincide.*

A very nice property of sequential equilibria is that one always exists in finite games. A very nice property of this very nice property is that the existence proof demonstrates the relationship between perfect equilibria in normal form games and sequential equilibria in extensive form games.

Recall that we can always represent an extensive form game as a normal form game; each player selects her information set contingent strategies simultaneously. Examples of this equivalence appear at the beginning of Chapter 7. For our purposes we need to think about a slightly different normal from representation.

DEFINITION 8.7 *Given an extensive form game, the agent normal form attributes a different identity to the agent that moves at each information set.*

For example, in the Centipede extensive form game depicted in Figure 7.2 the agent normal form game involves five players. Abusing notation slightly, for any strategy profile $\sigma(\cdot)$ in the agent normal form, let $\sigma(\cdot)$ also denote the corresponding strategy profile in the extensive form game. So if player i moves at multiple information sets in the extensive form game her strategy profile is the composition of the strategies of multiple players from the agent normal form.

Converting the extensive form game into normal form game allows us to make the following comparison of equilibrium sets.

PROPOSITION 8.10 *Consider a finite extensive form game. If $\sigma_a(\cdot)$ is a perfect equilibrium in the agent normal form representation of the game then there exists a belief $b(\cdot)$ such that the pair $(\sigma(\cdot), b(\cdot))$ is a sequential equilibrium in the extensive form game.*

Aside from providing a connection between these two concepts this result is valuable for a second reason. Because Selten (1965) proved that finite games possess perfect equilibria, the following result is an immediate corollary.

PROPOSITION 8.11 *(Selten) Every finite extensive form game has at least one sequential equilibrium.*

6.2. The Intuitive Criterion. The concept of sequential equilibrium sometimes eliminates implausible PBEs, but not always. Thus, Kreps and Cho (1987) propose the *intuitive criterion* to restrict the equilibrium set in some signaling games further. Kreps and Cho postulate that beliefs should be concentrated on those sender types with the greatest incentive to defect. They illustrate their concept with the Beer and Quiche game. Because this is the simplest possible demonstration, we utilize it but with some political embellishments. Consider the game between Saddam Hussein and George Bush on the eve of the American invasion of Iraq. Consider a two-player signaling game in which the sender, Hussein, has two possible types. He can have weapons of mass destruction, $\theta = w$, or not, $\theta = \tilde{w}$. The receiver, Bush, can either attack, $s_b = a$, or not, $s_b = \tilde{a}$. Bush, demonstrating supreme confidence, has no concerns about winning if he attacks. He does, however, need to justify the attack with the claim that Hussein has weapons of mass destruction. Accordingly, he prefers to attack if w and not to attack if $\tilde{w}$. Prior to Bush's decision, Hussein decides whether to allow weapons inspections, $s_h = y$ or $s_h = \tilde{y}$. The result of a weapons inspection is not publicized before Bush's decision of whether or not to attack. We assume that regardless of Bush's decision, type w suffers a cost of 1 from inspection, a proven violation of UN resolutions. Type $\tilde{w}$ receives a benefit of 1 from inspection, public vindication. Regardless of Hussein's type he prefers not to be attacked. In fact, the cost of being attacked is sufficiently large that either type of Hussein is willing to allow UN inspections if this action prevents attack. Alternatively, Bush does not care directly about the inspections but prefers attacking so long as the probability of $\theta = w$ is sufficiently high (greater than $1/2$). Figure 8.10 depicts the game.

There are pooling equilibria in which weapons inspectors are allowed ($s_h = y$), and there are pooling equilibria in which they are not allowed ($s_h = \tilde{y}$). In any pooling equilibria, Bush's posterior must correspond to the prior. Thus if the prior probability w is sufficiently low, Bush

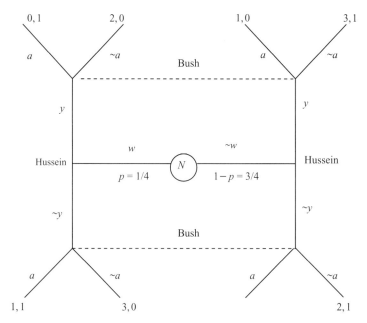

Figure 8.10. Bush-Hussein Game.

does not attack. To support pooling at $s_h = y$, it is necessary that both Hussein types prefer y to $\tilde{y}$. This results in the incentive compatibility conditions

$$3 \geq EU_H(\tilde{y}, \tilde{w})$$
$$2 \geq EU_H(\tilde{y}, w).$$

Let $\Pr(a \mid \tilde{y})$ denote the probability that Bush attacks after observing y. The incentive compatibility conditions require that

$$3 \geq 0\Pr(a \mid \tilde{y}) + 2(1 - \Pr(a \mid \tilde{y}))$$
$$2 \geq 1\Pr(a \mid \tilde{y}) + 3(1 - \Pr(a \mid \tilde{y})).$$

These conditions are true as long as $\Pr(a \mid \tilde{y}) \geq 1/2$. If Bush uses a strategy in which $\Pr(a \mid \tilde{y}) \geq 1/2$, his posterior belief about Hussein's type conditional on the off-the-path action $\tilde{y}$ must satisfy $\Pr(w \mid \tilde{y}) \geq 1/2$. This posterior, however, cannot be determined by Bayes' rule. Recall that the on-the-path belief $\Pr(w \mid y) = 1/4$ corresponds to the prior and is pinned down in a pooling equilibrium. So we have shown that there is a PBE (and by Proposition 8.9, a SE) in which both types of Husseins pool at y and Bush does not attack.

To support the other pooling equilibrium where both types of Hussein select $\tilde{y}$ and Bush again does not attack, we need only specify off-the-path beliefs $\Pr(w \mid y) \geq 1/2$. Following these beliefs, Bush attacks with probability at least $1/2$ and so both Hussein types prefer to select $\tilde{y}$ and avoid attack.

Although both equilibria are PBE and SE, Cho and Kreps argue that only one of these pooling equilibria is reasonable. Consider the equilibria in which both Hussein types select $\tilde{y}$. This equilibrium requires that the off-the-path beliefs satisfy $\Pr(\omega \mid y) \geq 1/2$. Is it reasonable for Bush to believe that Hussein is more likely to have weapons if he allows inspections than if he does not? Recall that in this equilibrium, type w gets his maximal payoff. No inspections and no attack result in a payoff of 3. The defection to y and not attack results in a payoff of 2 for w. Such a deviation is not desirable under the assumption that the deviation does not trigger an attack. If y triggers an attack, the defection is even less attractive. On the other hand, consider the potential incentive for type $\tilde{w}$ to deviate. In equilibrium he gets a payoff of 2. If his defection does not result in an attack, he gets utility of 3 (and thus improves his situation). Thus, it seems *intuitive* that if a defection were observed it is most likely to be committed by $\tilde{w}$. Cho and Kreps argue that Bush would be foolish to interpret y as evidence of w. Instead they imagine that the only justification for such an off-the-path deviation is that Hussein type $\tilde{w}$ might deviate to y and send the following justification.

> Dear W:
>   Sorry for past squabbles with your old man. About this recent disagreement: I know that you are expecting me to choose $\tilde{y}$ and this doesn't tell you anything – it's a pooling equilibrium after all (you remember pool tables, from Yale, don't you?). But I am not going to do this, because I actually don't have any weapons and I want to show this to the world, so I am going to make myself even better off. You should trust that this action indicates that I really have no weapons because if I did have weapons and I expected you not to attack if I didn't allow the inspections (which is the equilibrium we are playing), then I would only hurt myself by letting in the inspectors. If I had weapons this deviation would not possibly help me.
>   Sincerely,
>   SH

Of course this type of communication is not modeled in standard signaling games. The point is, given the Bush strategy, one type can possibly gain from the off-the-path deviation, while the other type can only lose. In such a setting, the off-the-path beliefs should be concentrated on the type that stands to gain. Note that the y pooling equilibrium is immune from this criticism. The only type that possibly stands to gain from choosing ˜y is w. So the beliefs justifying Bush's attack following ˜y are justified.

We now present the intuitive criterion in a somewhat more rigorous manner requiring a bit more notation. Let Γ^s denote a simple signaling game with two periods and two players. Player 1 has a type space Θ and a message space M. Player 2 observes player 1's message m and selects an action from A. For simplicity, all of these sets are finite. For the more complicated case of nonfinite sets, the following conditions can be modified but some technical issues are encountered. Although player 1 knows her type, player 2 only knows that 1's type is drawn from some probability function $f(\cdot)$ on Θ and player payoffs are given by utility functions $u_s(m, a, \theta)$ and $u_r(m, a, \theta)$. Accordingly, a mixed strategy profile is a message function $\sigma_s(\theta)$ that selects a lottery on M for every θ and an action function $\sigma_r(m)$ that selects a lottery over actions for each possible message. Let $\sigma_s(m, \theta)$ and $\sigma_r(a, m)$ denote the probability that m is played by a sender with type θ and the probability that a is played by an r that has observed m, respectively. A sequential equilibrium also involves a belief $\mu(\theta \mid m)$. Given a signaling game and a sequential equilibrium to the game, let $U_s^*(\theta)$ denote expected utility to player 1 of type θ from the equilibrium profile. Finally let Δ denote the set of probability distributions on Θ and let $BR_r(m) = \cup_{p(\theta) \in \Delta} \{\arg\max_{a \in A} \sum u_r(m, a, \theta) p(\theta)\}$ denote the set of actions by r that maximize the receiver's expected utility for some beliefs about θ. We say an action r is rationalizable if it is an element of $BR_r(m)$.

DEFINITION 8.8 *An SE $(\sigma_s(\cdot), \sigma_r(\cdot), \mu(\cdot \mid \cdot))$ satisfies the intuitive criterion if for any message m such that $\sum \sigma_r(m, \theta) f(\theta) = 0$, the posterior belief $\mu(\theta \mid m) > 0$ only if $U_s^*(\theta) < \max_{a \in BR_r(m)} u_s(m, a, \theta)$.*

In words, an intuitive equilibrium (more precisely an SE satisfying the intuitive criterion) requires that out-of-equilibrium beliefs put 0 probability on types that could not gain from the observed deviation under some expectation that the receiver responds to the deviation by playing a strategy from her set of best responses.

As further demonstration, we modify the entry deterrence game considered earlier. Now instead of restricting the message space to be $\{WC, \tilde{\ }WC\}$ we allow the incumbent to select a level of fund-raising $s_I \in \mathbb{R}_+^1$ at a cost cs_I where c is either c_w or c_s depending on the incumbent's type. Let the value of office be 1 for the incumbent, so if in equilibrium she accumulates s' and wins with probability π her payoff is $\pi - cs'$. There are multiple pooling, partially pooling, and separating equilibria to this game. There is, however, only one intuitive equilibrium, that is separating. We leave the analysis of this game as an exercise.

The literature on refinements is quite large and refinements to the intuitive criterion have appeared in many applications. Commonly, models with type spaces with more than two elements require stronger refinements. This is because several types might gain from a defection for different best responses by the receiver. In such situations, stronger refinements such as *universal divinity* (Banks and Sobel 1987) might restrict the equilibrium set.[11] Because universal divinity has been used in numerous political applications, we present a definition and an example.

DEFINITION 8.9 *An SE or PBE* $(\sigma_s(\cdot), \sigma_r(\cdot), \mu(\cdot \mid \cdot))$ *satisfies universal divinity if for any message m such that $\sum \sigma_r(m, \theta) f(\theta) = 0$, the posterior belief $\mu(\theta \mid m) > 0$ only if there exists an action $a \in BR_r(m)$ such that $U_s^*(\theta) < u_s(m, a, \theta)$ and for every $\theta' \neq \theta$ $U_s^*(\theta') \geq u_s(m, a, \theta')$.*

Universal divinity is more stringent than the intuitive criterion. It allows the posteriors to place positive probability on a smaller set of types. In the case of universal divinity, the posteriors only place weight on a type if there is a rationalizable action that makes the deviation desirable for this type and no other. Informally, universal divinity requires that off-the-path beliefs put weight only on the types "most likely" to deviate.

To contrast the intuitive criterion and universal divinity, consider an application of Michael Spence's signaling model to political reform (Spence 1975). Suppose a developing country has type $\theta \in \{1, 2, 3\}$ with θ measuring the nation's potential to repay debts successfully (higher numbers are better). Let π_1 and π_2 denote the probability of

---

[11] We encourage motivated students to seek out the original Cho and Kreps (1987) and Banks and Sobel (1987) pieces. In addition, Banks (1991) is an exemplary presentation of signaling games and refinements in applications dealing with political science.

Packages f

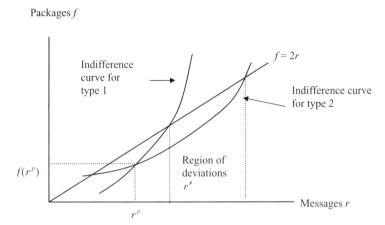

Figure 8.11. International Aid and Reform Game.

types 1 and 2 (with type 3's occurring with probability $1 - \pi_1 - \pi_2$). The country must select a level of observable political reform $r \in \mathbb{R}_+^1$. The pain associated with reform is dependent on the nation's type. After observing r, the IMF determines a financial package $f \in \mathbb{R}_+^1$ for the nation. The receiver's goal is to match f with the product θr. Payoffs are as follows: given type θ, reform r, and package f, the nation's utility is $f - r^2/\theta$.

We first consider the case of $\pi_1 + \pi_2 = 1$ (so there are just two types of developing countries). In this case, there are pooling, partially-pooling, and separating PBEs. The intuitive criterion, however, selects a unique equilibrium. We sketch the argument here. Consider Figure 8.11, which depicts indifference contours over pairs of messages and responses for senders of types 1 and 2. Because all senders prefer more funds and fewer reforms, movements to the northwest quadrant are desirable.

Consider a pooling (or partially pooling) equilibrium in which both sender types select the same level r^p with positive probability. After observing r^p the receiver knows that the posterior probability of $\theta < 2$ is greater than 0. Thus in any PBE the package corresponding to r^p, $f(r^p)$, must be less than $2r^p$. So there exists a message $r' > r^p$ such that if $f(r') = 2r'$ a type 2 nation prefers the deviation, and a type 1 nation does not. In this case the intuitive criterion implies that beliefs must place probability 1 on $\theta = 2$ if r' is chosen. Given these beliefs, following r' the package $f(r') = 2r'$ is the unique sequentially rational package for the receiver. In the preceding notation, we have

$$U_r^*(2) = f(r^P) - \frac{(r^P)^2}{2}$$

$$u_r(r', 2r', 2) = 2r' - \frac{(r')^2}{2}$$

$$U_r^*(1) = f(r^P) - (r^P)^2$$

$$u_r(r', 2r', 1) = 2r' - (r')^2.$$

Accordingly, $U_r^*(1) > u_r(r', 2r', 1)$ requires $f(r^P) > (r')^2 - (r^P)^2$, whereas $U_r^*(2) < u_r(r', 2r', 2)$ requires

$$f(r^P) < 2r' - \frac{(r')^2 - (r^P)^2}{2}.$$

Both of these inequalities can be simultaneously satisfied. See Figure 8.11 for the region of such values of r'. To recap, in a pooling or partially pooling equilibrium in which both types play r^P with positive probability, the intuitive criterion requires that beliefs assign probability 1 to type $\theta = 2$ following the (possibly off-the-path) message of r'. Thus, if r' is played the financial package is $2r'$. The value r' was chosen so that type 2s strictly prefer message r' to r^P meaning that type 2s cannot put positive probability on the message r^P. This contradicts the assumption of an intuitive equilibrium in which both types play r^P with positive probability. Having ruled out all but separating equilibria, we claim that the intuitive criterion selects a unique separating equilibrium. We leave this as an exercise.

Now assume that $\pi_1 + \pi_2 < 1$ so that $\theta = 3$ occurs with probability $1 - \pi_1 - \pi_2 > 0$. The first question to address is whether the intuitive criterion continues to eliminate all pooling or partially pooling equilibria. The answer is no. Suppose that types 1 and 2 are both playing a message r^P with positive probability, and $\theta = 3$ plays a pure strategy $r^3 > r^P$. It can be shown that this happens in some PBEs. Our argument before was that the intuitive criterion required that following some reform $r' > r^P$ posterior beliefs are concentrated at the higher type. With the third type present, however, this turns out not to be the case. We now satisfy the intuitive criterion with posteriors putting

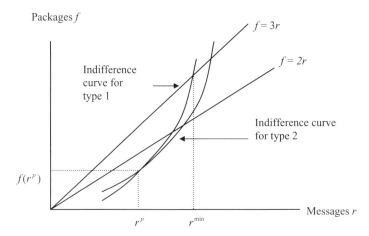

Figure 8.12. International Aid and Reform Game.

weight on $\theta = 3$ following a reform $r' > r^p$. With such beliefs, the sequentially rational choices of f might lead $\theta = 1$ to prefer the deviation to the equilibrium payoff. More specifically, the requirement that
$f(r') \le 2r'$ need no longer hold. Now, only $f(r') \le 3r'$ needs to hold.
With $f(r') \ge 3r'$, type $\theta = 1$ might prefer to deviate with the expectation that a deviation results in $f(r')$. Accordingly in order for type
$\theta = 2$ to signal that it is not type 1, it needs to send a message at least as
high as the level $r^{\min}$ depicted in Figure 8.12. For every level of $r > r^{\min}$,
however, there are possible best responses $f(r)$ that make type 2 worse
than under equilibrium play. Notice that there is space between type
2's indifference curve and the line $f = 2r$. Because the intuitive criterion only requires that type 2 expect a response of $f > 2r$ for an r
greater than $r^{\min}$, it cannot be certain that the deviation is desirable.

   This partial-pooling equilibrium cannot be a universally divine equilibrium, however. Again suppose that types 1 and 2 are both playing
a message r^p with positive probability, and $\theta = 3$ plays a pure strategy $r^3 > r^p$. Under universal divinity, a message of r' that is slightly
larger than r^p must result in a posterior concentrated at $\theta = 2$; for
values of r to the right of r^p type 1's indifference curve is above
type 2's. For pairs $(r', f(r'))$ that lie between the two indifference
curves, $U_s^*(2) < u_s(r', f(r'), 2)$ and $U_s^*(1) > u_s(r', f(r'), 1)$. Moreover,
because type 3 is getting $f = 3r$, his utility is higher in the equilibrium
than the deviation. Accordingly, universal divinity requires that a message of r' result in beliefs concentrated at $\theta = 2$, and sequential rationality requires that $f(r') = 2r'$. Type 2 gains from the deviation. It is

left as an exercise to show that there is exactly one universally divine equilibrium in the game with three types.

7. Exercises

EXERCISE 8.1 *Consider the game of Figure 8.6 where the payoff to the path B, NR is (5, 0) instead of (4, 0). Characterize all of the PBEs (mixed and pure strategy) to the game.*

EXERCISE 8.2 *Consider the game of Figure 8.6 where the payoff to the path ND is $(w, 5)$ instead of $(0, 5)$. Here w is an exogenous parameter known to the agents that ranges from -2 to 5. For what values of w are there PBEs in which ND occurs with positive probability?*

EXERCISE 8.3 *In the game depicted in Figure 8.7, show that there is no PBE in which $m(\theta) = \begin{cases} b \ if \ \theta = a \\ a \ if \ \theta = b \end{cases}$.*

EXERCISE 8.4 *Find all of the PBEs of the game depicted in Figure 8.13.*

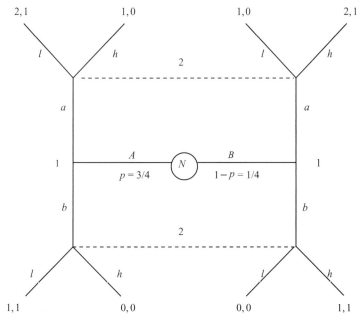

Figure 8.13. Signaling Game.

EXERCISE 8.5 *A model of political repression: Suppose that in each of two periods, society must decide whether to protest the policies of the state. The state may either acquiesce or repress. Society gets* 1 *if the state acquiesces,* −1 *if the state represses, and* 0 *if it does not protest.*

Suppose there are two types of states: Moderate and Hardline. The moderate state (M) gets 0 if the protest does not take place, −2 *if it acquiesces, and* −3 *if it represses. The hardline (H) state gets 0 for no protest,* −2 *for repression, and* −3 *for acquiescing. Let p_0 be the prior probability that the state is M.*

(1) *In the second period, what is the critical value p^* such that S protests if $p_1 \geq p^*$ (where p_1 is S's updated belief that the state is M)?*

(2) *Is there ever a separating equilibrium with these strategies?*

> *M :{acquiesce, acquiesce}*
> *H :{repress, repress}*
> *S :{protest, stay home if repressed in period 1}*

If so, for what values of p_0 does it hold?

(3) *Is there a pooling equilibrium in the first period with these strategies?*

> *M :{repress, acquiesce}*
> *H :{repress, repress}*
> *S :{protest, stay home if repressed in period 1}*

If so, for what values of p_0 does it hold? Is it consistent with the intuitive criterion?

(4) *Is there a pooling equilibrium in the first period with these strategies?*

> *M :{repress, acquiesce}*
> *H :{repress, repress}*
> *S :{stayhome, stay home if repressed in period 1}*

If so, for what values of p_0 does it hold? Is it consistent with the intuitive criterion?

(5) *Compute a semipooling equilibrium where M represses in the first period with probability q. For what values of p_0 does S protest?*

EXERCISE 8.6 *Compute the remaining partial-pooling equilibria for the War Chest game.*

EXERCISE 8.7 *Show that there are no partial-pooling equilibria in the open rule version of the Gilligan-Krehbiel model.*

EXERCISE 8.8 *Consider the open rule version of the Gilligan-Krehbiel model described earlier, but suppose that their are two committee members with $c > \theta$ that observe the state and make simultaneous messages to the floor. Does a separating equilibrium exist? Now suppose that there are three committee members. Does a separating equilibrium exist?*

EXERCISE 8.9 *Show that for any finite extensive form game, if $\sigma(\cdot), b(\cdot)$ constitutes a sequential equilibrium, then $\sigma(\cdot)$ is subgame perfect.*

EXERCISE 8.10 *Show that in a one-sender, one-receiver signaling game if the sender's type space has two elements the sets of PBE and SE coincide.*

EXERCISE 8.11 *Prove Proposition 8.9.*

EXERCISE 8.12 *Prove Proposition 8.10.*

EXERCISE 8.13 *Show that in the Hussein-Bush game the equilibrium pooling on y does not violate the intuitive criterion.*

EXERCISE 8.14 *Can one modify the probability of w in Figure 8.10 to support the observed path of play ($\tilde{y}$ and a) as a PBE?*

EXERCISE 8.15 *Characterize the levels of s_I and entry lotteries that are supportable in a PBE to the modified war chest game where the message space is the positive real numbers.*

EXERCISE 8.16 *Characterize the unique intuitive equilibrium to the modified war chest game where the message space is the positive real numbers.*

EXERCISE 8.17 *In the loan guarantee game with two types, show that the unique intuitive equilibrium involves $r(1) = \arg\max\{r - r^2\} = 1/2$ and $r(2) = \arg\max\{r - r^2/2\} = 1$.*

EXERCISE 8.18 *In the loan guarantee game with three types, show that the unique universally divine equilibrium involves $r(1) = \arg\max\{r - r^2\} = 1/2$ and $r(2) = \arg\max\{r - r^2/2\} = 1$ and $r(3) = \arg\max\{r - r^2/3\} = 3/2$.*

9 Repeated Games

Many models in political game theory involve agents' playing the same game repeatedly. In many of these cases, the focus is on how certain social practices such as conventions, norms, cooperation, and trust are sustained when actors have short-run incentives to deviate from these practices. Another significant application of "repeated games" is the study of how to solve social dilemmas such as the Prisoner's Dilemma without recourse to centralized authority (Taylor 1976).

The most interesting conceptual issue in such games is the extent to which repetition creates the opportunity to sustain more behavior as Nash equilibria than is possible in single-shot games. In general, the set of Nash equilibria is much larger in repeated games than in the corresponding static versions; expectations that future play is dependent on current behavior can create incentives for behavior that is not optimal in a one-shot interaction. Repeated games, however, generate an opposite problem; the proliferation of equilibria is so great that generating precise predictions becomes difficult.

To see how expectations about the future can influence behavior, consider the normal form game[1] in Table 9.1.

If this game is played once there are only two Nash equilibria: (M, M) and (B, R) (starred in the table). Although the strategy profile (T, L) provides the highest aggregate payoff, it is not a Nash equilibrium; player 1 unilaterally defects to B and player 2 unilaterally defects to R. What happens if this game is played twice with players' caring about their combined two-period payoffs? Suppose player 1 chooses the strategy "Play T in period 1; if player 2 plays L in period 1 play M in period 2;

---

[1] By this point in the book, we assume that students are quite comfortable with games that do not have motivating stories.

Table 9.1

1\2	L	M	R
T	8, 8	0, 0	1, 9
M	0, 0	5, 5*	0, 0
B	9, 1	0, 0	3, 3*

otherwise play B in period 2." Moreover, suppose that player 2 chooses the strategy "Play L in period 1; if player 1 plays T in period 1 play M in period 2; otherwise play R in period 2." This pair of strategies is a Nash equilibrium if the stage game is played twice. In this equilibrium the agents play the "good" outcome (T, L) in the first period. If either player defects, her payoff is $9 + 3 = 12$, less than the equilibrium utility of $8 + 5 = 13$. In fact, not only do these strategies constitute a Nash equilibrium, but the equilibrium is subgame perfect. Because (M, M) and (B, R) are Nash equilibria of the one-shot game, playing them in the proper subgames is consistent with subgame perfection. A strategy playing (T, L) in the second period, however, cannot be supported in a Nash equilibrium.

1. The Repeated Prisoner's Dilemma

One of the most studied games is the repeated Prisoner's Dilemma. Consider an application focused on trade policy. Suppose that the world economy performs better when all nations agree to free trade, but that individual countries prefer to protect their domestic economy. Given this tension, how are free trade regimes sustained? One answer is that free trade can be supported as an equilibrium in a repeated game where a trade war begins whenever a major country defects from the trade agreement. To illustrate this argument, consider Table 9.2, a representation of a trade policy dilemma between the United States (U.S.) and the European Union (EU).

Table 9.2. Free Trade Game

U.S.\EU	Free Trade	Protect
Free Trade	10, 10	1, 12
Protect	12, 1	4, 4

Obviously, if the game is played once, the unique Nash equilibrium is the strategy profile (*Protect*, *Protect*). If it is played twice, then the strategy sets for each player are

$$\{FT_1\,FT_2\,FT_2,\ FT_1\,FT_2\,P_2,\ FT_1\,P_2\,FT_2,\ FT_1\,P_2\,P_2,\ P_1\,FT_2\,FT_2,\ P_1\,FT_2\,P_2,$$
$$P_1\,P_2\,FT_2,\ P_1\,P_2\,P_2\},$$

where $FT_1 FT_2 P_2$ means "Play FT in period 1 and play FT in period 2 if the other country plays FT in period 1; otherwise play P." Table 9.3 depicts the normal form representation of the two-period game (we ignore the discounting of future payoffs).

Unlike the example of Table 9.1, repeating the game once does not affect behavior as $(P_1 P_2 P_2, P_1 P_2 P_3)$ is the only Nash equilibrium. This result can be generalized to any finite number of periods. In the last period, each country protects. This is known in the penultimate period, so it is not possible for penultimate period behavior to affect final period behavior. Thus, each country has an incentive to protect in this period as well. This process unravels until each country is protecting in every period.

We could induce first-period cooperation in Table 9.1 because first-period behavior helps coordinate among multiple equilibria in the second period. The good equilibrium is used as a reward whereas the bad equilibrium is used as a punishment. Because the Prisoner's Dilemma has only one Nash equilibrium, it is impossible to encourage cooperation with the promise of coordinating on a good equilibrium or the threat of coordinating on a bad equilibrium.

If the game lasts an infinite number of periods, however, this ceases to be an issue. Suppose that the "good equilibrium" is free trade in every period and the "bad equilibrium" is protection in every period. As we will now see, if there is no last period, the good equilibrium need not unravel as it does in the finite case. Thus, in every single period, cooperation is sustained by the reward of the good equilibrium and the sanction of the bad.

2. The Grim Trigger Equilibrium

To see how infinite repetition eliminates the "last-period" problem, consider the following strategy: "Play free trade in every period until the other country protects, then protect forever." This is known as the *grim trigger strategy*, because any failure to cooperate leads to the noncooperative equilibrium in all future periods. If each country plays this strategy, both receive 10 in every period. If both countries discount the future at a common factor of δ, the long-term utility of this strategy is $10/(1 - \delta)$.[2] To show that this strategy is a Nash equilibrium, we must

---

[2] See Chapter 3 for a discussion of time discounting and the calculation of infinite sums of discounted utilities.

Table 9.3. Two-Period Free Trade Game

U.S.\EU	$FT_1FT_2FT_2$	$FT_1FT_2P_2$	$FT_1P_2FT_2$	$FT_1P_2P_2$	$P_1FT_2FT_2$	$P_1FT_2P_2$	$P_1P_2FT_2$	$P_1P_2P_2$
$FT_1FT_2FT_2$	20, 20	20, 20	11, 22	11, 22	11, 22	11, 22	2, 24	2, 24
$FT_1FT_2P_2$	20, 20	20, 20	11, 22	11, 22	13, 13	13, 13	5, 16	5, 16
$FT_1P_2FT_2$	22, 11	22, 11	14, 14	14, 14	11, 22	11, 22	2, 24	2, 24
$FT_1P_2P_2$	22, 11	22, 11	14, 14	14, 14	13, 13	13, 13	5, 16	5, 16
$P_1FT_2FT_2$	22, 11	13, 13	22, 11	13, 13	14, 14	5, 16	14, 14	5, 16
$P_1FT_2P_2$	22, 11	13, 13	22, 11	13, 13	16, 5	8, 8	16, 5	8, 8
$P_1P_2FT_2$	24, 2	16, 5	24, 2	16, 5	14, 14	5, 16	14, 14	5, 16
$P_1P_2P_2$	24, 2	16, 5	24, 2	16, 5	16, 5	8, 8	16, 5	8, 8*

Table 9.4. Generalized Prisoner's Dilemma

1\2	Cooperate	Don't Cooperate
Cooperate	a, a	d, c
Don't Cooperate	c, d	b, b

show that neither player prefers to defect. Because each stage game is identical, either a player wants to defect in every period or never prefers to defect. Defection gives the defector 12 in the period of the defection. Because the other country protects forever after the defection, the defector's best response is also to protect forever. Therefore, the defector gets 4 in every period after the defection. The total utility from defecting is therefore $12 + \delta4/(1 - \delta)$. Thus, the grim trigger strategies are a Nash equilibrium to the repeated Prisoner's Dilemma if and only if $10/(1 - \delta) \geq 12 + \delta4/(1 - \delta)$. This inequality is satisfied if and only if $\delta \geq 1/4$. As long as the players are sufficiently patient (δ is large), the grim trigger strategy is a Nash equilibrium. The grim trigger equilibrium is also subgame perfect. A proper subgame to this game is also an infinitely repeated Prisoner's Dilemma; thus playing protect forever is a Nash equilibrium in any subgame in which at least one player has previously protected. A subgame following only free trade looks identical to the original game. Thus, because this strategy profile is a Nash equilibrium, it is a Nash equilibrium in a subgame of this type.

Now consider a generalized Prisoner's Dilemma, shown in Table 9.4. where $c > a > b > d$. Using exactly the same arguments, the grim trigger strategy is a SPNE if and only if $a/(1 - \delta) \geq c + \delta b/(1 - \delta)$. Rearranging yields the condition

$$\delta \geq \frac{c - a}{c - b}.$$

Thus, cooperation is harder to sustain (requires a higher discount factor) when

(1) c is large relative to a and b
(2) a and b are roughly equal.

3. Tit-for-Tat Strategies

The grim trigger strategy is not the only equilibrium of the infinitely repeated Prisoner's Dilemma that sustains the cooperative outcome. Many authors find the grim trigger equilibrium unrealistic and undesirable, because cooperation disappears forever after a single defection. Moreover, it is not robust to mistakes by the players. Finally, following a breakdown of cooperation the players cannot renegotiate to return to the cooperative phase, something they clearly have an incentive to do. If players can engage in such renegotiation, however, the incentive for cooperation diminishes; the uncooperative path is no longer a credible deterrent.

An alternative Nash equilibrium is based on "tit-for-tat" strategies of the form "Cooperate in the first period and then in any subsequent period play the action that the other player chose in the previous period." In order to check whether tit-for-tat strategies form a Nash equilibrium, consider a unilateral deviation by player i, *don't cooperate* in period t. Player i's payoff in period t is c. In period $t + 1$, she gets either d or b, depending on how she plays. Return to tit-for-tat in period $t + 1$ results in the oscillating sequence $d, c, d, c, d, c, \ldots$. So the future stream of payoffs from a one-period defection and return to tit-for-tat is $c + \delta d + \delta^2 c + \delta^3 d + \delta^4 c + \cdots = c + \delta d + \delta^2 (c + \delta d) + \delta^4 (c + \delta d) + \cdots = (c + \delta d)/(1 - \delta^2)$. If i plays *don't cooperate* in all subsequent periods starting in t then the stream of payoffs is simply $c + \delta b/(1 - \delta)$. We leave as an exercise to show that the best deviation from tit-for-tat results in one of these two payoff streams. Recall that the stream of payoffs from equilibrium play is $a/(1 - \delta)$. Accordingly, tit-for-tat is a Nash equilibrium if and only if

$$\frac{a}{1 - \delta} \geq \max\left\{\frac{c + \delta d}{1 - \delta^2}, c + \delta\left(\frac{b}{1 - \delta}\right)\right\}$$

Rearranging allows us to express this as a condition on the discount rate. The inequality

$$\frac{a}{1 - \delta} \geq \frac{c + \delta d}{1 - \delta^2}$$

reduces to $\delta \geq (c - a)/(a - d)$. The inequality

$$\frac{a}{1 - \delta} \geq c + \delta\left(\frac{b}{1 - \delta}\right)$$

reduces to $\delta \geq (c - a)/(c - b)$. Thus tit-for-tat is a Nash equilibrium if and only if

$$\delta \geq \max\left\{\frac{c-a}{a-d}, \frac{c-a}{c-b}\right\}.$$

Is tit-for-tat subgame perfect? When players use this strategy there are two types of subgames to consider:

(1) A subgame where, following cooperation in the previous period, both players are expected to cooperate in the next period. This is the cooperation phase.
(2) A subgame where following cooperation by one player and defection by the other, the defector is supposed to cooperate and the other player is supposed to punish the defector by not cooperating in the next period. This is the punishment phase.

In fact there are also subgames in which both players are supposed to defect, but these subgames are not reached by a unilateral deviation from the equilibrium path when players use the tit-for-tat strategy. The incentives for a deviation in the cooperation phase can be understood by appealing to the single-deviation principle. In presenting subgame perfection we proved that the single-deviation principle holds for finite games. It also holds for infinitely repeated games when payoffs are discounted with a discount rate $\delta < 1$. We leave the proof of this result as an exercise.[3] A unilateral single deviation from tit-fot-tat yields the payoff stream $c + \delta d + \delta^2 c + \delta^3 d + \delta^4 c + \cdots$, and the preceding analysis demonstrates that this deviation is not desirable if $\delta \geq (c - a)/(a - d)$.

Now consider the punishment phase and suppose that agent i is supposed to play *don't cooperate* and agent j is supposed to play *cooperate*. A unilateral single-period deviation by player i in period t results in cooperation by both players in all periods after period t. Accordingly, the payoff stream to i from this deviation is $a + \delta a + \delta^2 a + \cdots = a/(1 - \delta)$. The stream of payoffs from following the equilibrium strategy in the payoff phase is $c + \delta d + \delta^2 c + \delta^3 d + \cdots = (c + \delta d)/(1 - \delta^2)$. Thus,

---

[3] The difficulty in extending the principle to infinite horizon games is that it is possible for a strategy that is not subgame perfect to be beaten only by a deviation in an infinite number of periods. With discounting, however, deviations that are sufficiently distant cannot influence payoffs very much, and thus if a strategy is not subgame perfect there must be a better alternative strategy that has deviation in only a finite number of periods. From this, the intuition captured in the finite game result applies.

agent i prefers to play tit-for-tat in the punishment stage as long as $(c + \delta d)/(1 - \delta^2) \geq a/(1 - \delta)$. This inequality is the reversal of the condition for tit-for-tat to be a Nash equilibrium. In order to follow through on the punishment i needs to prefer the oscillation between c and d over the perpetual stream of c. In order for i to prefer playing tit-for-tat to an initial deviation, however, she must prefer the perpetual stream of a's to the oscillation stream. Accordingly, tit-for-tat is only a subgame perfect Nash equilibrium if $\delta = (c - a)/(a - d)$, a very knife-edge condition.

An alternative version of tit-for-tat avoids the problem of oscillation in the punishment phase. Milgrom, North, and Weingast (1990) argue for the strategy "Start out playing *cooperate*. Unless you selected *don't cooperate* in period $t - 2$, play *cooperate* in period t if the other player selected *cooperate* in period $t - 1$. If you selected *don't cooperate* in period $t - 1$, then select *cooperate* in periods t and $t + 1$." Although this strategy seems convoluted, it has a natural interpretation. It suggests that following any deviation, the deviating player must cooperate for one period while his opponent defects. This strategy pair punishes the deviator with the low payoff of d. After this one-period punishment, both players return to cooperating. As an exercise the reader is asked to show that this *modified tit-for-tat* strategy is subgame perfect as long as δ is large enough.

4. Intermediate Punishment Strategies

The grim trigger and tit-for-tat strategies represent just two of the possible strategies that sustain cooperative outcomes. These strategies can be generalized to include strategies that involve punishment phases of intermediate length. Consider the following strategies:

(1) Cooperate until your opponent defects. If your opponent defects do not cooperate for the next k periods but then return to cooperation; if you defect do not cooperate for the next k periods but then return to cooperation. Once you have returned to cooperation, cooperate until a defection occurs. Following a defection use the preceding punishment strategy.

(2) Cooperate until your opponent defects. If your opponent defects do not cooperate for k periods. If she cooperates in each of the k periods return to cooperation, ending the punishment

phase. If she fails to cooperate in any period of the punishment phase, then the punishment phase starts over: that is, don't cooperate for k more periods. If your own failure to cooperate caused the punishment phase then cooperate during the punishment phase.

Strategy 1 is similar to the grim trigger strategy in that a punishment consists of a reversion to the strategy pair (*don't cooperate, don't cooperate*). But now the punishment phase is finite. The second strategy is similar to the subgame perfect version of tit-for-tat in that a defector is punished by the need to cooperate while the other player does not.

Consider strategy 1 first. There is no incentive to defect during a punishment phase: noncooperation is a best response to noncooperation in terms of current period payoffs, and deviation only lengthens the punishment phase. Consider a defection from mutual cooperation. The payoff stream from a single defection during a cooperative phase consists of the one-period gain from defecting, b for k periods, and an infinite stream of a beginning $k + 1$ periods in the future. Again because of the single-deviation principle for subgame perfection, we need only worry about a single deviation. Thus, using the rules for computing infinite sums, the utility of defecting during the punishment phase is

$$c + \frac{\delta - \delta^{k+1}}{1 - \delta} b + \frac{\delta^{k+1}}{1 - \delta} a.$$

Consequently, sustaining cooperation requires that

$$a \left(1 - \delta^{k+1}\right) \geq (1 - \delta) c + \left(\delta - \delta^{k+1}\right) b.$$

Although we cannot generate a closed form for the critical value of δ, we can rewrite this expression as

$$\delta > \frac{c - a}{c - b} + \delta^{k+1} \frac{a - b}{c - b}.$$

The first term on the right side of the inequality is the critical value for the grim trigger strategy, and the second term is positive for any finite k. Not surprisingly, it is harder to sustain cooperation with a finite punishment phase. In a model where players make mistakes, however, this equilibrium may be preferred to the grim trigger strategy.[4]

Now consider strategy 2 and a defection from the cooperation phase. The payoff from a defection consists of a one-period benefit c, a punishment payoff of d for k periods, and a return to cooperative payoffs a at the end of the punishment. Summing these up generates $c + (\delta - \delta^{k+1})d/(1 - \delta) + \delta^{k+1}a/(1 - \delta)$. Because $a > d$, this expression is declining in k. Thus, increasing the length of the punishment phase decreases the incentive to defect from the cooperative phase.

Increasing k, however, may not make such an equilibrium easier to sustain because it reduces the incentive to comply in the punishment phase. Consider the payoffs from defecting from the punishment phase. These payoffs consist of b for one period, d for k periods, and then return to a for a total payoff of $b + (\delta - \delta^{k+1})d/(1 - \delta) + \delta^{k+1}a/(1 - \delta)$. The payoffs from adhering to the equilibrium in the punishment phase depend on the current period of the punishment phase. Because we must verify compliance in each period, we need to ensure compliance in the period when the payoff to compliance is lowest. This period is the first one of the punishment phase. Thus, the utility for complying with the punishment in this period is $(1 - \delta^k)d/(1 - \delta) + \delta^k a/(1 - \delta)$. Thus, compliance with the punishment requires

$$\delta > \left(\frac{b - d}{a - d}\right)^{\frac{1}{k}}.$$

This critical value is clearly diminishing in k.

5. The Folk Theorem

A common theme of these examples is that so long as the agents are sufficiently patient, outcomes that are not Nash equilibria in static games may be Nash equilibria or subgame perfect equilibria of infinitely repeated games. In fact, any payoff vector to an infinitely repeated game that satisfies *individual rationality* can be sustained as a SPNE so long

---

[4] Like the grim trigger SPNE, punishment is not renegotiation proof. Once the agents reach a punishment phase they both gain from negotiating a settlement that moves to cooperation in fewer than k periods.

as agents are sufficiently patient. This result has been well known for so long that it has been afforded the status of a *folk theorem*. In this section, we formally prove one version.

The primitives of a repeated game are a normal form stage game $\Gamma = \langle N, S, u \rangle$ and vector of agent discount rates $\delta = (\delta_1, \ldots, \delta_n)$. In each period $t \in \{1, 2, 3, \ldots\}$, the agents play normal form game Γ. Before agent i selects her strategy in period t, $s_i^t \in S_i$, she observes the strategy profile s^{t-1} played in period $t - 1$. We assume perfect recall so that s_i^t can be conditioned on the history $h^{t-1} = (s^1, \ldots, s^{t-1}) \in S^{t-1} := \prod_{j=1}^{t-1} S$. The null history is $h^0 = \emptyset$. A pure strategy for player i is then a sequence of mappings $\{s_i^t(h^{t-1}) : S^{t-1} \to S_i\}_{t=1}^{\infty}$. A mixed strategy is a sequence of mappings $\{\sigma_i^t(h^{t-1}) : S^{t-1} \to \Delta(S_i)\}_{t=1}^{\infty}$. Given a sequence of lotteries over stage game profiles $\{\sigma^t\}_{t=1}^{\infty}$ agent i's expected utility is $\mathbb{E}U_i(\{\sigma^t\}_{t=1}^{\infty}) = (1 - \delta_i) \sum_{t=1}^{\infty} \delta_i^{t-1} \mathbb{E}_{\sigma^t} u_i(s^t)$ where $\mathbb{E}_{\sigma^t} u_i(s^t)$ takes the expectation of $u_i(s^t)$ over the mixture σ^t. The multiplier $(1 - \delta_i)$ is included so that for a constant sequence σ^t, $\mathbb{E}U_i(\{\sigma^t\}_{t=1}^{\infty}) = \mathbb{E}u_i(\sigma^t)$. The repeated game induced by a stage game is denoted $\Gamma^{\infty} = \langle N, S, u, \delta \rangle$. Of course a repeated game is also an extensive form game so that Nash equilibria and subgame perfect Nash equilibria are well defined in the repeated game.

We focus on repeated games generated by finite normal form stage games. From Nash's theorem, every such stage game has at least one mixed strategy Nash equilibrium. It is not surprising, therefore, that every such repeated game has a mixed strategy subgame perfect Nash equilibrium; strategies that use the stage game equilibrium strategies in each period regardless of the history form a SPNE in Γ^{∞}.

THEOREM 9.1 *If σ^* is a subgame perfect Nash equilibrium of the stage game then the repeated game profile $\sigma_i^t(h^{t-1}) = \sigma_i^*$ for every (h^{t-1}) for every t for every i is a subgame perfect Nash equilibrium of the repeated game.*

An interesting feature of repeated games is that the set of subgame perfect Nash equilibria is usually very large. The folk theorems serve to quantify the set of equilibrium payoffs that are supportable in such an equilibrium. We prove a particularly useful and simple folk theorem. First, we require several definitions.

DEFINITION 9.1 *The payoff vector* $v = (v_1, \ldots, v_i, \ldots, v_n) \in \mathbb{R}^n$ *is individually rational if*

$$v_i \geq \min_{s_{-i} \in S_{-i}} \left\{ \max_{s_i \in S_i} u_i(s_i, s_{-i}) \right\}$$

for each $i \in N$.

The value $\min_{s_{-i} \in S_{-i}} \left\{ \max_{s_i \in S_i} u_i(s_i, s_{-i}) \right\}$ is the minimal stage game utility that player i attains from any strategy profile in which she plays a best response to s_{-i}. This value is identified by letting players $-i$ select s_{-i} so as to minimize the utility to i of playing a best response to s_{-i}.

DEFINITION 9.2 *The payoff vector* $v \in \mathbb{R}^n$ *is feasible if there is some pure strategy profile* s *such that for each* $i \in N$, $u_i(s)/(1 - \delta_i) = v_i$.

THEOREM 9.2 *For every feasible and individually rational payoff vector* $v \in \mathbb{R}^n$ *there is an n-tuple of discount rates* δ' *such that the payoff vector* v *occurs in a Nash equilibrium of the repeated game if each coordinate of* δ *is at least that of* δ'.

Proof Assume that v is feasible and individually rational. Let $\{s^{vt}\}$ be a strategy profile that plays the strategy that attains the payoff vector v as long as no one has previously deviated from this strategy or more than two players have deviated. If exactly one player, say i, has deviated, this strategy calls for $\{s_i^{pt} = \arg\min_{s_{-i} \in S_{-i}} \{\max_{s_i \in S_i} u_i(s_i, s_{-i})\}\}$. This strategy punishes the deviating player in all subsequent periods. At any period t the payoff to i of playing $\{s^{vt}\}$ is v_i and the payoff to deviating is bounded by

$$(1 - \delta_i^t)v_i + \delta_i^t(1 - \delta_i) \max_{s \in S} u_i(s) + \delta_i^{t+1} \min_{s_{-i} \in S_{-i}} \left\{ \max_{s_i \in S_i} u_i(s_i, s_{-i}) \right\}.$$

This value is less than v_i if

$$\delta_i \geq \frac{\max_{s \in S} u_i(s) - v_i}{\max_{s \in S} u_i(s) - \min_{s_{-i} \in S_{-i}} \left\{ \max_{s_i \in S_i} u_i(s_i, s_{-i}) \right\}}.$$

Because $\max_{s \in S} u_i(s) \geq v_i \geq \min_{s_{-i} \in S_{-i}} \left\{ \max_{s_i \in S_i} u_i(s_i, s_{-i}) \right\}$ the right-hand side is strictly less than 1. As long as this condition is satisfied for each $i \in N$, the conjectured strategy profile is a Nash equilibrium to the repeated game. □

The equilibria used in the proof need not be SPNE as the punishment can be very costly to impose. We can quantify a set of payoff vectors supportable in SPNE to the repeated game using reversion to stage game Nash strategies as the punishment. We leave the following result as an exercise.

THEOREM 9.3 *If $v \in \mathbb{R}^n$ is a feasible payoff vector and for each $i \in N$ there is some mixed strategy stage game Nash equilibrium that yields the expected payoff vector v' with $v'_i < v_i$ there is an n-tuple of discount rates δ' such that there is subgame perfect Nash equilibrium in the repeated game that yields the payoff vector v if each coordinate of δ is at least that of δ'.*

Most applications of folk theorems in political science are covered by these two propositions. Scholars, however, have extended these results in many directions and we refer interested readers to Abreu (1988) and Fudenberg and Maskin (1986).

6. Application: Interethnic Cooperation

Fearon and Laitin (1996) use infinitely repeated games to understand how interethnic cooperation is sustained. Consider two groups A and B both with n (even) members. In each period t, players are randomly matched to play the Prisoner's Dilemma in Table 9.5, where $\alpha > 1$, $\beta > 0$, and $(\alpha - \beta)/2 < 1$. Further suppose that each group member has a common discount factor $\delta \in (0, 1)$. In each period m members of each group are selected to be paired with members of the other group, and the remaining $n - m$ are matched with members of their own group. This random matching process suggests that each player has a $p = m/n$ probability of being matched with an "out-group" member.

Table 9.5. Interethnic Cooperation Game

1\2	Cooperate	Defect
Cooperate	1, 1	$-\beta, \alpha$
Defect	$\alpha, -\beta$	0, 0

To capture the dynamics of intergroup and intragroup interaction, Laitin and Fearon assume that the result of in-group pairings is observed by all members of the group. The history of play for members of the other group is not observed, however. Thus, interethnic cooperation is hard to sustain because those who defect in intergroup interactions cannot be singled out for punishment by members of the other group. Nevertheless, Fearon and Laitin argue that cooperation can be sustained even in the absence of these direct sanctions. They consider two such equilibria to this game. The first is the *spiral* equilibrium. In this equilibrium, cooperation is supported within groups by k^{in} periods of punishment against individual defectors. Intergroup cooperation is sustained by the threat of group-specific punishment phases of k^{out} periods. During these punishment phases, all members of a given group are punished by the other group if any has defected in an intergroup interaction. The second equilibrium is the *in-group policing* equilibrium in which there is no cross-group punishment, but each group punishes its own for defections against the other group. In the following, we analyze the in-group policing equilibrium and refer the reader to the original article for the discussion of the spiral equilibrium.

6.1. The In-Group Policing Equilibrium. We focus on group A as the analysis extends easily to the strategies of group B. Let $s_t = (k_1, k_2, \ldots, k_n)$ be the *state* of the system where k_i is the number of periods remaining in the punishment period for player i at the beginning of period t. If $k_i = 0$, player i is a cooperator and if $k_i > 0$ player i is a defector. The strategy for the in-group policing equilibrium involves nice play (i.e., no player initiates defection). Off the equilibrium path, defectors are punished for a fixed number of periods by members of their own group. Defectors, themselves, cooperate with the cooperators who are punishing them; punishers defect against defectors. All types cooperate with out-group members. Fearon and Laitin describe the strategy as follows:

> Play C in all out-group pairings. For in-group pairings, always play C against any partner not in punishment phase, and always play D against any player in punishment phase. A player enters or restarts a punishment phase for k^{gp} periods if she defects against either an out-group or an in-group cooperator.

For a given state s_t and any integer $l > 0$, let n_{t+l} be the number of members of group A who will be cooperators in period $t + l$, assuming that each plays the equilibrium strategy from period t to period $t + l$. Therefore, $q_{t+l} = (n_{t+l})/(n - 1)$ is the probability of facing a cooperator in an in-group interaction.

To demonstrate that these strategies constitute a subgame perfect Nash equilibrium, we must verify the following conditions:

(1) A cooperator i has no incentive to
   (a) defect against any out-group player
   (b) defect against any in-group cooperator
   (c) cooperate with any in-group defector.
(2) A defector i has no incentive to
   (a) defect against an out-group player
   (b) defect against an in-group cooperator
   (c) cooperate against an in-group defector.

Clearly, conditions 1(c) and 2(c) are satisfied; those deviations lower utility in the current period without affecting strategies of any other player, that is, do not trigger punishments. Note that 1(a) and 1(b) reflect the same trade-offs; both deviations generate a payoff of α in period t followed by k^{gp} periods of punishment. Thus, we must only establish that there is no incentive to deviate in cases 1(a), 2(a), and 2(b).

The utility for cooperation against an in-group cooperator or out-group member is

$$1 + \sum_{l=1}^{\infty} \delta^l (p + (1 - p)(q_{t+l} + (1 - q_{t+l})\alpha)),$$

and the utility from deviations 1(a) and 1(b) is

$$\alpha + \sum_{l=1}^{k^{gp}} \delta^l (p + (1 - p)(-q_{t+l}\beta + (1 - q_{t+l})0))$$

$$+ \sum_{l=k^{gp}+1}^{\infty} \delta^l (p + (1 - p)(q_{t+l} + (1 - q_{t+l})\alpha)). \qquad (9.1)$$

The net utility of cooperating is therefore

$$1 - \alpha + \sum_{l=1}^{k^{gp}} \delta^l ((1 - p)(q_{t+l}(1 + \beta) + (1 - q_{t+l})\alpha)). \qquad (9.2)$$

So that deviations 1(a) and 1(b) are not profitable, equation 9.2 must be positive for all states and resulting sequences of q_{t+l}. If $\alpha > 1 + \beta$, equation 9.2 is minimized by $q_{t+l} = 1$ for $l = 1, \ldots, k^{gp}$. This is the path following $s_t = (0, 0, \ldots, 0)$. The net utility is positive following this state if and only if

$$\delta^{k^{gp}} \leq 1 - \frac{(1 - \delta)(\alpha - 1)}{\delta(1 - p)(1 + \beta)}. \tag{9.3}$$

Now consider the case where $1 + \beta > \alpha$. The net utility is minimized at $q_{t+l} = 0$ for $l = 1, \ldots, k^{gp}$. Given the definition of q this is an infeasible sequence, because all players are assumed to cooperate in their punishment phases and terminate their punishments after k^{gp} periods. Thus, the minimizing sequence is one where all players defect in time $t - 1$ and return to cooperation status in period $t + k^{gp} - 1$. The sequence of q is therefore $q_{t+l} = 0$ for $l = 1, k^{gp} - 1$, and $q_{t+k^{gp}} = 1$. Some algebra yields the requirement that

$$\frac{\left(\delta - \delta^{k^{gp}}\right)}{1 - \delta} \frac{\alpha}{(1 + \beta)} + \delta^{k^{gp}} \geq \frac{\alpha - 1}{(1 - p)(1 + \beta)}. \tag{9.4}$$

Now we need to check to see whether a defector at time t wishes to make deviation 2(a). Suppose that a defector with k_i is paired against an out-group player. The utility of cooperating is

$$1 + \sum_{l=1}^{k_i - 1} \delta^l(p + (1 - p)(-q_{t+l}\beta + (1 - q_{t+l})0))$$

$$+ \sum_{l=k_i}^{\infty} \delta^l(p + (1 - p)(q_{t+l} + (1 - q_{t+l})\alpha)),$$

and the utility of the deviation is equation 9.1. Thus, the defector cooperates with an out-group member so long as

$$\sum_{l=k_i}^{k^{gp}} \delta^l((1 - p)(q_{t+l}(1 + \beta) + (1 - q_{t+l})\alpha)) \geq \alpha - 1.$$

The right side of this inequality is minimized when $k_i = k^{gp}$ so we require

$$\delta^{k^{gp}}((1-p)(q_{t+k^{gp}}(1+\beta)+(1-q_{t+k^{gp}+l})\alpha)) \geq \alpha - 1.$$

Because all players play according to the equilibrium strategy, $q_{t+k^{gp}} = 1$ for all s_t. Therefore, the defection is profitable unless

$$\delta^{k^{gp}} \geq \frac{\alpha - 1}{(1-p)(1+\beta)}. \tag{9.5}$$

Finally, we need to rule out deviation 2(b). Assume a defector with $k_i = 1$ is paired against a cooperator. The utility of cooperating is

$$-\beta + \sum_{l=1}^{k_i-1} \delta^l(p + (1-p)(-q_{t+l}\beta + (1-q_{t+l})0))$$

$$+ \sum_{l=k_i}^{\infty} \delta^i(p + (1-p)(q_{t+l} + (1-q_{t+l})\alpha)).$$

The utility of defecting is given by

$$\sum_{l=1}^{k^{gp}} \delta^l(p + (1-p)(-q_{t+l}\beta + (1-q_{t+l})0))$$

$$+ \sum_{l=k^{gp}+1}^{\infty} \delta^i(p + (1-p)(q_{t+l} + (1-q_{t+l})\alpha)).$$

Consequently, the net utility of cooperating is $\sum_{l=k_i}^{k^{gp}} \delta^i((1-p)(q_{t+l}(1+\beta)+(1-q_{t+l})\alpha)) - \beta$. Using the same argument as in case 2(a), a SPNE requires

$$\delta^{k^{gp}} \geq \frac{\beta}{(1-p)(1+\beta)}. \tag{9.6}$$

Now we have a full set of equilibrium conditions. First, consider the case $\alpha > 1 + \beta$; where a SPNE requires equations 9.3, 9.5, and 9.6. Equation 9.6 holds whenever 9.5 does. Less obviously, we can show that equation 9.5 implies equation 9.3. We can rewrite equation 9.3 as

$$\delta \left(\delta^{k^{gp}} - \frac{\alpha - 1}{(1-p)(1+\beta)} \right) \le \delta - \frac{(\alpha - 1)}{(1-p)(1+\beta)}. \tag{9.7}$$

If equation 9.5 holds, both sides of equation 9.7 are positive and the right side must be larger because $1 > \delta > \delta^{k^{gp}}$. Thus, equation 9.5 is necessary and sufficient for the in-group policing strategies to be a subgame perfect Nash equilibrium if $\alpha > 1 + \beta$.

Now consider the case $\alpha < \beta + 1$ where a SPNE requires equations 9.4, 9.5, and 9.6 to hold. Here equation 9.6 implies equation 9.5. Also, if equation 9.6 holds, the following holds:

$$\delta^{k^{gp}} \ge \frac{\beta}{(1-p)(1+\beta)} > \frac{\alpha - 1}{(1-p)(1+\beta)}$$
$$> \frac{\alpha - 1}{(1-p)(1+\beta)} - \frac{\left(\delta - \delta^{k^{gp}}\right)}{1-\delta} \frac{\alpha}{(1+\beta)}.$$

Therefore, equation 9.6 implies equation 9.4 so that equation 9.6 is necessary and sufficient for the in-group punishments to constitute a subgame perfect Nash equilibrium. We have proved the following proposition:

PROPOSITION 9.1 *The in-group punishment strategy with k^{gp}-period punishments is a subgame perfect Nash equilibrium if and only if*

$$\delta^{k^{gp}} \ge \min \left\{ \frac{\alpha - 1}{(1-p)(1+\beta)}, \frac{\beta}{(1-p)(1+\beta)} \right\}.$$

A few features of this SPNE are worth noting. First, if

$$\delta^{k^{gp}} \ge \min \left\{ \frac{\alpha - 1}{(1-p)(1+\beta)}, \frac{\beta}{(1-p)(1+\beta)} \right\}$$

holds for $k^{gp} > 1$, it must hold for $k^{gp} = 1$. Thus, no more than a single period of punishment is required to sustain the equilibrium. In fact, longer punishments are counterproductive; they lower the incentives of defectors to cooperate in order to end the punishments.

A second important point about this subgame perfect Nash equilibrium is that it can only be sustained if p, the probability of out-group interactions, is low enough. Because the SPNE requires

$$\min\left\{\frac{\alpha-1}{(1-p)(1+\beta)}, \frac{\beta}{(1-p)(1+\beta)}\right\} \leq 1,$$

it does not exist if

$$p > \min\left\{\frac{1}{1+\beta}, 1-\frac{\alpha-1}{1+\beta}\right\}.$$

When the probability of interaction with the out-group is large, the probability of punishment for any deviation is low because punishments are meted out only by in-group players. This effect generates the somewhat counterintuitive implication that interethnic cooperation is impeded by too much interethnic interaction. Fearon and Laitin argue that this result provides an endogenous rationale for groups' wanting to preserve ethnic boundaries.

7. Application: Trade Wars

Consider a generalization of the free trade game as presented in Table 9.6.

We now interpret Θ_i as the value to each country of the other country's open markets and ρ as each country's gain from protecting its own markets. As before, free trade can be supported by grim trigger strategies if an only if $\Theta_i/(1-\delta) \geq \Theta_i + \rho + \delta\rho/(1-\delta)$ or

$$\delta \geq \frac{\rho}{\Theta_i}$$

for both players.

Supporting this equilibrium depends crucially on each country's ability to observe the policies of the other country perfectly. This is not a very realistic assumption if countries use invisible trade barriers. Also

Table 9.6. Generalized Free Trade Game

1\2	Free Trade	Protection
Free Trade	Θ_1, Θ_2	$0, \Theta_2 + \rho$
Protection	$\Theta_1 + \rho, 0$	ρ, ρ

because trade flows vary with a number of market conditions unrelated to trade policy, a fall in trade between countries need not require malfeasance by the other side.

To model these issues, assume that each country cannot directly observe the policies of the other country but observes only the value of its trade Θ_i, which is a random variable. To keep matters as simple as possible, assume that when country j engages in free trade $\Theta_i = \theta > 0$ with probability π and $\Theta_i = 0$ with probability $1 - \pi$. If country j protects its markets, $\Theta_i = 0$ with probability 1. Consequently, following $\Theta_i = \theta$ country i can infer that j selected free trade; following $\Theta_i = 0$ country i faces uncertainty about country j's policy choice. Let $\pi\theta > \rho$ so that each county prefers the free trade outcome to mutual protectionism in expectation.[5]

Clearly, there are SPNEs in which protection occurs in every period. We investigate whether there are equilibria that sustain some level of free trade. Obviously, such an equilibrium requires some form of punishment when $\Theta_i = 0$ is observed.

First, consider a grim trigger strategy in which country i protects forever following any observation of $\Theta_i = 0$. Thus, the payoffs to free trade in the first period are $\pi\theta + (1 - \pi)0$. Free trade continues to the next period so long as $\Theta_1 = \Theta_2 = \theta$, which occurs with probability π^2. Thus, country i's payoffs in the second period are $\pi^2(\pi\theta + (1 - \pi)0) + (1 - \pi^2)\rho = \pi^3\theta + (1 - \pi^2)\rho$. Continuing the same logic to period 3, we get $\pi^5\theta + (1 - \pi^4)\rho$. Thus, the infinite discounted sum of utilities from free trade is

$$V^{FT} = \pi\theta + \delta \left(\pi^3\theta + (1 - \pi^2)\rho \right) + \delta^2 \left(\pi^5\theta + (1 - \pi^4)\rho \right) + \cdots$$
$$V^{FT} = \pi\theta(1 + \delta\pi^2 + \delta^2\pi^4 + \cdots) + \delta(1 - \pi^2)\rho + \delta^2(1 - \pi^4)\rho + \cdots.$$

The first series is $\pi\theta/(1 - \delta\pi^2)$ while the second series can be further reduced to $\delta\rho/(1 - \delta) - \delta\pi^2\rho/(1 - \delta\pi^2)$. Consequently,

$$V^{FT} = \frac{\pi\theta - \delta\pi^2\rho}{1 - \delta\pi^2} + \frac{\delta\rho}{1 - \delta}.$$

The utility from defecting to protection is more straightforward. The one-period payoff is $\pi\theta + \rho$, and the future payoff is $\delta\rho/(1 - \delta)$ so that

---

[5] This model is based loosely on Green and Porter's (1984) model of imperfect collusion and price wars in economic cartels.

$V^P = \pi\theta + \rho/(1-\delta)$. Thus, country i chooses free trade if and only if $V^{FT} \geq V^P$ or

$$\delta > \frac{\rho}{\pi^3\theta}.$$

For comparison, note that if policies were observable, a subgame perfect Nash equilibrium in grim trigger strategies exists so long as $\delta > \rho/(\pi\theta)$. Thus, the grim trigger strategy is significantly more difficult to sustain when policies are unobservable. In fact, if $\rho > \pi^3\theta$, there are no discount rates for which grim trigger strategies constitute a SPNE. The grim trigger strategy is also very costly because bad realizations of Θ_i can generate infinite punishments. Although no player defects from free trade without first observing $\Theta_i = 0$, the equilibrium results almost certainly in the breakdown of trade.

Following Green and Porter (1984), we consider finite trigger strategies. If either country observes $\Theta_i = 0$, a trade war begins in which both countries protect their markets for $k \geq 1$ periods. We now establish conditions under which free trade is the optimal policy if there is no ongoing trade war.[6] Let V_i^k be the value of the k periods of payoffs for country i in a k-period trade war. It is easy to see that

$$V_i^k = \frac{(1-\delta^k)\rho}{1-\delta}.$$

Let V^{FT} be the expected payoff of the infinite stream of payoffs beginning at a period in which the countries are in a free trade phase. Therefore,

$$V^{FT} = \pi\left(\theta + \pi\delta V^{FT}\right) + \left(1 - \pi^2\right)\delta\left(V_i^k + \delta^k V^{FT}\right).$$

Simple algebra yields

$$V^{FT} = \frac{\pi\theta + \left(1 - \pi^2\right)\delta V_i^k}{1 - \pi^2\delta - (1-\pi^2)\delta^{k+1}}.$$

Using the single-deviation principle, the value of a deviation, V^P, is

$$V^P = \pi\theta + \rho + \delta\left(V_i^k + \delta^k V^{FT}\right).$$

---

[6] Since mutual protection is a Nash equilibrium, we do not need to check the optimality of protecting during a trade war.

In equilibrium it must be the case that $V^{FT} \geq V^P$. This requires that

$$\frac{\delta - \delta^{k+1}}{1 - \delta^{k+1}} > \frac{\rho}{\pi^3 \theta}. \tag{9.8}$$

The left side of this expression is increasing in k so let $k^{\min}(\delta)$ be the smallest integer such that the inequality holds for a given δ. We have proved the following proposition:

PROPOSITION 9.2 *If $\delta > \rho/(\pi^3 \theta)$ and $k \geq k^{\min}(\delta)$, the following strategies form a SPNE:*

(1) Begin the game, free trading.
(2) Free trade until $\Theta_i = 0$ for either country.
(3) Following a period in which $\Theta_i = 0$, protect for k periods.
(4) After k periods, return to free trade.

Note that a SPNE can be supported with trade wars of any length greater that $k^{\min}(\delta)$. If countries can coordinate on the optimal duration of trade wars, however, the model provides a theory of their duration. Intuitively, because trade wars are costly, the countries should coordinate on the minimal length war that sustains cooperation, that is, $k^{\min}(\delta)$. This intuition can be verified by checking that V^{FT} is strictly decreasing in k so long as $\pi \theta > \rho$. Thus, we derive empirical predictions by examining equation 9.8. Recall that the left side is increasing in k; this implies that $k^{\min}(\delta)$ is increasing in the value of protectionism and decreasing in the value of free trade. This conclusion is reasonable; trade wars should be longer when the incentive problems are more severe. The duration of trade conflict is decreasing in π. Suppose that we interpret $1 - \pi$ as the volatility of trade flows (the probability of low trade during a free trade regime). This interpretation suggests that trade volatility increases the duration of trade wars. This is necessary to prevent countries from enacting barriers and blaming the drop in trade on natural volatility. In equilibrium, the countries never protect outside trade wars so that they know with certainty that $\Theta_i = 0$ is caused by natural volatility. Ironically, although country j never defects, country i must respond to $\Theta_i = 0$ with a costly, lengthy trade war; this is necessary to ensure that barriers are, in fact, not erected.

8. Exercises

EXERCISE 9.1 *Consider the infinitely repeated game with stage game:*

1\2	l	m	r
u	1, 1	8, 3	1, 2
c	1, 6	5, 5	1, 4
d	1, 2	4, 1	2, 2

Assume that players have a common discount rate δ (with $0 < \delta < 1$).

(1) Is there a Nash equilibrium to the repeated game in which (u, m) is played in every period? Does the answer depend on the value of the discount rate δ?

(2) Find the smallest value of δ such that the following is a Nash equilibrium in the repeated game: Play (c, m) in the first period and in any period in which (c, m) was played in every previous period. If in some previous period (c, m) was not played then play (d, r) forever.

(3) Find the smallest value of δ such that there is a Nash equilibrium in which (u, m) is played in every period.

EXERCISE 9.2 *Show that in the Prisoner's Dilemma of Table 9.4, the best deviation from tit-for-tat results in one of the following payoff streams: $c + \delta d + (c + \delta d)/(1 - \delta^2)$ or $c + \delta b/(1 - \delta)$.*

EXERCISE 9.3(*) *Prove that the single-deviation principle applies for subgame perfect equilibria in infinitely repeated games if agents use discount rates less than 1.*

EXERCISE 9.4 *Find the range of discount rates for which the modified tit-for-tat strategy is subgame perfect in the repeated Prisoner's Dilemma with payoffs given by Table 9.4.*

EXERCISE 9.5 *Prove Proposition 9.1.*

EXERCISE 9.6 *Prove Proposition 9.2.*

EXERCISE 9.7 *Find conditions for the existence of the spiral SPNE to the Fearon and Laitin model. This equilibrium is based on the following strategies:*

In in-group pairings, always play C with cooperator, and always play D against a defector, regardless of one's status. A player enters or restarts the in-group punishment phase for k^{in} periods by defecting against a cooperator. In out-group pairings, play C if neither group is in an out-group punishments phase. Otherwise play, D. A group enters the out-group punishment phase for k^{out} periods if any member defects in a cross-group pairing when neither group is in the out-group punishment phase.

EXERCISE 9.8 *Consider the model of trade wars. Construct the following "probabilistic grim trigger SPNE." Instead of reverting to protectionism forever the first time $\Theta_i = 0$ is observed, assume that country i plays a mixed strategy and protects forever with probability μ.*

10 Bargaining Theory

If political science is the study of "who gets what, when and how," then bargaining theory lies at its foundation.[1] Legislators and executives bargain over new legislation. States bargain to reach new international agreements and to settle crises. Political parties bargain over coalition governments. And so on.

Not surprisingly, given bargaining's importance, the application of game theoretic models of bargaining to study political processes is a very active area of research. These models focus on two sets of issues. The first are questions of distribution – "who wins" and "who loses." Does the president get his preferred legislation? Which country gets to control the disputed region? Which parties receive government portfolios? The second important question concerns the efficiency of political bargaining. Does the bargaining process itself consume resources or fail to reach outcomes that make everyone better off? Does legislative bargaining end in gridlock or a veto even though there are policy compromises that all prefer? Do international disputes end in costly militarized conflicts and wars? Why does it take so long to form new coalition governments?

In this chapter, we review some of the most important bargaining models and their application to political science.

1. The Nash Bargaining Solution

One of the earliest attempts to model bargaining is the framework developed by John Nash. His approach is axiomatic; it stipulates a number

---

[1] See Lasswell (1936).

of features that should characterize the outcome of any bargaining situation. Before discussing these axiomatic requirements, we describe his "solution" to the bargaining problem. Our discussion closely mirrors that of Muthoo (1999).

Suppose that two players A and B negotiate over the allocation of X units of some resource. X is infinitely divisible; the feasible allocations are x_A and x_B such that $x_A + x_B \leq X$. Both players receive utility based on their allocations, $u_A(x_A)$ and $u_B(x_B)$. The utility functions $u_i(\cdot)$ are strictly increasing and concave for both players $i \in \{A, B\}$. If no agreement is reached, each player receives a default utility, *disagreement value* or *outside option* of $\underline{u}_i > u_i(0)$. Finally, to ensure that the bargaining problem is nontrivial, there exists at least one allocation (x_A, x_B) such that $u_i(x_i) > \underline{u}_i$ for each i and $x_A + x_B \leq X$. This ensures at least one feasible allocation that both players prefer to their disagreement values.

In analyzing Nash's solution to this problem, it is useful to convert it into one of allocations of utilities (u_A, u_B) rather than one of allocations of X. We, therefore, define the feasible utility allocations as the set $\Omega = \{(u_A, u_B) : u_A(x_A) = u_A, \ u_A(x_B) = u_B, \text{ and } x_A + x_B \leq X\}$. Given our assumptions about the utility functions, the boundary of this feasible set is a locus of points such as in Figure 10.1. This locus is the function

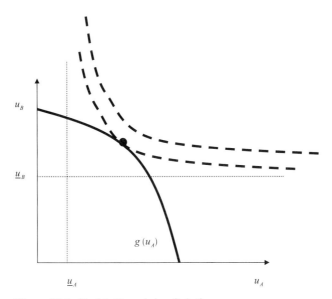

Figure 10.1. Nash's Bargaining Solution.

$g(u_A) = u_B(X - u_A^{-1}(u_A))$. Muthoo (1999) provides a proof that g is both decreasing and concave in u_A. To simplify our exposition, we assume that it is twice-differentiable.

Now we can state Nash's solution to the bargaining problem. His solution, based on the axioms discussed later, is the utility allocation $(u_A, u_B) \in \Omega$ that maximizes

$$(u_A - \underline{u}_A)(u_B - \underline{u}_B)$$

subject to $u_A \geq \underline{u}_A$ and $u_B \geq \underline{u}_B$.

The requirement that $u_A \geq \underline{u}_A$ and $u_B \geq \underline{u}_B$ is illustrated by the dotted lines in Figure 10.1. Thus, the constraint set is $g(u_A)$ on the range $[\underline{u}_A, g^{-1}(\underline{u}_B)]$. Because g is concave and decreasing, the feasible set is convex. It is easy to see that the *Nash product* $(u_A - \underline{u}_A)(u_B - \underline{u}_B)$ is quasi-concave in both u_A and u_B. Thus, its level curves in the region where the product is positive are the heavy dotted lines in Figure 10.1.

The unique Nash bargaining solution is located at the tangency of g and the iso-product curves. Mathematically, the solution to this constrained optimization problem is

$$-g'(u_A) = \frac{u_B - \underline{u}_B}{u_A - \underline{u}_A}$$

and

$$u_B = g(u_A).$$

Before proceeding to general results about the Nash bargaining solution, it is useful to consider some special cases. Assume that $X = 1$ and $u_i(x_i) = x_i$. The Nash bargaining solution for this model is

$$u_A = x_A = \frac{1 + \underline{u}_A - \underline{u}_B}{2} \text{ and } u_B = x_B = \frac{1 - \underline{u}_A + \underline{u}_B}{2}.$$

This solution has two important features. First, each player does better when a disagreement provides her with a higher utility and worse when the opponent has a better outside option. Second, if both players have equally valuable outside options, the resources are split evenly. In this case, bargainers insist upon their disagreement values and equally split the surplus $1 - \underline{u}_A - \underline{u}_B$. This split generates a utility of $\underline{u}_i + (1 - \underline{u}_A - \underline{u}_B)/2$.

Turning to the general case, the Nash bargaining solution (in terms of shares) is provided by the following proposition:

THEOREM 10.1 *The Nash bargaining shares are the solution to*

$$\frac{u_A(x_A) - \underline{u}_A}{u'_A(x_A)} = \frac{u_B(X - x_A) - \underline{u}_B}{u'_B(X - x_A)}.$$

Proof Direct application of the previous result using the fact that $g'(u_A) = -u_A^{-1'}(X - u_A^{-1}(u_A)) \cdot u'_B(X - u_A^{-1}(u_A)) = -u'_B(X - u_A^{-1}(u_A))/u'_A(X - u_A^{-1}(u_A))$ and $u_A^{-1}(u_A) = x_A$. $\square$

A direct implication of this result is that if the disagreement values and utility functions are the same for both players, the Nash bargaining shares are $x_A = x_B = \frac{1}{2}X$. Finally, given our assumptions about g, payoffs increase in one's own disagreement value and decline in the opponent's.

THEOREM 10.2 *Assume that g is twice-differentiable; then $\partial u_i/\partial \underline{u}_i > 0$ and $\partial u_j/\partial \underline{u}_i < 0$ for $i \neq j$.*

Proof Because g is twice-differentiable, we can use implicit differentiation on the solution $(g(u_A) - \underline{u}_B)/(u_A - \underline{u}_A) + g'(u_A) = 0$. Because the second-order condition is satisfied (i.e., $(g'(u_A)(u_A - \underline{u}_A) - (g(u_A) - \underline{u}_B))/(u_A - \underline{u}_A)^2 + g''(u_A) < 0$), the result follows from $-1/(u_A - \underline{u}_A) < 0$, $(g(u_A) - \underline{u}_B)/(u_A - \underline{u}_A)^2 > 0$, and $g'(u_A) < 0$. $\square$

1.1. Application: Risk Aversion and the Nash Bargaining Solution.

Intuitively, risk is an important component of bargaining. Bargainers always have to contend with the possibility that an agreement will not be reached, and they will be left with their outside options. Also we expect that if a player makes a more aggressive demand, she increases the probability that the negotiations collapse. Consequently, it seems natural to think that bargainers who are more willing to tolerate risk should do better, because they make tougher demands and reject more offers. Although the Nash bargaining model "black boxes" the negotiation process, its solution is consistent with this intuition.

Assume that each player has a utility function given by $u_i(x_i) = x_i^{\alpha_i}$ where $0 < \alpha_i < 1$, disagreement values $\underline{u}_i = 0$, and $X = 1$. The different values of α capture the player's risk aversion; the lower α the greater the risk aversion.[2] It is easiest to compute the equilibrium shares by using the formula from Theorem 10.1. The solution is

$$x_A = \frac{\alpha_A}{\alpha_A + \alpha_B} \text{ and } x_B = \frac{\alpha_B}{\alpha_A + \alpha_B}.$$

In these results, each bargainer's share decreases in his own risk aversion and increases in the risk aversion of his opponent. This effect is consistent with the intuition that bargainers who are risk acceptant enough to take tough positions (i.e., increase the likelihood of disagreement) receive larger allocations.

1.2. Nash's Axioms. In this section we outline the axioms that underlie Nash's bargaining solution. Informally, the axioms encapsulate the following principles:

(1) The bargainers maximize expected utility.
(2) Bargaining is efficient. The players fully allocate all of the available resources, and no player does worse than her disagreement value.
(3) The allocation depends only on the player's preferences and disagreement values.
(4) The bargaining solution is not affected by eliminating from consideration allocations other than the solution.

To formalize these axioms, recall that Ω is the set of feasible utility levels (u_A, u_B) that can be reached through some allocation of X. The set of Pareto optimal allocations is $\Omega^e = \{\omega \in \Omega : u_A \geq \underline{u}_A \text{ and } g(u_A) \geq \underline{u}_B\}$. A generic bargaining situation is a pair $(\Omega, \underline{u})$ where $\underline{u}$ is the vector of disagreement values. Finally, the set of all bargaining games is Σ, and a bargaining solution is a function $F : \Sigma \to R^2$. Let F_i denote the utility allocated to agent i.

The following axioms form the basis of Nash's solution.

AXIOM 10.1. *Invariance to Equivalent Utility Representations: Let $u_i' = \alpha_i u_i + \beta_i$ and $\underline{u}_i' = \alpha_i \underline{u}_i + \beta_i$ for $\alpha_i > 0$ and define Ω' accordingly. Then $F_i(\Omega', \underline{u}') = \alpha_i F_i(\Omega, \underline{u}) + \beta_i$ for $i = A, B$.*

---

[2] A standard measure of risk aversion is $-u''/u'$. For these utility functions, $-u''/u' = -(\alpha(\alpha - 1)r^{\alpha-2})/(\alpha r^{\alpha-1}) = (1 - \alpha)/x$.

Affine transformations of utility functions and disagreement utilities do not alter the bargaining outcomes. Because the utility allocations are adjusted by the same transformations as the utility functions, the resource allocations are the same in both bargaining solutions. Formally, $u_i^{-1}(F_i(\Omega, \underline{u})) = u_i'^{-1}(F_i(\Omega', \underline{u}'))$. From Chapter 3, this axiom implies that the players are expected utility maximizers.

AXIOM 10.2. *Pareto Efficiency: If $F(\Sigma) = (u_A, u_B)$, then there are no other allocations $(u'_A, u'_B) \in \Omega$ such that $u'_i > u_i$ for some i and $u'_j \geq u_j$ for $j \neq i$.*

The Pareto axiom holds that the bargainers are not able to improve upon the bargaining solution by choosing an allocation that makes one of the bargainers better off without reducing the utility of the other.

AXIOM 10.3. *Symmetry: Let $\underline{u}_A = \underline{u}_B$ and assume that $(u_1, u_2) \in \Omega$ if and only if $(u_2, u_1) \in \Omega$. Then $F_A(\Omega, \underline{u}) = F_B(\Omega, \underline{u})$.*

The basic idea of this axiom is that if neither player is advantaged by having a better disagreement outcome or a utility level unreachable by her opponent, then the bargainers receive the same utility allocations.

AXIOM 10.4. *Independence of Irrelevant Alternatives. Consider two bargaining situations $(\Omega, \underline{u})$ and $(\Omega', \underline{u})$ such that $\Omega' \subset \Omega$ and $F(\Omega, \underline{u}) \subset \Omega'$. Then $F(\Omega, \underline{u}) = F(\Omega', \underline{u})$.*

The intuition behind the IIA axiom is that, holding the disagreement points constant, a smaller feasible set of allocations only changes the bargaining solution if it makes the original allocation infeasible.

From our analysis of the Nash bargaining solution in the previous section, it is clear that it satisfies all of these axioms. The next proposition establishes that it is the only solution satisfying all four axioms.

THEOREM 10.3 *A bargaining solution $F : \Sigma \to R^2$ satisfies axioms 1–4 if and only if it is the Nash bargaining solution.*

Muthoo (1999) presents a straightforward proof. The conscientious reader should independently complete the part of the proof described in the exercises.

2. Noncooperative Bargaining

Although it makes a number of reasonable empirical predictions, the Nash bargaining solution is best interpreted as a normative argument about what bargaining outcomes should look like rather than a positive theory about how actual bargaining takes place. In this section, we turn to noncooperative game theoretic models to deduce behavior of bargainers under different extensive forms.

The starting point for the application of noncooperative game theory to bargaining is the model of Rubinstein (1982). Suppose that two players try to decide how to divide \$1. The players take turns making offers so that player 1 proposes in periods 0, 2, 4, and so on, and player 2 makes proposals in the other periods. The game continues (possibly infinitely) until a proposal is accepted by the other player.

In each period that she is the proposer, player 1 makes an offer (x_1, x_2) where x_1 is player 1's share and x_2 is player 2's share where $x_1 + x_2 \leq 1$. If player 2 accepts, the game ends and the dollar is divided accordingly. If player 2 rejects, then she gets to make an offer (x_1, x_2), and the game continues if player 1 rejects. To simplify matters, both players have linear utility functions $u_1(x_1, x_2) = x_1$ and $u_2(x_1, x_2) = x_2$. Each player has a discount factor δ_i: players value proposal (x_1, x_2) accepted t periods in the future as $(\delta_1^t x_1, \delta_2^t x_2)$.

Just as in the bargaining game encountered in Chapter 7, there are lots of Nash equilibria. For example, consider the strategy pair "Player 1 demands $x_1 = 1$ and refuses all other offers, and player 2 always offers $x_1 = 1$ and accepts any offer." This equilibrium, however, is not subgame perfect. If player 2 rejects player 1's first offer and offers $x_1 > \delta_1$, player 1 accepts; the best it can get is the whole dollar next period discounted by δ_1. So we focus on subgame perfect Nash equilibria.

2.1. Subgame Perfect Equilibria. Rubinstein shows that there is a unique SPNE to this game based on playing the following strategies in every period:

Player 1 proposes

$$\left(\frac{1 - \delta_2}{1 - \delta_1 \delta_2}, \frac{\delta_2 (1 - \delta_1)}{1 - \delta_1 \delta_2} \right)$$

and accepts player 2's offer if and only if

$$x_1 \geq \frac{\delta_1 (1 - \delta_2)}{1 - \delta_1 \delta_2}.$$

Player 2 proposes

$$\left(\frac{\delta_1(1-\delta_2)}{1-\delta_1\delta_2}, \frac{1-\delta_1}{1-\delta_1\delta_2}\right)$$

and accepts player 1's offer if and only if

$$x_2 \geq \frac{\delta_2(1-\delta_1)}{1-\delta_1\delta_2}.$$

We begin by verifying that these strategies are in fact a SPNE. First we check whether player 1 has an incentive to defect in any subgame. Consider a subgame beginning with a proposal by player 1 (i.e., an even period). In the equilibrium, player 1 proposes the split $((1-\delta_2)/(1-\delta_1\delta_2), (\delta_2(1-\delta_1))/(1-\delta_1\delta_2))$, which is accepted by player 2. Clearly, player 1 cannot gain by lowering x_1; such a proposal is accepted and player 1 gets a lower share. If player 1 raises x_1, then she must lower x_2 to maintain feasibility. Any $x_2 < (\delta_2(1-\delta_1))/(1-\delta_1\delta_2)$ is rejected, however. Following such a rejection, player 2 proposes $x_1 = (\delta_1(1-\delta_2))/(1-\delta_1\delta_2)$, and player 1 accepts. Note that we are using the single-deviation principle by considering a deviation that changes proposal behavior but not accepting behavior. Thus, player 1's utility of this defection is $(\delta_1^2(1-\delta_2))/(1-\delta_1\delta_2)$, which is less than her equilibrium utility of $(1-\delta_2)/(1-\delta_1\delta_2)$ because $\delta_1 < 1$.

Now consider whether player 1 defects when player 2 is the proposer (i.e., an odd period). Player 2 proposes $((\delta_1(1-\delta_2))/(1-\delta_1\delta_2), (1-\delta_1)/(1-\delta_1\delta_2))$. Note that accepting and rejecting the offer lead to the same utility; the best that player 1 can do is to have $x = (1-\delta_2)/(1-\delta_1\delta_2)$ accepted one period later.

The process of showing that player 2 does not defect is exactly the same.

2.2. Computing the Equilibrium. The problem with the preceding proof is that it does not give much of a sense of how the result is derived. Now we consider a more constructive proof. Let v_1 and v_2 be the utilities of player 1 and 2 for subgames in which they are the proposer, for example, if player 1 makes a proposal x_1 that is accepted $v_1 = x_1$. If player 1's proposal is rejected, v_1 is the discounted value of the maximum of what player 2 offers and what player 1 gets by rejecting and proposing in his next turn. Given that the postulated strategies are the same in every period, these values are independent of t. These are *continuation values* because they also reflect the utility of rejecting a proposal and moving to the next subgame. Consider a subgame where player 1 is the proposer. She must offer player 2 at least $\delta_2 v_2$. Thus, $x_1 = 1 - \delta_2 v_2$. Because this offer is accepted $v_1 = x_1 = 1 - \delta_2 v_2$. Consider a subgame where player 2 is the proposer. She must offer at least $\delta_1 v_1$ so that $v_2 = 1 - \delta_1 v_1$.

Solving these two equations leads to $v_1 = (1 - \delta_2)/(1 - \delta_1 \delta_2)$ and $v_2 = (1 - \delta_1)/(1 - \delta_1 \delta_2)$. These continuation values are consistent with the strategies presented in the last section. In fact the strategies presented earlier represent the only feasible way to attain these continuation values.

2.3. Uniqueness. Although we have shown that Rubinstein's equilibrium is a subgame perfect Nash equilibrium, we have not ruled out the possibility that there are others. We now show that this equilibrium is the unique SPNE by proving that v_1 and v_2 defined earlier are the only continuation values consistent with a SPNE. Suppose there are more than one SPNE. Let $\overline{v}_i$ and $\underline{v}_i$ be player i's highest and lowest SPNE continuation values for any subgame where player i is the proposer. Let $\overline{w}_i$ and $\underline{w}_i$ be player i's highest and lowest SPNE continuation values for any subgame where player i is not the proposer.

When player 1 makes a proposal, she never offers more than $\delta_2 \overline{v}_2$ because player 2 cannot expect more than $\overline{v}_2$ by rejecting and making her own proposal in the next round. Thus, player 1's lowest possible continuation value must satisfy $\underline{v}_1 \geq 1 - \delta_2 \overline{v}_2$. By a symmetric argument, $\underline{v}_2 \geq 1 - \delta_1 \overline{v}_1$. Because the other player never offers more than $\delta_i \overline{v}_i$ we also know that $\overline{w}_i \leq \delta_i \overline{v}_i$.

Now consider player 1's strategy. When she proposes the best she can do is pay $\delta_2 \underline{v}_2$ or trigger a rejection to get $\delta_1 \overline{w}_1$. Thus, we know that her continuation value satisfies $\overline{v}_1 \leq \max\{1 - \delta_2 \underline{v}_2, \delta_1 \overline{w}_1\} \leq \max\{1 - \delta_2 \underline{v}_2, \delta_1^2 \overline{v}_1\} = 1 - \delta_2 \underline{v}_2$. Similarly, $\overline{v}_2 \leq 1 - \delta_1 \underline{v}_1$. Thus, the following four inequalities must be satisfied:

$$\underline{v}_1 \geq 1 - \delta_2 \overline{v}_2$$
$$\underline{v}_2 \geq 1 - \delta_1 \overline{v}_1$$
$$\overline{v}_2 \leq 1 - \delta_1 \underline{v}_1$$
$$\overline{v}_1 \leq 1 - \delta_2 \underline{v}_2.$$

Combining the first and third inequalities generates $\underline{v}_1 \geq 1 - \delta_2(1 - \delta_1 \underline{v}_1)$, which implies that $\underline{v}_1 \geq (1 - \delta_2)/(1 - \delta_1 \delta_2)$. Similarly, combining the second and fourth inequalities generates $\overline{v}_1 \leq 1 - \delta_2(1 - \delta_1 \overline{v}_1)$ or $\overline{v}_1 \leq (1 - \delta_2)/(1 - \delta_1 \delta_2)$. These conditions imply that $\overline{v}_1 = \underline{v}_1 = (1 - \delta_2)/(1 - \delta_1 \delta_2)$. With similar arguments, we can also establish that $\overline{v}_2 = \underline{v}_2 = (1 - \delta_1)/(1 - \delta_1 \delta_2)$. Thus, there is a single continuation value for each player and the postulated strategies are the only SPNE.

2.4. Implications. The model suggests a very simple path of play. In period zero, player 1 proposes $((1 - \delta_2)/(1 - \delta_1 \delta_2), (\delta_2(1 - \delta_1))/(1 - \delta_1 \delta_2))$, player 2 accepts, and the game ends. Because the whole dollar is allocated and there is no delay, the subgame perfect Nash equilibrium is efficient. It is easy to see that the SPNE has the following implications:

(1) If both players have the same discount factor, there is a first mover advantage because $(1 - \delta)/(1 - \delta^2) > \delta(1 - \delta)/(1 - \delta^2)$. Intuitively, because player 2 discounts the future, player 1 only needs offer her a fraction of what she gets for being the proposer next period. Because both players are identical, player 2 is getting only a fraction of what player 1 gets.

(2) Both players' shares are increasing in their discount factors and declining in their opponent's: it pays to be patient. When player 2's discount factor is high, player 1 has to offer her more to secure immediate agreement. Conversely, when player 1's discount factor is high, player 2 must offer him more to reach agreement in the event that player 2 gets to make an offer. Thus, rejecting player 1's offer is less valuable for player 2, suggesting that player 1 gets to keep more in the first period.

(3) If $\delta_1 = \delta_2 = \delta$, then both players' shares converge to $1/2$ as δ converges to 1. As both players become perfectly patient, they are less willing to accept offers that are less than what they can get as the proposer next period. In the limit, they demand exactly what they expect to get next period. One way to think about the discount rates' converging to 1 is to consider a situation in which offers and counteroffers can be made very quickly so that rejecting an offer creates only infinitessimal delay. In such a case, the equilibrium involves equal division and corresponds to the Nash bargaining solution.

2.5. Asymmetric Disagreement Values. In the canonical Rubinstein game, the players get 0 in any period for which there is no agreement. We now modify the game in two ways. First, players receive an allocation of (d_1, d_2) in each period prior to an agreement where $d_1 + d_2 < 1$. After an agreement, (x_1^*, x_2^*), is reached, the bargainers receive this allocation in every period over an infinite horizon. This contrasts with the model of the last section where the allocation is "consumed immediately."[3] To keep matters simple, we assume that $\delta_1 = \delta_2 = \delta$. Thus, the utilities of reaching agreement (x_1^*, x_2^*) in period t are

$$\left(\frac{\left(1 - \delta^{t-1}\right) d_1 + \delta^t x_1^*}{1 - \delta}, \frac{\left(1 - \delta^{t-1}\right) d_2 + \delta^t x_2^*}{1 - \delta} \right).[4]$$

Let v_i be i's continuation values for any period in which she proposes. If an agreement (x_1^*, x_2^*) is reached in such a period, $v_i = x_i^*/(1 - \delta)$. Consider player 2's decision to accept or reject an offer of x_2. If she accepts, she generates a value of $x_2/(1 - \delta)$ whereas if she rejects she gets d_2 in the current period and a continuation value v_2 in the next. Thus, she accepts so long as $x_2 > (1 - \delta)(d_2 + \delta v_2)$. Now consider player 1's choice. If he makes the minimal acceptable offer $x_2 = (1 - \delta)(d_2 + \delta v_2)$, his continuation value is $v_1 = (1 - (1 - \delta)(d_2 + \delta v_2))/(1 - \delta) = 1/(1 - \delta) - d_2 - \delta v_2$. Similarly, if player 2 wishes to secure an agreement to her proposals, we require $v_2 = 1/(1 - \delta) - d_1 - \delta v_1$. The solution to these two equations is given by

$$v_1 = \frac{1 - d_2 + \delta d_1}{1 - \delta^2} = \frac{d_1}{1 - \delta} + \frac{1 - d_1 - d_2}{1 - \delta^2}$$

$$v_2 = \frac{1 - d_1 + \delta d_2}{1 - \delta^2} = \frac{d_2}{1 - \delta} + \frac{1 - d_1 - d_2}{1 - \delta^2}.$$

To show that these are in fact equilibrium continuation values, we must show that each player prefers to make the equilibrium proposal rather

---

[3] This modification rules out strategies where the bargainers delay infinitely in the hope the discounted sum of d_i exceeds the one-period agreement. We can easily adjust the original model to correspond to the assumption that the agreement is over a flow of utilities rather than one-shot consumption. We would simply use the original model and assume that the players were allocating $1/(1 - \delta)$.

[4] We assume that any agreement results in the same allocation in each period. However, because the players are risk neutral, there might be agreements to random allocations that generate the same payoffs.

than defect and get the disagreement value for an additional period. Thus, we require $v_1 > d_1 (1 + \delta) + \delta^2 v_1$ or $v_1 > d_1/(1 - \delta)$. Similarly, our equilibrium requires that $v_2 > d_2/(1 - \delta)$. These facts are easily verified. The techniques of Section 2.3 can easily be generalized to show that this is the unique SPNE.

This equilibrium has a number of qualitative similarities to the Nash bargaining solution. Note that each player's continuation value increases in her disagreement value and decreases in her opponent's disagreement value. This equilibrium also has a surplus-splitting interpretation. Note that each player's continuation value has two components. The first is $d_i/(1 - \delta)$ which is the utility each player can guarantee herself in the absence of any agreement. The second component $(1 - d_1 - d_2)/(1 - \delta^2)$ corresponds to the equilibrium continuation value in a game to split $1 - d_1 - d_2$ when the players have outside option values of 0. Thus, a useful interpretation of this equilibrium is that both players take what they are entitled to and bargain over the rest.

3. Majority-Rule Bargaining Under a Closed Rule

A key feature of the Rubinstein model is that unanimous consent is required to reach an agreement on the allocation. This rules out a number of important political settings where only a simple majority or a supermajority is required for agreement. Baron and Ferejohn (1989) have extended Rubinstein's model to simple majority rule with more than two bargainers.

Suppose that there are N (odd) players bargaining and any proposal requires $n = (N + 1)/2$ votes. Instead of assuming alternating offers, Baron and Ferejohn consider a bargaining protocol with a *random recognition rule*. According to this protocol, in each period, every player is chosen to make a proposal with an equal probability $(1/N)$. In this section, we focus on bargaining under a *closed rule* where the proposer makes a take-it-leave-it offer for the current legislative session. The proposer in each period makes an offer $(x_1, x_2, \ldots, x_N)$ such that x_i is the share for player i. Feasibility requires that $\sum x_i \leq 1$. If this proposal is rejected, the session ends, discounting occurs, and a new proposer is chosen at the beginning of the next session. Later we consider open rule bargaining where proposals can be amended within the current session. To simplify, we assume that each player has the same discount factor δ.

This game has lots of subgame perfect equilibria. In fact, for large N and δ, there is a SPNE that can support any division of the dollar. If the players are patient enough, they can design punishment strategies to guarantee \$0 to any defector. These strategies require, however, that each player know the whole (possibly infinite) history of the game in order to know which actions are consistent with the prescribed punishment. Thus, following Baron and Ferejohn, we analyze only *stationary* equilibria. A stationary equilibrium to this game is one in which

(1) A proposer proposes the same division every time she is recognized regardless of the history of the game.
(2) Voters vote only on the basis of the current proposal and expectations about future proposals. Because of assumption 1, future proposals have the same distribution of outcomes in each period.

These two assumptions imply that the game essentially starts over in every period. Therefore, the continuation value of each player is the expected utility of the game. Let v_i be the continuation value for player i. We focus on symmetric equilibria so that $v_i = v$ for all i. Finally, we consider only equilibria in which voters do not choose weakly dominated strategies in the voting stages. Therefore, a voter accepts any proposal that provides her at least as much as the discounted continuation value. Therefore, any voter who gets $x_i \geq \delta v$ votes in favor of the proposal whereas any voter who receives less than δv votes against it.

Given these voting strategies, an optimal proposal gives δv to $n - 1$ other players, $z = 1 - (n - 1)\delta v$ to the proposer, and 0 to the rest. We assume (although you should show that it must be true) that the proposer chooses her coalition partners randomly. Now we can compute v. Because the continuation value is just the expected value of the game starting next period, it is simply z times the probability of being chosen as proposer $1/N$, δv times the probability of being included in the winning coalition $(n - 1)/N$, and 0 times the remaining probability. Thus,

$$v = \frac{z}{N} + \frac{n - 1}{N}\delta v.$$

Substituting for z and simplifying yields

$$v = \frac{1}{N}$$

Thus, the continuation value is a proportional share of the dollar. Because v is also the expected utility of the game, this result implies that bargaining is efficient because the sum of player utilities is maximized. As shown in the exercises, this efficiency result may not hold if voters are risk averse.

Finally, given our solution for v, we compute the proposer's share:

$$z = 1 - \delta \frac{n-1}{N} = 1 - \delta \frac{N-1}{2N}.$$

To ensure that the proposer prefers to make an acceptable proposal, we must check that $z > \delta v$; otherwise a proposer would prefer to punt and wait for the next period. This condition is easily verified.

Among the important implications of the model are its predictions about proposal power. One measure of proposal power is the difference between z and δv or $1 - \delta(N+1)/2N$. First, note that proposal power increases in N. When N increases, the proposer has more potential coalition partners to play off one another. This increases the competition for inclusion in the winning coalition and drives down what the proposer must pay. Second, proposal power is decreasing in δ. When δ is higher, the voters are more willing to vote down proposals and wait for a chance to propose themselves. Thus, the proposer must be relatively more generous to secure agreement.

3.1. Supermajority Rule. The model can be easily extended to capture situations where more than a simple majority is required for passage of the bill. Now assume that $k > n$ votes are required. If is easy to see that the proposer's share is now

$$z = 1 - (k-1)\delta v$$

and the continuation values are now given by

$$v = \frac{z}{N} + \frac{k-1}{N}\delta v.$$

Simple algebra reveals that once again $v = 1/N$. This is not terribly surprising given that the supermajority rule preserves the symmetry of the majority rule game. The proposer's equilibrium share is now lowered to $z = 1 - \delta(k-1)/N$, however. Thus, the primary consequence of supermajority rules is to mitigate the proposer's advantage.

3.2. Asymmetric Proposal Power. A limitation of the preceding models is the assumption that all legislators have the same probability of being recognized to make the proposal. In real world legislative institutions, membership in certain committees and parties may affect the probability that an individual legislator gets to make a proposal.

To show how the model generalizes, suppose that the members are divided into two parties A and B. Party A has $N - m \geq (n + 1)/2$ members so that it is the majority party. Each member of A has a proposal power $p > 1/N$. Alternatively, there are m members of B who have proposal power $q < 1/N$. For consistency, we require that $(N - m)p + mq = 1$.

Again we assume symmetry so that every legislator with the same recognition probability plays the same strategy and has the same continuation value. The members of the two parties have continuation values v_A and v_B, respectively. We conjecture for now (and prove later) that $v_A > v_B$. Given these continuation values, a member of party A votes for any proposal that provides her at least δv_A and a member of party B votes for a proposal giving her at least δv_B. Given these strategies and the assumption that $v_A > v_B$, a proposer from party A gives δv_B to the m members of party B and δv_A to $n - m - 1$ members of party A. Recall that $n = (n + 1)/2$. Thus, the proposer's share is

$$z_A = 1 - (n - m - 1)\delta v_A - m\delta v_B.$$

A member of B gives positive allocations to $m - 1$ members of B and $n - m$ members of A so that the proposer's share is

$$z_B = 1 - (n - m)\delta v_A - (m - 1)\delta v_B.$$

Note that $z_A > z_B$. We can now compute v_A and v_B

$$v_A = p z_A + p(n - m - 1)\delta v_A + qm(n - m)\delta v_A/(N - m)$$
$$v_B = q z_B + (1 - q)\delta v_B.$$

Thus, we have four equations with four unknowns. Solving this system is straightforward. Writing down the solution is tedious, so we consider a simple example. Let $N = 3, m = 1$. Note that $q = 1 - 2p < 1/3$.

Therefore, the equilibrium conditions are the following:

$$z_A = 1 - \delta v_B$$
$$z_B = 1 - \delta v_A$$
$$v_A = p z_A + q \delta v_A / 2$$
$$v_B = q z_B + (1 - q) \delta v_B.$$

After some tedious algebra, we find that

$$v_A = \frac{(1 - q)(1 - \delta)}{2 + q\delta - 2\delta}$$
$$v_B = \frac{q(2 - \delta)}{2 + q\delta - 2\delta}.$$

We still need to check our assumption that $v_A \geq v_B$. This occurs when

$$q < \frac{1 - \delta}{3 - 2\delta} \leq \frac{1}{3}.$$

Because this upper bound is always less than $1/3$ when $\delta > 0$, the asymmetry in proposal power must be substantial to give an advantage to party A. The reason is that its greater proposal power makes members of A unattractive coalition partners. Thus, the likelihood of being the proposer must be large enough to offset this effect. It is easy to show, however, that v_A is decreasing and v_B is increasing in q.

To complete our analysis, we need to consider what happens when $(1 - \delta)/(3 - 2\delta) < q \leq 1/3$. We can rule out $v_B > v_A$ as this would imply that the member of B is never in a coalition with the proposer. Thus,

$$v_B = q z_B = q(1 - \delta v_A)$$
$$v_A = p z_A + (1 - p)\delta v_A = p(1 - \delta v_A) + (1 - p)\delta v_A.$$

This leads to $v_A = (1 - q)/(2(1 - \delta q))$ and $v_B = q(2 - \delta - \delta q)/(2(1 - \delta q))$. Note that $v_B > v_A$ only if $q \geq (1 + 2\delta)/(3 - 2\delta) \geq 1/3$, which violates our original assumption about q. Thus, the only possible outcome for $(1 - \delta)/(3 - 2\delta) < q \leq 1/3$ is $v_A = v_B$. To support this equilibrium, proposers from A must choose a mixed strategy that randomizes between forming a coalition with the remaining members of A and forming one with the member of B. We leave computation of the equilibrium mixed strategy as an exercise.

3.3. Asymmetric Veto Powers. Another institutional variation in legislative institutions is that certain players are privileged with the ability to block legislation such as the president, an upper chamber, or a court. In this section, we provide a simple example of how to incorporate vetoes into the Baron-Ferejohn model.[5] Now suppose that one member of our three-person legislature has absolute veto power in that she must approve every proposal. Let party B have the veto player. To keep matters simple, we return to the case of equal proposal powers.

Because B has an absolute veto, any proposer must include B and at least one member of A in her coalition so that

$$z_A = 1 - \delta v_B$$
$$z_B = 1 - \delta v_A.$$

Computing the continuation values, we obtain

$$v_A = \frac{1}{3} z_A + \delta \frac{1}{3} v_A$$
$$v_B = \frac{1}{3} z_B + \delta \frac{2}{3} v_B.$$

Thus, we can solve for

$$v_A = \frac{3(1 - \delta)}{\delta^2 - 9\delta + 9} \text{ and } v_B = \frac{3 - 2\delta}{\delta^2 - 9\delta + 9}.$$

Note that $v_A < v_B$ so long as $\delta > 0$.

4. The Baron-Ferejohn Model Under Open Rule

The preceding sections focus exclusively on models where proposals cannot be amended within the current legislative session. The model can be extended, however, to allow proposals to be amended before a final passage vote. Now following each proposal a member is selected at random from the remaining $N - 1$ legislators. The selected legislator

---

[5] This variation of the Baron-Ferejohn game was developed in McCarty (2000a, 2000b)

has two choices. First, she may *call the question* and bring about a final passage vote on the proposal. Alternatively, she may make a new offer or *amendment*. The amendment is paired against the current offer. The winner of this vote is the proposal on the floor at the beginning of the next session. In the next session, a new legislator is chosen either to amend or to call the question.

Now a legislative proposer has two considerations. First, just as before, a simple majority must receive their discounted continuation values in order to support the proposal on final passage. Second, the proposer must craft a proposal that deters others from amending it. This can be accomplished by allocating sufficient resources that the next proposer prefers to move the initial proposal rather than have her own proposal on the floor at the beginning of the next session.

To keep matters simple, we focus again on $N = 3$. First, consider a scenario where the proposer keeps z, provides $(1 - z)/2$ to both other legislators, and each legislator moves the question. To solve for the optimal z, define $v_i^2(z)$ as the continuation value of beginning a session with a proposal giving z to player i and $(1 - z)/2$ to the other two legislators. Because we focus on symmetric equilibria, we suppress the subscript i. Thus, $v^2(z)$ is the expected utility of this strategy for the first proposer and that of any proposer who successfully amends a proposal.

Given this definition, a proposer must give each legislator at least $\delta v^2(z)$ to induce her to call the question Otherwise, a legislator selected in the amendment stage defects, making a proposal giving herself z. Therefore, the equilibrium requires that $(1 - z)/2 \geq \delta v^2(z)$. So long as this condition holds, the proposer gets z with probability 1 so that $v^2(z) = z$. Thus, the proposer maximizes z subject to $(1 - z)/2 \geq \delta v^2(z)$. This leads to a solution of

$$v^2(z) = z = \frac{1}{1 + 2\delta}.$$

Although the proposer secures $z = 1/(1 + 2\delta)$ with certainty, she may prefer to secure the support of only one legislator and risk the defeat of her proposal if the excluded legislator is selected to make an amendment. So now assume that the proposer keeps z, gives $1 - z$ to some other legislator, and gives 0 to the third legislator. The legislator who receives $1 - z$ moves the question if selected. The legislator who receives 0 offers an amendment giving z to herself, 0 to the original proposer, and $1 - z$ to the other legislator. Such an amendment carries with the votes of the legislators who receive positive allocation in the amended proposal.

To compute the optimal z, we must consider two values. Let $v_i^1(z)$ be the value to legislator i of beginning the period with a proposal giving z to i and $1 - z$ and 0 to the others. Similarly, let $v_i^1(0)$ be the value to i of the game starting from a proposal that gives 0 to agent i and z and $1 - z$ to the others. Again because of symmetry we drop the subscripts.

First, we compute $v(z)$. With probability $1/2$, the proposal is moved and approved, giving the proposer z. With probability $1/2$, however, the proposal is amended so that the original proposer gets 0 in the proposal in play at the beginning of the next session. Therefore, $v^1(z) = z/2 + \delta v^1(0)/2$. Now consider the value of starting the period with 0. With probability $1/2$, the proposal is moved and passed, leading to a payoff of 0. With probability $1/2$, the member is selected and amends the proposal so that she gets z in the standing proposal at the beginning of the next session. Therefore, $v^1(0) = \delta v^1(z)/2$. Putting these two values together, we get $v^1(z) = z/2 + \delta^2 v^1(z)/4$ or

$$v^1(z) = \frac{2z}{4 - \delta^2}.$$

Finally, we must ensure that the legislator receiving $1 - z$ prefers to move the question rather than amend. This requires that $1 - z \geq \delta v^1(z)$ or $z \leq 1 - \delta v^1(z)$. Therefore, the proposer chooses z to maximize $v^1(z)$ subject to this constraint. The solution is $z = (4 - \delta^2)/(4 + 2\delta - \delta^2)$ leading to a continuation value of

$$v^1(z) = \frac{2}{4 + 2\delta - \delta^2}.$$

To determine which strategy the proposer chooses, we simply need to compare $v^1(z)$ and $v^2(z)$. Straightforward algebra shows that $v^1(z) > v^2(z)$ when $\delta > \delta^* \equiv \sqrt{3} - 1$. Intuitively, when players are patient and value the future, it is very expensive to inhibit amendments from both legislators. Therefore, the proposer prefers to buy off only one member and take his chances with an amendment from the other.

There are two interesting features of the open rule model. First, it is possible that coalitions are greater than minimal winning. This occurs when $\delta < \delta^*$ so that the proposer spreads resources sufficiently to deter all amendments. Second, there can be equilibrium delay in agreement.

This occurs when $\delta > \delta^*$ and the proposer gives 0 to one member. If that member is then selected, she makes a successful amendment, which precludes agreement in the first session.

It is useful to compare the equilibrium allocations from the open rule with those from the closed rule. The literature has paid particular attention to the proposer's share.[6] Recall that for the closed rule with $N = 3$, the proposer keeps $(3 - \delta)/3$. This share is always greater than $v^2(z)$ and is greater than $v^1(z)$ when $\delta > \delta^*$. Thus, the open rule lowers the proposer's advantage. Proposal power can also be mitigated by the use of supermajority rules. Consider the case of $k = N = 3$. The proposer's share is $(3 - 2\delta)/3$, which is always lower than $v^1(z)$. Thus, when $\delta > \delta^*$, the unanimity rule lowers proposal power below that of the open majority rule without incurring costly delay.

5. Bargaining with Incomplete Information

In all of the bargaining models discussed so far the agents know the disagreement or continuation values of their opponents. Consequently, they know with certainty which offers are accepted and which are rejected.[7] This assumption is obviously unrealistic in many political contexts. A legislature does not know whether an executive will sign a particular bill, states do not know whether the peace terms will be accepted or whether the opponent will prefer to continue fighting, and so on. In this section, we provide a bare bones model of bargaining with incomplete information. We then elaborate the model with examples from executive-legislative bargaining and crisis bargaining in international relations.

5.1. A Basic Model. Consider the setup of the Nash bargaining problem where two players negotiate over the division of X. Now there is uncertainty about player A's disagreement value. With probability π, the disagreement value is $\underline{u}_A = 0$; with probability $1 - \pi$ it is $\underline{u}_A = d > 0$. We refer to $\underline{u}_A = 0$ as the "weak" type and $\underline{u}_A = d$ as the "strong" type. To keep matters as simple as possible, player B makes

---

[6] This is not only an important equity consideration. In models of allocating the benefits of costly projects, institutions that limit the proposer's share reduce the incentive to pass inefficient projects (Baron 1991; McCarty 2000b; Primo 2004).

[7] In the open rule Baron-Ferejohn game, the uncertainty is about which player will be selected to offer an amendment, but not whether a particular player prefers an amendment to the proposal.

a take-it-or-leave-it offer to A of $(u_A, u_B) \in \Omega$. If A accepts, the offer is implemented. If A rejects, the payoffs are $(\underline{u}_A, \underline{u}_B)$.

Clearly, A only accepts an offer that gives her $u_A \geq \underline{u}_A$. Because B does not know the value of $\underline{u}_A$, she does not know how much utility to transfer to A to secure her agreement. If she offers less than A's disagreement value, A rejects, leading to $(\underline{u}_A, \underline{u}_B)$. Let $P(u_A | \underline{u}_A)$ be the probability that A accepts u_A when her disagreement value is $\underline{u}_A$. We can write B's expected utility as a function of her offer

$$EU_B(u_A) = [\pi P(u_A|0) + (1 - \pi) P(u_A|d)] g(u_A)$$
$$+ [1 - \pi P(u_A|0) - (1 - \pi) P(u_A|d)] \underline{u}_B$$

where $g(u_A) = g(u_A) = u_B(X - u_A^{-1}(u_A))$. Sequentially rational behavior by A requires that $P(u_A | \underline{u}_A) = 1$ if $u_A \geq \underline{u}_A$ and 0 otherwise. Consequently, we can rewrite B's utility as

$$EU_B(u_A) = \begin{cases} \pi g(u_A) + (1 - \pi)\underline{u}_B \text{ if } d > u_A \geq 0 \\ g(u_A) \text{ if } u_A \geq d \end{cases}.$$

Given that $g(u_A)$ is decreasing in u_A, the only possible solutions are $u_A = d$ or $u_A = 0$. We call $u_A = 0$ the aggressive offer and $u_A = d$ the accommodating offer. B chooses the aggressive offer if and only if $\pi g(0) + (1 - \pi)\underline{u}_B > g(d)$ or

$$\pi > \frac{g(d) - \underline{u}_B}{g(0) - \underline{u}_B}.$$

Although it is very simple, the model makes a number of sensible predictions. First, B is more likely to make the aggressive offer of $u_A = 0$ when

- The probability that A is the weak type is high
- Her disagreement value $\underline{u}_B$ is good
- The utility difference between the aggressive and accommodating offers, $g(0) - g(d)$, is large

Given the assumptions of one-sided incomplete information and a single take-it-or-leave-it offer, this model is very limited. Rather than generalize this abstract model, we review a number of political science applications that relax these assumptions.

6. Application: Veto Bargaining

In Chapter 7, we studied the application of the Romer-Rosenthal agenda setting model to the presidential veto. Although this complete information model provides an excellent tool for studying veto power, it cannot provide a basis for studying vetoes; it predicts that vetoes do not occur. We now turn to a simple model for studying vetoes, rather than veto power. In this model, vetoes do occur. This simple incomplete information model in turn provides the foundation for building more complex models of veto bargaining that incorporate reputation, learning, and dynamics.[8]

In order to explain the fact that vetoes occur, it is necessary to dispense with at least one of the assumptions underlying the basic model. Although the model presented in Chapter 7 has a number of very restrictive assumptions, few of them are actually consequential in the prediction that vetoes do not occur. One important exception is the assumption that C has complete information about the preferences of P and O. When the legislature faces uncertainty, vetoes may occur as the legislature overestimates its ability to extract concessions from the president or the override pivot.

Relaxing the assumption of complete information has been the starting point for most of the recent work on veto bargaining (Matthews 1989; McCarty 1997; Cameron 1999). To present the basic flavor of these models, we consider a model without an override possibility so that q remains the policy in the event of a veto. To capture the uncertainty that the proposer C faces about the receiver P's preferences, we assume she believes P is one of two preference types, a moderate with ideal point m or an extremist with ideal point e. We maintain the convenient assumption that all agents have linear preferences given by $-|x - i|$ for policy $x \in \mathbb{R}$ and ideal point $i \in \{c, e, m\}$ where $e < m < c$. Let π be the probability that P is the extreme type.

The main implication of uncertainty about preferences is that C no longer knows for sure which bills the president accepts and which he vetoes. To see this, consider Figure 10.2, where $q < e$. Here the set of

---

[8] This section draws heavily on Cameron and McCarty (2004).

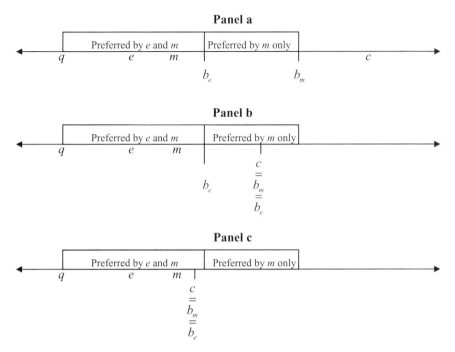

Figure 10.2. Veto Bargaining Under Incomplete Information.

bills the extremist type accepts over the status quo is only a subset of those the moderate type accepts. Thus, C can force a more attractive bill (from her perspective) on the moderate receiver than she can on the extremist one. C's dilemma is whether to propose a bill that she finds relatively less attractive but that both types accept – a bill such as b_e – or be more aggressive and propose a bill – such as b_m – she finds more attractive but only the moderate receiver accepts. Clearly, the attractiveness of the gamble depends on C's beliefs about P's type. If π is high (so C believes P is probably an extremist), C is likely deterred from making the aggressive proposal. On the other hand, if π is low (so C believes P is probably a moderate), C may well find the gamble attractive. If she offers it, on occasion it proves a poor choice: P turns out to be the extreme type and vetoes it.

Now we compute the necessary conditions for an equilibrium veto to occur. First, assume the preference configuration of Figure 10.2 holds (i.e., $q < e < m < c$). Let $B_t(q)$ be the sets of bills that each type $t \in \{e, m\}$ accepts over the status quo. Just as in our analysis of the complete information version of the model, these sets are $[q, 2t - q]$ if

$t > q$ and $[2t - q, q]$ otherwise. For any q, president m accepts higher bills than president e accepts. Because $e > q$, $B_e(q) = [q, 2e - q] \subset B_m(q) = [q, 2m - q]$. Consequently, any bill that e accepts m accepts, but the converse is not true. Therefore, C faces a trade-off. It can propose $2e - q$, which both types accept, or can propose $2m - q$, which e vetoes. Given C's beliefs the latter strategy result in a veto with probability π.

Case 1: $c > 2m - q$. Given C's linear preferences, her utility from $b = 2e - q$ is $2e - q - c$, while her expected utility from $b = 2m - q$ is $\pi q + (1 - \pi)(2m - q) - c$. Thus, if $\pi \leq (m - e)/(m - q)$, she prefers $b = 2m - q$ and a veto occurs with probability π.

Case 2: $2e - q < c < 2m - q$. C's payoff from $b = 2e - q$ remains $2e - q - c$, but now m accepts $b = c$. Thus, proposing her ideal point leads to an expected utility of $\pi(q - c)$. Thus, C proposes $b = c$ if $\pi \leq (c + q - 2e)/(c - q)$. Note that the critical value of π is lower than in case 1, making a veto less likely for this preference configuration.

Case 3: $c < 2e - q$. Now both types accept $b = c$. So C proposes its ideal point for all values of π and no vetoes occur.

The punch line of this simple model is that vetoes are less likely to occur when C's preferences are closer to m and e. Empirically, Cameron (1999) finds that vetoes are less likely to occur during periods of unified party control of Congress and presidency: a finding he interprets as evidence for this prediction.

6.1. Models with Reputation, Learning, and Dynamics. An interesting feature of the incomplete information model is that a moderate P does better if the proposer C believes P is the extreme type. This raises the possibility that P might attempt to manipulate C's beliefs about his type (i.e., reputation). In this section, we examine three models in which the actors try to manipulate P's reputation. All are signaling models, because an informed player takes an action that conveys information about P's type. In the first two models, the veto threat and sequential veto bargaining (SVB) models, the informed player is P. In the third model, the "blame game" veto model, both C and P take actions to convey information to uninformed voters.

6.1.1. Veto Threats. Ranging from the dramatic "read my lips" variety to the much more mundane "statements of administration policy" routinely produced by the Office of Management and Budget, the veto threat is an important feature of legislative politics in the United States.

Figure 10.3. Best Responses in Cheap Talk Veto Bargaining Model.

None of the models reviewed thus far provides any leverage on understanding this phenomenon. Matthews (1989), however, provides an influential model of veto threats where the president uses cheap talk to reveal information about his preferences and veto intentions.

To illustrate this model, it is helpful to increase the number of presidential types from two to four. Therefore, to m and e, we add the two following types: r the *recalcitrant* type and a the *accommodating* type. We assume that each president type and C have linear preferences and that $r < q < e < m < c < a$ as in Figure 10.3. President r is called recalcitrant because he vetoes any bill that C prefers to the status quo. President a is accommodating because he prefers c to the status quo. The probabilities of each type are π_r, π_e, π_m, and π_a. In this game, the president first makes a "speech" (i.e., a costless signal to the legislature). Each of these messages has no literal meaning, just a contextual one derived from the equilibrium that is being played. Following the speech, C updates her beliefs about the president's preferences and then makes a proposal that the president either accepts or rejects.

As a baseline, first consider an equilibrium where the president's speeches contain no information because each type chooses the same mixed strategy over the set of possible speeches.[9] In this babbling equilibrium, C simply chooses the bill from $b_r = q$, $b_e = 2e - q$, $b_m = 2m - c$, or $b_a = c$ to maximize her utility. For any such choice, those with lower types veto. For example, if C chooses b_m, types e and r veto so that the probability of veto is $\pi_e + \pi_r$. The formulae for the conditions for each proposal are not presented; rather, illustrated graphically in Figure 10.4. The first figure shows which proposal is made in the babbling equilibrium for different values of π_m and π_e for given values of π_a and π_r. Note that the proposal $b_r = q$ is never made because C does at least as well with a vetoed proposal. This babbling equilibrium is somewhat bad from the president's perspective. If the president is

---

[9] This randomization over all speeches implies that there are no off-the-equilibrium histories. There are no universally divine babbling equilibria where all types give the same speech. We leave this proof as an exercise.

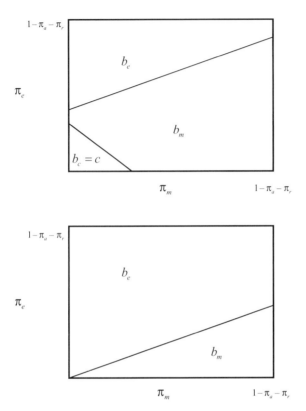

Figure 10.4. *Top*, Proposals in "Babbling Equilibrium"; *bottom*, Proposals in "Two-Message Equilibrium" Following Compromising Message.

type a, there is a utility loss associated with the fact that C may propose the less desirable policies b_m and b_e. For president m, there are losses associated with the fact that C might propose c (which he then vetoes) rather than his preferred b_e. Because presidents r and e obtain their status quo utility from all proposals, they are not affected. C is also affected by the lack of information as it may force her either to accommodate more than necessary or to risk a veto.

So given the bad outcomes from the babbling equilibrium, it is reasonable to ask whether there are other equilibria where more information is transmitted. Matthews shows that some information about presidential preferences, but not all of it, can be revealed in presidential speeches. First, consider why a separating equilibrium where every presidential type gives a distinct speech cannot be an equilibrium. If C could learn the president's type from the speech, she would optimally propose b_r to r, b_e to e, and so forth. Because m prefers b_e to b_m, however, m prefers to defect and give e's speech. Thus, a separating equilibrium cannot exist. Matthews shows that the most informative equilibrium is one where type a reveals his type with an "accommo-dating" speech and the other types all make the same "threatening" speech. Following an accommodating speech, C correctly infers that the president will accept her ideal point and thus proposes c. Type a makes the accommodating speech because she clearly prefers c to b_m or b_e. Following the threatening speech, C learns that the president is not a and updates her beliefs accordingly. Given these beliefs, C chooses between b_m and b_e. The second panel of Figure 10.4 illustrates the op-timal proposal as a function of π_m and π_e for given values of π_a and π_r. There are two important points to note. First, it is more likely that C proposes b_e because the knowledge that the president is not type a makes the probability that b_m is vetoed much higher. Thus, C makes a larger concession to the president's preferences after a threatening speech than after an accommodating speech.

It is important to note that an informative equilibrium is not guar-anteed to exist. Suppose type a preferred b_m to c to b_e; an informative equilibrium would exist only if C's best response to the threatening message were b_e. Otherwise, a defects to the threatening speech. Sim-ilarly, if a prefers b_e to c, no informative equilibrium exists.

For some configurations of preferences the veto threat is simply a bluff. Consider what happens if m was moved in Figure 10.3 so far to the right that he prefers c to q (thus became an accommodator) but still preferred b_e to c. In the informative equilibrium, m gives the threatening speech, but it is a bluff in the sense that he would sign C's ideal point.

The informative equilibrium makes C better off (if it did not she could just turn off the TV and ignore the speech). It is possible, how-ever, that some presidential types are worse off. Suppose that a were repositioned so that his preference ordering were such that he prefers b_m to c to b_e. Further, suppose that the babbling equilibrium produces b_m while a threat in the more informative equilibrium produces b_e. Then a would clearly prefer the outcome of the babbling equilibrium to the informative equilibrium.

6.1.2. Sequential Veto Bargaining with Incomplete Information. Often, the proposer can make multiple offers, learning about the receiver as she does so. For example, if the receiver rejects a tough offer early, the proposer may believe the receiver is genuinely tough. If so, the pro-poser's next offer is likely to be more accommodating. This "haggling" dynamic is very common in many types of bargaining, and one might well expect to see it in veto bargaining as well. But a complicating factor is misdirection: the receiver often has an incentive to reject early offers in order to build a reputation that leads to better offers later in the game. But knowing this, why should the proposer actually make the compromises? The sequential veto bargaining model (SVB) model explores these questions about learning and credibility.

A simple example conveys many of the basic ideas. First, consider a situation in which $q = 0, e = .25, m = .6$, and $c = 1$. By now it should be clear that in a one-shot game (without a veto threat) $b_e = .5$ and $b_m = c$. Using the results of the one-shot incomplete information model, it is easy to see that C offers $b_m = c$ if $\pi < 1/2$ and $b_e = .5$ otherwise. But suppose this is not a one-shot game, so that C may make a second offer if the first is rejected. More specifically, suppose bargaining breaks down with probability ρ, but otherwise a second offer can be made. The probability of a bargaining breakdown reflects the inherent uncertainty of the legislative and other political processes. Is a haggling equilibrium possible, that is, one in which C first makes a tough offer then, following a veto and no bargaining breakdown, makes a more accommodating offer?

In such a haggling equilibrium, the moderate president must accept the tough offer in the first round (if both types rejected the tough offer, then C should make the accommodating offer lest a breakdown saddle her with the unappealing status quo). Therefore, the following incentive compatibility constraint must hold:

$$(m - c) \geq (1 - \rho)(m - 2e + q) + \rho(q - m)$$

or

$$\rho \geq \frac{c - q - 2(m - e)}{2(e - q)}.$$

The incentive compatibility constraint indicates that accepting the tough offer in the first round is better for the moderate type than rejecting the offer and holding out for the more proximate accommodating offer, taking into account the probability of a bargaining breakdown. In the example, the critical value for the breakdown probability is .6. Let $\mu(e)$ be C's belief that the president is the extreme type, following a veto. Note the following: in a haggling equilibrium, it must be the case that $\mu(e) \geq 1/2$; otherwise, following a veto, C makes the tough offer again in the final period (this was proved earlier). But if the probability of a breakdown is greater than .6, then the moderate type accepts the initial offer, so that by Bayes' rule $\mu(e) = 1$, following a veto, and C indeed makes the accommodating offer in the second round.

There remains an additional incentive compatibility constraint to examine, however. Congress must find it more appealing to make a tough offer followed by an accommodating offer (conditional on a veto and no breakdown), rather than make an initial accommodating offer that would surely be accepted. This requires that

$$\pi\left[(1-\rho)(2e-q-c)+\rho(q-c)\right] \geq \rho(2e-q-c)$$

or

$$\pi \leq \frac{c-2e-q}{c-2e(1-\rho)+q(1-2\rho)}.$$

In the example, this condition becomes $\pi \leq 1/(1+\rho)$. We can now indicate a haggling equilibrium in the two-period, two-type sequential veto bargaining model with the ideal points indicated earlier. If $.6 \leq \rho \leq 1$ and $\pi \leq 1/(1+\rho)$, then C offers $b_1 = b_m = c$ and $b_2 = b_e = .5$. Presidential type m accepts both b_e and b_m in both periods, while type e accepts offer b_e and vetoes b_m in both periods. Finally, C's belief that the president is an extreme type is $\mu(e) = 1$ following a veto.

6.1.3. Bargaining over Multiple Bills. The last section shows that in- complete information can affect the dynamics of bargaining on a sin- gle issue, but McCarty (1997) considers how informational and reputa- tional incentives alter the bargaining across multiple issues over time. He considers a model of veto bargaining with incomplete information where P and C bargain over a series of policies with status quo points q_1 and q_2. In each of the two periods, C proposes b_t and the president decides whether to accept or reject. Thus, bargaining over each pol- icy is modeled as a one-shot game such that if P vetoes b_t the status quo q_t is the policy outcome. Because the president's ideal point is assumed to be constant across policies, the outcome on policy 1 may provide information to C prior to her making an offer on policy 2. Because in the last period, the game is identical to the one-shot incom- plete information game described earlier, type m does better on the second policy by having C believe that he is the extreme type if preferences correspond to those given in panel a or b. Thus, given those preference configurations, m may be willing to use a first-period veto to build a reputation as the extreme type in order get a better outcome on policy 2. This involves rejecting bills that he, but not type e, prefers to q_1. Thus, reputational incentives increase the likelihood of a veto on policy 1. Given that C understands these incentives, she may be sufficiently accommodating on the first policy to discourage type m from vetoing on reputational grounds. Thus, McCarty's model predicts a "honeymoon" pattern of accommodating policies early in the president's term followed by less accommodating policies toward the end when reputational incentives are diminished. He notes, however, that because the existence of reputational incentives depends on preference configurations such as those in panels a and b, this honeymoon effect is unlikely when the expected difference between P and C is small as in the case of unified governments.

6.2. Blame Game Vetoes. Groseclose and McCarty (2000) argue that vetoes are less a product of legislative uncertainty than of electoral politics. Their article presents a model in which the legislative agenda setter uses its proposal power to signal that the president has policy views out of step with the voters'. In this "blame game" model, vetoes occur when the agenda setter receives a larger payoff from signaling that the president has extreme preferences than she does from enacting a new policy. Thus, the electorate's uncertainty about the president is critical, but uncertainty of legislators is not.

To illustrate a simple version of this model, consider a new actor V, the voter. V has linear preferences and an ideal point v. Following the notation of the last section, V believes the president is type e with probability π and type m otherwise. We focus on the case where $e < m < v$. We assume the voter evaluates the president on the basis of the expected distance between the president's ideal point and her own ideal point. Therefore, the voters' evaluation is just

$$w(e, m, \pi; v) = -\pi |v - e| - (1 - \pi) |v - m| = \pi e + (1 - \pi) m - v.$$

An important feature of this model is that P and C care how much expected utility V gets from the president's position. The most interesting case is one of conflict, in which the president gets greater utility when the voter believes he is a moderate and Congress gets greater utility when the voter believes the president is an extremist. Such a case would plausibly arise when Congress and the presidency are controlled by different political parties or factions, especially when those parties are highly polarized, and the median voter is moderate. In such a case, C and P trade gains from enacting policy with gains from political posturing. More specifically, the president prefers actions that lead the public to lower π while the legislature prefers actions that lead the public to increase π. We allow C and P to value these trade-offs differently by letting λ_c and λ_p be the respective weights each place on policy. Therefore, the utility functions for C and P are

$$-\lambda_c|x - c| + (1 - \lambda_c)(\pi e + (1 - \pi)m - v)$$

and

$$-\lambda_p|x - p| - (1 - \lambda_p)(\pi e + (1 - \pi)m - v).$$

An important assumption of this model is that while V is relatively uninformed about P's preferences, C is fully informed. Therefore, C may be able to communicate its information about π through its choice of bill. Similarly, the president's decision whether to veto particular proposals may also provide information to voters about his preferences.

A particularly interesting equilibrium is one in which C proposes an acceptable bill when P is moderate and submits a bill that is rejected when the president is extreme. It exists if and only if the following two conditions hold:

$$\frac{\lambda_p - \lambda_c}{\lambda_p \lambda_c}(1 - \pi)(m - e) \geq 2(e - q) \tag{10.1}$$

and

$$2 \geq \frac{\lambda_p - \lambda_c}{\lambda_p \lambda_c}\pi. \tag{10.2}$$

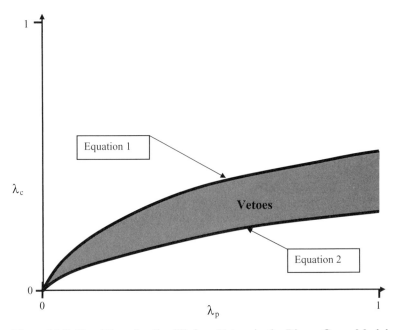

Figure 10.5. Conditions for Equilibrium Vetoes in the Blame Game Model.

These conditions produce a number of predictions about the occurrence of vetoes.[10] First, condition 10.1 cannot be satisfied if $m = e$ or $\pi = 1$. Thus, voter uncertainty about the president's preferences is crucial. Without this uncertainty, orchestrating a veto has no signaling value to C so she prefers to make acceptable proposals to both types. Second, both conditions are easier to satisfy when π is lower. Because the ex ante evaluation of the president is decreasing in π (the probability he is extreme), the model suggests that vetoes occur more often when the public believes the president is moderate (that is, believes the president is ideologically proximate). Intuitively, Congress finds the blame game most attractive when it has negative information about the president's policy preferences that contradicts the voter's beliefs.

The next three predictions are based on C and P's willingness to trade policy gains for political gains. Figure 10.5 illustrates how the policy weights λ_p and λ_c affect each of the conditions. The area under the higher line represents combinations of λ_p and λ_c that satisfy

---

[10] These conditions are necessary for the case of $c > 2m - q + (m - e)(1 - \lambda_p)/(\lambda_p)$. Different positions of c result in slightly modified but qualitatively similar conditions.

condition 10.1. Alternatively, the area above the lower line represents those satisfying condition 10.2. The blame game equilibrium described earlier exists in the intersection of these regions. First, note that condition 10.1 is met only when $\lambda_p > \lambda_c$, suggesting that the president must put relatively more weight on the policy outcome than does Congress. If this is not the case, C prefers the policy gains of passing mutually attractive bills rather than the electoral advantage of passing bills the president rejects. Condition 10.2 puts an upper bound on the difference in policy weights. If λ_p is much greater than λ_c, C loses the ability to signal credibly with its proposals. One final prediction emerges from the fact that only extreme types veto in the blame game model. Because only type e vetoes, every veto is followed by a reduction of voter support.

7. Application: Crisis Bargaining

One of the limitations of bargaining theory is that solutions are generally highly dependent on the bargaining protocol and are therefore not robust to changes in the extensive form. In the context of veto bargaining, this is not such a large problem because its protocol is often codified in constitutional provisions and well-established legislative procedures. In crisis bargaining among sovereign states, however, it is clearly less desirable to have bargaining solutions depend heavily on particular extensive forms; the relevant protocols are generally more informal, noncodified, and unobservable because of secrecy concerns.

Recognizing this problem, Banks (1990) considers what equilibria of a large class of crisis bargaining games must have in common. Consider the following crisis bargaining scenario. Two states 1 and 2 bargain over 1 unit of territory. Let x be the share that goes to country 1. Following Banks, we assume that both countries are risk neutral so that country 1's payoff from a settlement is x and country 2's is $1 - x$. Failure to reach an agreement on the division of the territory leads to a war.[11] Country 1's expected utility of a war is u and country 2's is v. These expected utilities encapsulate expectations about the probability of winning the war, the benefits of winning and losing, and the allocation of territory that the winner can secure.

---

[11] We include in the set of possible agreements a settlement in which the status quo remains intact.

Banks assumes that country 1 has an informational advantage vis-a-vis country 2 about the values of (u, v). Following the usual practice, he models this asymmetric information by assuming that country 1's type is some $t \in T$ defined such that country 1's expected benefits of war, $u(t)$, are increasing in its type. Although country 1 learns t prior to negotiations, country 2 has only a prior $f(t)$, which is common knowledge.

Given this framework, standard game theoretic models specify a set of decisions available to the countries, a (probabilistic) outcome function specifying the probability of a war, and the distribution of settlements as a function of these decisions. From this model, we can derive equilibrium strategies $(\sigma_1(t), \sigma_2)$ that produce the equilibrium probability of war $p(t)$ and expected settlement $x(t)$. In such an equilibrium, country 1's payoffs are

$$U(t; x, p) = p(t)u(t) + (1 - p(t))x(t).$$

Clearly, not every $p(t)$ and $x(t)$ can arise from a Bayesian equilibrium. In particular, a Bayesian equilibrium has two requirements. The first is incentive compatibility. Type t cannot prefer the outcomes $p(t')$ and $x(t')$ to $p(t)$ and $x(t)$. Otherwise it would defect from its equilibrium strategy $\sigma_1(t)$. Incentive compatibility requires that for every t and t'

$$p(t)u(t) + (1 - p(t))x(t) \geq p(t')u(t) + (1 - p(t'))x(t') \quad (10.3)$$
$$p(t')u(t') + (1 - p(t'))x(t') \geq p(t)u(t') + (1 - p(t))x(t). \quad (10.4)$$

The second condition imposed by Bayesian equilibrium is individual rationality.[12] The value $u(t)$ cannot be greater than $x(t)$ unless $p(t) = 1$. Otherwise, t withdraws from the agreement and starts a war with probability 1. The individual rationality constraint is

$$p(t)u(t) + (1 - p(t))x(t) \geq u(t). \quad (10.5)$$

Although incentive compatibility and individual rationality are minimal requirements, they impose quite a bit of structure on bargaining outcomes. The most important feature of Bayesian equilibria concerns the monotonicity of p, x, and U in t.

---

[12] The similarity of Banks's approach to mechanism design should be obvious to the attentive reader (at least after the next chapter is digested).

LEMMA 10.1 *If p and x are incentive compatible and individually rational, then p(t) is weakly increasing on T.*

Proof Let $t' > t$. We can subtract the right side of equation 10.3 from the left side of equation 10.4 and the left side of equation 10.3 from the right side of 10.4 to produce

$$p(t')[u(t') - u(t)] \geq p(t)[u(t') - u(t)].$$

Because $u(t)$ is strictly increasing, $u(t') - u(t) > 0$ so that it must be the case that $p(t') \geq p(t)$.   □

This lemma shows that in any Bayesian equilibrium the probability of war cannot decrease as country 1's expected utility of war increases. Not only is this a feature of strategic models, it is consistent with the assumptions of a number of decision theoretic models of war.

For the next result, we define the set of types who resolve the dispute through bargaining with a positive probability given p, x. Let $T_b = \{t \in T : p(t) < 1\}$. Note that individual rationality requires that $x(t) \geq u(t)$ for any $t \in T_b$.

LEMMA 10.2 *If p and x are incentive compatible and individually rational, then x(t) is weakly increasing on T_b.*

Proof Let $t, t' \in T_b$, and $t' > t$. This means that Lemma 10.1 implies $1 > p(t') \geq p(t)$. Because $x(t) \geq u(t)$ for all $t \in T_b$, we know that

$$p(t)u(t') + (1 - p(t))x(t') \geq p(t')u(t') + (1 - p(t'))x(t'). \quad (10.6)$$

We can combine this result with equation 10.4 to produce

$$p(t)u(t') + (1 - p(t))x(t') \geq p(t)u(t') + (1 - p(t))x(t),$$

which reduces to $x(t') \geq x(t)$ after dividing by $(1 - p(t))$, which we know is positive because $t \in T_b$.   □

Not surprisingly, country 1 must do at least as well in the bargaining outcome when its war utility improves. Taken together Lemmas 10.1 and 10.2 suggest that in any Bayesian equilibrium higher types get better bargaining outcomes but incur a greater risk for war.[13] Incentive compatibility, however, requires that these trade-offs benefit higher types (or else they would mimic lower types). Let $T_w = \{t \in T : p(t) > 0\}$ so that T_w is the set of types that go to war with some probability.

LEMMA 10.3 *If p and x are incentive compatible and individually rational, then $U(t; x, p)$ is weakly increasing on T and strictly increasing on T_w.*

Proof Let $t' > t$, and $t', t \in T_w$. Suppose (contra the lemma) that $U(t) \geq U(t')$ so that

$$p(t)u(t) + (1 - p(t))x(t) \geq p(t')u(t') + (1 - p(t'))x(t').$$

Because $u(t') > u(t)$, this implies that

$$p(t)u(t') + (1 - p(t))x(t) \geq p(t')u(t') + (1 - p(t'))x(t'). \quad (10.7)$$

Because $t', t \in T_w$, $p(t)$ and $p(t')$ are greater than 0 so that equation 10.7 violates equation 10.4. Thus, $U(t') > U(t)$. This strict equality does not hold on $T\backslash T_w$, however. If $t, t' \in T\backslash T_w$, then $p(t) = p(t') = 0$ so that equations 10.3 and 10.4 clearly imply that $x(t) = x(t')$ and $U(t) = U(t')$. $\qquad \square$

Thus, a better expected utility of war cannot make country 1 worse off. In fact, for types that go to war with a nonzero probability, higher war payoffs lead to strictly higher equilibrium payoffs.[14]

Although the incentive compatibility approach can go a long way toward telling us what predictions are generic to crisis bargaining models, there are a number of questions it cannot resolve. For example, we do not learn how country 2's perceptions of country 1's war utilities, as measured by the priors $f(t)$, affect the likelihood of war or the bargaining settlement. For that we turn to more explicit models of crisis bargaining.

---

[13] Banks also shows that if x and p are incentive compatible and individually rational then $x(t') > x(t)$ if and only if $p(t') > p(t)$ for $t' > t$ and $t, t' \in T_b$.

[14] Banks also shows that $U(t; x, p)$ is continuous in t, but we refer the reader to his article.

7.1. Models of Crisis Bargaining. Fearon's (1995) article explores several models in the class covered by Banks's results. He gives a specific form to (u, v). Fearon assumes that each country has a cost of war $c_i > 0$, country 1 wins any war with probability $\pi \in (0, 1)$, and the winner of the war can impose its most preferred settlement ($x = 1$ for country 1 and $x = 0$ for country 2). Therefore, $u = \pi - c_1$ and $v = 1 - \pi - c_2$. Let x_0 be the status quo allocation of the territory.

Given this framework, we can define the set of agreements that each side accepts in lieu of going to war. For country 1, we require that $x > \pi - c_1$ and for country 2 we require $1 - x > 1 - \pi - c_2$. Therefore, any allocation $x \in [\pi - c_1, \pi + c_2]$ prevents conflict. Because the costs of war are positive, the set of peaceful agreements is nonempty. Under perfect information, we expect that one of these agreements is reached and war is prevented.[15]

Fearon considers a simple model with incomplete information about country 1's costs. Although he assumes a continuous distribution of c_1, it suffices to consider a cost distribution where c_1 takes on only two values, $\bar{c} > \underline{c}$. The common knowledge prior is that $c_1 = \underline{c}$ with probability λ. Fearon first considers a model where country 2 makes a single take-it-or-leave-it offer to country 1. If country 1 rejects it, war ensues.

In analyzing this model, note that if country 2 offers $x \geq \pi - \underline{c}$ both country 1 types accept and war is avoided. Clearly, country 2 has no incentive to pay higher than $\pi - \underline{c}$, so let $\underline{x} = \pi - \underline{c}$. If country 2 offers $x \in (\pi - \bar{c}, \pi - \underline{c}]$, only the low-cost type accepts, so that war starts with probability λ. Of these offers, country 2 prefers $\bar{x} = \pi - \bar{c}$. Finally, if country 2 offers $x < \pi - \bar{c}$ both types reject, and a war starts with certainty. This generates a payoff to country 2 of $v = 1 - \pi - c_2$. Thus, country 2's choice boils down to a choice of three utilities, $1 - \underline{x}$, $\lambda v + (1 - \lambda)(1 - \bar{x})$, or v. We can easily dismiss the third option. Because the interval $[\pi - \underline{c}, \pi + c_2]$ is nonempty, we know that $1 - \underline{x} > v$. Thus, country 2 never chooses to sabotage the negotiations to generate a war with probability 1. Now we can determine country 2's preferences over the remaining offers. Clearly, $\lambda v + (1 - \lambda)(1 - \bar{x}) \geq 1 - \underline{x}$ whenever

$$\lambda \leq \frac{\bar{c} - \underline{c}}{c_2 + \bar{c}}.$$

---

[15] This statement of course assumes that the territory is infinitely divisible so that an agreement in this region is feasible. This may not be the case in some disputes. Problems of this form are likely to arise when the territory involves religious or ideational significance.

When the probability that country 1 has low costs is sufficiently low, country 2 takes an aggressive bargaining stance that risks war in the event that country 1 actually does have low costs. Note that the critical threshold is decreasing in country 2's costs; it is less willing to take such a risk when its military capabilities are low.

We can easily check that Banks's results hold trivially for this model. When $\lambda > (\bar{c} - \underline{c})/(c_2 + \bar{c})$, both types receive the same allocation and generate 0 probabilities of going to war. When $\lambda \leq (\bar{c} - \underline{c})/(c_2 + \bar{c})$, both types are still offered the same allocation but $\underline{c}$ goes to war with probability 1.

As Fearon notes there are reasons to be skeptical of informational explanations for war. Perhaps opportunities for communication should resolve such informational asymmetries and prevent war. Given that the countries have diametrically opposed preferences over the allocations, however, it is easy to show that cheap talk does not influence bargaining or the probability of war. Let country 1 announce H or L as a signal of its costs $\bar{c}$ and $\underline{c}$, respectively.[16] Following the message, let λ^* be country 2's updated beliefs about 1's costs. Clearly, on the basis of the these updated beliefs, country 2 uses the same cutpoint rule as before. First we consider whether there are separating equilibria where type $\bar{c}$ reports H and $\underline{c}$ reports L. In such a case, $\lambda^*(H) = 0$, $\lambda^*(L) = 1, x(H) = \bar{x}$, and $x(L) = \underline{x}$. The probability of war is 0. Separating messages, therefore, require the incentive compatibility conditions $x(H) \geq x(L)$ and $x(L) \geq x(H)$. These conditions clearly fail because $\underline{x} > \bar{x}$. We leave it to the reader to verify that there are no partially informative semipooling equilibria.

7.2. A Model of Escalation*. This section is based on Fearon (1994), which develops a version of the war of attrition to explore how "audience costs" imposed on states who back down in international disputes affect the dynamics of crisis escalation.

Two states 1 and 2 are in a dispute over a prize worth $v > 0$. The game is played in continuous time beginning at $t = 0$. At every instant each state can choose among three strategies: *attack, quit,* or *escalate.* The game continues until one or both of the states quit or attack. If both states escalate, the game continues . If either state attacks before the other quits they both receive their expected payoffs from war $w_i < 0$.

---

[16] The restriction to two messages or endowing them with literal meaning is not consequential.

Fearon interprets these payoffs as resolve; the state with the higher w_i is relatively more willing to engage in military conflict to settle the dispute.

Fearon wants to understand how sanctions imposed on leaders who back down during disputes affect crisis behavior. Therefore, he assumes that if state i quits before state j at time t it suffers audience costs $a_i(t)$ that are strictly increasing in t. The dependence on t reflects the intuition that it is more costly to back down during a protracted dispute than a short one.

A pure strategy in this game specifies a rule for any subgame beginning at time t' specifying a finite time $t \geq t'$ at which to *attack* or *quit*.[17] We write these strategies as $\{t, attack\}$ meaning "escalate until t and then attack" or $\{t, quit\}$ to represent "escalate until time t and then quit."

Before considering the more general model where each side is uncertain of the other's resolve, it is instructive to consider the case of complete information. For each state, we can compute the time t at which it strictly prefers to attack rather than back down. Clearly, this occurs when $w_i \geq -a_i(t)$. Let

$$\bar{t}_i = -a_i^{-1}(w_i).$$

Suppose $\bar{t}_1 < \bar{t}_2$ because either state 1's resolve or its audience costs are higher than state 2's. Thus, at $\bar{t}_1$, state 2 prefers to quit rather than to be attacked; thus it quits. Let $Q_i(t; t')$ be the probability that state i quits before time t conditional on its not quitting before t' and $Q_i(t)$ be the unconditional probability of quitting by time t.

Thus, at every subgame $0 \leq t' < \bar{t}_1$, state 2 receives $-a_2(t')$ for quitting immediately and $Q_1(t; t')v - (1 - Q_1(t; t'))a_2(t)$ for $\{t, quit\}$. Consider state 1's strategy, however. From subgame $0 \leq t' < \bar{t}_1$, strategy $\{\bar{t}_1, attack\}$ has a payoff of v while $\{t, quit\}$ has a payoff of $Q_2(t; t')v - (1 - Q_2(t; t'))a_2(t) < v$. Therefore, $Q_1(t; t') = 0$ for all $t < \bar{t}_1$. Now we can see that state 2's payoff from $\{t, quit\}$ is $-a_2(t) < -a_2(t')$. Thus, state 2 quits immediately at every subgame $0 \leq t' < \bar{t}_1$, including 0. The equilibrium with complete information therefore involves state 2's stopping immediately and state 1's claiming the prize.

---

[17] Not including "never quit" in the strategy set eliminates the uninteresting equilibrium where both sides choose this strategy and escalate forever.

The complete information equilibrium has the property that both high resolve and audience costs lead to better crisis bargaining outcomes. It predicts, however, that no crises ever occur, and the weaker side capitulates immediately. Therefore, Fearon also considers an incomplete information version of the game where each side is uncertain of the other's resolve. The resolve of state i is distributed according to the cumulative distribution function F_i on the interval $[\underline{w}_i, 0]$.

Just as in the complete information game, the equilibrium depends on defining a time point after which neither state wishes to quit. Fearon refers to such a time point as the *horizon* of the crisis game. Formally, this horizon point is t_h, the earliest time point at which $Q_i(t)$ is not increasing for $t > t_h$ for $i = 1, 2$.

Fearon observes that the following must be true in any PBE:[18]

(1) Both states quit simultaneously with probability 0. Suppose state 1 quits with positive probability mass at t'. Then clearly state 2 has an incentive to wait until at least $t' + \varepsilon$ (for some small positive number ε) before quitting; this increases its probability of winning v substantially with only an infinitesimal increase in its audience costs. Similarly, there is no PBE where a state quits contemporaneously with an attack from the other state. Again, if state 2 expects that state 1 quits with probability mass at point t', it should hold off its attack until $t' + \varepsilon$. This implies that both states cannot plan to quit at t_h.

(2) State i does not attack at time t' if $Q_j(t)$ is increasing at t'. Because attacks have negative expected utility, it pays to wait longer in the hope that the opponent will drop out prior to the attack.

(3) Both states quit with positive probability in time intervals arbitrarily close to t_h. By the definition of t_h, at least one state must quit with positive probability in the arbitrarily small interval before t_h. Suppose that this is true for state i. Now suppose to the contrary that state j quits with 0 probability after time $t' < t_h$. Clearly from observation 2, state 2 does not attack between t' and t_h. Therefore, quitting with positive probability after t', state 1 unnecessarily increases its audience costs – it knows it will quit before state 2 yet it keeps escalating.

---

[18] For formal statements of these observations and their proofs, see Fearon (1994).

(4) Both states attack with probability 0 for $t < t_h$. This follows directly from observations 2 and 3. Therefore, the utility of strategy $\{t > t_h, \text{attack}\}$ for state i is

$$U_i^a(t, w_i) = Q_j(t_h)v + (1 - Q_j(t_h))w_i \qquad (10.8)$$

while the utility of $\{t < t_h, \text{quit}\}$ is

$$U_i^q(t) = Q_j(t)v - (1 - Q_j(t_h))a_i(t). \qquad (10.9)$$

Because $U_i^q(t)$ does not depend on w_i, $\{t < t_h, \text{quit}\}$ is only a best response if it is constant at some value k_i for all t. Suppose this were not true and let $U_i^q(t') > U_i^q(t)$ for some $t' < t_h$ and all $t < t_h$. Then all types such that $U_i^q(t') > U_i^a(t_h, w_i)$ quit at exactly t'. State j's best response would then be $\{t > t', \text{quit}\}$, making $U_i^q(t') = -a_i(t')$, which contradicts $U_i^q(t') > U_i^q(t)$ for all $t < t_h$.

On the basis of these observations, the following lemmas help to characterize the perfect Bayesian equilibria for this game.

LEMMA 10.4 *In any equilibrium in which both states choose to escalate with positive probability, there must exist a finite horizon t_h.*

The logic of this Lemma is straightforward. Suppose to the contrary that there were a PBE where $Q_i(t)$ were increasing for all t. By observation 2, state j never attacks. In turn observation 4 suggests that $U_i^q(t)$ is constant for all t. This implies that

$$Q_j(t) = \frac{k_i + a_i(t)}{v + a_i(t)}.$$

But because j never attacks, it must be the case that $\lim_{t \to \infty} Q_j(t) = 1$. This is only true if $k_i = v$ or $\lim_{t \to \infty} a_i(t) = \infty$. If $k_i = v$, $Q_j(0) = 1$ implying that j does not escalate with certainty. If $\lim_{t \to \infty} a_i(t) = \infty$, i prefers not to choose $\{t, \text{quit}\}$ for arbitrarily large t.

LEMMA 10.5 *In any equilibrium with t_h as the horizon and in which escalation may occur, (1) if state i chooses $\{t, \text{attack}\}$ it must be the case* *that $t \geq t_h$; and (2) state i chooses $\{t, attack\}$ where $t \geq t_h$ if $w_i > -a_i(t_h)$ and only if $w_i \geq -a_i(t_h)$.*

Part 1 of this lemma follows directly from observations 2 and 3. Ignoring several technical complications, part 2 follows from the fact that $U_i^a(t, w_i) \geq U_i^q(t)$ if and only if $w_i \geq -a_i(t_h)$.[19]

From Lemma 10.5, the ex ante probability that state j attacks at t_h is $(1 - F_j(-a_j(t_h)))$. Thus, state i's ex ante utility of escalating up to t_h and then backing down is

$$u_i(t_h) = F_j(-a_j(t_h))v - (1 - F_j(-a_j(t_h)))a_i(t_h).$$

We define t_i^* such that $u_i(t_i^*) = 0$. Thus, t_i^* has the property that state i is indifferent between escalating to time t_i^* and conceding immediately.[20]

PROPOSITION 10.1 *Let t_i^* be the unique solution $u_i(t_i^*) = 0$ and $t^* = \min\{t_1^*, t_2^*\}$. For any equilibrium in which escalation occurs with positive probability, the horizon must be t^*.*

If t_h is greater than t^*, the state with the lower t_i^* has an incentive to quit with probability 1 before t_d. This contradicts observation 3. If t_d is greater than t^*, then both states have an incentive to bluff a little longer at t_d before quitting. This contradicts the definition of t_d. These conclusions lead directly to the main result.

PROPOSITION 10.2 *Label the players so that $t^* = t_2^* < t_1^*$. Let $k_1 = u_1(t^*) > 0$. The following describes equilibrium strategies for state $i = 1, 2$ as a function of type w_i:*

For $w_i \geq -a_i(t^*)$, state i plays $\{t, attack\}$ for any $t > t^*$.

For $w_i < -a_i(t^*)$, state i plays $\{t, quit\}$ with any pure strategies that yield the following cumulative distributions:

$$\Psi_1(t) = \frac{1}{F_1(-a_1(t^*))} \frac{a_2(t)}{v + a_2(t)}$$

$$\Psi_2(t) = \frac{1}{F_2(-a_2(t^*))} \frac{k_1 + a_1(t)}{v + a_1(t)}.$$

---

[19] The technical complications involve ruling out situations were $Q_i(t)$ has mass points.

[20] We implicitly assume that the range of $a_i(t)$ is sufficiently large that there is a unique solution to $u_i(t_i^*) = 0$.

For $t \leq t^*$, state i believes that the probability that j does not back down is given by

$$\Pr(w_j \geq -a_j(t^*)|t) = \frac{v + a_i(t)}{v + a_i(t^*)}.$$

For $t > t^*$, state i's beliefs follow Bayes' rule in accord with the opponent's strategy for attacking. For any $t > t^*$ off the equilibrium path, let i believe that $w_j > -a_j(t^*)$ and is distributed according to F_j truncated at $-a_j(t^*)$.

Proof Let $Q_i(t)$ be the unconditional probability that state i quits by time t. From Lemma 10.5 and Proposition 10.1, $Q_i(t^*) = F_i(-a_i(t^*))$. The utility to state i of $\{t, \text{quit}\}$ is therefore

$$Q_j(t)v - (1 - Q_j(t))a_i t.$$

To ensure that i is indifferent between quitting and continuing for any $t < t^*$, we require that $Q_j(t)v - (1 - Q_j(t))a_i(t) = u_i(t^*)$ or

$$Q_j(t) = \frac{u_i(t^*) + a_i(t)}{v + a_i(t)}.$$

Because only types $w_j < -a_j(t^*)$ ever quit, these types must quit at rates

$$\frac{Q_j(t)}{F_j(-a_j(t^*))}$$

so that

$$\Psi_j(t) = \frac{1}{F_j(-a_j(t^*))} \frac{u_i(t^*) + a_i(t)}{v + a_i(t)}.$$

We know that by time t, $\Psi_j(t)$ of the types in the interval $[\underline{w}_j, a_j(t^*))$ have dropped out so that

$$\begin{aligned}
\Pr(w_j \geq -a_j(t^*)|t) &= \frac{1 - F_j(-a_j(t))}{1 - F_j(-a_j(t)) + F_j(-a_j(t))(1 - \Psi_j(t))} \\
&= \frac{1 - F_j(-a_j(t))}{1 - Q_j(t)} = \frac{(1 - F_j(-a_j(t)))(v + a_i(t))}{v - u_i(t^*)} \\
&= \frac{v + a_i(t)}{v + a_i(t^*)}.
\end{aligned}$$

$\sqcap$

In this PBE, types with low-resolve from state i drop out at a rate designed to keep the low-resolve types of state j indifferent between dropping out and escalating through time t^*. At time t^*, both states attack because they know that all of the low-resolve types for the other state have dropped out and escalating simply leads to larger audience costs.

It is instructive to explore why low-resolve types of state j quit at a rate to make low-resolve types of state i indifferent between dropping out and escalating. If they dropped out at a faster rate, all low-resolve types in state i conclude at each t that state j is more likely to be a strong type. This leads low-resolve types of state i to quit more quickly. Then state j would then begin to infer that the pool of state i types is stronger and begin to drop more quickly. In the limit, all low-resolve types would quit at $t = 0$, but this cannot be an equilibrium (recall observation 1).

Now consider what happens if low-resolve types from state i drop out at a slower rate than the equilibrium. Then at each t, state j would infer that the pool of remaining types is weaker than the corresponding equilibrium pool. This leads state j types also to drop out at a slower rate, which in turn induces state i to escalate more, and so on. Such a dynamic leads to all types' preferring to escalate until t^*. This cannot be an equilibrium; low-resolve types would have a clear preference for dropping out before t^* over attacking at t^*.

An important substantive feature of the model is that it is beneficial to be able to incur large audience costs. A high-cost state is better able to convince its opponent that it is "locked in" to the conflict (i.e., a larger set of types are willing to escalate to the horizon and then attack). This runs counter to a simple intuitive prediction that those with the most to lose from backing down surrender earlier. Conditional upon starting a crisis, the signaling value outweighs this effect. By modifying his model slightly to include an explicit initiation phase, Fearon argues that this framework provides a justification for why democracies (highly sensitive to audience costs) may be less likely to initiate conflict, but are more likely to prevail.

8. Exercises

EXERCISE 10.1 *Let $u_i(x_i) = \ln x_i$ for $i \in \{A, B\}$. Solve for the Nash bargaining solution as a function of the disagreement values.*

EXERCISE 10.2 *Prove that the only bargaining solution satisfying the four Nash axioms is the Nash bargaining solution.*

EXERCISE 10.3 *In the Rubinstein bargaining model with $\delta_1 = \delta_2$ and $d_1 = d_2 = 0$, assume that $u_i(x_i) = x_i^\alpha$ where $0 < \alpha < 1$. Compute the SPNE shares. What is the effect of risk aversion (lower α)?*

EXERCISE 10.4 *Consider the closed rule Baron-Ferejohn model where $u_i(x_i) = x_i^\alpha$. Show that the initial proposer's share is decreasing in α.*

EXERCISE 10.5 *In the model described in Section 10.3.2 with $N = 3$ and $m = 1$, suppose that $(1 - \delta)/(3 - 2\delta) < q \leq 1/3$. Compute a mixed strategy equilibrium where $v_A = v_B$.*

EXERCISE 10.6 *In the model described in Section 10.3.2, compute v_A and v_B for generic values of N and m.*

EXERCISE 10.7 *Consider an extension of the model considered in Section 10.3.3. Assume that there are two groups of bargainers, 1 and 2. Let m_i be the number of members of group i so that $m_1 + m_2 = N$. Suppose that all members of group i have a qualified veto power in that if they object to the proposal k_i votes are required to override their veto where $0 < k_i < N$. Assume that $k_1 > k_2$. Compute continuation values for members of each group.*

EXERCISE 10.8 *Consider an extension of the model described in Section 10.5.1. First assume that there are two rounds of bargaining so that A makes a counteroffer if it rejects B's initial offer. Assume that the payoffs are discounted by a factor δ if agreement is reached in the second round. What is the PBE to this game? Now assume that there is incomplete information about B's disagreement value where $\underline{u}_B = 0$ with probability π and $\underline{u}_B = d$ with probability $1 - \pi$. Construct a PBE to this game. Is it unique?*

EXERCISE 10.9 *Prove that there are no universally divine equilibria to the Matthews model depicted in Figure 10.10.3 where all presidential types make the same speech.*

EXERCISE 10.10 *In the model described in Section 10.7.1, assume that c_1 is distributed uniformly on the interval $[\underline{c}, \overline{c}]$. Compute the perfect Bayesian equilibrium. Now consider the extension with prebargaining cheap talk. Show that if $\overline{c}$ is sufficiently large, there is a PBE where the high-cost types reveal information about their cost to country 2.*

11 Mechanism Design and Agency Theory

So far we have discussed techniques that analyze how strategic agents behave in specific games. In certain social settings where the rules are fairly clear, this approach is a powerful source of intuition and empirical predictions. An alternative approach asks a slightly different question: Given a desired outcome, what games among strategic agents produce it? Do such games even exist?

The field of game theory asking such questions is *mechanism design*. In this framework, a designer or *principal* selects a Bayesian game, or *mechanism*, for agents to play. Examples of mechanism design include the design of tax codes that induce agents to reveal their willingness to fund public projects, the design of auctions that maximize revenue, and the choice of reelection functions by voters that create incentives for government officials to behave well in office.

Typically, the choice of mechanisms is a maximization problem: the designer chooses a game to maximize her utility subject to the constraint that the agents play the game rationally. If the designer's preferences correspond to some notion of social preferences, mechanism design is a normative exercise. A classic example of the normative approach is the selection of rules that determine the provision of public goods to maximize the sum of individual utilities. Given its normative interpretation, mechanism design is closely related to social choice theory. A version of mechanism design known as *implementation* theory seeks to uncover choice functions (mappings from agent types to collective decisions) for which there exists a mechanism that achieves the choice function. Choice functions of this type are said to be implementable. The Gibbard-Sattherwaite theorem is an example of this type of work.

Although applications of mechanism design are often prescriptive, we also may use it to make positive predictions. For example, mechanism design is often used to study principal-agent relations. The goal is to investigate whether a poorly informed principal such as a legislature or executive can induce well-informed agents such as committees or bureaucrats to act on her behalf.

In most economic applications, the designer can choose from a very rich set of games. She usually can commit to contracts with very elaborate reward and punishment schemes. Such assumptions are reasonable in economic settings where third parties such as courts can enforce complex agreements and where large monetary rewards and sanctions are considered legitimate. In political applications, however, it is often unreasonable to assume that principals can precommit to a reward scheme because third-party enforcement is often unavailable. Also, monetary incentives are often legally or socially proscribed. Accordingly, after presenting some basic concepts and results of mechanism design, we focus on incentives when the principal is more constrained.

1. An Example

Consider one of the classic examples – a political science department of n members and a chair that is deciding whether to purchase a shiny new Saeco espresso maker. The coffee maker has a cost c, and the chair wants to learn whether the department members value the machine sufficiently to justify the expense. Each member's valuation of the coffee maker is $\theta_i \in \mathbb{R}^1_+$. The chair, a Benthamite and non–coffee drinker,[1] wishes to purchase the machine if and only if $\sum_{i=1}^n \theta_i \geq c$. Unfortunately, the chair does not know the valuations of individual department members. Instead she believes that each member's type is drawn from the probability distribution $F(\cdot)$.

What should the chair do? One solution is to ask each member privately for his valuation and purchase the espresso maker with department funds if the total revealed valuations exceed c. The problem is that some colleagues might find it advantageous to inflate their valuations in order to increase the likelihood that the machine is purchased.[2]

---

[1] Jeremy Bentham (1748–1832) was a prominent British philosopher who advocated an ethical system based on pursuing the "greatest good for the greatest number." Historians record that he was also a coffee drinker.

[2] We assume here that department members do not concern themselves with the other ways that the department budget can be used.

Thus, this scheme induces a game where each faculty member's best response is to report a valuation exceeding its actual level. So this solution will not do a very good job in determining whether the espresso maker should be purchased. A better solution is to ask each member to contribute her valuation and purchase the maker if the total contributions exceed c and keep the surplus to pay for coffee beans. If the contributions do not reach c, the chair returns them. This mechanism is also flawed. Now the strategic scholars would understate their valuations hoping to free ride on the contributions of their colleagues. This rule creates a collective action problem.

Although neither of these schemes works well, we can use the theory of mechanism design to uncover a class of particularly simple mechanisms that can be used to learn the faculty's preferences. Groves (1973) and Clarke (1971) show that the following mechanism has desirable properties.

- Ask each faculty member to e-mail her valuation m_i to the chair.
- If $\sum_{i=1}^{n} m_i \geq c$ purchase the coffee maker; otherwise do not.
- If the coffee maker is purchased, collect from faculty member i the amount $t_i(m_i, m_{-i}) = c - \sum_{j \neq i} m_j$.
- If the coffee maker is not purchased, collect no money.

Under this mechanism each faculty member has an incentive to reveal her true valuation regardless of the other members' valuations. A key property is that member i's message affects her contribution only indirectly through its effect on the ultimate decision of whether to purchase the espresso maker. The amount that each member pays depends on the messages of all the other members.

To see that all members have an incentive to offer truthful messages, consider the decision of member i with type θ_i. Suppose that she lies by announcing $m_i' < \theta_i$. This understatement affects the outcome only if alters the likelihood that the machine is purchased, or if

$$\sum_{j \neq i} m_j + m_i' < c < \sum_{j \neq i} m_j + \theta_i.$$

Under these circumstances, $c - \sum_{j \neq i} m_j < \theta_i$ so that the contribution required from a truthful announcement, $c - \sum_{j \neq i} m_j$, is less than the member's value of the new espresso maker. This deviation from a truthful response can only make the department member worse off. Now consider whether a member has an incentive to overstate her demand for espresso with a message $m'_i > \theta_i$. This fabrication only affects i's utility if the inflated message results in purchasing the machine when the truthful message would not have. Such a scenario requires that

$$\sum_{j \neq i} m_j + m_i > c > \sum_{j \neq i} m_j + \theta_i$$

so that $c - \sum_{j \neq i} m_j > \theta_i$. Thus, member i's contribution is more than her valuation of the coffee maker. So lying does not pay.

Beyond promoting honesty in departmental affairs, the Groves-Clarke mechanism has the desirable property that the espresso maker is purchased if and only if the aggregate valuation of the department exceeds its cost. It has a less desirable property, however; it is not "budget balancing." When the machine is purchased, the chair collects

$$\sum_{i=1}^{n} t_i(m_i, m_{-i}) = nc - \sum_{i=1}^{n} \sum_{j \neq i} m_j,$$

an amount greater than or equal to c. Of course, this is not much of a problem so far as the chair is concerned – a little compensation for having to send and read all those e-mail messages.

2. The Mechanism Design Problem

We now consider the mechanism design problem more abstractly. Consider a set N of n agents and a mechanism designer (denoted agent 0). The designer ultimately selects a policy $x \in X$. Each agent has a type $\theta_i \in \Theta$ that is private information. The type vector θ is drawn from the joint distribution function $F(\theta)$. Agents also have Bernoulli utility functions $u_i(x, \theta) : X \times \Theta^n \to \mathbb{R}^1$ that depend on the chosen policy and the agents' types. The mechanism designer has a Bernoulli utility function $u_0(x, \theta)$. In many applications agents care only about their own type, but we allow agents' payoffs to be a function of the entire profile. The primitives of a mechanism design problem are therefore $\langle \Theta, F(\cdot), X, u \rangle$.

In a typical application, the mechanism designer elicits a vector of signals from the agents. The designer chooses a message space for each agent, M_i, and a policy function $p(m) : \prod_{i \in N} M_i \to X$, that selects a policy for every possible profile of messages $m - (m_1, m_2, \ldots, m_n) \in M = \prod_{i \in N} M_i$. Accordingly, a mechanism is a pair $\langle M, p(\cdot) \rangle$.

For a given choice of message spaces and policy function, the n agents play the Bayesian normal form game with the strategy sets $S_i = M_i$ and payoffs given by the composition of u and p, $u_i(p(m), \theta)$.

It is straightforward to see how the espresso mechanism maps into this framework. Clearly, the chair is the designer who selects the message space $M = \Theta$ and implements the policy "buy if $\sum_{i=1}^{n} m_i \geq c$ and charge $c - \sum_{j \neq i} m_j$ to agent i." The faculty members then play a Bayesian normal form game.

Given a mechanism, determining how agents behave requires specifying a form of rationality. One possibility is to make predictions only if the agents have dominant strategies in the induced game. These are known as *dominance solvable* mechanisms. Alternatively, the agents might play a Bayesian Nash equilibrium. Clearly, the question of how well the mechanism performs rests on assumptions about how the agents play the induced game.

In this chapter we focus on Bayesian Nash equilibria. A large literature exists in economics using other solution concepts. For example, the Groves-Clarke mechanism originated in the literature on implementation in dominant strategies. Given the focus on Bayesian Nash equilibria, we wish to highlight the types of choice functions $g : \Theta \to X$ that satisfy the following condition: there exists a mechanism $\langle M, p(\cdot) \rangle$ such that if agents play a Bayesian Nash equilibria to the mechanism then the final outcome corresponds to the policy that would be selected by the choice function, that is, $p(m(\theta)) = g(\theta)$ for each $\theta \in \Theta$.

From the mechanism designer's perspective the mechanism is instrumental to achieving a particular choice function. If the designer wishes to implement the function $g(\cdot)$ in Bayesian Nash strategies then she must select a mechanism $\langle M, p(\cdot) \rangle$ such that the corresponding game has a Bayesian Nash equilibrium where the agents use strategies $m_i^*(\cdot)$ so that $p(m_1^*(\theta_1), m_i^*(\theta_i), \ldots, m_n^*(\theta_n)) = g(\theta)$. Thus, the choice of a mechanism is informed by knowledge of the incentives created by the mechanism. The designer anticipates how these incentives shape behavior by anticipating that agents play equilibrium strategies to the mechanism.

DEFINITION 11.1 *For a mechanism design problem* $\langle \Theta, F(\cdot), X, u \rangle$, *the choice function* $g(\cdot)$ *is implementable in Bayesian Nash strategies if there exists a mechanism* $\langle M, p(\cdot) \rangle$ *with a Bayesian Nash equilibrium* $m_i^*(\cdot)$ *in which* $p(m_1^*(\theta_1), m_i^*(\theta_i), \ldots, m_n^*(\theta_n)) = g(\theta)$ *for every* $\theta \in \Theta$.

If a game is dominance solvable, the surviving strategy profile is a Bayesian Nash equilibrium. This means that given a mechanism design problem the set of choice functions that are implementable in dominant strategies is a subset of those that are implementable in Bayesian Nash strategies. Now that we have defined implementability, a hard question arises. How do we know which choice functions are implementable given that the number of possible mechanisms is quite large?

Our first result, the *revelation principle,* dramatically simplifies the search for implementable choice functions by allowing us to focus on the smaller set of *direct mechanisms.* Direct mechanisms are those in which the agents are asked to report their types directly. Thus, direct mechanisms involve $M_i = \Theta_i$. The revelation principle says that if there exists a mechanism that implements the choice function $g(\cdot)$, then there must exist a direct mechanism that implements $g(\cdot)$. This powerful result tells us that we need not consider all possible mechanisms – just the direct ones.

Although the revelation principle is quite general, its proof is very straightforward.

THEOREM 11.1 *(Revelation Principle in Bayesian Nash strategies) Given a mechanism design problem $\langle \Theta, F(\cdot), u \rangle$, if the choice function $g(\cdot)$ is implementable in Bayesian Nash strategies, there exists a direct mechanism $\langle \Theta, p(\cdot) \rangle$ that implements $g(\cdot)$ in Bayesian Nash strategies.*

Proof Assume that there is a nondirect mechanism $\langle M, p'(\cdot) \rangle$ that implements $g(\cdot)$ in Bayesian Nash strategies. We use this mechanism to construct a direct mechanism that also implements the choice function $g(\cdot)$. Let $s_i(\cdot)$ denote the strategy that player i deploys in one of the Bayesian Nash equilibria to the game induced by $\langle M, p'(\cdot) \rangle$, which implements $g(\cdot)$. Consider the direct mechanism in which agents are asked to announce messages $m_i \in \Theta_i$ and then the policy is chosen by the function $p(\theta) = p'(s_1(\theta_1), \ldots, s_i(\theta_i), \ldots, s_n(\theta_n))$ for each $\theta \in \Theta$. We need only verify that under the direct mechanism, truthful announcements of $m_i(\theta_i) = \theta_i$ form a Bayesian Nash equilibrium. First, suppose that all agents $N\backslash\{i\}$ are playing truthful strategies. If agent i also uses a truthful strategy then the final outcome will be $g(\theta)$ for each θ. Now suppose that there is a desirable deviation $m'_i \neq \theta'_i$ in the direct mechanism for agent i with type $\theta'_i \in \Theta_i$. If agent i can select m'_i in the direct mechanism, it must be the case that $m'_i \in \Theta_i$. Because $s_l(\theta_l) : \Theta_l \to M_l$ in the game induced by $\langle M, p'( ) \rangle$, however, it must be the case that $s_i(m') \in M_i$ exists. This implies that

$$\int_{\theta_{-i} \in \Theta_{-i}} u_i(p'(s_1(\theta_1), \ldots, s_i(m'), \ldots, s_n(\theta_n)))dF(\theta_{-i} \mid \theta_i) >$$

$$\int_{\theta_{-i} \in \Theta_{-i}} u_i(p'(s_1(\theta_1), \ldots, s_i(\theta_i'), \ldots, s_n(\theta_n)))dF(\theta_{-i} \mid \theta_i).$$

This expression contradicts the fact that $s_i(\cdot)$ is a best response in the equilibrium of the Bayesian game induced by $\langle M, p'(\cdot) \rangle$. Thus, the result is established.   □

One cautionary note is in order. We focus only on the existence of a mechanism that implements a choice function as the outcome of a Bayesian Nash equilibrium. Clearly, there may be other equilibria that result in different collective choices. We refer readers to Palfrey and Srivastava (1989) for a treatment of mechanism design when mechanisms are required to have unique equilibria.

We can extend the revelation principle to a very large class of equilibrium concepts. As mentioned, one important example is the case of implementation in dominant strategies. Exercise 3 of this chapter provides the appropriate definitions and asks the reader to prove this revelation principle. The intuition behind the result is quite similar. Suppose a player has a dominant strategy to play a particular strategy in one mechanism. Then under a suitably defined direct mechanism that provides the payoff of the original mechanism for a truthful message, truthfulness is a dominant strategy.

Given the revelation principle, the question of whether a particular choice function is implementable can be answered by focusing on truthful direct mechanisms. If a choice function cannot be implemented by such a mechanism, it cannot be implemented by any mechanism.

We now consider a few examples before returning to the development of the theory.

3. Application: Polling

Suppose that there are $N = \{1, 2, \ldots, n\}$ (where n is odd – of course) voters with symmetric single-peaked preferences on $\mathbb{R}^1$. The mechanism designer does not know the agents' ideal points but may ask each voter a question and select a policy $x \in \mathbb{R}^1$. Each ideal point θ_i is drawn from a distribution $F(\cdot)$ on $\mathbb{R}^1$. A natural question to ask is whether there are any mechanisms that induce agents to reveal their ideal points in dominant strategies. Herve Moulin (1980) shows that the answer is yes. Consider the mechanism that asks each agent to announce his ideal point $m_i \in \mathbb{R}^1$ and then chooses policy equal to the median announcement, $x(m) = median(m)$. To see that truthful response is a best response, consider a respondent with ideal point y_i. Let $x(m_i, m_{-i})$ denote the median of the profile of messages that includes m_i and the responses of the other $n - 1$ respondents. Further, let $\underline{x}(m_{-i})$ and $\overline{x}(m_{-i})$ be the lower and upper bounds of $median\,(m_{-i})$.[3]

Suppose that agent i reports y_i. If $y_i < \underline{x}(m_{-i})$, then $\underline{x}(m_{-i})$ becomes the median report so that $x(y_i, m_{-i}) = \underline{x}(m_{-i})$. Similarly, if $y_i > \overline{x}(m_{-i})$, $x(y_i, m_{-i}) = \overline{x}(m_{-i})$. Finally, if $y_i \in [\underline{x}(m_{-i}), \overline{x}(m_{-i})]$, y_i is the median report so that $x(y_i, m_{-i}) = y_i$. Thus, a deviation to y_i can result in only three types of outcomes $\underline{x}(m_{-i}), \overline{x}(m_{-i})$, and $y_i \in [\underline{x}(m_{-i}), \overline{x}(m_{-i})]$.

Clearly, the defection cannot pay if $\theta_i \in [\underline{x}(m_{-i}), \overline{x}(m_{-i})]$ because the agent obtains her ideal point by reporting $m_i = \theta_i$. So suppose that $\theta_i < \underline{x}(m_{-i})$. Now agent i's best feasible outcome is $\underline{x}(m_{-i})$. This outcome can be obtained by any message less than $\underline{x}(m_{-i})$, including θ_i. Similarly, if $\theta_i > \overline{x}(m_{-i})$, announcing $m_i = \theta_i$ weakly maximizes her utility. Regardless of the responses of the other players, agent i's best strategy is to announce $m_i = y_i$.

Moulin focuses on mechanisms in which respondents are asked to announce a number (interpreted as their ideal point). He requires that the mechanism satisfy two criteria: anonymity, and efficiency. The first condition, anonymity, requires, simply, that the mechanism treat individuals identically.

DEFINITION 11.2 *A mechanism* $g : \mathbb{R}^n \to X$ *is anonymous if for any permutation* $\pi : N \to N$, $g(m_1, \ldots, m_i, \ldots, m_n) = g(m_{\pi(1)}, \ldots, m_{\pi(i)}, \ldots, m_{\pi(n)})$.

The efficiency condition is essentially identical to Arrow's Pareto condition.

DEFINITION 11.3 *A mechanism* $g : \mathbb{R}^n \to X$ *is efficient if for every profile of types* $y = (y_1, \ldots, y_n)$ $g(y)$ *is Pareto efficient (i.e., there is not*

---

[3] Recall that if a set of real numbers has an even number of distinct elements, it has two medians.

some other policy $z \neq g(y)$ such that every agent weakly prefers z to $g(y)$ and some agent strictly prefers z to $g(y)$.

Moulin proves the following result:

THEOREM 11.2 *If preferences are single peaked then every efficient and anonymous strategy-proof mechanism has the following form: Take the announcements $m_1, m_2, \ldots, m_n$ and add k fixed numbers $a_1, \ldots, a_k$, and select the median of this longer list.*

Because the argument for why such a mechanism is strategy-proof has already been sketched out, the proof of Moulin's result is left as an exercise. Meirowitz (2004a) considers the incentives for information revelation in polls when candidates use the polls to inform policy selection decisions. He finds that it is typically the case that respondents have an incentive to be dishonest. An exercise asks the reader to develop some of this logic.

4. Auction Theory

Because of the role of auctions in allocating everything from broadcast spectra to bric-a-brac on e-Bay, economists have developed a large body of theory on how to structure auctions optimally to generate maximal revenue and achieve allocative efficiency. Although political scientists are generally not concerned with these applications, there are a couple of reasons to consider some of the basics of auction theory. First, several important aspects of politics can be modeled as particular types of auctions. Second, auction theory demonstrates how mechanism design can be used to study the choice of institutions.

It is not, however, the case that auction theory has been ignored in political science. A classic application of auction theory are models of favor buying where competing interest groups offer bribes to secure public contracts or policy concessions from politicians. Recently one of us has argued for modeling electoral competition as a form of an auction (Meirowitz 2004b).

The standard auction problem involves a seller (agent 0) and a population of potential bidders, $N = \{1, \ldots, n\}$. Each bidder places a valuation of $\theta_i \in \mathbb{R}^1_+$ on the item up for auction. These valuations are the private information of each buyer. The common prior belief is that bidder valuations are independent and identical draws from a twice-differentiable distribution function $F(\cdot)$. In an auction model the utility of a bidder i with valuation θ_i who wins the item by paying b_i is $\theta_i - b_i$. The payoff of a losing bidder who pays b_i is $-b_i$. If a losing bidder is not required to pay, the payoff is 0. We begin with a few commonly studied auction mechanisms.

4.1. Second-Price and Ascending-Price Auctions. Consider two auction designs. In a second-price auction, each participant submits a sealed bid b_i and the one who makes the highest bid wins the object. The winner only pays the amount equal to the second-highest bid, and all other bidders pay nothing. In an ascending-price auction, all participants begin with their placards up, and the auctioneer announces an ascending sequence of prices, \$10, \$11, \$12,.... When a price is announced, causing the second to last placard to fall, the item is sold to the remaining bidder with an upright placard at the announced price.

Both of these auctions are commonly used and the experience of bidding under these schemes may seem to vary greatly. Nonetheless, from a game theoretic perspective the mechanisms are identical. Note that the auctions induce different games (one is a Bayesian game with simultaneous moves and the other is a Bayesian game with sequential moves). Nonetheless, the incentives are identical. To see this we use the logic of the revelation principle. Imagine that each bidder enters his valuation θ_i into a computer that does two things: (1) It submits the valuations into a second-price auction (i.e., it uses strategy $b_i = \theta_i$). (2) It has a robot play the following strategy in an ascending-price auction: hold the placard up until the announced price exceeds the valuation, θ_i. In both cases the bidder with the highest valuation wins the item and pays the amount of the second-highest valuation.

In the second-price auction bidding $b_i = \theta_i$ is a dominant strategy. Consider any other bid $b_i \neq \theta_i$. Let $b_{-i}^{\max} = \max_{j \neq i} b_j$ denote the highest bid submitted by all the other agents. There are three possibilities, either $b_{-i}^{\max} = \theta_i$, $b_{-i}^{\max} < \theta_i$, or $b_{-i}^{\max} > \theta_i$. In the first case $b_i = \theta_i$ results in a tie with an expected utility equal to 0. The strategy $b_i > \theta_i$ results in victory at the price $b_{-i}^{\max} = \theta_i$ – also resulting in a utility of 0. Finally under the strategy $b_i < \theta_i$ agent i loses the item's and receives utility of 0. In the second case, $b_i = \theta_i$ results in agent i winning and paying $b_{-i}^{\max}$. Thus, her payoff is $\theta_i - b_{-i}^{\max} > 0$. Under $b_i > \theta_i$, agent i wins and pays $b_{-i}^{\max}$. Again her payoff is $\theta_i - b_{-i}^{\max}$. Under the strategy of $b_i < \theta_i$ agent i loses and receives a payoff of 0. In the last case, under the strategy of $b_i = \theta_i$ agent i does not win and receives payoff of 0. Under the strategy $b_i > \theta_i$ agent i wins and pays $b_{-i}^{\max}$ for an item that she only values at $\theta_i < b_{-i}^{\max}$ or she loses and gets a payoff of 0. Thus the strategy of $b_i = \theta_i$ does at least as well as any other strategy and prevents two types of regret: not winning an item at a price one is willing to pay and winning an item at a price that one does not want to pay.

Similarly, lowering the placard once the price exceeds θ_i is a dominant strategy in the ascending-price auction. Is there a reason to lower the placard before the price reaches θ_i? Doing so ensures that the agent loses the item, resulting in a payoff of 0. Early resignation cannot improve upon the conjectured strategy. Moreover, if it is the case that all other agents lower their placards at a price $p' < \theta_i$ then the conjectured strategy results in victory at a price of p' and utility $\theta_i - p'$. Now consider the potential consequences of deviating to a strategy of keeping the placard up after the price exceeds θ_i. In this case either the agent loses and receives a utility 0 or she is the winner, paying a price in excess of her valuation.

4.2. First-Price and Descending-Price Auctions*. In a first-price auction, agents simultaneously submit bids. The highest bidder wins the object and pays her bid. In a descending-price auction each bidder has a placard. The auctioneer begins with a high price and lowers it as the auction progresses, \$100, \$99, \$98, ... The bidder who raises her placard first wins the item and pays the most recent price. As in the case of second-price and ascending-price auctions, the simultaneous move and extensive form versions of the game are similar. We focus only on the analysis of the first-price auction, leaving as an exercise the construction of a PBE to the descending-price auction. Following Krishna (2002), we present an informal derivation of the equilibrium strategies. We begin with a conjecture about equilibrium strategies and verify that the conjecture is consistent with a Bayesian Nash equilibrium.

Suppose that bidders $j \neq i$ have strategies represented by the differentiable and strictly increasing function $b(\cdot) : \mathbb{R}_+^1 \to \mathbb{R}_+^1$. A bidder's expected utility is 0 if she pays her valuation or loses. Let the random variable $b_{-i}^{\max}$ be the highest bid from the bidders $N \backslash \{i\}$ when they use the conjectured strategy. Because the payoff from losing the item is 0, the expected utility to a bidder with type θ_i from using strategy

$b_i = b(\theta_i)$ is

$$\Pr(b^{\max}_{-i} < b_i)\,[\theta_i - b_i]\,.$$

If the other bidders use $b(\cdot)$, the term $\Pr(b^{\max}_{-i} < b_i)$ is the probability that $n-1$ draws of θ_j from $F(\cdot)$ all have values lower than $b^{-1}(b_i)$. Because the types are independent draws, the expression for this probability is $F(b^{-1}(b_i))^{n-1}$. Accordingly, the expected utility is

$$F(b^{-1}(b_i))^{n-1}\,[\theta_i - b_i]\,.$$

An optimal b_i solves the first-order necessary condition

$$(n-1)F(b^{-1}(b_i))^{n-2}f(b^{-1}(b_i))\frac{db^{-1}(b_i)}{db_i}\,[\theta_i - b_i] - F(b^{-1}(b_i))^{n-1} = 0.$$

In the conjectured equilibrium $b(\theta_i) = b_i$ so that

$$(n-1)F(\theta)^{n-2}f(\theta)\theta = \frac{db(\theta)}{d\theta}F(\theta)^{n-1} + (n-1)F(\theta)^{n-2}f(\theta)b(\theta).$$

The right-hand side is $\frac{d}{d\theta}\left(F(\theta)^{n-1}b(\theta)\right)$. This allows us to reexpress the first-order condition as

$$\frac{d}{d\theta}\left(F(\theta)^{n-1}b(\theta)\right) = (n-1)F(\theta)^{n-2}f(\theta)\theta.$$

The first theorem of calculus ($\int \frac{df}{dx}dx = f(x)$) allows us to reexpress this equation as

$$b(\theta) = \frac{\int_0^\theta \theta'(n-1)F(\theta')^{n-2}f(\theta')d\theta'}{F(\theta)^{n-1}}. \tag{11.1}$$

The right-hand side of equation 11.1 is the conditional expectation of $b^{\max}_{-i}$ given that $b^{\max}_{-i} < \theta$. Verifying that $b(\cdot)$ is in fact an equilibrium bid function amounts to determining whether the local extrema characterized by equation 11.1 is a global maximum. We leave this as an exercise.

4.3. The Revenue Equivalence Principle*. First-price and second-price auctions result in different bidding strategies. Given this, a natural question is which auction the seller prefers. This question is answered by the fundamental result in auction theory, the *revenue equivalence principle* (Riley and Samuelson 1981; Myerson 1981). This principle guarantees that when the types are independent the expected revenue of an auction depends only on the probability that a seller wins as a function of her type θ_i and the utility realized by a seller with the lowest possible type. An immediate consequence of this result is that, assuming independent evaluations, all of the preceding auctions yield the same expected revenue to the seller. In this section we develop this logic.

Returning to the notation from the beginning of this chapter, let $M = \Theta$ denote the space of possible messages. Each of the n players has a valuation independently drawn from the differentiable distribution $F(\cdot)$ on Θ with density $f(\cdot)$. For convenience Θ is an interval of the form $[0, k]$. The set $\Delta(N)$ contains all lotteries over the bidders N. Let $w(m_1, \ldots, m_n) : M^n \to \Delta(N)$ and $t(m_1, \ldots, m_n) : M^n \to \mathbb{R}_+^n$ denote a mechanism that specifies for each message profile m a lottery over the identity of the winner and a transfer profile. Thus, the first-price auction involves winner

$$w(m) = \begin{cases} \frac{1}{\#\{\arg\max\{m_j\}\}} & \text{if } i \in \arg\max\{m_j\} \\ 0 \text{ otherwise} \end{cases}$$

and transfers

$$t_i(m) = \begin{cases} \frac{m_i}{\#\{\arg\max\{m_j\}\}} & \text{if } i \in \arg\max\{m_j\} \\ 0 \text{ otherwise.} \end{cases}$$

Ignoring ties, these terms simplify to 1 and m_i if $i = \arg\max\{m_j\}$ and 0 and 0 otherwise. An all-pay, first-price auction, which we analyze later, involves $t_i(m) = m_i$.

The revenue equivalence result concerns the expected revenue generated by Bayesian Nash equilibria in the auction. Standard auctions have the "winner takes it with certainty" mapping $g(m)$ defined earlier. Given an increasing bid function $b(\theta_i)$, the expected revenue is $ER = \sum_{i=1}^{n} \int_0^k t_i(b(\theta_i)) dF(\theta_i)$. We can now state the result.

THEOREM 11.3 *Let valuations be independently and identically distributed. In every standard auction, every symmetric and increasing* *equilibrium in which the expected payment of a bidder with value 0 is 0 yields the same value of expected revenue.*

Proof Consider a fixed standard auction where a symmetric and increasing equilibrium is characterized by the function $b(\cdot)$. Let $t^+(\theta_i)$ denote the expected payment of a bidder with value θ_i. Suppose that bidder i's valuation is θ_i' and consider the bid $z = b(\theta_i'')$. When all other bidders use the strategy $b(\cdot)$ the expected utility of bid z to bidder i is

$$\theta_i' F(\theta_i'')^{n-1} - t^+(\theta_i'').$$

Differentiating this expected utility with respect to the type θ_i'' yields the first-order condition

$$(n-1)\theta_i' f(\theta_i'')^{n-2} = \frac{\partial t^+(z)}{\partial z}\Big|_{z=\theta_i''}.$$

Because $b(\cdot)$ is an equilibrium, $z = b(\theta_i'') = b(\theta_i')$ solves this condition, yielding

$$(n-1)\theta_i' f(\theta_i')^{n-2} = \frac{\partial t^+(z)}{\partial z}\Big|_{z=\theta_i'}.$$

But this differential equation yields the solution

$$t^+(\theta_i') = t^+(0) + \int_0^{\theta_i'} (n-1)\theta_i' f(\theta_i')^{n-2} d\theta_i'.$$

Thus, under the assumption that $t^+(0) = 0$, we have

$$t^+(\theta_i') = \int_0^{\theta_i'} (n-1)\theta_i' f(\theta_i')^{n-2} d\theta_i'$$

independently of the details of the auction. Because

$$ER = \sum_{i=1}^n \int_0^k t_i(b(\theta_i)) dF(\theta_i) = n \int t^+(\theta_i') f(\theta_i') d\theta_i',$$

the proof is complete. □

5. Application: Electoral Contests and All-Pay Auctions*

An all-pay auction requires that contestants pay their bids regardless of whether they win. Many contests may take this form. Special interests pay bribes, and the group that makes the largest payment receives its preferred policy. Candidates compete for office and the one who spends the most money wins. We develop this second application in some detail and use the revenue equivalence principle to reach some conclusions about the efficiency of imperfect voting. A special case of this model was analyzed directly in Chapter 6.

Consider a pool of candidates, $C = \{1, 2, \dots, c\}$. Each candidate has a nonnegative, real-valued type $\theta_p \in \mathbb{R}^1_+$ that corresponds to his overall efficiency at governing. The social goal is to select one of the most efficient candidates $p^* \in \arg\max_{p \in C} \theta_p$. The quality types $\boldsymbol{\theta} = (\theta_1, \dots, \theta_c)$ are private information – only candidate p knows θ_p. For simplicity, the types are independent and identical draws from the distribution $F(\cdot)$ with density function $f(\cdot)$. Let $M_c = \max\{\theta_j\}_{j \neq 1}$ denote the maximal type from $c - 1$ draws of θ. Given θ_p the probability that $M_c \leq \theta_p$ is $F_c(\theta_p) \equiv F(\theta_p)^{c-1}$. Differentiating yields the density of M_c, $f_c(\theta_p) = (c - 1)F(\theta_p)^{c-2} f(\theta_p)$.

Our baseline model involves two periods. In the first period each candidate simultaneously selects a level of campaign effort a_p. In the second period the candidate with the highest level of effort wins office. The key assumption is that a candidate's cost of campaign effort is decreasing in her governing efficiency. That is, if candidate 1 has a lower cost of campaign effort than candidate 2, candidate 1 is likely to be a more effective leader than is candidate 2. This assumption can be justified on the grounds that competence translates into good management in office and good management on the campaign trail. For simplicity, we consider the case where campaigning costs are inversely proportional to efficiency. Candidate payoffs are then

$$
Eu(a_p, \theta_p) = \begin{cases} 1 - \frac{a_p}{\theta_p} & \text{if } a_p > \max_{j \neq p}\{a_j\} \\ -\frac{a_p}{\theta_p} & \text{if } a_p < \max_{j \neq p}\{a_j\} \\ \frac{1}{\#\{j : a_j = a_p\}} - \frac{a_p}{\theta_p} & \text{if } a_p = \max_{j \neq p}\{a_j\} \end{cases} ,
$$

where the last line of the expression follows from assuming that ties are broken through randomization. Multiplying each candidate's utility function by θ_p translates this payoff function into that of a standard all-pay auction where the prize has value θ_p and bids have unitary cost. We now characterize a symmetric, pure strategy equilibrium in which each candidate's effort level $\alpha(\theta_i)$ is a strictly increasing and differentiable function of her efficiency type θ_i. So candidate p with type θ_p who selects effort a_p generates an expected utility of

$$\pi(a_p, \theta_p) = F(\alpha^{-1}(a_p))^{c-1} - \frac{a_p}{\theta_p}.$$

In order for a_p to be optimal it must solve the first-order condition

$$(c-1)F(\alpha^{-1}(a_p))^{c-2} f(\alpha^{-1}(a_p))\frac{d\alpha^{-1}}{da_p} = \frac{1}{\theta_p}.$$

In a symmetric equilibrium, $\alpha(\theta_p) = a_p$, so that $\alpha^{-1}(a_p) = \theta_p$. Thus the first-order condition reduces to

$$\frac{d\alpha^{-1}}{da_p} = \frac{1}{\theta_p(c-1)F(\theta_p)^{c-2} f(\theta_p)}$$

or

$$\frac{d\alpha}{d\theta} = \theta_p(c-1)F(\theta_p)^{c-2} f(\theta_p).$$

Integration yields the required solution,

$$\alpha(\theta) = \int_0^\theta x(c-1)F(x)^{c-2} f(x)dx$$

$$= \int_0^\theta x f_c(x)dx.$$

This function is strictly increasing in θ so it remains only to verify that this solution satisfies the sufficient second-order condition. This result follows from Theorem 2 of Krishna and Morgan (1997), so we do not reproduce the proof.

PROPOSITION 11.1 *A symmetric equilibrium in which effort $\alpha(\theta_i)$ is strictly increasing in efficiency exists. In this equilibrium the best candidate $p^* = \arg\max_{p\in\mathcal{C}}(\theta_p)$ is chosen with probability 1.*

A few comments are in order. First, because $\int_0^\theta x f_c(x)dx < \theta$, $\alpha(\theta_i) < \theta_i$ so that the winning candidate achieves a strictly positive payoff. Second, the derivative of the effort functions with respect to c is

$$\frac{\partial \alpha(\theta)}{\partial c} = \int_0^\theta x(c-1)\ln(F(x))F(x)^{c-2}f(x)dx.$$

This derivative is negative because $F(x) \le 1$. Thus for $c < c'$, $\alpha_c(\theta) > \alpha_{c+1}(\theta)$ where $\alpha_n(\theta)$ denotes the equilibrium effort function when $c = n$. Consequently, the effort that each candidate puts into winning decreases as the number of candidates increases. Third, because the model is equivalent to a first-price all-pay auction with independent values and $\alpha(0) = 0$, the revenue equivalence principle implies that the expected total effort, $A_c = c \int_0^\infty \alpha(x)f(x)dx$, must be the same as the expected payment of the winner in a second-price auction in which player values are drawn from $F(\cdot)$. This value is simply the expected value of the second highest of c draws from $F(\cdot)$, which is

$$Total\ effort = \int_0^\infty xc(c-1)(1 - F(x))F(x)^{c-2}f(x)dx.$$

This term is increasing in c. Thus, the total effort is increasing in the number of candidates.

It is reasonable to think that the social objective of elections is the maximization of $\theta_{p_c^*}$. If the actual effort of campaigning is wasteful, however, there is a trade-off between increasing the expected value of the winning candidate's quality, $\mathbb{E}\theta_{p_c^*}$, and decreasing the expected campaign costs $\mathbb{E}\sum_{p=1}^c \alpha(\theta_p)/\theta_p$. Letting $v(\cdot)$ and $u(\cdot)$ denote twice-differentiable increasing functions with $v'' < 0$ and $u'' > 0$, we consider a social welfare function of the form

$$V_c = \mathbb{E}v(\theta_{p_c^*}) - \mathbb{E}u\left(\sum_{p=1}^c \frac{\alpha(\theta_p)}{\theta_p}\right).$$

Although the all-pay auction aspect of campaigns does an excellent job selecting the best-quality candidate, the costs $\sum_{p=1}^c \alpha(\theta_p)/\theta_p$ may be considered undesirable. This perspective motivates a natural question. How does one select good candidates while preventing excessive wasteful campaigning? One answer to this question involves imperfect voting – something that seems to happen occasionally in Florida if not elsewhere.

The baseline model assumes that elections are perfect screening devices selecting the candidate with the highest level of a. In reality voting is imperfect. In this section we consider elections with probabilistic outcomes – the candidate with the highest level a wins with probability $q + (1 - q)/c$ and the remaining candidates win with probability $(1 - q)/c$. In this setting the candidate payoffs are

$$Eu(a_p, \theta_p) = \begin{cases} q + \frac{1-q}{c} - \frac{a_p}{\theta_p} & \text{if } a_p > \max_{j \neq p}\{a_j\} \\ \frac{1-q}{c} - \frac{a_p}{\theta_p} & \text{if } a_p < \max_{j \neq p}\{a_j\} \\ \frac{q}{\#\{j:a_j=a_p\}} + \frac{1-q}{c} - \frac{a_p}{\theta_p} & \text{if } a_p = \max_{j \neq p}\{a_j\} \end{cases}.$$

Given this utility function, the derivation of equilibrium strategies is similar to the baseline model (the baseline model sets $q = 1$). If each player uses a strictly increasing and differentiable strategy $\alpha(\theta_i)$, candidate p with type θ_p selecting accumulation a_p has an expected utility of

$$\pi(a_p, \theta_p, q) = q F(\alpha^{-1}(a_p))^{c-1} - \frac{a_p}{\theta_p} + \frac{1-q}{c}.$$

For a_p to be optimal, it must solve the first-order condition

$$q(c - 1) F(\alpha^{-1}(a_p))^{c-2} f(\alpha^{-1}(a_p)) \frac{d\alpha^{-1}}{da_p} = \frac{1}{\theta_p}. \qquad (11.2)$$

For all q, a symmetric equilibrium mapping requires $\alpha(\theta_p; q) = a_p$ so that $\alpha^{-1}(a_p; q) = \theta_p$. Thus equation 11.2 reduces to

$$\frac{d\alpha^{-1}}{da_p} = \frac{1}{\theta_p q(c - 1) F(\theta_p)^{c-2} f(\theta_p)}$$

so that

$$\frac{d\alpha}{d\theta} = \theta_p q(c - 1) F(\theta_p)^{c-2} f(\theta_p).$$

Integration yields the required solution,

$$\alpha(\theta;q) = \int_0^\theta xq(c-1)F(x)^{c-2}f(x)dx$$

$$= q\int_0^\theta xf_c(x)dx$$

$$= q\alpha(\theta;1). \tag{11.3}$$

Accordingly, when the election is imperfect, each candidate reduces her effort proportionally to the imperfection parameter q.

For the remainder of this section we focus on two candidate contests and consider the optimal level $q \in [0, 1]$. In this case the strategies are

$$\alpha(\theta;q) = q\int_0^\theta xf(x)dx.$$

The social welfare associated with q is

$$V(q) = q\int_0^\infty v(x)2F(x)f(x)dx + (1-q)\int_0^\infty v(x)2(1-F(x))f(x)dx$$

$$-\int_0^\infty u\left(\frac{2q}{\theta}\int_0^\theta xf(x)dx\right)df(\theta).$$

The optimal value q satisfies the first-order condition

$$\int_0^\infty v(x)F(x)f(x)dx - \int_0^\infty v(x)(1-F(x))f(x)dx$$

$$= \int_0^\infty \left(\left[\frac{1}{\theta}\int_0^\theta xf(x)dx\right]u'\left(\frac{2q}{\theta}\int_0^\theta xf(x)dx\right)\right)f(\theta)d\theta.$$

The optimal value q^* is less than 1 if

$$\int_0^\infty v(x)F(x)f(x)dx - \int_0^\infty v(x)(1-F(x))f(x)dx$$

$$< \int_0^\infty \left(\left[\frac{1}{\theta}\int_0^\theta xf(x)dx\right]u'\left(\frac{2}{\theta}\int_0^\theta xf(x)dx\right)\right)f(\theta)d\theta$$

and greater than 0 if

$$\int_0^\infty v(x)F(x)f(x)dx - \int_0^\infty v(x)(1 - F(x))f(x)dx$$

$$> \int_0^\infty \left(\left[\frac{2}{\theta} \int_0^\theta xf(x)dx \right] u'(0) \right) f(\theta)d\theta.$$

Accordingly, if $v(\cdot)$ is relatively flat and $u(\cdot)$ is relatively steep then imperfect elections are efficiency enhancing. If v and u are linear, the first-order condition does not depend on q and the optimal q is either 1 or 0 – it is either efficient to maximize the probability that the best candidate serves or to minimize the campaigning costs.

6. Incentive Compatibility and Individual Rationality

In our Saeco purchasing and polling examples, we considered mechanisms for which truthfully reporting one's type was a best response. Although the revelation principle proves that focusing on direct mechanisms does not limit the choice functions under consideration, it is silent about what types of choice functions are implementable. In other words, it fails to answer the question, Which types of mechanisms induce agents to be truthful? Incentive compatibility is the requirement that given the mechanism and the belief that all other agents are being truthful, agent i prefers being truthful to lying.

Consider a model with agents N, choice space X, type space Θ, prior joint density function over types $f(\theta)$, and state-contingent utility functions $u_i(x, \theta)$ for each $i \in N$. A direct mechanism is a mapping $p(\theta) : \Theta \to X$. For there to be a Bayesian Nash equilibrium with truthful strategies to the game induced by the mechanism the following *incentive compatibility* condition must hold:

DEFINITION 11.4 *(Incentive Compatibility) For every $i \in N$ and every distinct θ_i and θ_i' in Θ_i*

$$\int_{\Theta_{-i}} u_i(p(\theta_i, \theta_{-i}), \theta_i)f_{-i}(\theta_{-i})d\theta_{-i} \geq \int_{\Theta_{-i}} u_i(p(\theta_i', \theta_{-i}), \theta_i)f_{-i}(\theta_{-i})d\theta_{-i}.$$

$$\text{(IC)}$$

The incentive compatibility (or IC) condition requires that truthful messages are a best response if other agents are using truthful messages. The easiest way to ensure that the IC condition is satisfied is to select a mechanism for which $\int_{\Theta_{-i}} u_i(p(m_i, \theta_{-i}), \theta_i) f_{-i}(\theta_{-i}) d\theta_{-i}$ is constant in m_i. Consider the following example. Let ω be a random state variable that affects the players' payoffs from various policies. Assume that $n \geq 3$ agents observe ω so that $\theta_i = \omega$ with probability 1. The mechanism designer can implement a choice function $x(\omega)$ that maps a profile of messages into policies x by using the following simple type of mechanism:

$$p(\theta) = \begin{cases} x(\omega') \text{ if } \#\{j \in N : \theta_j = \omega'\} \geq n - 1 \\ x(w^*) \text{ otherwise} \end{cases}$$

where $\#\{j \in N : \theta_j = \omega'\}$ denotes the number of individuals announcing $\theta_j = \omega'$ and w^* is an arbitrary value of ω. Because a single defection does not alter the policy choice, this mechanism satisfies incentive compatibility.

The mechanism in the preceding example, however, does not provide a strong incentive to be truthful. In the auction theory incentive compatibility is satisfied by a second-price auction because the expected utility (ignoring ties) is

$$u_i(p(m_i, \theta_{-i}), \theta_i) = \begin{cases} \theta_i - \max_j \theta_j \text{ if } m_i > \max_j \theta_j \\ 0 \text{ otherwise} \end{cases}.$$

This function is constant in m_i if $m_i > \max_j \theta_j$ and constant in m_i for $m_i < \max_j \theta_j$. The variable component of the function jumps from 0 to $\theta_i - \max_j \theta_j$, which is positive only if $m_i > \max_j \theta_j$. In contrast the first-price auction is not incentive compatible. In other words, truthful bidding is not a Bayesian Nash equilibrium to the first-price auction.

To generate some intuition for incentive compatibility conditions we return to the coffee machine problem. Consider an arbitrary transfer schedule $t_i(m_i, m_{-i})$ that maps a message profile into the amount that member i is charged. Let $p(m)$ be a policy function that maps the message profile into the probability that the coffee maker is purchased.

Given this transfer schedule, the expected utility to department member i from announcement m_i is

$$Eu(m_i, \theta_i) \equiv \int [\theta_i \, p(m_i, \theta_{-i}) - t_i(m_i, \theta_{-i})] \, f_{-i}(\theta_{-i}) d\theta_{-i}.$$

Incentive compatibility requires that $m_i = \theta_i$ maximize $Eu(m_i, \theta_i)$. If we assume that p and t are differentiable functions, then it is easy to analyze a *local incentive compatibility condition* based on the first-order condition

$$\frac{\partial Eu(m_i, \theta_i)}{\partial m_i} \Big|_{m_i = \theta_i} = 0.$$

Interchanging the order of integration and differentiation leads to

$$\theta_i \int \frac{\partial p(m_i, \theta_{-i})}{\partial m_i} f_{-i}(\theta_{-i}) d\theta_{-i} \Big|_{m_i = \theta_i}$$

$$= \int \frac{\partial t(m_i, \theta_{-i})}{\partial m_i} f_{-i}(\theta_{-i}) d\theta_{-i} \Big|_{m_i = \theta_i}.$$

Intuitively, this condition requires that in an incentive compatible mechanism the expected decrease in transfers associated with a slight underreporting of θ_i is exactly offset by the reduction in the expected likelihood of coffee maker purchase times the valuation θ_i.

Although incentive compatibility requires a willingness of players to reveal their private information, to implement a choice function participants must also be willing to play the game. Analysis of these constraints is somewhat simpler and ad hoc. The key intuition is that a player rationally participates only if her expected payoff from equilibrium play is at least as high as her expected payoff from nonparticipation. In some settings, these constraints are trivial: agents have no choice but to participate. In other settings it is necessary to be explicit about the value to players of not participating. Formally, we have the following additional constraint.

DEFINITION 11.5 *(Individual Rationality constraint) Let the value of not participating in the mechanism be given by $v_i(\theta, \theta_{-i})$ and the value to being truthful in a direct mechanism be $u_i(\theta_i, \theta_{-i})$. For each $i \in N$ and* *each* $\theta_i \in \Theta$

$$\int u_i(\theta_i, \theta_{-i})dF(\theta_{-i}) \geq \int v_i(\theta_i, \theta_{-i})dF(\theta_{-i}). \qquad \text{(IR)}$$

A weaker notion of the *individual rationality* (or IR) constraint is that players prefer to play the game ex ante (i.e., before they learn their type). Such a constraint is called an ex ante IR constraint whereas the condition defined previously is an *ex interim* IR constraint.[4]

7. Constrained Mechanism Design

Classical mechanism design allows the planner to commit to one of a large number of mechanisms. Incentive compatibility and individual rationality are the only constraints. In many political settings, however, principals often lack the ability to commit to a mechanism or to use certain incentives such as direct monetary transfers. We devote the remainder of this chapter to examples illustrating how political scientists use constrained mechanism design to address problems of institutional design.

Models in political science generally fall within the principal-agent paradigm: there are a set of principals or bosses and a set of agents or subordinates. Principals like "good" agents and want them to do a "good job." Monitoring problems, however, preclude principals from directly observing whether the agents are good or doing a good job. Conversely, agents want to convince the principal that they are "good" and doing a "good job." Agents, however, typically prefer shirking to performing well. In most political science models, the principal has a limited number of instruments available for influencing the agents' behavior. In the language of mechanism design, the principal is the planner and doing a "good job" or revealing whether one is a "good" type corresponds to selecting appropriate messages in a direct mechanism. The limited number of instruments corresponds to constraints on the mechanisms that can be enacted. Before turning to more interesting applications, we demonstrate these concepts in a simple delegation problem.

---

[4] We apologize for the potential confusion between this concept and the usage of individual rationality in the discussion of repeated games. The literature has used the phrase in both of these related, but distinct ways.

Suppose there are a principal and two agents. Agents have one of two possible types $\theta_i \in \{good, bad\}$. Each agent is a good type with probability π. If an agent is chosen to perform a task she can devote one of two levels of effort $a_i \in \{high, low\}$. Effort level $a_i = high$ imposes a cost c on the agent while $a_i = low$ is costless. The principal must select one of the two agents to perform a task and the chosen agent must decide which effort level to choose. The fundamental question of *principal-agent models* (or agency models) can then be phrased as follows: How can the principal design institutions to select a *good* type agent and induce the chosen agent to select *high*? The former aspect, designing institutions to select *good* types, is called solving *adverse selection*. The latter aspect, designing institutions to create incentives for *high* effort, is called solving *moral hazard*.

If the principal can observe a label on the agent's shirt that indicates his type, and if the choice of effort is readily observable, then there is no monitoring or observability problem. In this case, matters are easy for the principal. She simply hires only good types and fires them if they give low effort. More interesting situations involve private information about agent types and imperfectly observed effort.

7.1. Electoral Accountability. Ferejohn (1986) models accountability in repeated elections as a principal agent problem. We work through a simplified version of Ferejohn's model. Ferejohn focuses only on the moral hazard problem, so for now we ignore the possibility of different types. There are two identical parties that can serve in office. Suppose that the party in government selects an effort level, but the voters observe only a noisy policy outcome $x \in \{high, low\}$ that has the following form. If $a = high$ then x is *high* with probability $q > 1/2$ and *low* with probability $1 - q$; if $a = low$ then x is low with probability q and high with probability $1 - q$. Finally, suppose the governing party receives a rent r each period it is in office and discounts the future at rate δ. The opposition party gets a payoff of 0 each period it is out of office.

The voter chooses a reelection rule specifying the values of x that result in the reelection of the incumbent. Can the voter select a rule that creates incentives for the government always to select $a = high$? A simple rule is to retain the incumbent party if $x = high$ and replace it otherwise. If the voter uses this rule in each period, the governing party faces a simple decision problem. Selection of $a = high$ in the current period results in the expected utility

$$r - c + q\delta V_I + (1 - q)\delta V_O \tag{11.4}$$

where V_I is the value of the game starting next period if the party is in office at the beginning of next period, and V_O is the value of the game starting next period if the party is out of office at the beginning of next period.[5] If the government selects $a = low$ then her expected utility is

$$r + (1 - q)\delta V_I + q\delta V_O. \tag{11.5}$$

If the voter's rule works, so that the incumbent finds it optimal to select $a = high$ in every period, the values of the game are

$$V_I = r - c + q\delta V_I + (1 - q)\delta V_O$$

and

$$V_O = (1 - q)\delta V_I + q\delta V_O.$$

Solving these four equations results in

$$V_I = \frac{r - c + cq\delta - qr\delta}{2q\delta^2 - \delta^2 - 2q\delta + 1} \tag{11.6}$$

and

$$V_O = \frac{r\delta - c\delta + cq\delta - qr\delta}{2q\delta^2 - \delta^2 - 2q\delta + 1}. \tag{11.7}$$

Incentive compatibility for all governments to select $a = high$ requires that equation 11.4 is no less than equation 11.5. This incentive constraint is

$$V_I - V_o \geq \frac{c}{(2q - 1)\delta}.$$

[5] See Chapter 3 for a discussion of Bellman equations and value functions.

Substituting equations 11.6 and 11.7 leads to the requirement that

$$r - c - r\delta + c\delta \geq \frac{c(2q\delta^2 - \delta^2 - 2q\delta + 1)}{(2q - 1)\delta}. \tag{11.8}$$

Equation 11.8 is necessary for the voting rule to induce $a_i = high$ in every period. If the exogenous parameters satisfy equation 11.8, the moral hazard problem is solved by a rule that retains the governing party only if $x = high$. Because the voter prefers $x = high$ to $x = low$, she has no problem committing to this rule: the rule represents an equilibrium strategy given the government decision rule. This is true because all governments select $a_i = high$ and all governments have the same type (i.e., there is no adverse selection problem). Accordingly, if the preceding condition is satisfied, we have characterized a Nash equilibrium to the game between the two parties and the voter: parties in office select $a_i = high$, and voters reelect only if $x = high$.

Now consider an adverse selection version of the problem. Suppose the government does not select an effort level but has private information about its type. For simplicity now each party has a type that is *high* with probability $\pi > 1/2$ and *low* with probability $1 - \pi$. These draws are independent across parties. In each period the voter only observes x that takes the value *high* with probability $z > 1/2$ if the government is a high type and the value of *low* with probability $1 - z$ if the government is a high type. If the government is a low type, $x = high$ with probability $1 - z$ and *low* with probability z. Once again the voter may choose the simple rule: retain if $x = high$ and replace otherwise. This rule, however, may throw out high-quality governments that are temporarily unlucky. A better rule uses information from previous periods. For any finite number of periods k_i that party i was in office let h_i denote the number of these periods for which x was *high*. It follows that in $k_i - h_i$ of those periods $x = low$. The posterior probability that party i is of type *high* after h_i realizations of *high* from k_i trials is given by Bayes' rule:

$$\Pr(\theta_i = high \mid k_i, h_i) = \frac{\pi z^{h_i}(1 - z)^{k_i - h_i}}{\pi z^{h_i}(1 - z)^{k_i - h_i} + (1 - \pi)(1 - z)^{h_i} z^{k_i - h_i}}.$$

An optimal rule is to retain the original incumbent until $\Pr(\theta_i = high \mid k_i, h_i)$ falls below π, the ex ante expected quality of party j. Going forward, the voter should dump party j as soon as $\Pr(\theta_i = high \mid k_i, h_i) >$

$\Pr(\theta_j = high \mid k_j, h_j)$. This discussion of agency theory is intended only as an introduction. We now discuss several applications of agency theory to the study of delegation.

7.2. A Model of Delegation to Bureaucrats.

7.2. A Model of Delegation to Bureaucrats. One of the key questions in the study of the modern administrative state is the trade-off between political control of an agency and the autonomy that an agency requires to apply its expertise to policy problems. Principal-agent theory has been a natural approach to this question. Originally applied in politics to study when and how the U.S. Congress delegates rule-making authority to regulatory agencies, principal-agent theory has been applied to many other political systems and to many other types of political bodies including political parties and international organizations. In this section, we consider a version of a model that Epstein and O'Halloran (1994) apply to the study of statutory delegation in the United States.

Suppose that a legislature L is considering how much authority to delegate to a bureaucratic agency A. The policy space X is a subset of $\mathbb{R}$. Each of the n legislators has quadratic policy preferences with ideal points $l_1 < \cdots < l_n$. The agency is treated as a unitary actor with quadratic policy preferences and an ideal point a.

The members of L are uninformed about the consequences of various policy choices $p \in X$ whereas A is fully informed. We model this uncertainty as Gilligan and Krehbiel (1989) do in their study of legislative committees; assume that the policy outcome x is a function of the policy choice p and an error term ε. To keep matters as simple as possible, let $x = p - \varepsilon$. Each legislator has a common knowledge prior that ε has mean 0 and is distributed according to a distribution function $F(\varepsilon)$ with density $f(\varepsilon)$. The agency knows ε with certainty. This informational structure captures the idea that bureaucrats are policy experts on whom legislators rely to improve policy formulation.

Rather than solve for the optimal mechanism from the L's perspective, we limit the analysis to a very simple class of mechanisms: L chooses a set of allowable policies $P \subset X$. As is standard in the literature, it is assumed that the legislature selects a P that is unbeatable under majority rule. The sanction against an agency that chooses $p \notin P$ is so large that this type of deviation is never made. Given a set of allowable policies, P, and the state of the world ε, A chooses p to solve the problem

$$\max_p \left\{ -(a - p + \varepsilon)^2 \right\} \text{ subject to } p \in P.$$

Thus, whenever $a + \varepsilon \in P$, the agency gets her ideal outcome by choosing $p = a + \varepsilon$. If $a + \varepsilon \notin P$, A chooses the point in P closest to $a + \varepsilon$.

Given A's best response, we turn to the legislature's choice of P. In principle P can be any subset of X. However, the optimal P is always a closed interval $\left[\underline{p}, \overline{p} \right] \subset X$.

PROPOSITION 11.2 P^* *is a closed interval* $\left[\underline{p}, \overline{p} \right] \subset X$.

We refer the reader to Gailmard (2005) for the details of the proof, but here is some intuition. Suppose that P has a "hole" in it (e.g., $P = \left[\underline{p}, p' \right] \cup [p'', \overline{p}]$ where $p' < p''$). Then whenever $p' < a + \varepsilon < (p' + p'')/2$, A chooses p' and when $(p' + p'')/2 < a + \varepsilon < p''$, she chooses p''. Thus, the policy outcome as a function of ε appears as the solid line of Figure 11.1. It is easy to see the variance in the policy

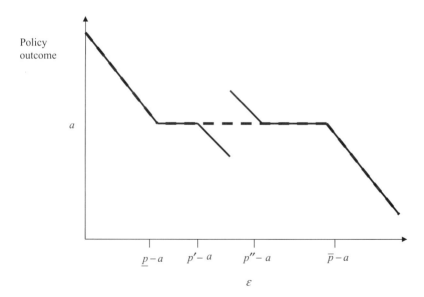

Figure 11.1. Policy Outcomes from the Epstein-O'Halloran Model.

outcome is lowered by moving p' and p'' closer together. Because all legislators are risk averse, they want to reduce the variance so long as the expected policy outcome does not change. The reader can verify that it is always possible to move p' and p'' closer together without changing the mean policy outcome.[6]

Given the proposition, it is clear that the legislature's collective choice problem is to choose $\underline{p}$ and $\overline{p}$. Therefore, the agency's best response function is

$$p^* = \begin{cases} \underline{p} \text{ if } a + \varepsilon < \underline{p} \\ \overline{p} \text{ if } a + \varepsilon > \overline{p} \\ a + \varepsilon \text{ otherwise} \end{cases}.$$

The dotted line of Figure 11.1 gives this best response.

A complication arises in modeling L's collective choice in that it must decide over two dimensions, the lower bound and the upper bound. Fortunately, the majority rule decision is the P^* preferred by the legislator with the median ideal point l_m. To see this, note that given A's best response, l_i prefers the combination of $\underline{p}$ and $\overline{p}$ that maximizes

$$-\int_{\overline{p}-a}^{\infty} (l_i - \overline{p} + \varepsilon)^2 f(\varepsilon) d\varepsilon - \int_{\underline{p}-a}^{\overline{p}-a} (l_i - a)^2 f(\varepsilon) d\varepsilon - \int_{-\infty}^{\underline{p}-a} (l_i - \underline{p} + \varepsilon)^2 f(\varepsilon) d\varepsilon.$$

The first-order conditions are found by differentiating[7] with respect to $\overline{p}$ and $\underline{p}$,

$$2 \int_{\overline{p}-a}^{\infty} (l_i - \overline{p} + \varepsilon) f(\varepsilon) d\varepsilon = 0$$

$$2 \int_{-\infty}^{\underline{p}-a} (l_i - \underline{p} + \varepsilon) f(\varepsilon) d\varepsilon = 0.$$

Whenever $l_i < a$, $\partial/\partial \underline{p} < 0$ for any finite $\underline{p}$. Thus, the optimal choice is $\underline{p}^* = -\infty$. Why? When $l_i < a$ the agency always wants a higher policy

---

[6] Of course, eliminating holes does not prove that the interval must be closed. Closedness is required to make A's best response well defined.

[7] This differentiation involves use of Leibnitz's rule and some simplification.

than legislator i would want if she were informed. Thus, legislator i never finds it in her interest to constrain A from choosing low policies. Similarly, if $l_i > a$, $\partial/\partial \overline{p} > 0$ and $\overline{p}^* = \infty$. Combining these observations, we see that any policy other than the one that is optimal for the legislator with ideal point l_m can be defeated in a majority vote.

PROPOSITION 11.3 *The majority rule outcome for P* is the closed interval* $\left[\underline{p}, \overline{p}\right]$ *preferred by the legislator with ideal point* l_m.

Because the majority rule outcome is the median's ideal statute, the delegation game becomes one between the agency and legislative median. Thus, the allowable policies for the agency are given by the solutions

$$\underline{p}^* = -\infty$$

$$\int_{\overline{p}^*-a}^{\infty} (l_m - \overline{p}^* + \varepsilon) f(\varepsilon) d\varepsilon = 0$$

if $l_m < a$ and

$$\overline{p}^* = -\infty$$

$$\int_{-\infty}^{\underline{p}^*-a} (l_m - \underline{p}^* + \varepsilon) f(\varepsilon) d\varepsilon = 0$$

if $l_m > a$.

Consider the intuition for the expressions for the finite constraint. If $l_m < a$, we can rewrite the expression for $\overline{p}^*$ as

$$l_m = \int_{\overline{p}^*-a}^{\infty} (\overline{p}^* - \varepsilon) \frac{f(\varepsilon)}{1 - F(\overline{p}^* - a)} d\varepsilon.$$

This condition implies that the expected outcome conditional on the constraints on A must equal the median legislator's ideal point. If this expected outcome were greater than l_m, the median could do better in expectation by further constraining A's choice to generate lower policies. Similarly, we can write the condition for $\underline{p}^*$ when

$l_m > a$ as

$$l_m = \int_{-\infty}^{\underline{p}^* - a} (\underline{p}^* - \varepsilon) \frac{f(\varepsilon)}{F(\underline{p}^* - a)} d\varepsilon.$$

To generate some more specific results, assume that ε is distributed uniformly on $[-E, E]$ so that $F(\varepsilon) = (\varepsilon + E)/(2E)$ and $f(\varepsilon) = 1/(2E)$. Then if $l_m < a$, we can solve for $\overline{p}^* = 2l_m - a + E$. We can see that if the agency and the median move closer together, either by raising l_m or by decreasing a, the legislature passes a more permissive statute – one with a greater upper bound. Intuitively, the legislature delegates more authority to an agency that shares its preferences. Also, when there is more policy uncertainty (e.g., E is larger), the agency is granted more authority. Thus, when information asymmetries are greater, the legislature is more dependent on the informed agency to formulate policy.[8]

7.3. Bureaucratic Capacity. One of the important assumptions of the Epstein and O'Halloran (1994) model and other models of delegation is that the agency can implement its policy choice perfectly without error. This may be a reasonable assumption for advanced democracies with cadres of professional, highly trained bureaucrats, but it is far less applicable in developing states or earlier historical eras.

Because of the limitations of the standard models, Huber and McCarty (2004) develop a model in which bureaucracies vary in their capacity to implement policies. In that model, if A attempts to implement policy p, the resulting policy is $\tilde{p} = p - \omega$ where ω is an implementation error with mean 0 and variance σ_ω^2. Bureaucracies with high capacity are better able to implement policies and therefore have lower values of σ_ω^2. Conversely, low-capacity bureaucracies implement policy with imprecision so that σ_ω^2 is high. Let $G(\omega)$ be the distribution function for ω and $g(\omega)$ be the associated density.

Huber and McCarty embed this model of capacity into a delegation model very similar to that of Epstein and O'Halloran. The legislature wants to delegate to the agency because the agency is better informed

---

[8] If $l_m > a$, the solution is $\underline{p}^* = 2l_m - a - E$. The reader can verify that this lower bound is less restrictive if $\overline{l}_m$ and a are close together and if E is large.

about the consequences of various policy choices. As earlier, the agency knows ε but the legislature knows only that it is distributed uniformly on $[-E, E]$. Again members of L and A have quadratic preferences over the policy space, X. We retain the notation from the previous section.

The legislature moves first and creates a statute specifying the set of acceptable policies $P = \left[\underline{p}, \overline{p} \right]$.[9] The agency then attempts to implement policy p that results in policy $\widetilde{p} = p - \omega$ and outcome $x = \widetilde{p} - \varepsilon$. Compliance with the statute requires that $\widetilde{p} \in P$. Thus, even if the agency attempts to comply (i.e., $p \in P$), implementation errors may generate a noncompliant outcome. If $\widetilde{p} \notin P$, the agency incurs a cost δ as a sanction for noncompliance.[10] Unlike in the Epstein and O'Halloran model, in this model the agency may choose to be noncompliant. Alternatively, noncompliance may be a result of implementation errors. Because it is assumed that L cannot observe p, the sanction for noncompliance must be the same regardless of the ultimate cause. Thus, A is sanctioned when $p - \omega > \overline{p}$ or when $p - \omega < \underline{p}$. Given a choice of p, the probability of sanction is $G(p - \overline{p}) + 1 - G(p - \underline{p})$.

To facilitate the exposition, note that a number of features of the Epstein-O'Halloran model generalize to this model. First, it can be shown that the majority rule choice of P maximizes the utility of the legislator with ideal point l_m. We assume throughout this section that $a > l_m$. Second, it can be shown that in the current model $\underline{p}^* = -\infty$ if $a > l_m$.

Given this setup and the assumption that $a > l_m$, A's utility function is [11]

$$-\int_{-\infty}^{\infty} (a - p + \omega + \varepsilon)^2 g(\omega) d\omega - \delta \left[G(p - \overline{p}) \right] =$$

$$-(a - p + \varepsilon)^2 - \sigma_\omega^2 - \delta \left[G(p - \overline{p}) \right].$$

---

[9] A note to the industrious reader who refers to the original publication is in order. In Huber and McCarty, the political principal is a generic politician rather than a legislature. We have adjusted the nomenclature and notation to parallel our discussion of Epstein and O'Halloran.

[10] Actually, Huber and McCarty assume that noncompliance is detected probabilitisically. However, our simplification does not alter the results.

[11] The second line follows from a useful fact about expected utilities of quadratic functions, $\int_{-\infty}^{\infty} (x + \phi)^2 f(\phi) d\phi = (x - E(\phi))^2 + var(\phi)$, where E is the expectations operator and var is the variance operator.

The first-order condition for a maximum is

$$2(a - p + \varepsilon) - \delta g(p - \overline{p}) = 0.$$

The first term in this expression represents the marginal benefit of moving the expected policy closer to the agency's ideal point a. The second term represents the net marginal cost of increasing the intended policy in terms of the probability of sanction. Increasing p increases the probability of $p + \omega > \overline{p}$ by $g(p - \overline{p})$. Clearly, A chooses p to equate the marginal policy benefits with marginal sanction costs. To get an explicit solution for p^*, Huber and McCarty assume that $g(\omega) = (\Omega - |\omega|)/\Omega^2$. This density is "tent shaped" on the interval $[-\Omega, \Omega]$ and satisfies the condition $\sigma_\omega^2 = \Omega^2/6$. Thus, Ω represents a measure of bureaucratic incapacity.

Given these assumptions about the functional form, Figure 11.2 plots the marginal policy benefit curve and the marginal compliance costs for three values of $\overline{p}$ as a function of p. The marginal benefit line is the bold downward-sloping line. The marginal policy benefit is independent of the location of $\overline{p}$ and declines as the bureaucrat's action approaches the bureaucrat's most-preferred action, $a + \varepsilon$. The marginal cost curves depend on the location of $\overline{p}$, and are depicted in Figure 11.2 by the three triangles centered at $\overline{p}_1, \overline{p}_2$, and $\overline{p}_3$. These triangles represent the function $\delta g(p - \overline{p})$. If $\overline{p}$ is too high or too low, the marginal costs are

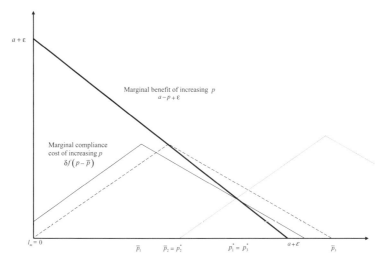

Figure 11.2. Policy Choice in Huber-McCarty Model.

0 at the bureaucrat's ideal intended action, $a + \varepsilon$. Consequently, the bureaucrat chooses its ideal action. For non-extreme statutes, the bureaucrat's best response lies at the intersection of the marginal benefit curve with the relevant marginal cost curve.[12] Statute $\overline{p}_1$, for example, leads to optimal action p_1^*. For any $p > p_1^*$, the marginal policy benefits of increasing the policy action (toward the bureaucrat's most preferred) exceed the marginal compliance costs, and for any $p < p_1^*$, the reduction in compliance costs of moving the action away from the bureaucrat's most-preferred action exceed the policy loses.

From Figure 11.2, the effect of changes in $\overline{p}$ on the bureaucrat's best-response depends on whether the apex of the "compliance cost" triangle is to the left or right of the policy benefit line (i.e., to the left or right of $\overline{p}_2$ in Figure 11.2). For $\overline{p}_1 < \overline{p} < \overline{p}_2$, $p^* > \overline{p}$. In this range, increases in $\overline{p}$ increase the marginal compliance costs of any $p > \overline{p}$, inducing the bureaucrat to move toward the politician's ideal point. At $\overline{p}_2$, however, this effect reverses. For $\overline{p} > \overline{p}_2$, $p^* < \overline{p}$, and increases in $\overline{p}$ decrease the marginal compliance cost of any $p^* < \overline{p}$, inducing the bureaucrat to adjust his action closer to his ideal point. Consequently, the minimal action that the legislature can induce is given by $p^*(\overline{p}_2)$.

Huber and McCarty show that formal solution to the agent's maximization problem is

$$
p^* = \begin{cases}
a + \varepsilon & \text{if } \overline{p} - \varepsilon \leq a - \Omega \\
\frac{\Omega^2(a+\varepsilon)-\delta(\overline{p}+\Omega)}{\Omega^2 - \delta} & \text{if } a - \Omega \leq \overline{p} - \varepsilon \leq a - \frac{\delta}{\Omega} \\
\frac{\Omega^2(a+\varepsilon)-\delta(\overline{p}-\Omega)}{\Omega^2 + \delta} & \text{if } \overline{p} - \varepsilon \leq a + \Omega \leq \overline{p} - \varepsilon \leq a + \Omega \\
a + \varepsilon & \text{if } \overline{p} - \varepsilon \geq a + \Omega
\end{cases}
$$

A few features of A's best response are worth emphasizing. First, for extreme statutes ($\overline{p} \leq a - \Omega + \varepsilon$ or $\overline{p} \geq a + \Omega + \varepsilon$), A's best response is to attempt to implement her ideal point. If the statute is too lax or too constraining, the marginal compliance cost at A's ideal policy is 0. Second, l_m can only induce policies in the interval $[a - (\delta/\Omega) + \varepsilon, a + \varepsilon]$. He cannot induce a lower policy because A complies less often under a more restrictive statute. This minimal policy is

---

[12] McCarty and Huber assume that $\Omega^2 > \delta$, which guarantees that there is a unique intersection of the marginal benefit and cost curves and it represents a global maximum. Given their interest in systems where bureaucratic capacity and the ability to sanction noncompliance are low, this assumption seems reasonable.

increasing in Ω. Thus, l_m's ability to control A decreases when capacity is lower. The intuition is that a low-capacity bureaucracy is noncompliant a large part of the time regardless of the policies it chooses. Moreover the probability of noncompliance is not very responsive to the agency's choices. Therefore, the agency chooses to implement policies closer to its ideal point because there is little penalty for doing so at the margin. The model identifies one important effect of low bureaucratic capacity: bureaucrats are harder to control through statutes.

Given their interest in the bureaucratic politics of low-capacity systems, Huber and McCarty focus on the optimal statute when bureaucratic capacity is sufficiently low.[13] Under these assumptions the optimal statute is

$$\overline{p}^* = a - \frac{\delta}{\Omega} + \frac{\delta E}{\Omega^2}.$$

Like the Epstein-O'Halloran model, the Huber-McCarty model predicts that L delegates more authority when E is larger. Its prediction about preference divergence is the exact opposite, however. In the Huber-McCarty model, the statute is more permissive if a and $l_m = 0$ are further apart. This is because low-capacity bureaucrats are more likely to defect to their ideal point in response to restrictive statutes. This defection is extremely costly to L if a is far from l_m. Thus, L grants more latitude to extreme bureaucrats to provide stronger incentives for statutory compliance. Finally, the Huber-McCarty model generates another prediction at odds with the standard models. These models generally show that if ex post sanctions are high, the principal delegates more authority. In the Huber-McCarty model, high δ is associated with a more restrictive statute. High sanctions induce even low-capacity bureaucrats to comply. Thus, L need not grant more discretion solely to induce compliance.

7.4. Generalized Models of Delegation. Most game theoretic treatments of delegation maintain a number of stylized assumptions. First, principals and agents are assumed to be risk averse. Indeed in most applications, they have quadratic preferences. Second, the policy space and shocks are assumed to be one dimensional. Third, most models assume that policy outcomes are additive functions of policy choices

---

[13] "Sufficiently low capacity" means $\Omega > \min\left\{E, \delta/a, \sqrt{\delta}\right\}$.

and shocks. Although these simplifying assumptions allow us to specify parsimonious models, Bendor and Meirowitz (2004) argue that these modeling choices make it difficult to generalize to other political environments. In particular, the assumptions limit our ability to determine specifically which features are most important in the decision to delegate. For example, is the selection of an agent or are the available monitoring and control mechanisms more important? We sketch the key points of Bendor and Meirowitz's argument.

There are a single principal and n subordinates.[14] All agents have ideal points in $\mathbb{R}^d$ and the principal's ideal point is the 0 vector. Preferences over outcomes are represented by the utility function $u_i(x) = h(-\|x - y_i\|)$ where $h(\cdot)$ is a strictly increasing continuous function, $\|z\|$ is the Euclidean norm, and y_i is i's ideal vector in $\mathbb{R}^d$. Quadratic preferences over a single-dimensional policy are a special case of this assumption. As in Epstein-O'Halloran and Huber-McCarty, Bendor and Meirowitz assume that the principal is less informed than the subordinates, but their model allows for (1) arbitrary functional forms and (2) heterogeneity in the uncertainty associated with different policy selections. Formally, for any policy p, outcome $x(p)$ is a random variable generated by the conditional distribution $F(x \mid p)$. This treatment allows for the possibility that there is more uncertainty about the consequences of some policies than others. The principal knows only the family of conditional distributions and the informed subordinates know the deterministic mappings from p into x. Bendor and Meirowitz also invoke a condition they call *perfect shock absorption*. It implies that an informed agent can implement any policy outcome x by choosing the appropriate p. Epstein and O'Halloran's assumption that $x = p + \varepsilon$ is a special case. Because of the implementation shocks, the shock absorption assumption holds only in expectation in the Huber-McCarty model.

Whereas in the Huber-McCarty model bureaucrats lack the ability to implement their intended policies, Bendor and Meirowitz consider variation in the agent's competence as variation in expertise. With probability q_i agent i learns the random shock and selects p to attain any x. With probability $1 - q_i$, however, subordinate i is uninformed and knows no more than the principal does.

---

[14] Some extensions in Bendor and Meirowitz consider the case of multiple principals, however.

In the basic delegation model, the principal decides whether or not to delegate. If she does not delegate, she selects policy according to her prior beliefs about the policy shock. If she delegates, she chooses an agent and grants that agent complete discretion over the policy choice. The selected agent chooses policy p, and the game ends. We now highlight a few of the key findings. For now assume that all agents have high expertise, $q_i = 1$ for all $i \in N$.

PROPOSITION 11.4 *The principal is willing to delegate to agents whose ideal point falls in a closed ball* $B(\varepsilon, 0)$ *centered at* 0 *with radius* ε. $B(\varepsilon, 0)$ *is known as the delegation set.*

The construction of $B(\varepsilon, 0)$ is straightforward. If agent i controls policy, she selects a policy that generates outcome $x = y_i$. Accordingly, the principal delegates to i only if the outcome y_i is preferred to the lottery generated by the principal's optimal policy choice. As long as the principal is uncertain, her utility of implementing policy herself, u_0', is less than the utility associated with reaching $x = 0$ with probability 1, $h(0)$. Clearly, the principal delegates to an agent with ideal point $y_i = 0$. The set of ideal points sufficiently close to 0 to merit delegation solves the inequality

$$h(- \| y_i \|) \leq u_0'.$$

Given that $h(\cdot)$ is strictly increasing and continuous, for any value of u_0' the set $\{ y : h(- \| y \|) \leq u_0' \}$ is a closed ball.

Because little structure has been placed on $h(\cdot)$, this conclusion shows that the informational rationale for delegation in spatial settings hinges only on the desire to prevent bad outcomes: risk preferences, dimensionality, and the nature of uncertainty are secondary issues. It is easy to see that relaxing the assumption of perfect competence does not have a qualitative effect. As competency decreases the delegation set shrinks – if the principal is going to give authority to someone else who is not likely to know anything more than she does, the agent had better have preferences very close to the principal's.

If several agents have ideal points in the delegation set, the choice of whom to delegate to can be subtle. The traditional literature has often stressed the *ally principle*: if the principal delegates, she selects an agent whose preferences most closely match hers. With homogeneous competence (i.e., q_i the same for all i) and the stylized assumption that

$x = p - \varepsilon$ (a multidimensional version of the assumption in Epstein-O'Halloran), the ally principle holds. The proof is left as an exercise.

With heterogeneity in q_i or a more general policy outcome function, the ally principle may fail. As an example with heterogeneous competence, consider the case of $x = p - \varepsilon$ and two agents with $\|y_1\| < \|y_2\|$. Would the principal ever choose to delegate to agent 2 instead of the more proximate agent 1? Bendor and Meirowitz show that if $q_2 > q_1$ then possibly yes. They conclude only that the principal never selects an agent who is dominated by another agent in the sense that agent i dominates agent j if $\|y_i\| \le \|y_j\|$ and $q_i \ge q_j$ with one of the inequalities strict. A more subtle finding is that once we relax the assumption that $x = p - \varepsilon$ even if $q_1 = q_2$ agent 2 might still be chosen over agent 1. This result may arise because the uncertainty associated with different policies need not be the same. In the general model it is possible that an uninformed agent 1's most preferred policy, p_1, results in more uncertainty than an uninformed agent 2's most preferred policy, p_2. This can be the case if attempting to enact certain types of outcomes (such as ones far from the status quo) is harder and perhaps subject to larger errors than attempting to enact other types of outcomes (such as those close to the status quo). For an example suppose the policy and outcome spaces are $\mathbb{R}^1$ and consider two agents with ideal points $y_1 = -1 + \delta$ and $y_2 = 1$. Thus, agent 1 is closer to the principal. Suppose that $F(x \mid p)$ is as follows: if $p > 0$ then $x = p + .1$ or $x = p - .1$ with equal probability and if $p < 0$ then $x = p + .2$ or $x = p - .2$ with equal probability. In this case, both agents select $p = y_i$ if they do not learn the shock. Consequently, agent 1's uninformed policy choice entails more outcome risk. Accordingly if $h(\cdot)$ is strictly concave and δ is sufficiently small then the principal prefers to delegate to agent 2 although her ideal point is farther from the principal than agent 1's. An example of this argument is left as an exercise.

Another violation of the ally principle may arise from free-riding among agents when information acquisition is costly. Suppose now that the shock can be learned at a cost, c, by any agent or principal. Any player who chooses to incur the cost observes the shock with probability 1. Further suppose that the principal selects an agent and then observes whether she invests the cost c to learn the shock. If the agent does not learn, the principal may retake control and decide whether to invest c to learn the shock and select policy. Alternatively the principal can select policy in ignorance. In this setting, the delegation set is a multidimensional "doughnut." If the principal delegates to an agent with an ideal point very close to her own, the agent has the choice of paying c to get the outcome utility $h(0)$ or not investing, with the knowledge that the principal will then retake control and invest c herself. Thus, learning implies utility $h(0) - c$ while free-riding yields utility $h(-\|y_i\|)$. Thus for agents with ideal points closer than $h^{-1}(h(0) - c)$, free-riding on the principal is preferred. Accordingly the principal will not delegate to agents who are very close to her in the policy space. Of course agents who are very distant select undesirable outcomes and are not in the delegation set.

PROPOSITION 11.5 *If information acquisition has cost c and the principal can retake control if the selected agent does not invest, the delegation set consists of agents in the original delegation set with ideal points farther from 0 than $d = h^{-1}(h(0) - c)$.*

Bendor and Meirowitz also consider the effect of competition among agents in settings where there are many agents and one principal. Suppose that agents are perfectly competent and simultaneously announce outcomes in X. The principal then selects an agent and the agent selects policy (knowing the shock) to enact the outcome she announced. If the outcome space is one dimensional and there are agents on either side of the principal, the game is similar to Downsian competition. In every equilibrium at least two agents promise to enact the principal's ideal outcome. This conclusion holds regardless of the dimensionality of the policy space.

DEFINITION 11.6 *Preferences satisfy diversity either (1) if there does not exist a vector $s \in X$ such that for all $i \in N$ $x_i = \lambda_i s$ for some $\lambda_i \in R^1$ or (2) if such a vector does exist then there must be two agents i and j with $\lambda_i > 0$ and $\lambda_j < 0$.*

Diversity requires either that preferences are not collinear or that there are agents on either side of the principal.

PROPOSITION 11.6 *If preferences satisfy diversity then at least two agents commit to enacting $x = 0$ and the principal selects one of these agents in every equilibrium.*

It is clear that if one agent promises to enact 0 the commitments of the other agents are payoff irrelevant. So any strategy profile in which at least two agents make this commitment is an equilibrium. Now suppose that no agents are making this commitment. When there are at least two agents at least one of the agents can move the final outcome closer to her ideal point by committing to an outcome that is closer to the principal's than the closest commitment of the remaining agents. Thus, there cannot be an equilibrium in which the principal does not get her ideal outcome.

7.5. Application: Electoral Accountability Revisited*. Returning to the issue of electoral accountability, we consider a model closer to Ferejohn's moral hazard model than the binary choice example we analyzed earlier. In each period $t = 1, 2, \ldots$, an officeholder privately observes a shock $\theta_t \in [z, 1 + z]$ for some constant $z \in (0, 1)$. She then selects a level of effort $a_t \in [0, 1]$. Each period's shock, θ_t, is an identical and independent draw from the uniform distribution on $[z, 1 + z]$. Effort is costly: a politician suffers disutility ca_t from effort level a_t. The politician, however, benefits b from holding office in period t. A representative voter cares about output $x_t = \theta_t a_t$; higher output is better than lower output. In each period t, the voter receives payoff x_t but does not observe the value of θ_t or a_t. The voter then decides whether to retain the politician or replace him. If a politician is replaced, its payoff is 0 for all future periods. Because this is a model only of moral hazard and not adverse selection, all possible politicians have the same payoffs, and the distribution of θ is the same across politicians. Finally, assume that politicians and the voter discount with the common discount rate δ. Ferejohn shows that if the voter uses pure strategies optimal equilibria involve a cutoff rule – retain if x_t is greater than some threshold, x^*, and replace if x_t is less than x^*. In an equilibrium of this form, the politician in office chooses $a_t = 0$ if θ_t is below a threshold θ^* and chooses $a_t = x^*/\theta_t$ if θ_t is above θ^*. We leave it as an exercise to characterize equilibrium thresholds x^* and θ^*.

Using the concept of incentive compatibility, however, we can construct mixed strategy equilibria that make the voter better off than in Ferejohn's equilibria. Suppose that the voter randomizes over retention and replacement and selects the probability of retention as a function of the observed output x_t. Is it possible to select such a probability of retention function that creates incentives for high effort? If all politicians select the same level of effort in equilibrium, the voter is indifferent between retention and replacement. Consequently, randomization is a best response. Let $p(x)$ denote the probability that the politician is retained as a function of x. Given this function, the expected payoff to the politician of selecting a_t in period t when θ_t is observed is

$$p(\theta_t a_t)\delta V^{in} - ca_t$$

where V^{in} is the expected utility of the game in which the politician is in office at the beginning of the next period. In an equilibrium in which the politician always works as hard as possible ($a_t = 1$ regardless of θ_t) the value V^{in} satisfies the recursive relation

$$V^{in} = b - c + V^{in} \int_a^{1+a} p(\theta)d\theta.$$

Solving for V^{in} yields

$$V^{in} = \frac{b - c}{1 - \int_a^{1+a} p(\theta)d\theta}.$$

Note that $\int_a^{1+a} p(\theta)d\theta$ is just the expected probability of retention when θ is unknown and $a_t = 1$. In order to induce full effort, $a_t = 1$, an incentive compatibility condition must be satisfied. The function $p(\cdot)$ must be chosen so that $a_t = 1$ maximizes $p(\theta_t a_t)\delta V^{in} - ca_t$. Thus, $a_t = 1$ needs to solve the following first-order condition;

$$p'(\theta_t a_t) \mid_{a_t=1} = \frac{c}{\theta_t \delta V^{in}} \tag{11.9}$$

or

$$p'(x) = \frac{c\left(1 - \int_a^{1+a} p(\theta)d\theta\right)}{x\delta (b - c)}. \tag{11.10}$$

Equation 11.10 implicitly defines the function $p(\cdot)$ by relating its first derivative and integral. Because $d\ln(x)/dx = 1/x$, $p(x) = \gamma \ln(x) + k$ satisfies equation 11.10 (where γ and k are positive constants). In an equilibrium in which $a_t = 1$ regardless of θ_t, the relevant values of x are contained in the set $[z, (1 + z)]$. In order for the probability of retention to be a proper probability, boundary conditions $p(z) \geq 0$ and $p(1 + z) \leq 1$ need to be satisfied. Thus, the question of whether a mixed strategy equilibrium inducing $a_t = 1$ exists is the same as whether there exist values of γ and k such that

$$\gamma \ln(z) + k \geq 0 \tag{11.11}$$
$$\gamma \ln(1 + z) + k \leq 1$$
$$\frac{\gamma}{x} = \frac{c}{x\delta(b - c)}\left(1 - k - \gamma \int_z^{1+z} \ln(x)dx\right).$$

A possible solution to system 11.11 involves $\gamma \ln(z) + k = 0$. With this substitution, the first and second inequalities can be satisfied as long as $\gamma \ln(1 + z) - \gamma \ln(z) \leq 1$. The value of γ is positive for the corresponding value of k. Solving for γ yields

$$\gamma = \frac{c}{\delta(b - c)}\left(1 + \gamma \ln(z) - \gamma \int_z^{1+z} \ln(x)dx\right)$$

or

$$\gamma = \left(\frac{c}{\delta(b - c) - \ln(z) + \int_z^{1+z} \ln(x)dx}\right). \tag{11.12}$$

Because $az < 1$ and $1 + z < e$, $-\ln(z)$ is positive. Because $\ln(\cdot)$ is increasing and $z < 1$, $\ln(z) < \int_z^{1+z} \ln(x)dx$. This means that $-\ln(z) + \int_z^{1+z} \ln(x)dx \geq 0$. So for $b > c$ the solution to equation 11.12 is positive. In fact we have worked harder than necessary to develop the mixed strategy. Recall that condition 11.9 is the condition that makes $a_t = 1$ optimal. In fact if the upper bound of effort is 1, γ does not need to equal the solution in equation 11.12 exactly. Our solution guarantees that a value of a_t greater than 1 is less attractive than a value of $a_t = 1$. As an exercise, the reader can relax the constraint that $a_t \in [0, 1]$ and instead assume that $a_t \geq 0$ and find conditions supporting an equilibrium in which $a_t = \alpha$ for some fixed value $\alpha > 0$.

8. Mechanism Design and Signaling Games

As is the case in much of the literature, we have discussed mechanism design and signaling independently. We think, however, that some intuition can be gained by exploring the connections between these two normally distinct topics.

Suppose that the sender's (player's s) type is $\theta \in \Theta = [0, 1]$ and the message space is $M = [0, 1]$. It is common knowledge that θ is drawn from a distribution $F(\cdot)$ on Θ. Following s's message $m \in M$, the receiver (player r) selects a policy $p \in X = [0, 1]$. Even without specifying payoffs, we can use incentive compatibility to specify necessary conditions for the existence of an equilibrium in which the sender's message is fully revealing (i.e., $m^{-1}(m(\theta)) = \theta$). In an equilibrium in which $m(\theta)$ is one-to-one, consistent beliefs must be concentrated at the correct θ. Thus, beliefs can be represented by the probability distribution

$$B(\theta \mid m') = \begin{cases} 1 \text{ if } \theta \geq m^{-1}(m') \\ 0 \text{ otherwise} \end{cases}.$$

Given a fully revealing message, sequential rationality by r requires that $p(m') \in P(m') \equiv \arg\max_p u_r(p, m^{-1}(m'))$. Sequential rationality by s requires that she not have an incentive to mislead r by behaving as if her type were θ' when it is θ''. Given the mapping $p(\cdot)$, this incentive compatibility condition is $u_s(p(\theta''), \theta'') \geq u_s(p(\theta'), \theta'')$ for all $\theta', \theta'' \in \Theta$. Alternatively, the receiver's best response requires $u_r(p(\theta''), \theta'') \geq u_r(p(\theta'), \theta'')$ for all $\theta', \theta'' \in \Theta$. Thus, a requirement of a separating equilibrium is that $p(m')$ maximize both $u_s(p, m^{-1}(m'))$ and $u_r(p, m^{-1}(m'))$.

PROPOSITION 11.7 *A separating PBE exists only if the preferences of the players are similar – specifically for every $\theta \in \Theta$ it must be the case that $\{\arg\max_{p \in X} u_r(p, \theta)\} \cap \{\arg\max_{p \in X} u_s(p, \theta)\}$ is nonempty.*

Given this result, it is clear that truthful revelation in cheap talk signaling with one sender requires strong similarity between sender and receiver payoffs. As an example, recall our version of the open rule Gilligan-Krehbiel (1989) model from Chapter 8. There we showed that the best response by F to informative signals is $p(-\theta) = \theta$ and $p(-\theta) = \theta$. The proposition specifies that a separating equilibrium exists if and only if

$$u_F(\theta \mid -\theta) \geq u_F(-\theta \mid -\theta)$$
$$u_F(-\theta \mid \theta) \geq u_F(\theta \mid \theta)$$
$$u_C(\theta \mid -\theta) \geq u_C(-\theta \mid -\theta)$$
$$u_C(-\theta \mid \theta) \geq u_C(\theta \mid \theta).$$

We know the first two inequalities hold since $p(-\theta) = \theta$ and $p(-\theta) = \theta$ so the crucial conditions are $-c^2 \geq -(2\theta + c)^2$ and $-c^2 > -(2\theta - c)^2$. Note that these both hold if $c < \theta$. This is exactly the condition of preference divergence derived earlier.

Now we extend the general model so that there are two senders 1 and 2 who each observe θ but have possibly different preferences. The question of whether there is a PBE in which the receiver learns θ can be modeled as a type of mechanism design problem. In such a model, the receiver's choice of a mapping $p(m_1, m_2) : M^2 \rightarrow X$ is analogous to selection of a mechanism. In contrast to mechanism design, a PBE of a signaling game requires that the receiver's decision be sequentially rational given consistent beliefs. Thus, we are not free to choose just any mechanism that satisfies the sender's incentive compatibility conditions. Baron and Meirowitz (2004), however, show that in many cases the constraint that the receiver's actions must be sequentially rational is not binding.

In the mechanism design problem, suppose the receiver wishes to induce truthfulness by punishing senders if their messages do not coincide. Suppose that there exists a bad policy p^b that is worse for both senders than the receiver's best response to any truthful pair of messages. Formally, p^b is defined so that for every θ

$$u_1(\arg\max_{p \in X} u_r(p, \theta), \theta) \geq u_1(p^b, \theta) \qquad (11.13)$$

$$u_2(\arg\max_{p \in X} u_r(p, \theta), \theta) \geq u_2(p^b, \theta).$$

Given this definition of p^b, the following mechanism satisfies the incentive compatibility conditions for both senders to be truthful:

$$p(m_1, m_2) = \begin{cases} \arg\max_{p \in X} u_r(p, m) \text{ if } m_1 = m_2 \\ p^b \text{ otherwise} \end{cases}.$$

Given this policy function, condition 11.13 implies that sender 2's best response to a truthful announcement by sender 1 is a truthful announcement to prevent the dreaded p^b. A similar argument applies for sender 1's incentive to be truthful. Within the mechanism design framework, the mere existence of p^b is enough to induce truthfulness regardless of the receiver's utility from p^b. In signaling models, however, we must to worry about whether choosing p^b is sequentially rational for the receiver. Accordingly it must be the case that p^b is an optimal policy for the receiver given the beliefs she forms at all information sets where $m_1 \neq m_2$. This suggests that our mechanism design trick is not very compelling to those committed to the signaling tradition. But recall that weak consistency only constrains beliefs at information sets that occur with positive probability. In an equilibrium in which the senders are truthful $m_1 \neq m_2$ does not occur. Accordingly, satisfying sequential rationality and credibly committing to enact p^b if $m_1 \neq m_2$ are not very challenging. All that is required is that there exists some distribution $b^b(\cdot)$ on Θ such that $p^b \in \arg\max_p \int u_r(p, \theta) d\, b^b(\theta)$. Adding a state θ^b in which $p^b \in \arg\max_p u_r(p, \theta^b)$ suffices. Using this argument Baron and Meirowitz (2004) reach the following conclusion.

THEOREM 11.4 *Suppose two senders observe θ. As long as there are a policy $p^b \in X$ satisfying condition 11.13 and a distribution $b^b(\cdot)$ on Θ such that $p^b \in \arg\max_p \int u_r(p, \theta) d\, b^b(\theta)$ a truthful PBE exists.*

In response to Gilligan and Krehbiel's (1989) work on heterogeneous legislative committees, Krishna and Morgan (2001) demonstrate that with two senders there are PBEs in which the receiver learns the state θ. This equilibrium does not hinge on a punishment policy p^b but uses out-of-equilibrium beliefs to rationalize a policy that punishes any agent who has an incentive to lie. Krehbiel (2001) criticizes this approach on the grounds that the off-the-path responses to some messages are highly discontinuous and tend to move in the wrong direction. Although in equilibrium high policies are best responses to low messages, Krishna and Morgan's PBE calls for low policies in response to high out-of-equilibrium messages.

Battaglini (2002) shows that if in fact the policy and state spaces are multidimensional (say, for example, $X = \Theta = [0, 1]^2$) then truthful equilibria can be constructed that do not depend on beliefs in such a peculiar manner. As an example of this model, consider a receiver and two senders with Euclidean preferences over two dimensions. The receiver has an ideal point of $(0, 0)$, sender 1 has ideal point $(1, 0)$, and sender 2 has ideal point $(0, 1)$. In this model, each sender observes the shock $\theta \in \Theta$ perfectly, and the outcomes x are a random function of policy p where $x = p + \theta$. A message is $m_s = (m_s^1, m_s^2)$ for $s \in \{1, 2\}$. Similarly, outcomes and policies are vectors ($x = (x^1, x^2)$, $p = (p^1, p^2)$). A particularly simple direct mechanism can be constructed on the basis of the realization that although neither sender has the same preferences as the receiver,[15] each sender has the same preferences as the receiver over one dimension. Sender 1 and the receiver both want the second dimension of the outcome as close to 0 as possible, and sender 2 and the receiver both want the first coordinate of the outcome as close to 0 as possible. Suppose that sender 1 with ideal point $(1, 0)$ is given complete control of the second coordinate, so that $p^1 = -m_1^1$ and that sender 2 with ideal point $(0, 1)$ is given complete control of the first coordinate, so that $p^2 = -m_2^2$. Given this mechanism, announcement of $m_s(\theta) = \theta$ is a best response, and thus the mechanism is incentive compatible. Can this receiver strategy be supported in a PBE? If so we need to find weakly consistent beliefs for which this policy function is sequentially rational. Because the mapping $p(m)$ described previously is a direct mechanism at every reached information set, Bayes' rule results in concentrated beliefs $\theta = m_1 = m_2$. It remains to specify beliefs for information sets in which $m_1 \neq m_2$ that make policy function $p(m)$ sequentially rational for the receiver and the truthful messages sequentially rational for the senders. An easy way to do this is to let the beliefs ignore m_2^1 and m_1^2. In other words, the beliefs are concentrated at $\theta = (m_1^1, m_2^2)$. Battaglini shows that, in the Euclidean preferences setting with at least two dimensions and two senders, separating PBEs exist as long as the ideal points of the three players are not on a line.

We have seen that under certain preference profiles separating PBEs exist with two senders. With three perfectly informed senders $\{1, 2, 3\}$, we do not need to make any assumptions about preferences to characterize a simple separating PBE. Let $p^*(\theta)$ denote a selection from the correspondence $\arg\max u_r(p, \theta)$ and suppose that $p^+ \in p^*(\theta)$ for some θ. Similarly to the earlier example, suppose the receiver can commit to the following mechanism that depends on the messages m_1, m_2, m_3:

$$p(m) = \begin{cases} p^*(\theta) \text{ if } \theta = m_i = m_j \text{ for some } i, j \in \{1, 2, 3\} \\ p^+ \text{ otherwise} \end{cases}.$$

Truthful messages are a best response because if i and j are truthful then k's message is outcome inconsequential. Supporting this policy function as sequentially rational is easy. Any belief mapping that is

---

[15] By proposition 11.7 there is no truthful equilibrium in the one sender game.

concentrated on θ if $m_1 = m_2 = m_3 = \theta$ is weakly consistent, and any beliefs that are concentrated at θ if $\theta = m_i = m_j$ for some i, $j \in \{1, 2, 3\}$ make the policy mapping a best response for the receiver.

The conclusion of Baron and Meirowitz is that any direct mechanism that (1) following truthful messages selects an optimal policy for the receiver and (2) following nontruthful messages selects a policy that is optimal given some belief on Θ can be supported in some PBE to the signaling game.

9. Exercises

EXERCISE 11.1 *Instead of maximizing the welfare of her department, the department chair wants to maximize her surplus (contributions minus expenditures on the espresso maker). Does she still want to implement the Groves-Clarke mechanism?*

EXERCISE 11.2 *Consider a mechanism design problem involving two agents. The mechanism designer selects a policy $p \in [0, 1]$ to maximize the sum of the payoffs for agents 1 and 2. Each agent's payoff is $u_i(p, y_i, \beta_i) = -\beta_i |y_i - x|$. Each coordinate of each agent's type (y_i, β_i) is drawn from a uniform distribution. Assume that the draws are independent. (1) Write down an example of a direct mechanism. (2) Do any direct mechanisms implement (in Bayesian Nash strategies) the objective of the planner?*

EXERCISE 11.3 *This exercise is to prove a version of the revelation principle. A choice function, $g(\theta)$, is implementable in dominant strategies if there exists a mechanism $\langle M, p(\cdot) \rangle$ in which each agent has a dominant strategy to play the strategy $m_i(\theta)$ for each $\theta \in \Theta$ given policy function $p(m(\theta)) = g(\theta)$. Prove the following theorem: given a mechanism design problem $\langle \Theta, F(\theta), u \rangle$, there exists a direct mechanism $\langle \Theta, p(\cdot) \rangle$ that implements $g(\theta)$ in dominant strategies if the choice function $g(\theta)$ is implementable in dominant strategies.*

EXERCISE 11.4 *Prove Moulin's result (Proposition 11.2).*

EXERCISE 11.5 *Consider a population of agents with private information about their ideal points and quadratic preferences. Assume that they are asked to announce their ideal point and the policy $x(m) - (1/n) \sum m_i$ is enacted (i.e., the average ideal point is the implemented policy). Show that truthful response does not form a Bayesian Nash equilibrium to this game.*

EXERCISE 11.6 *Prove that the strategies described by equation 11.1 form an equilibrium to the first-price auction.*

EXERCISE 11.7 *Demonstrate that use of the strategy "Hold up placard until the price exceeds $b(\theta)$" constitutes a PBE in the descending-price auction.*

EXERCISE 11.8 *Find the expected revenue of a standard auction if $F(\cdot)$ is the uniform distribution on $[0, 1]$.*

EXERCISE 11.9 *Consider Ferejohn's model with moral hazard. Assume that equation 11.8 does not hold. Construct a mixed strategy equilibrium where the government sometimes chooses $a = low$ and the voter always removes the government when $x = low$ and occasionally removes it when $x = high$.*

EXERCISE 11.10 *Prove that in the Epstein-O'Halloran model P^* is a closed interval $\left[\underline{p}, \overline{p}\right] \subset X$.*

EXERCISE 11.11 *In the Epstein-O'Halloran model, show that the majority rule outcome for P^* is that preferred by the legislator with ideal point l_m.*

EXERCISE 11.12 *In the Epstein-O'Halloran model, assume that ε is distributed $N(0, \sigma^2)$. Compute the optimal statute P. How does P depend on l_m, a, and σ^2? Hint: $E(\varepsilon|\varepsilon < m) = -\sigma\phi(m/\sigma)/\Phi(m/\sigma)$.*

EXERCISE 11.13 *This exercise is related to McCarty (2004). Augment the Epstein-O'Halloran model by assuming that governor G with ideal point $g > l_m$ appoints A (i.e., selects a) prior to L's choosing P. Assume that A learns ε but that G and L believe that ε is distributed uniformly on $[-E, E]$. Show that the governor's optimal appointment is $a^* \in (l_m, g)$. How does a^* depend on l_m and E? What if the governor appoints A after P is selected?*

EXERCISE 11.14 *In the context of the Bendor-Meirowitz model, prove that $\{y : h(\|y\|) \le u_0'\}$ is a closed ball.*

EXERCISE 11.15 *In the Bendor-Meirowitz model, show that if q_i is the same for all i and $x = p - \varepsilon$ (with ε distributed according to $F(\cdot)$ on $\mathbb{R}^d$), the ally principle holds.*

EXERCISE 11.16 *In the Bendor-Meirowitz model, suppose that $q_1 = q_2 = 3/4$ and $u(x) = -x^2$. Find the minimal value of δ such that the principal prefers delegation to agent 2.*

EXERCISE 11.17 *In the continuous version of Ferejohn's model assume that a_t can be any nonnegative level of effort and characterize equilibrium values of x^* and θ^* as functions of the exogenous parameters b, c, z, δ.*

EXERCISE 11.18 *In the continuous version of Ferejohn's model assume that a_t need only be positive (it can be greater than 1). For a fixed value $\alpha > 0$ characterize an equilibrium in which $a_c = \alpha$ in every period regardless of θ_t.*

EXERCISE 11.19 *Construct a fully separating PBE in a version of the Battaglini model in which sender 1 has ideal point $(1, 1)$ and sender 2 has ideal point $(0, 1)$.*

EXERCISE 11.20 *Consider a problem in which a policymaker must select a policy $p \in \mathbb{R}^3$. The outcome is given by $x = p + \varepsilon$ where ε is a random shock. The policymaker's prior is that ε is given by the distribution function $F(\cdot)$. Assume that there are five agents. Agents 1, 2, 3 all perfectly observe coordinate 1 of the shock (ε^1) but observe nothing about the remaining dimensions of the shock. Agents 4 and 5 observe only the second and third dimensions of the shock ($\varepsilon^2, \varepsilon^3$). Assume that the policymaker's ideal point is the 0 vector. The remaining agents have arbitrary ideal points in $\mathbb{R}^3$. All agents have quadratic preferences over the outcome x. Are there any games of cheap talk communication that possess a perfect Bayesian equilibrium in which the outcome chosen always corresponds to the policymaker's most preferred outcome 0? If so, give an example and characterize such an equilibrium. If not, prove it.*

12 Mathematical Appendix

Mathematics is the study of axiomatic systems and the true propositions of these systems. Mathematics as a language facilitates communication about these systems and the resulting propositions. In comparison to ordinary language, mathematical statements tend to be more transparent, revealing how assumptions and conclusions are related. Mathematical propositions are true or correct if they follow from the structure of the system that generates them. For example, Euclidean geometry is the set of all statements that are true if parallel lines never intersect. So the statement that the shortest distance between points is a straight line is true in Euclidean geometry. The claim that the quickest way to get from Central Park to Princeton is a straight line may or not be true. The answer might depend on traffic between these two points, the quality of paving, or other factors. Thus, just as the extent to which a mathematically true proposition about distance accurately describes a problem we care about is unclear, mathematically correct propositions about game theoretic models may or may not accurately describe politics. Students and scholars interested in pursuing more about truth and the value of models and formalism should seek out epistemologists. From our perspective, a critical step is determining what the mathematically correct propositions are. In this appendix we first give explicit definitions to mathematical terminology. We then define the standard axioms of the mathematical system in which most, albeit not all, applications in political game theory are assumed to exist. We then summarize the more important mathematical propositions used in political game theory.

1. Mathematical Statements and Proofs

As in any other language, the fundamental unit of mathematics is the statement, which we denote P. We review the types of mathematical statements that readers are likely to encounter.

- *Universal Statement:* P is always true within a given mathematical system.

Consider the following example of a universal statement. Let x be a real number, $\forall x$, $x \leq |x|$, where the symbol $\forall$ means "for all" or "for every." To prove such a statement, we require it to be proved for a generic x where we can only use the properties common to every value of x.

- *Existential Statement:* There are conditions under which P is true.

The following is such an example: $\exists x$ such that $x = |x|$ where $\exists$ means "there exist(s)." To prove an existential statement, we must only find a value of x in the given system for which P is true. Of course in this example, $x \geq 0$ is the needed condition.

Mathematics also has well-defined procedures for verifying that a given statement is true. Now we consider the types of *proofs* that are encountered in the text.

1.1. Deduction. Proofs by deduction are those for which a statement is true because it is logically connected to a statement either known or presupposed to be true. Suppose we know P to be true; then we establish that Q is true if we can prove "if P, then Q" or $P \Rightarrow Q$. Obviously, this can take place via a number of steps such as

$$P \Rightarrow R$$
$$R \Rightarrow S$$
$$S \Rightarrow Q.$$

Sometimes when we work it out mentally, showing $S \Rightarrow Q$ may be the first step. When communicating the logic of the proof, however, it should be written in the order given. Deduction is used to prove both existential and universal statements.

1.2. The Contrapositive. Sometimes it is easier to establish $P \Rightarrow Q$ by formulating it in terms of the negative statements $\tilde{\ }Q$ and $\tilde{\ }P$ where $\tilde{\ }$ means "not." It is logically true that $(\tilde{\ }Q \Rightarrow \tilde{\ }P) \Rightarrow (P \Rightarrow Q)$.

EXAMPLE 12.1 *If 7m is an odd integer, then m is an odd integer.*

Thus, $P = \{7m \text{ is odd}\}$, $Q = \{m \text{ is odd}\}$, $\tilde{\ }P = \{7m \text{ is even}\}$, and $\tilde{\ }Q = \{m \text{ is even}\}$. We show $P \Rightarrow Q$ by showing $\tilde{\ }Q \Rightarrow \tilde{\ }P$.

$$\tilde{\ }Q \Rightarrow m = 2k \text{ for some integer } k$$
$$\Rightarrow 7m = 7(2k)$$
$$\Rightarrow 7m = 2(7k)$$
$$\Rightarrow 7m = 2n \text{ for some integer } n$$
$$\Rightarrow \tilde{\ }P.$$

1.3. Contradiction. One way to prove that the statement P is true is to demonstrate that $\tilde{\ }P$ is false. Proving a statement is false is quite easy: we only need to provide a counterexample. A single counterexample showing $\tilde{\ }P$ to be false implies that P is true. This procedure works best when arguing against a universal statement or in favor of an existential statement.

EXAMPLE 12.2 *Let n be any integer and let $P = \{there\ exists\ n > 0\ such\ n^2 + n + 17\ is\ not\ a\ prime\ number\}$ or $P = \{\exists n > 0 \ni n^2 + n + 17\ is\ not\ a\ prime\ number\}$ where $\exists$ means "there exists" and $\ni$ means "such that."*

We now construct $\tilde{\ }P = \{\forall\ n > 0, n^2 + n + 17 \text{ is a prime number}\}$. But $\tilde{\ }P$ is false because $n = 17$ implies that $n^2 + n + 17 = 17 \cdot 19$ and is thus not prime. Thus, P is true.

We may also establish $\tilde{\ }P$ is false by deriving a series of implications from $\tilde{\ }P$ that lead to a false statement.

$$\tilde{\ }P \Rightarrow n + 1 + 17/n \text{ is not an integer for all } n$$
$$\Rightarrow 17/n \text{ is not an integer for all } n$$
$$\Rightarrow 1 \text{ is not an integer.}$$

The final statement is obviously false.

1.4. Mathematical Induction. Some statements describe a property of an index number n (an integer) and may be written as $P(n)$. One way to prove that the statement $P(n)$ is true for each natural number n is to demonstrate that $P(1)$ is true and that if $P(n)$ is true then $P(n + 1)$ must be true.

EXAMPLE 12.3 *Let $P(n)$ be the event that $2n < n^2$. For $n \geq 3$, $P(n)$ is true. For $n = 3$, $6 < 9$ and thus $P(3)$ is true. Now assume that $P(n)$ is true, implying that $2n < n^2$. Because $2(n + 1) = 2n + 2$ and $(n + 1)^2 = n^2 + 2n + 1$, the assumption implies that if $2 < 2n + 1$ then $P(n + 1)$ is true. But this simplifies to $1/2 < n$, which is true for $n > 3$.*

2. Sets and Functions

2.1. Sets. A set is a collection of distinct objects. The objects of sets are called elements. We denote sets either by enumerating them or by describing them. Suppose S is the set of all positive integers less than 10. We may write S as $S = \{1, 2, 3, 4, 5, 6, 7, 8, 9\}$ or $S = \{n | n$ is an integer and $0 < n < 10\}$. The second statement is read as "S is the set of all numbers that are integers and are greater than 0 and less than 10." Sets either have a finite number of elements as here or an infinite number such as $I = \{n \mid n$ is integer greater than 7$\}$ or $J = \{x \mid 0 < x < 1\}$. Infinite sets are either countable or uncountable. I is countable because it is possible to associate each element of I with a distinct integer. J is uncountable because it is impossible to associate each element with an integer.

EXAMPLE 12.4 *A rational number is one that can be written as a fraction p/q where p and q are integers. Prove that $\mathbb{Q} = \{x \mid x$ is rational$\}$ is infinite but countable.*

We denote that some element belongs to a set with the symbol "$\in$." Therefore, the following are truthful statements: $3 \in S$, $9 \in I$, $.345678 \in J$, and $.8 \in \mathbb{Q}$. We can also designate which elements are not in a particular set with "$\notin$" so that $10 \notin S$, $7 \notin I$, $0 \notin J$, and $\pi \notin \mathbb{Q}$.

2.2. Set Relations and Operations. The following are some useful relationships between different sets.

- **Equality:**

$S_1 = S_2$ implies that $x \in S_1$ if and only if $x \in S_2$. In other words, if $S_1 = S_2$, S_1 and S_2 contain exactly the same elements.

- **Subset:**

S_1 is said to be a subset of S_2 or $S_1 \subseteq S_2$ if $x \in S_1$ implies $x \in S_2$. Thus, S_1 is a subset of S_2 if all of the elements of S_1 are also in S_2. Note that if $S_1 = S_2$, then $S_1 \subseteq S_2$ and $S_2 \subseteq S_1$. We can also define a "proper" subset that rules out the possibility of equality. $S_1 \subset S_2$ implies that for all $x \in S_1$, $x \in S_2$ and $\exists y \in S_2$ such that $y \notin S_1$. In other words, all elements of S_1 are in S_2 but S_2 contains additional elements not found in S_1. We use the symbols $\supset$ and $\supseteq$ to write such statements in the opposite order. Finally, the symbol $\nsubseteq$ means "not a subset of."

- **Disjoint:**

Two sets are said to be disjoint if they have no elements in common. Formally, S_1 and S_2 are disjoint if $x \in S_1$ implies that $x \notin S_2$ and $x \in S_2$ implies that $x \notin S_1$.

There is a special set $\varnothing$ known as the null set or empty set defined by the following properties: $\varnothing$ contains no elements and for all S, $\varnothing \subset S$. Clearly, $\varnothing$ is the smallest possible set. It is sometimes convenient to talk about a large set U such that for all S that we are considering $S \subseteq U$. This set is called the universal set.

A number of mathematical operations on sets are useful.

- **Unions:**

The union of two or more sets is the total set of elements that are contained in at least one of the sets. Formally, the union of S_1 and S_2 is $S_1 \cup S_2 = \{x \mid x \in S_1 \text{ or } x \in S_2\}$. The union of a large number of sets indexed by i is $\bigcup_{i=1}^{n} S_i = S_1 \cup S_2 \cup \ldots \cup S_n$. For an infinite collections of sets, with the index set I, we may write $\bigcup_{i \in I} S_i$.

- **Intersections:**

The intersection of two or more sets is the set of elements common to all of the sets. Formally, the intersection of S_1 and S_2 is $S_1 \cap S_2 = \{x \mid x \in S_1 \text{ and } x \in S_2\}$. The intersection of a large number of sets indexed by i as $\bigcap_{i=1}^{n} S_i = S_1 \cap S_2 \cap \cdots \cap S_n$. If S_1 and S_2 are disjoint, $S_1 \cap S_2 = \varnothing$. Because the sets have no elements in common, the only subset in the intersection must be the null set. For an infinite collection of sets, with the index set I, we may write $\bigcap_{i \in I} S_i$.

- **Complements:**

Given a universal set U and a subset S, the complement of S is $S^c = U \backslash S = \{x \mid x \in U \text{ and } x \notin S\}$.

- **De Morgan's Laws:**

Let A, B, C, and D be sets. Then the operations on these sets must satisfy the following properties:

Commutative: $A \cup B = B \cup A$ and $A \cap B = B \cap A$

Associative: $(A \cup B) \cup C = A \cup (B \cup C)$ and
$\qquad \qquad (A \cap B) \cap C = A \cap (B \cap C)$

Distributive: $A \cup (B \cap C) = (A \cup B) \cap (A \cup C)$ and
$\qquad \qquad A \cap (B \cup C) = (A \cap B) \cup (A \cap C)$

- **Products:**

The product of two sets A and B denoted $A \times B$ is the set of ordered pairs, (a, b) such that $a \in A$ and $b \in B$. For indexed sets we write $\prod_{i=1}^{n} S_i = S_1 \times S_2 \times \cdots \times S_n$. Some authors use the notation $\times_{i=1}^{n} S_i$ to denote $\prod_{i=1}^{n} S_i$. For an infinite collections of sets, with the index set I, we may write $\prod_{i \in I} S_i$.

2.3. Correspondences and Functions. Another way to relate two sets to one another is to specify which elements of each set "correspond" or "go with each other." In general a correspondence is a rule, f, that links the elements of S_1 to S_2. Formally, we write $f : S_1 \rightarrow\rightarrow S_2$ where the set S_1 is called the domain (or preimage) set and S_2 is the range (or image) set. For example, consider Figure 12.1 where the correspondence f relates $x \in S_1$ to elements $y, z \in S_2$.

A function is a special type of correspondence that relates each element of the domain to a unique point of the range. So if the correspondence $f : S_1 \rightarrow\rightarrow S_2$ is a function, $f(x)$ is a single element of S_2 for every $x \in S_1$. For functions we write $f : S_1 \rightarrow S_2$. With a function, multiple points of the domain may map into the same point in the range. In Figure 12.2, the function relates $x, w, v \in S_1$ to elements $y, z \in S_2$.

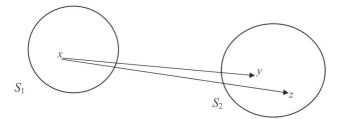

Figure 12.1. Correspondences.

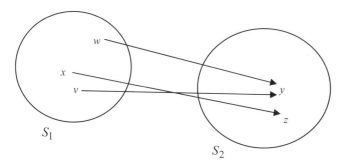

Figure 12.2. Functions.

Because each element of the domain maps into a single element in the range, we may write $y = f(x)$ for $x \in S_1$ and $y \in S_2$. We also represent the function by a set of ordered pairs such as $\{(y, x) \mid y = f(x)$ for some $x \in S_1\}$.

Consider a function $f : A \to B$. Two important properties are the following:

- Injectivity: For all a_1 and $a_2 \in A$, $f(a_1) = f(a_2)$ if and only if $a_1 = a_2$. Each point in the range is associated with a single point in the domain. This property is also known as "one-to-one."
- Surjectivity: $\forall b \in B$ there exist $a \in A$ such that $f(a) = b$. This property is also known as "on to."

If a function has these two properties, it is known as a *bijection*, and there exists an inverse function mapping points in B to points in A. We write this inverse function as $f^{-1} : B \to A$ or $f^{-1}(b) = a$ for $b \in B$ and $a \in A$.

EXAMPLE 12.5 $y = 2x$ *is a bijection. Because every y maps to a single x, we can write the inverse function* $f^{-1}(x) = y/2$.

EXAMPLE 12.6 $y = x^2$ *is not injective because x and −x produce the same y. If we restrict the domain to positive numbers, however, we can write* $f^{-1}(x) = \sqrt{y}$

3. The Real Number System

The real number system, $\mathbb{R}$, consists of all the integers as well as the rational numbers (ratios of integers) and the irrational numbers (numbers that are not the ratio of integers). The real number system is a set of numbers with some additional structure. The system also includes two operators, $+$ and $\times$, which map from $\mathbb{R} \times \mathbb{R}$ into $\mathbb{R}$ and a weak ordering, $\geq$, that is a subset of $\mathbb{R} \times \mathbb{R}$. These are the familiar operators of addition and multiplication and the ordering is "greater than or equal to." Axiomatically, the system is characterized by fourteen axioms. For our purposes it is sufficient to highlight only a subset of these conditions. The real number system is a field; that means that the operations $+$ and $\times$ behave the way we learned in elementary school: the order of addition (or multiplication) does not matter, multiplication is distributive (meaning that $\forall x, y, z \in \mathbb{R} \ x(y + z) = xy + xz$), multiplication and addition by 0 and 1 have the expected consequences, and every number has a multiplicative inverse (so that $x \times 1/x = 1$). In addition the real number system satisfies order axioms that ensure that $\geq$ behaves the way we expect it to. One axiom, completeness, is probably unfamiliar, so we define it formally.

DEFINITION 12.1 *Completeness Axiom:* *For every nonempty subset $S \subset \mathbb{R}$ if there exists an upper bound b of S (meaning $x \in S \Longrightarrow x \leq b$) then there exists a least upper bound c (meaning c is an upper bound of S and if z is an upper bound of S then $c \leq z$). In other words, every set with an upper bound has a least upper bound.*

An example of a space that is not complete is $\mathbb{R} \backslash \mathbb{Z}$, where $\mathbb{Z}$ is the set of integers. In this space the set $(0, 1)$ has an upper bound (example $3/2$) but it does not have a least upper bound. This axiom captures a version of the idea that the set of real numbers does not have any holes in it. Many of the properties of limits depend on this feature of the number system.

3.1. Limits of Real Sequences. A sequence of real numbers $\{x_n\}_{n=1}^{\infty}$, sometimes denoted $\{x_n\}$, is an infinite list of real numbers. More precisely a sequence is a function that maps the counting numbers $(1, 2, 3, \dots)$ into the real numbers. In this sense x_n is the value of this function evaluated at integer n. A subsequence is the sequence formed by considering only a subset of the integers.

DEFINITION 12.2 *The number $l \in \mathbb{R}$ is a limit of the sequence $\{x_n\}$ if for every $\varepsilon > 0$ there is an N such that for all $n > N$ we have $|x_n - l| < \varepsilon$. If l is a limit of the sequence $\{x_n\}$ we write $l = \lim x_n$.*

PROPOSITION 12.1 *A sequence has at most one limit.*

We include a proof of this statement as a lesson in how statements are proved.

Proof Suppose otherwise, then $a = \lim x_n = b$ and $a \neq b$. Because $a \neq b$ there exists some $\varepsilon > 0$ such that (1) $|a - b| > 2\varepsilon$. Since $a = \lim x_n = b$ it must be the case that for some N if $n > N$ (2) $|x_n - a| < \varepsilon$ and (3) $|x_n - b| < \varepsilon$. Without loss of generality assume that $a < b$. If $x_n < a < b$, then we have contradicted 1 or 3; if $a < b < x_n$, then we have contradicted 1 and 2; if $a < x_n < b$, then 1 implies that either 2 or 3 is violated. One of these three cases must be true. □

DEFINITION 12.3 *A sequence $\{x_n\}$ is a Cauchy sequence if for every $\varepsilon > 0$ there is an N such that for all $n, m > N$ we have $|x_n - x_m| < \varepsilon$.*

PROPOSITION 12.2 *A sequence has a limit if and only if it is a Cauchy sequence.*

DEFINITION 12.4 *A sequence $\{x_n\}$ converges to infinity ∞ $(-\infty)$ if for any $b \in \mathbb{R}$ there is some N such that (s.t.) $x_n > (<)b$ for all $n > N$.*

DEFINITION 12.5 *The number $l \in \mathbb{R}$ is a cluster point of the sequence $\{x_n\}$ if for every $\varepsilon > 0$ and every N there exists some $n > N$ such that $|x_n - l| < \varepsilon$.*

The sequence $x_n = -1^n$ has two cluster points 1 and -1 but no limit.

PROPOSITION 12.3 *Point l is a cluster point of $\{x_n\}$ if and only if it is the limit of a subsequence $\{x_{n'}\}$.*

DEFINITION 12.6 *The number $l \in \mathbb{R}$ is the limit superior (limsup) of the sequence $\{x_n\}$ if (1) for any $\varepsilon > 0$ there is an N such that for all $n > N$ we have $x_n < l + \varepsilon$, and (2) for any $\varepsilon > 0$ and any N there exists some $n > N$ such that we have $x_n > l - \varepsilon$. We write $l = \limsup x_n$.*

DEFINITION 12.7 *l is the limit inferior (liminf) of the sequence $\{x_n\}$ if $l = -\limsup(-x_n)$.*

An alternative definition that may be more intuitive follows.

DEFINITION 12.8 *The limsup is the greatest cluster point and the liminf is the least cluster point.*

PROPOSITION 12.4 *For any sequence $\{x_n\}$ $\limsup x_n \geq \liminf x_n$ and if equality holds then $\lim x_n$ exists and $\lim x_n = \limsup x_n = \liminf x_n$.*

4. Points and Sets

We now consider arbitrary spaces endowed with a particular structure. These spaces are called metric spaces. These spaces are endowed with a distance function satisfying several properties.

DEFINITION 12.9 *A metric space (X, d) is a set of points X and a distance function $d(x, y) : X \times X \to \mathbb{R}$, satisfying the conditions*

(1) $d(x, y) \geq 0$
(2) $d(x, y) = 0$ if and only if $x = y$
(3) $d(x, y) = d(y, x)$ for any $x, y \in X$
(4) $d(x, z) \leq d(x, y) + d(y, z)$ for any $x, y, z \in X$.

For any distance function, we can define regions around points known as "balls." For any scalar $\varepsilon > 0$ and point $x \in X$, the ε-ball around x is $B(x, \varepsilon) = \{y \in X : d(x, y) < \varepsilon\}$. There are two important properties of sets.

DEFINITION 12.10 *A set $A \subset X$ is open if for every $x \in A$ there is some $\varepsilon > 0$ such that $B(x, \varepsilon) \subset A$. A set $A \subset X$ is closed if its complement $X \backslash A$ is open.*

Conventionally X and $\varnothing$ are both open and closed. We state several results about open and closed sets. These results demonstrate how one can operate on closed and open sets and ensure that the resulting product inherits openness or closedness.

PROPOSITION 12.5

(1) *If O_1 and O_2 are open then $O_1 \cap O_2$ is open.*
(2) *Given a collection of open sets $O_1, O_2, \dots,$ the set $\cup_i O_i$ is open.*
(3) *If C_1 and C_2 are closed then $C_1 \cup C_2$ is closed.*
(4) *Given a collection of closed sets $C_1, C_2, \dots,$ the set $\cap_i C_i$ is closed.*

It is not the case that the infinite intersections of open sets are open. An example is the collection of open sets $(-1/n, 1/n)$. Each such set is open but the intersection is just the set $\{0\}$, which is not open.

Another property of sets is the following.

DEFINITION 12.11 *A set $A \subset X$ is bounded if there exists some finite scalar k such that for every $x, y \in A$ we have $d(x, y) < k$.*

If X is a subset of finite-dimensional Euclidean space $\mathbb{R}^n = \{(x_1, x_2, \dots, x_n) : x_i \in \mathbb{R}\}$ we have the following definition:

DEFINITION 12.12 *A set $A \subset \mathbb{R}^n$ is compact if A is closed and bounded.*

In arbitrary metric spaces a more general definition of compactness is needed. The more general (or topological) definition of compactness deals with open covers.

DEFINITION 12.13 *Given a set A, an open covering of A is a collection of sets $\{O_\theta\}_{\theta \in \Theta}$ where Θ is an arbitrary index set and O_θ is open for every $\theta \in \Theta$ such that $A \subset \{\cup_{\theta \in \Theta} O_\theta\}$. In other words, if $x \in A$ then there is some $\theta \in \Theta$ such that $x \in O_\theta$.*

A set is compact if every open covering has a finite subcovering. Formally, this definition takes the following form:

DEFINITION 12.14 *A set A is compact if $\{O_\theta\}_{\theta \in \Theta}$ an open covering of A implies that for some finite set $B \subset \Theta$, $\{O_\theta\}_{\theta \in B}$ is a covering of A.*

Given that addition is defined in our metric space, as is the case for $\mathbb{R}^n$, the following definition is useful:

DEFINITION 12.15 *A set A is convex if for every $x, y \in A$ and every scalar $\lambda \in [0, 1]$ the point $\lambda x + (1 - \lambda)y$ is also in A.*

The following result turns out to be of interest in social choice theory and bargaining. For example, if individual preferences are strictly convex, then the following result ensures the convexity of the preferred (or upper contour sets) for a collection of individuals.

PROPOSITION 12.6 *Given an indexed collection of sets A_i for $i \in \alpha$, if A_i is convex for each $i \in \alpha$, $\cap_{i \in \alpha} A_i$ is a convex set.*

5. Continuity of Functions

An important property of functions is *continuity*. Let X and Y be subsets of metric spaces. The metrics for these spaces are d_X and d_Y. The motivating example is $X = Y = \mathbb{R}$, but the following applies to any functions that map one metric space into another.

DEFINITION 12.16 *A function $f : X \to Y$ is continuous at $x \in X$ if for any $\varepsilon > 0$ there is some $\delta > 0$ such that $d_Y(f(x), f(y)) < \varepsilon$ for all $y \in X$ with $d_X(x, y) < \delta$. A function is continuous if it is continuous at every point in its domain.*

The following definition is equivalent.

DEFINITION 12.17 *A function $f : X \to Y$ is continuous if for every open set $B \subset Y$ the inverse image $f^{-1}(B) := \{x \in X : f(x) \in B)\}$ is open.*

Of particular interest are functions for which the range is a subset of the real line. These functions are called real-valued functions. For real-valued functions another definition of continuity is often useful.

DEFINITION 12.18 *Given a function* $f : X \rightarrow \mathbb{R}$, *the upper contour sets are a collection of sets of the form* $U_\alpha = \{x \in X : f(x) \geq \alpha\}$ *for every* $\alpha \in R$. *The lower contour sets are the sets* $L_\alpha = \{x \in X : f(x) \leq \alpha\}$.

Continuity can be restated in terms of the contour sets.

PROPOSITION 12.7 *The function* $f : X \rightarrow \mathbb{R}$ *is continuous if and only if all of the upper and lower contour sets are closed.*

5.1. Extrema, Solutions, and Fixed Points*. The following are sufficient conditions for optimization problems to have solutions.

THEOREM 12.1 *If* $f : X \rightarrow \mathbb{R}$ *is continuous and* X *is compact and nonempty, there exists a point* $x^* = \arg\max_{x \in X}\{f(x)\}$.

Another fundamental result follows.

THEOREM 12.2 *(Bolzano Intermediate Value Theorem) If* $f:[a, b] \rightarrow \mathbb{R}$ *is continuous with* $f(a) < y < f(b)$ *[or* $f(b) < y < f(z)$*], then there is a* $c \in (a, b)$ *with* $f(c) = y$.

Proof Consider the lower contour set of y, $L_y = \{x \in [a, b] : f(x) \leq y\}$. Now L_y is nonempty as $a \in L_y$. This set is also bounded so by completeness it has a least upper bound. Call this point c. Either $c \in L_y$ (that is, $f(c) \leq y$) or c is a cluster point. If c is a cluster point then there is some sequence $\{x_n\}$ of numbers in L_y with $\lim x_n = c$. Because f is continuous this implies that $\{f(x_n)\}$ converges to $f(c)$. Because $f(x_n) < y$ for every n it is the case that $f(c) \leq y$. Thus, we know that $c \in L_y$. Now consider the upper contour set of y, U_y. Now U_y is nonempty as $b \in U_y$. This set is also bounded so by completeness it has a greatest lower bound. Call this point c. Either $c \in U_y$ (that is, $f(c) \geq y$) or c is a cluster point. If c is a cluster point then there is some sequence $\{x_n\}$ of numbers in U_y with $\lim x_n = c$. Because f is continuous this implies that $\{f(x_n)\}$ converges to $f(c)$. Because $f(x_n) > y$ for every n it is the case that $f(c) \geq y$. Thus, we know that $c \in U_y$. Thus, $c \in U_y \cap L_y$, implying that $f(c) = y$. $\square$

This result proves useful in showing that certain types of equations have solutions. In fact, one natural connection between the intermediate value theorem and game theory is through fixed point theorems – which are typically used to establish existence of equilibria.

DEFINITION 12.19 *Given a function* $f : X \to X$ *a fixed point is a point* $x \in X$ *such that* $f(x) = x$.

A key result is Brouwer's fixed point theorem.

THEOREM 12.3 *(Brouwer) If* $X \subset \mathbb{R}^n$ *is compact, convex, and nonempty and* $f : X \to X$ *is continuous then it has a fixed point.*

Although the proof for $n > 1$ is beyond the scope of this review, one can prove the one-dimensional version with the intermediate value theorem.

PROPOSITION 12.8 *If* $f : [a, b] \to [a, b]$ *is continuous then it has a fixed point.*

Proof Define the function $g(x) = f(x) - x$. This is a continuous function from $[a, b]$ into $[a - b, b - a]$. If for some $a', b' \in [a, b]$ we have $g(a') > 0$ and $g(b') < 0$ or $g(a') < 0$ and $g(b') > 0$ then the intermediate value theorem implies that for some $c \in [a', b'] \subset [a, b]$ we have $g(c) = 0$ so that $f(c) = c$ and c is a fixed point. The remaining cases are $g(x) > 0$ for all $x \in [a, b]$ or $g(x) < 0$ for all $x \in [a, b]$. These cases involve $f(x) > x$ for all x or $g(x) < x$ for all x. But because $b = \sup\{x \in [a, b]\} = \sup\{f(x) : x \in [a, b]$ and $a = \inf\{x \in [a, b]\} = \inf\{f(x) : x \in [a, b]\}$ this is not possible. $\square$

When X is a field (recall the real number system is a field), the following condition is relevant.

DEFINITION 12.20 *A function* $f : X \to \mathbb{R}$ *with* X *a convex set is quasi-concave if the upper contour sets are convex. That is, for every* $t \in \mathbb{R}$ *and* $x, x' \in X$ *and every* $\lambda \in (0, 1)$ *it is the case that* $f(x) \geq t$ *and* $f(x') \geq t$ *implies* $f(\lambda x + (1 - \lambda)x') \geq t$. *If the last inequality is always strict the function is strictly quasi-concave.*

A useful property of quasi-concave objective functions is easily obtained.

THEOREM 12.4 *If* X *is convex and* $f : X \to \mathbb{R}$ *is strictly quasi-concave then* $\arg\max_{x \in X}\{f(x)\}$ *contains at most one point.*

6. Correspondences**

Correspondences may have a number of important properties.

DEFINITION 12.21 *A correspondence* $f : X \twoheadrightarrow Y$ *is convex valued if for each* $x \in X$ *the set* $f(x)$ *is convex.*

Notions of continuity may also be extended to correspondences. First we define the upper and lower images.

DEFINITION 12.22 *The upper image of* $E \subset Y$ *under* f *(denoted* $f^+(E)$*), is defined by* $f^+(E) = \{x \in X : f(x) \subset E\}$.

The upper image of a set E is the set of points in X that map into subsets of E.

DEFINITION 12.23 *The lower image of* $E \subset Y$ *under* f *(denoted* $f^-(E)$*), is defined by* $f^-(E) = \{x \in X : f(x) \cap E \neq \varnothing\}$.

The lower image of a set E is the set of points in X that map into sets that intersect E. Just as continuity of functions pertains to properties of contour sets, continuity of correspondences relates to properties of these image sets.

DEFINITION 12.24 *A correspondence* $f : X \twoheadrightarrow Y$ *is upper hemicontinuous if for each* $x \in X$, *whenever* $x \in f^+(E)$ *for* E *an open set in* Y *there exists an open ball* $B(x, \varepsilon)$ *with* $B(x, \varepsilon) \subset f^+(E)$.

DEFINITION 12.25 *A correspondence* $f : X \twoheadrightarrow Y$ *is lower hemicontinuous if for each* $x \in X$, *whenever* $x \in f^-(E)$ *for* E *an open set in* Y *there exists an open ball* $B(x, \varepsilon)$ *with* $B(x, \varepsilon) \subset f^+(E)$.

DEFINITION 12.26 *A correspondence* $f : X \twoheadrightarrow Y$ *is continuous if it is both upper and lower hemicontinuous.*

For most problems in political game theory we can settle for an alternative condition that is more intuitive than upper hemicontinuity.

DEFINITION 12.27 *A correspondence* $f : X \twoheadrightarrow Y$ *is closed at* $x \in X$ *if* $x_n \to x$, $y_n \in f(x_n)$ *and* $y_n \to y$ *imply* $y \in f(x)$. *If a correspondence is closed at each point in its domain it is closed.*

PROPOSITION 12.9 *If* Y *is compact then* $f : X \twoheadrightarrow Y$ *is upper hemicontinuous if and only if it is closed.*

The following result is an early version of what is called the theorem of the maximum. Alternative versions exist, but the basic point for formal theory is clear: the solutions of well-behaved optimization problems respond smoothly to changes in parameters.

THEOREM 12.5 *(Berge) If* $u : X \to \mathbb{R}$ *is a continuous function and* $\Gamma : Y \twoheadrightarrow X$ *such that for each* $y \in Y$, $\Gamma(y) \neq \varnothing$ *then*

(1)   the function $v : Y \to \mathbb{R}$ *defined by* $v(y) = \max\{u(x) \text{ such that } x \in \Gamma(y)\}$ *is continuous and*

(2)   the correspondence $a : Y \twoheadrightarrow X$ *defined by* $a(y) = \arg\max_{x \in \Gamma(y)}\{u(x)\}$ *is upper hemicontinuous.*

Our final result is a generalization of Brouwer's fixed point theorem.

THEOREM 12.6 *(Kakutani) Let* $A \subset R^n$ *be compact and convex and let* $f : A \twoheadrightarrow A$ *be closed (or upper hemicontinuous) with nonempty and convex values; then* f *has a fixed point,* $x \in A$ *such that* $x \in f(x)$.

7. Calculus

The preceding analysis results represent insights about problems that can be gained only on the basis of knowledge of topological features (compactness, continuity) and convexity features. With more structure and the use of calculus, more specific predictions can be obtained. In this section we provide a quick review of basic concepts of calculus that are used throughout the book. Readers are also referred to Gill (2004), Chiang (2004), and Simon and Blume (1994).

7.1. Calculus in $\mathbb{R}^1$. Many of the questions we ask in empirical political science involve what happens to variable y when we change variable x. If the variables are related by a function so that $y = f(x)$, the *derivative* allows us to describe and quantify the effects the variables have on

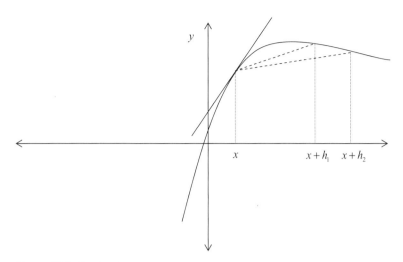

Figure 12.3. Derivatives.

one another. Suppose that $y = f(x)$. What happens if we increase x to $x + h$? The change in y per unit change in x is then given by

$$\frac{\Delta y}{\Delta x} = \frac{f(x+h) - f(x)}{h}$$

which is just the slope of the line drawn from $f(x + h)$ to $f(x)$. The difficulty of this measure is that it depends on h, as illustrated by the two heavy dotted lines corresponding to h_1 and h_2 in Figure 12.3. We prefer a measure that does not depend on h and describes the behavior of the function as close to x as possible. Such a measure is

$$\frac{dy}{dx} = \lim_{h \to 0} \frac{f(x+h) - f(x)}{h},$$

which is the *derivative* of f with respect to x. This is the solid heavy line in Figure 12.3. The notation $f'(x)$ is also used for the derivative with respect to x. It is common to write f' to denote the derivative of f. Although the numerator of this limit goes to 0, the denominator also goes to 0 so it can converge to any value. There is no guarantee that such a limit even exist. If it does exists, the function is *differentiable at x*. The limit cannot exist if f is not continuous at x. It may be continuous and not be differentiable, however. The function $f(x) = |x|$ is continuous but not differentiable at $x = 0$. For $f(x) = |x|$,

$$\lim_{h \to 0} \frac{f(x+h) - f(x)}{h} = \lim_{h \to 0} \frac{|h|}{h}.$$

Such a limit does not exist because a sequence of $h < 0$ converges to -1 whereas sequences with $h > 0$ converge to 1.

Because the derivative is a measure of the rate of change in y given a change in x, we use it to determine whether or not a function is increasing or decreasing. If $f'(x) > 0$, the function is increasing; if $f'(x) < 0$, the function is decreasing.

7.1.1. Some Special Derivatives. Many ordinary functions have derivatives with well-known functional forms. We now list these for reference.

(1) Constant: If $f(x) = c$ then $f'(x) = 0$.
(2) Linear: If $f(x) = a_0 + a_1 x$ then $f'(x) = a_1$.
(3) Polynomial: If $f(x) = ax^n$ then $f'(x) = nax^{n-1}$.
(4) Exponential: If $f(x) = e^{ax}$ then $f'(x) = ae^{ax}$.
(5) Natural logarithm: If $f(x) = a \ln(bx)$ then $f'(x) = a/x$.

7.1.2. Derivatives of Composite Functions. Taking derivatives of more complicated functions is easier if we can break them down into composite functions such as $f(x)$ and $g(x)$. The following rules help to compute such derivatives.

(1) The Addition and Subtraction Rule:

$$\frac{d(f+g)}{dx} = f' + g' \text{ and } \frac{d(f-g)}{dx} = f' - g'.$$

(2) The Product Rule:

$$\frac{d(f \cdot g)}{dx} = f' \cdot g + f \cdot g'.$$

(3) The Quotient Rule:

$$\frac{d(f/g)}{dx} = \frac{f' \cdot g - fg'}{g^2}.$$

(4) The Chain Rule: Let $z = g(y)$ and $y = f(x)$ so that $z = g(f(x))$; then

$$\frac{dz}{dx} = \frac{dz}{dy}\frac{dy}{dx} = f'(x)g'(y).$$

7.1.3. Higher Derivatives. Because derivatives of $f(x)$ (when they exist) are themselves functions of x, we can take derivatives of derivatives to learn more about the properties of the function. We represent the derivative of $f'(x)$, or the second derivative of $f(x)$ as $d^2 f/dx^2 = f''(x)$. As before, if $f'' > 0$, f' is increasing and if $f'' < 0$, f' is decreasing. The second derivative can also tell us about the behavior of the original function. If

- $f' > 0$, $f'' > 0$, then $f(x)$ is increasing at an increasing rate
- $f' > 0$, $f'' < 0$, then $f(x)$ is increasing at a decreasing rate
- $f' < 0$, $f'' > 0$, then $f(x)$ is decreasing at a decreasing rate
- $f' < 0$, $f'' < 0$, then $f(x)$ is decreasing at an increasing rate

Figure 12.4 plots a function that exhibits each of these properties on different ranges of x.

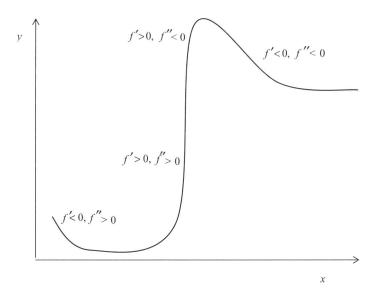

Figure 12.4. Second Derivatives.

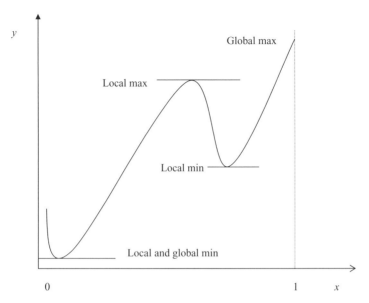

Figure 12.5. Extremum Points.

In principle, we can take nth-order derivatives, provided that they exist. We denote these as $d^n f/dx^n$ or $f^{(n)}(x)$.

7.1.4. Maxima and Minima of Functions. Much of the mathematical analysis in political game theory involves maximizing or minimizing functions. Voters maximize utility functions, and politicians maximize votes. States minimize the number of deaths in combat. The derivative is very handy in locating the local (as opposed to global) extrema of functions.

Intuitively, the local maximum (minimum) is the point where the function ceases to increase (decrease) and begins to decrease (increase). Therefore, the derivative must equal 0 unless the local extremum is global and located on the boundary of the domain. Figure 12.5 illustrates the distinctions between global and local maxima and minima as well as the intuition as to why derivatives must be 0 at local extrema. The derivative may be 0 at a point that is not a maximum or a minimum, however, as demonstrated by the function in Figure 12.6 that contains a "saddle point." Thus, a second-order condition must be satisfied to guarantee that a point satisfying the first-order condition is indeed an extremum. Approaching a local maximum, the derivative is positive, and it becomes negative after reaching it. So the derivative must be decreasing so that, the second derivative cannot be

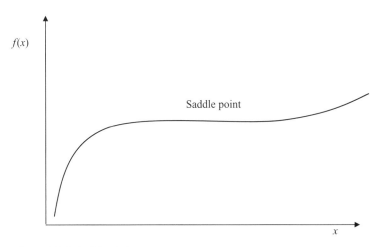

$f(x)$

Saddle point

x

Figure 12.6. Saddle Point.

positive. Conversely, at a local minimum the second derivative cannot be negative. At a saddle point, the second derivative is 0.

7.1.4.1. Some Formal Definitions. The following definitions are useful. Let $f : D \to \mathbb{R}$; then

- $f(x^*)$ is a global maximum if $f(x^*) \geq f(x)$ for all $x \in D$.
- $f(x^*)$ is a global minimum if $f(x^*) \leq f(x)$ for all $x \in D$.
- $f(x^*)$ is a local maximum if for some $\varepsilon > 0$ $|x^* - x| < \varepsilon$ implies $f(x^*) \geq f(x)$.
- $f(x^*)$ is a local minimum if for some $\varepsilon > 0$ $|x^* - x| < \varepsilon$ implies $f(x^*) \leq f(x)$.
- If $f(x^*)$ is a maximum, then x^* is known as $\arg\max_{D} f(x)$.
- If $f(x^*)$ is a minimum, then x^* is known as $\arg\min_{D} f(x)$.
- If $f'(x^*) = 0$, then x^* is a critical point of f.

EXAMPLE 12.7 *Application: Bureaucratic Resource Allocations. A bureaucrat has a budget B to spend on two activities that contribute to the output of the agency. The output of the agency is given by $O = \sqrt{x_1 x_2}$ where x_1 and x_2 are the expenditures on activities 1 and 2, respectively. Because $B = x_1 + x_2$, we can replace x_2 with $B - x_1$ so that $O = \sqrt{x_1 (B - x_1)}$. Now we wish to find the expenditure x_1 that maximizes the agency's output. First, we compute the critical values x_1^* to* *look for local maxima. The derivative of the output function is*

$$O' = \frac{\left(\frac{1}{2}B - x_1^*\right)}{\sqrt{x_1^* \left(B - x_1^*\right)}}.$$

Setting O' to 0 reveals that the only critical value is $x_1^* = B/2$. To determine whether this is indeed a maximizer, we compute the second derivative and evaluate it at x_1^*. The second derivative is $O'' = -((x_1^*(B - x_1^*))^{-1/2} - (B/2 - x_1^*)^2(x_1^*(B - x_1^*))^{-3/2})$. If we evaluate this second derivation at $x_1^* = B/2$, it reduces to $O'' = -2 < 0$. Thus, $x_1^* = B/2$ is a local maximizer and produces an output of $B/2$. It is easy to see that it is also a global maximizer because $O(x_1^*) = B/2$ is greater than $O(0) = O(B) = 0$.

7.1.5. Concavity and Convexity of Functions. Two important properties of functions are concavity and convexity. To illustrate these concepts, consider Figure 12.7. A function that curves downward as f_1 does is known as concave. We verify it is concave if for any points such as x_1 and x_2, the line between $f(x_1)$ and $f(x_2)$ lies below the function between those two points. Formally, $f : D \to \mathbb{R}$ is concave over the set D if and only if $f(\lambda x_1 + (1 - \lambda)x_2) \geq \lambda f(x_1) + (1 - \lambda)f(x_2)$ for all $\lambda \in [0, 1]$ and $x_1, x_2 \in D$.

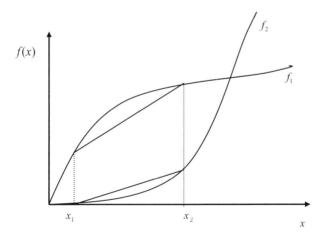

Figure 12.7. Convexity and Concavity.

Alternatively, a function that curves upward as does f_2 is convex. We can verify it is convex if for any points such as x_1 and x_2, the line between $f(x_1)$ and $f(x_2)$ lies above the function between those two points. Formally, $f : D \to \mathbb{R}$ is convex over the set D if and only if $f(\lambda x_1 + (1 - \lambda)x_2) \leq \lambda f(x_1) + (1 - \lambda) f(x_2)$ for all $\lambda \in [0, 1]$ and $x_1, x_2 \in D$. We can extend the definition to the case of strict concavity and convexity by replacing the weak inequalities with strict ones.

Concave and convex functions are critical because of the following:

- If $f : D \to \mathbb{R}$ is concave and $f'(x^*) = 0$, x^* is a global maximizer.
- If $f : D \to \mathbb{R}$ is convex and $f'(x^*) = 0$, x^* is a global minimizer.

These statements are true because if f' exists concavity implies that $f'' < 0$ and convexity implies that $f'' > 0$.

7.1.6. Integral Calculus. Let $F(x)$ be a function such that $F'(x) = f(x)$. Then we say that F is the antiderivative of $f(x)$. We typically write antiderivatives in terms of the indefinite integral:

$$F(x) = \int f(x)\, dx.$$

The laws of differentiation lead to the following results (where C is an arbitrary constant). Check by differentiating the left side of each.

(1) $\int af(x)dx = a \int f(x)\, dx.$
(2) $\int (f(x) + g(x))\, dx = \int f(x)dx + \int g(x)dx.$
(3) $\int x^n dx = \frac{x^{n+1}}{n+1} + C.$
(4) $\int \frac{1}{x}dx = \ln x + C.$
(5) $\int e^x dx = e^x + C.$
(6) $\int e^{f(x)} f'(x)dx = e^{f(x)} + C.$
(7) $\int (f(x))^n f'(x)dx = \frac{f(x)^{n+1}}{n+1} + C.$
(8) $\int \frac{f'(x)}{f(x)}dx = \ln f(x) + C.$

The most common use of the integral is to measure the area under a function. If F is the antiderivative of f, then the area underneath f

between points a and b is given by the definite integral

$$\int_a^b f(x)\,dx = F(b) - F(a).$$

7.1.7. Differentiation of the Definite Integral. The rules for differentiating definite integrals are the following

(1) $\frac{d}{dx}\int_a^b f(x)dx = \int_a^b f'(x)dx.$

(2) $\frac{d}{db}\int_a^b f(x)dx = f(b).$

(3) $\frac{d}{da}\int_a^b f(x)dx = -f(a).$

(4) $\frac{d}{d\alpha}\int_{a(\alpha)}^{b(\alpha)} f(x(\alpha))dx = \int_a^b f'(x(\alpha))\frac{\partial x}{\partial \alpha}dx + f(b(\alpha))\frac{\partial b}{\partial \alpha} - f(a(\alpha))\frac{\partial a}{\partial \alpha}.$

The last, most general, rule is sometimes referred to as Leibnitz's rule after one of the creators of the calculus, Gottfried Wilhelm Leibnitz.

7.2. Calculus of Several Variables*. This section presupposes some basic familiarity with matrix notation. A matrix is a rectangular array of numbers such as

$$A = \begin{bmatrix} a_{11} & a_{12} & a_{13} \\ a_{21} & a_{22} & a_{23} \end{bmatrix}.$$

It is convenient to refer to an arbitrary matrix element by reference to its row and column number (note the location of a_{23}, for example). A column vector is a column or numbers such as

$$B = \begin{bmatrix} b_1 \\ b_2 \end{bmatrix}.$$

A row vector is a row of numbers such as

$$C = \begin{bmatrix} c_1 & c_2 & c_3 \end{bmatrix}.$$

The transpose of a vector or matrix is denoted by the symbol $'$. It is formed by interchanging columns and rows. Thus,

$$A' = \begin{bmatrix} a_{11} & a_{21} \\ a_{12} & a_{22} \\ a_{13} & a_{23} \end{bmatrix}$$

and

$$B' = \begin{bmatrix} b_1 & b_2 \end{bmatrix}.$$

For this section we use boldface letters to denote vectors and non boldface letters to denote scalars. Consider the function $y = f(\mathbf{x})$. It is often useful to know how y changes given a change in one of the elements of $\mathbf{x}$. Typically, we look at the partial effects of x_i: that, is how does a change in x_i affect y if the other elements of $\mathbf{x}$ are held constant? This is equivalent to examining the behavior of the function within a given "slice." Formally, the partial derivative is

$$\frac{\partial f}{\partial x_i} = \lim_{h \to 0} \frac{f(\mathbf{x} + \mathbf{h}_i) - f(\mathbf{x})}{h}$$

where $\mathbf{h}_i$ is a vector of 0s with an h in the ith position. Partial derivatives are as easy to compute as regular derivatives because we treat all of the other variables as constants.

EXAMPLE 12.8 *Let* $f(x_1, x_2) = x_1/x_2$. *Then* $\partial f/\partial x_1 = 1/x_2$, $\partial f/\partial x_2 = -x_1/x_2^2$.

We often collect partial derivatives in a vector

$$D_{\mathbf{x}} f = \left(\frac{\partial f}{\partial x_1}, \frac{\partial f}{\partial x_2}, \dots, \frac{\partial f}{\partial x_n} \right)'.$$

This vector is called the gradient vector of f at $\mathbf{x}$. The gradient vector evaluated at $\mathbf{x}$ describes the behavior of the function near $\mathbf{x}$.

7.2.1. Higher-Order and Cross-Partial Derivatives. Just as with functions of a single variable, we can use higher-order partial derivatives to characterize the behavior of partial derivatives. The second partial derivative with respect to x_i is written as

$$\frac{\partial}{\partial x_i}\left(\frac{\partial f}{\partial x_i}\right) = \frac{\partial^2 f}{\partial x_i^2}.$$

We can interpret this quantity exactly the same way as in the case of a single variable. In the case of more than a single variable, however, we may want to know how a partial derivative changes when other variables change (i.e., how does changing x_j affect the partial derivative with respect to x_i?). We write the cross-partial derivative as

$$\frac{\partial}{\partial x_j}\left(\frac{\partial f}{\partial x_i}\right) = \frac{\partial^2 f}{\partial x_j \partial x_i}.$$

EXAMPLE 12.9 *Let* $f(x_1, x_2) = x_1/x_2$. *Then* $\partial^2 f/\partial x_1^2 = 0$, $\partial^2 f/\partial x_2^2 = -2x_1/x_2^3$, $\partial^2 f/(\partial x_1 \partial x_2) = -1/x_2^2$, *and* $\partial^2 f/(\partial x_2 \partial x_1) = -1/(x_2^2)$.

Note that $\partial^2 f/(\partial x_1 \partial x_2) = \partial^2 f/(\partial x_2 \partial x_1)$. This is true generally as $\partial^2 f/(\partial x_i \partial x_j) = \partial^2 f/(\partial x_j \partial x_i)$. Thus, the order of partial differentiation does not matter.

The Hessian matrix represents the collection of second- and cross-derivatives.

$$H(\mathbf{x}) = \begin{bmatrix} \frac{\partial^2 f(\mathbf{x})}{\partial x_1^2} & \frac{\partial^2 f(\mathbf{x})}{\partial x_1 \partial x_2} & \cdots & \frac{\partial^2 f(\mathbf{x})}{\partial x_1 \partial x_n} \\ \frac{\partial^2 f(\mathbf{x})}{\partial x_2 \partial x_1} & \frac{\partial^2 f(\mathbf{x})}{\partial x_2^2} & \cdots & \frac{\partial^2 f(\mathbf{x})}{\partial x_2 \partial x_n} \\ \vdots & \vdots & \ddots & \vdots \\ \frac{\partial^2 f(\mathbf{x})}{\partial x_n \partial x_1} & \frac{\partial^2 f(\mathbf{x})}{\partial x_n \partial x_2} & \cdots & \frac{\partial^2 f(\mathbf{x})}{\partial x_n^2} \end{bmatrix}$$

7.2.2. Implicit Function Theorem. Many equilibrium characterizations involve finding a value of $\mathbf{x} \in \mathbb{R}^n$ that solves a system such as

$$f(\mathbf{x}; \mathbf{y}) = 0$$

for a particular value of the parameters $\mathbf{y} \in \mathbb{R}^k$. When a closed form solution for the solution $\mathbf{x}^*$ exists, we can solve for an explicit relationship of the form

$$\mathbf{x}^* = g(\mathbf{y}).$$

If g is a differentiable function then comparative statics analysis (finding out how changes in **y** affect **x**) is straightforward. Sometimes, however, we can prove that a solution $\mathbf{x}^*$ exists for each **y** but we cannot directly solve for the function $g(\cdot)$. For example, a fixed point theorem may tell us that a solution to the system $f(\mathbf{x}; \mathbf{y}) = 0$ exists, but we may not be able to solve analytically for the vector **x** as a function of **y**.

Under suitable conditions the implicit function theorem lets us implicitly characterize the derivative $D_\mathbf{y}\mathbf{x}^*$. First, we present the result in the case of one endogenous and one exogenous variable.

THEOREM 12.7 *(Low-Dimension Implicit Function Theorem) Let $x^* \in \mathbb{R}$ solve $f(x, y) = 0$ at $y \in \mathbb{R}$. If $f(\cdot, \cdot)$ is continuously differentiable and $\partial f(x^*, y^*)/\partial x \neq 0$ then for some open set A containing x^* and an open set B containing y^* there exists a continuously differentiable function $\phi : B \to A$ with $f(\phi(y), y) = 0$. The derivative of this function at y^* is given by*

$$\frac{\partial \phi(y^*)}{\partial y} = -\frac{\frac{\partial f(x^*, y^*)}{\partial y}}{\frac{\partial f(x^*, y^*)}{\partial x}}.$$

To present the result for the more general case, we consider endogenous vectors of the form $\mathbf{x} = (x_1, \ldots, x_n) \in \mathbb{R}^n$ and exogenous vectors of the form $\mathbf{y} = (y_1, \ldots, y_k) \in \mathbb{R}^k$. Suppose the system $\mathbf{f}(\mathbf{x}, \mathbf{y}) = 0$ is of the form

$$f_1(x_1, \ldots, x_n; y_1, \ldots, y_k) = 0$$

$$\cdot$$
$$\cdot$$
$$\cdot$$

$$f_n(x_1, \ldots, x_n; y_1, \ldots, y_k) = 0.$$

The n-by-n Jacobian matrix of this system with respect to the endogenous variables is then the n-by-n matrix that stacks up the transpose of the gradient vectors:

$$J = D_\mathbf{x}\mathbf{f}(\mathbf{x}^*, \mathbf{y}^*) = \begin{bmatrix} D_\mathbf{x} f_1' \\ \cdot \\ \cdot \\ D_\mathbf{x} f_n' \end{bmatrix}.$$

When manipulating matrices, the analog to dividing is called taking the inverse. For an arbitrary $n \times n$ matrix, M, the matrix M^{-1} satisfies the equation $MM^{-1} = I$ where I is the identity matrix containing 1s on the main diagonal and 0s everywhere else. A matrix is said to be nonsingular if its inverse exists. We refer readers to Chiang (2004) and Simon and Blume (1994) or an introductory linear algebra book for details on the computation of inverses.

The $n \times k$ matrix

$$D_{\mathbf{y}}\mathbf{f}(\mathbf{x}^*, \mathbf{y}^*) = \begin{bmatrix} D_{\mathbf{y}} f_1' \\ \cdot \\ \cdot \\ \cdot \\ D_{\mathbf{y}} f_n' \end{bmatrix}$$

consists of the transposes of the derivatives of the equations in $\mathbf{f}(\cdot, \cdot)$ with respect to the exogenous variables.

THEOREM 12.8 *(Implicit Function Theorem) Let* $\mathbf{x}^* \in \mathbb{R}^n$ *solve* $\mathbf{f}(\mathbf{x}, \mathbf{y}) = 0$ *at* $\mathbf{y} \in \mathbb{R}^k$. *If* $f_1(\cdot)$ *through* $f_n(\cdot)$ *are continuously differentiable in each coordinate of* $\mathbf{x}$ *and* $\mathbf{y}$ *and the Jacobian matrix of the system with respect to the endogenous variables is nonsingular, then for some open set A containing* $\mathbf{x}^*$ *and an open set B containing y^* there exists a continuously differentiable function* $\phi : B \to A$ *with* $\mathbf{f}(\phi(\mathbf{y}), \mathbf{y}) = 0$. *The derivative of this function at* $\mathbf{y}^*$ *is given by the $n \times k$ matrix,*

$$D_{\mathbf{y}}\phi(\mathbf{y}^*) = -\left[D_{\mathbf{x}}\mathbf{f}(\mathbf{x}^*, \mathbf{y}^*) \right]^{-1} D_{\mathbf{y}}\mathbf{f}(\mathbf{x}^*, \mathbf{y}^*).$$

7.2.3. Optimization in $\mathbb{R}^n$. Recall that if we want to maximize $f : \mathbb{R} \to \mathbb{R}$, we solve for values of x for which $f'(x^*) = 0$.[1] If this condition does not hold, some other x in a neighborhood of x^* produces a larger value of $f(x)$.

The same logic holds for optimizing multivariate functions. In this case the derivative with respect to each element of $\mathbf{x}$ must be 0. Suppose $\partial f / \partial x_i > 0$. Then the value of the function increases for a small increase in x_i and decreases for a small decrease. Similarly, we cannot have $\partial f / \partial x_i < 0$ at an interior optimum. It is clear that a necessary condition

---

[1] Since the domain is $\mathbb{R}$, we need not worry about corner solutions.

for $\mathbf{x}^*$ to optimize $f : \mathbb{R}^n \to \mathbb{R}$ is that

$$Df(\mathbf{x}^*) = \mathbf{0}.$$

The second-order conditions for maxima and minima are based on the Hessian matrix and require some more advanced concepts in matrix algebra. The sufficient condition for a maximum (minimum) is that H is positive (negative) definite.

DEFINITION 12.28 *A $n \times n$ matrix M is positive definite if for all vectors $v \in \mathbb{R}^n$, $v'Mv > 0$. It is negative definite if $v'Mv < 0$ for all $v \in \mathbb{R}^n$. A matrix is positive or negative semidefinite if the inequalities are weak.*

We first state the following results for $\mathbb{R}^2$.

THEOREM 12.9 $\mathbf{x}^* \in \mathbb{R}^2$ *is a local maximizer if $Df(\mathbf{x}^*) = \mathbf{0}$, $\partial^2 f/\partial x_1^2 < 0$, $\partial^2 f/\partial x_2^2 < 0$, and $(\partial^2 f/\partial x_1^2)(\partial^2 f/\partial x_2^2) > (\partial^2 f/(\partial x_1 \partial x_2))^2$.*

THEOREM 12.10 $\mathbf{x}^* \in \mathbb{R}^2$ *is a local minimizer if $Df(\mathbf{x}^*) = \mathbf{0}$, $\partial^2 f/\partial x_1^2 > 0$, $\partial^2 f/\partial x_2^2 > 0$, and $(\partial^2 f/\partial x_1^2)(\partial^2 f/\partial x_2^2) > (\partial^2 f/(\partial x_1 \partial x_2))^2$.*

The higher-dimensional versions are similar.

THEOREM 12.11 $\mathbf{x}^* \in \mathbb{R}^n$ *is a local maximizer if $Df(\mathbf{x}^*) = \mathbf{0}$ and the Hessian matrix $H(\mathbf{x}^*)$ is negative definite.*

THEOREM 12.12 $\mathbf{x}^* \in \mathbb{R}^n$ *is a local minimizer if $Df(\mathbf{x}^*) = \mathbf{0}$ and the Hessian matrix $H(\mathbf{x}^*)$ is positive definite.*

If $Df(\mathbf{x}^*) = \mathbf{0}$ and the Hessian matrix $H(\mathbf{x}^*)$ is negative semidefinite, it is possible that $\mathbf{x}$ is a local maximum. But this need not be true. A similar statement holds for positive semidefinite Hessians. The following necessity results are, however, true.

THEOREM 12.13 *If $\mathbf{x}^* \in \mathbb{R}^n$ is a local maximizer and the objective function is twice differentiable then the Hessian matrix $H(\mathbf{x}^*)$ is negative semidefinite.*

THEOREM 12.14 *If $\mathbf{x}^* \in \mathbb{R}^n$ is a local minimizer and the objective function is twice differentiable then the Hessian matrix $H(\mathbf{x}^*)$ is positive semidefinite.*

EXAMPLE 12.10 *Party Resource Allocations. Suppose a political party wants to allocate its funds across two elections. The party values each of these seats by W_1 and W_2, respectively (the party gets 0 for each seat it loses). Let $x_i/(1 + x_i)$ be the probability that the party wins seat i where x_i is the amount of money it spends in election i. The cost of spending x_i is simply x_i. Therefore, the party wishes to choose (x_1, x_2) to maximize*

$$\frac{x_1}{1 + x_1} W_1 + \frac{x_2}{1 + x_2} W_2 - x_1 - x_2.$$

The first-order conditions are

$$\frac{W_1}{(1 + x_1)^2} - 1 = 0$$

$$\frac{W_2}{(1 + x_2)^2} - 1 = 0,$$

and the Hessian matrix of second derivatives is

$$\begin{bmatrix} -\frac{W_1}{(1 \mid x_1)^3} & 0 \\ 0 & -\frac{W_2}{(1+x_2)^3} \end{bmatrix}.$$

From the first-order conditions, there are four possible critical values: $\left(-\sqrt{W_1} - 1, -\sqrt{W_2} - 1\right)$, $\left(\sqrt{W_1} - 1, -\sqrt{W_2} - 1\right)$, $\left(-\sqrt{W_1} - 1, \sqrt{W_2} - 1\right)$, *and* $\left(\sqrt{W_1} - 1, \sqrt{W_2} - 1\right)$. *The second-order conditions require* $-W_i(1 + x_i)^3 < 0$ *or* $x_i > -1$. *Thus, because* $W_i > 0$, *the only critical value that satisfies the second-order condition is* $\left(\sqrt{W_1} - 1, \sqrt{W_2} - 1\right)$.

7.2.4. Concave and Convex Functions. The definitions of concavity and convexity generalize easily to $\mathbb{R}^n$.

DEFINITION 12.29 *Let $U \subseteq \mathbb{R}^n$ and $f : U \to \mathbb{R}$. The function f is concave if for all $\mathbf{x}, \mathbf{y} \in U$ and $\lambda \in [0, 1]$, $f(\lambda \mathbf{x} + (1 - \lambda)\mathbf{y}) \geq \lambda f(\mathbf{x}) + (1 - \lambda) f(\mathbf{y})$.*

DEFINITION 12.30 *Let $U \subseteq \mathbb{R}^n$ and $f : U \to \mathbb{R}$. The function f is convex if for all $\mathbf{x}, \mathbf{y} \in U$ and $\lambda \in [0, 1]$, $f(\lambda \mathbf{x} + (1 - \lambda)\mathbf{y}) \leq \lambda f(\mathbf{x}) + (1 - \lambda)f(\mathbf{y})$.*

Just as before, concavity guarantees that the critical values generate global maxima while convexity guarantees global minima.

THEOREM 12.15 *Let $f : U \to \mathbb{R}$ be be a twice-differentiable function where U is an open and convex subset of $\mathbb{R}^n$. If f is a concave function on U and $Df(\mathbf{x}^*) = 0$ for $\mathbf{x}^* \in U$, then $\mathbf{x}^*$ is a global maximizer of f on U. If f is a convex function on U and $Df(\mathbf{x}^*) = 0$ for $\mathbf{x}^* \in U$, then $\mathbf{x}^*$ is a global minimizer of f on U.*

7.2.5. Constrained Maximization

7.2.5.1. Equality Constraints. In a number of contexts in political game theory, it is useful to solve constrained maximization problems. Such constraints may arise either from feasibility constraints on agents' choices or from the behavior of other agents. Such problems take the form of

$$\max f(\mathbf{x}) \text{ subject to } g_1(\mathbf{x}) = 0$$
$$g_2(\mathbf{x}) = 0$$
$$\ldots$$
$$g_k(\mathbf{x}) = 0$$

where the function $f : \mathbb{R}^n \to \mathbb{R}^1$ and each of the functions $g_j : \mathbb{R}^n \to \mathbb{R}$ are twice differentiable. The solution to this constrained optimization problem can be found by setting up and solving a related unconstrained optimization. The trick is to incorporate the constraints as part of the objective function.

The Langrangian

$$L(\mathbf{x}, \lambda) = f(\mathbf{x}) - \sum_{j=1}^{k} \lambda_j g_j(\mathbf{x})$$

represents this translated objective function. It depends on both the choice variables $\mathbf{x}$ from our original problem and a new vector of k variables. These new variables are the constraint multipliers (as each constraint gets its own multiplier). The ordinal problem has a real-valued objective function and k constraints and the translation is an objective function formed by the sum of $k + 1$ real-valued functions. The first-order conditions for optimization of the Lagrangian are

$$\frac{\partial f(\mathbf{x})}{\partial x_i} = \sum_{j=1}^{k} \lambda_j \frac{\partial g_j(\mathbf{x})}{\partial x_i} \text{ for each } i = 1, \dots, n$$

$$g_j(\mathbf{x}) = 0 \text{ for each } j = 1, \dots, k.$$

Analysis of the first n conditions yields necessary conditions on $\mathbf{x}$ for a solution to the constrained problem. More formally:

THEOREM 12.16 *(Lagrangian Theorem) Assume that the gradient vectors of the k constraint functions are linearly independent vectors. If $\mathbf{x}^*$ solves the constrained problem then there exists a vector of Lagrangian multipliers $\lambda \in R^k$ for which $(\mathbf{x}^*, \lambda)$ solve the preceding first-order conditions.*

The motivation for translating the constrained problem to this unconstrained problem is best obtained by inspecting the first n first-order conditions of the Lagrangian. They require that any increase in the value of f obtained by changing $\mathbf{x}$ (from a solution to the first-order conditions) results in a corresponding change in the value of at least one of the constraint functions g. In other words, if $\mathbf{x}$ solves the Lagrangian then any improvement in f would be at the expense of violating the constraint. The independence requirement for the procedure to work is that the Jacobian of the constraints with respect to the variables x have rank k (that is, the gradient vectors of the k constraints are independent). Without this *constraint qualification* condition it need not be the case that a change in $\sum_{j=1}^{k} \lambda_j (\partial g_j(\mathbf{x})/\partial x_i)$ corresponds to a violation of the constraint.

EXAMPLE 12.11 *Party Resource Allocations Revisited. Suppose the party has a budget constraint that it must satisfy when allocating funds across districts. Now the party wishes to maximize*

$$\frac{x_1}{1 + x_1} W_1 + \frac{x_2}{1 + x_2} W_2$$

subject to $B = x_1 + x_2$.

The Lagrangian is $x_1 W_1/(1 + x_1) + x_2 W_2/(1 + x_2) + \lambda (x_1 + x_2 - B)$. The first-order conditions are $W_1/(1 + x_1)^2 - \lambda = 0$, $W_2/(1 + x_2)^2 - \lambda = 0$, and $x_1 + x_2 = B$. The first two conditions imply that

$$\frac{W_2}{W_1} = \frac{(1 + x_2)^2}{(1 + x_1)^2} \ or \ \sqrt{\frac{W_2}{W_1}} = \frac{(1 + x_2)}{(1 + x_1)}.$$

Together with the budget constraint, we have two equations and two unknowns. Using the positive roots, we have

$$+\sqrt{\frac{W_2}{W_1}} = \frac{(1 + B - x_1)}{(1 + x_1)},$$

which implies that

$$x_1^* = \frac{1 + B - \sqrt{\frac{W_2}{W_1}}}{\sqrt{\frac{W_2}{W_1}} + 1}$$

and

$$x_2^* = \frac{1 + \sqrt{\frac{W_2}{W_1}} (B - 1)}{\sqrt{\frac{W_2}{W_1}} + 1}.$$

7.2.5.2. Inequality Constraints. The problem considered earlier requires that the constraints are of the form $g_j (\mathbf{x}) = 0$. A larger class of optimization problems require only that a system of inequality or equality constraints be satisfied. The general problem is then

$$\max f (\mathbf{x}) \text{ subject to } g_j (\mathbf{x}) = 0 \text{ for } j = 1, \ldots, k$$
$$h_t (\mathbf{x}) \le 0 \text{ for } t = 1, \ldots, w.$$

Again we assume that all of the relevant functions are differentiable. The Kuhn-Tucker conditions are similar to the Lagrangian conditions except in the way the inequality constraints are treated. The relevant translated first-order conditions are

$$\frac{\partial f(\mathbf{x})}{\partial x_i} = \sum_{j=1}^{k} \lambda_j \frac{\partial g_j(\mathbf{x})}{\partial x_i} + \sum_{t=1}^{w} \lambda_t \frac{\partial h_t(\mathbf{x})}{\partial x_i} \text{ for each } i = 1, \dots, n$$

$$g_j(\mathbf{x}) = 0 \text{ for each } j = 1, \dots, k$$

$$\lambda_t h_t(\mathbf{x}) = 0 \text{ for each } t = 1, \dots, w.$$

The difference is that for inequality constraints, either the constraint binds (in the sense that $h_t(\mathbf{x}) = 0$) or the multiplier λ_t is 0.

7.2.5.3. The Envelope Theorem*. In applications the objective function or the constraints may also depend on exogenous variables $\mathbf{y} = (\mathbf{y}_1, \dots, y_l, \dots, y_z) \in \mathbb{R}^z$. Consider the problem

$$\max f(\mathbf{x}; \mathbf{y}) \text{ subject to } g_j(\mathbf{x}; \mathbf{y}) = 0 \text{ for } j = 1, \dots, k$$

$$h_t(\mathbf{x}; \mathbf{y}) \le 0 \text{ for } t = 1, \dots, w.$$

By $v(\mathbf{y})$ we denote the value function that is a mapping $v : \mathbb{R}^z \to \mathbb{R}^1$ with $v(\mathbf{y}) = f(\mathbf{x}^*(\mathbf{y}); \mathbf{y})$ where $\mathbf{x}^*(\mathbf{y})$ is a solution to the preceding optimization problem. The theorem of the maximum indicated that under suitable conditions the value function is continuous. We can use calculus to gain more insight into the dependence of the value function on the exogenous parameters.

THEOREM 12.17 *Assume that $v(\mathbf{y}')$ is differentiable at $\mathbf{y}'$ and that $(\mathbf{x}^*(\mathbf{y}'), \lambda(y'))$ solve the preceding problem and on some open set A containing $\mathbf{x}^*(\mathbf{y}')$ and some open set B containing $\mathbf{y}'$ the set of constraints that bind on the solution $x^* : B \to A$ is constant, then for each $i = 1, \dots, n$*

$$\frac{\partial v(\mathbf{y}')}{\partial y_l} = \frac{\partial f(\mathbf{x}^*(\mathbf{y}'); \mathbf{y})}{\partial y_l} - \sum_{j=1}^{k} \lambda_j \frac{\partial g_j(\mathbf{x}^*(\mathbf{y}'); \mathbf{y})}{\partial y_l} - \sum_{t=1}^{w} \lambda_t \frac{\partial h_t(\mathbf{x}^*(\mathbf{y}'); \mathbf{y})}{\partial y_l}.$$

The novelty of this result is that in characterizing $\partial v(\mathbf{y}')/\partial y_l$ we do not need to worry about $D_{y_l}\mathbf{x}^*(\mathbf{y})$.

EXAMPLE 12.12 *A party decides how to allocate its resources y over k electoral districts. Assume that it selects $r_i \in \mathbb{R}^1$ for districts $i = 1, 2, \dots, k$. It can only spend y on the election, so the constraint $y - \sum_{i=1}^{k} r_i \ge 0$ must be satisfied. Let $f(r) : \mathbb{R}^k \to \mathbb{R}^1$ denote the party's* *payoff from a particular allocation of resources. The envelope theorem says that if $v(y)$ is the value function from solving this problem and λ is the multiplier from the constraint, then $\partial v(y)/\partial y = \lambda$. Thus, the multiplier is the marginal value of a local increase in the party's resources.*

7.2.6. Multivariate Integrals. We calculate the area under multivariate functions with the use of the multivariate definite integral

$$\int\limits_{a_1}^{b_1} \cdots \int\limits_{a_n}^{b_n} f(x_1, \ldots, x_n)\, dx_1 \ldots dx_n.$$

Multivariate integrals are calculated by sequentially integrating with respect to one variable while holding the remaining constant. Suppose that we integrated with respect to x_1. Let $F_1(x_1, \ldots, x_n)$ be the partial antiderivative with respect to x_1; then

$$\int\limits_{a_1}^{b_1} \cdots \int\limits_{a_n}^{b_n} f(x_1, \ldots, x_n)\, dx_1 \ldots dx_n$$

$$= \int\limits_{a_2}^{b_2} \cdots \int\limits_{a_n}^{b_n} F_1(b_1, \ldots, x_n)\, dx_2 \ldots dx_n$$

$$- \int\limits_{a_2}^{b_2} \cdots \int\limits_{a_n}^{b_n} F_1(a_1, \ldots, x_n)\, dx_2 \ldots dx_n$$

We continue this iterative process by taking the partial antiderivative of F_1 with respect to x_2, and so on. It does not matter which definite partial integral we compute first.

EXAMPLE 12.13 *Consider $\int_1^2 \int_{1/2}^1 x^2 y\, dx\, dy$. Now we begin by computing $F_1(x, y) = x^3 y/3$. Then*

$$\int\limits_1^2 \int\limits_{\frac{1}{2}}^1 x^2 y\, dx\, dy = \int\limits_{\frac{1}{2}}^1 \frac{8}{3} y\, dy - \int\limits_{\frac{1}{2}}^1 \frac{1}{3} y\, dy$$

$$= \frac{8}{3}\left[\frac{1}{2} - \frac{1}{8}\right] - \frac{1}{3}\left[\frac{1}{2} - \frac{1}{8}\right] = \frac{7}{8}.$$

8. Probability Theory

As we saw in Chapter 3, models of decision making under uncertainty are heavily dependent upon probability theory. In this section, we outline the basics of probability and review some key results.

8.1. Outcomes and Events. The building blocks of probability theory are outcomes and events. Let S be the set of all possible outcomes that can be generated by a random process. Such a set is known as a *sample space*. A generic element $s \in S$ is called an *outcome*.

EXAMPLE 12.14 *Flipping two coins:* $S = \{HH, HT, TH, TT\}$.

EXAMPLE 12.15 *Unemployment rates:* $S = [0, 100]$.

The first example is that of a discrete sample space because the number of outcomes is finite, whereas the latter is a continuous sample space as the number of outcomes is infinite.

Given a sample space, we define an *event* as a subset $A \subseteq S$. Thus, an event is any combination of outcomes.

EXAMPLE 12.16 $A = \{TH, HT\}$: *"Flip 2 is different from flip 1."*

EXAMPLE 12.17 $A = [4, 13]$: *"Unemployment is between 4 percent and 13 percent."*

8.2. The Axioms of Probability Theory. Probability theory concerns itself with the likelihood that various events occur. We let $Pr(A)$ denote the probability that event A occurs. Classical probability theory is based on the following axiomatic statements about $\Pr(A)$:

AXIOM 12.1. *For any event* A, $\Pr(A) \geq 0$.

AXIOM 12.2. $\Pr(S) = 1$.

AXIOM 12.3. *Let* $A_1, A_2, \ldots$, *be a possibly infinite list of disjoint events; then* $\Pr\left(\bigcup_{i=1}^{\infty} A_i\right) = \sum_{i=1}^{\infty} \Pr(A_i)$.

Axiom 1 says that the probability of any event is nonnegative, and axiom 2 says that the probability that some event occurs is 1. Axiom 3 concerns the probability of mutually exclusive or *disjoint* events. It states that the probability of a set of mutually exclusive events is equal to the sum of the probabilities of the individual events. These axioms lead directly to a number of useful properties of probabilities.

The probability of the null event is 0.

THEOREM 12.18 $\Pr(\emptyset) = 0$.

Axiom 3 extends directly to the case of a finite number of disjoint events.

THEOREM 12.19 *Let A_1, A_2, ..., A_n be a finite list of disjoint events; then* $\Pr\left(\bigcup_{i=1}^n A_i\right) = \sum_{i=1}^n \Pr(A_i)$.

The previous theorem plus axioms 1 and 2 imply that the probabilities of an event and the probability of its complement sum to 1.

THEOREM 12.20 *Let $S|A$ be the complement of A; then* $\Pr(A) + \Pr(S|A) = 1$.

A direct implication of the previous theorem is that the probability of any event is less than 1 (weakly).

THEOREM 12.21 *For any event A, $0 \le \Pr(A) \le 1$.*

If the outcomes associated with event B are a proper subset of those associated with event A, the probability of event A has to be at least as large as the probability of B.

THEOREM 12.22 *If $B \subset A$, then $\Pr(A) \ge \Pr(B)$.*

The next two theorems concern the probability of a union of events. With just two events A and B, we can decompose $A \cup B$ into three disjoint sets $A \backslash B$, $B \backslash A$, and $A \cap B$. Thus, $Pr(A \cup B) = \Pr(A \backslash B) + \Pr(B \backslash A) + \Pr(A \cap B)$ from Theorem 12.19. Theorem 12.19 also suggests that $\Pr(A) = \Pr(A \backslash B) + \Pr(A \cap B)$ and $\Pr(B) = \Pr(B \backslash A) + \Pr(A \cap B)$. These results produce Theorem 12.23.

THEOREM 12.23 *For any two events A and B, $Pr(A \cup B) = Pr(A) + Pr(B) - Pr(A \cap B)$.*

Theorem 12.24 is a straightforward generalization of Theorem 12.23.

THEOREM 12.24 *For any n events $A_1, A_2, \ldots, A_n$,*

$$\Pr\left(\bigcup_{i=1}^{n} A_i\right) = \sum_{i=1}^{n}\left[\Pr(A_i) - \sum_{j>i}^{n}\Pr(A_i \cap A_j)\right.$$
$$\left. + \sum_{k>j>i}^{n}\Pr(A_i \cap A_j \cap A_k) - \cdots\right].$$

8.2.1. Dependence and Conditional Probability. We now turn to the question of how the likelihoods of distinct events are related. The main concern is whether the occurrence of one event affects the probability of another. Consider two events A and B. Suppose we know that event B has occurred; what is the probability that event A occurs?

One obvious possibility is that the likelihoods of the events are unrelated. We say that two events A and B are *independent* if $\Pr(A \cap B) = \Pr(A)\Pr(B)$. When events are independent, the realization of one event has no effect on the probability of the other. Suppose that event B occurs; then $\Pr(A \cap B)$ is simply $\Pr(A)$. Thus, the occurrence of A is not affected by the occurrence of B. This logic extends to a general definition of independence.

DEFINITION 12.31 *Let $A_1, \ldots, A_n$ be a set of events. They are independent if $\Pr\left(\bigcap_{i=1}^{n} A_i\right) = \prod_{i=1}^{n}\Pr(A_i)$.*

For this to be true, any subset of the events must also be independent. See DeGroot and Schervish (2001) for an example where three events are pairwise independent but are not independent.

Now we turn to cases where there is dependency among events. A key concept for analyzing such relationships is that of *conditional probability*. Given two events A and B, the conditional probability of A given B is the probability that A occurs given that B has occurred. We denote the conditional probability of A given event B as

$$\Pr(A|B) = \frac{\Pr(A \cap B)}{\Pr(B)} \text{ assuming } \Pr(B) > 0.$$

Note that if A and B are independent, $\Pr(A|B) = \Pr(A)$. It is also easy to see that conditional probabilities must satisfy $\Pr(A \cap B) = \Pr(A|B)\Pr(B) = \Pr(B|A)\Pr(A)$.

8.3. Bayes' Rule. One of the most important uses of probability theory in political game theory is that it makes predictions about how agents use observed events to make assessments about the probability of unobserved events. Bayes' rule specifies exactly how such assessments are formed. Stating and proving this theorem require an additional definition. A partition is simply a group of mutually exclusive events that cover the entire sample space.

DEFINITION 12.32 *A partition of a sample space S is a set of disjoint events $A_1, \ldots, A_k$ such that $\bigcup_{i=1}^{k} A_i = S$.*

We can now state Bayes' rule:

THEOREM 12.25 *If $A_1, \ldots, A_k$ form a partition of S and $\Pr(B) > 0$ then for any $B \subset S$ and $A_j \subset S$*

$$\Pr(A_j | B) = \frac{\Pr(A_j) \Pr(B | A_j)}{\sum_{i=1}^{k} \Pr(A_i) \Pr(B | A_i)}.$$

Proof The proof proceeds in a number of steps.

Claim 1: If $A_1, \ldots, A_k$ is a partition of S and B is a subset of S, the sets $A_1 \cap B, \ldots, A_k \cap B$ form a partition of B. This follows from the fact that $\bigcup_{i=1}^{k} (A_i \cap B) = \bigcup_{i=1}^{k} A_i \cap B = S \cap B = B$.

Claim 2: If $A_1, \ldots, A_k$ form a partition of S, $\Pr(B) = \sum_{i=1}^{k} \Pr(A_i \cap B)$. This is a direct application of Claim 1 and Theorem 12.19.

Claim 3: If $A_1, \ldots, A_k$ form a partition of S and $\Pr(A_i) > 0$ for all i, then $\Pr(B) = \sum_{i=1}^{k} \Pr(B | A_i) \Pr(A_i)$. This is an application of Claim 2 and the multiplication rule for conditional probabilities.

Now we prove the main result. Note that if $\Pr(B) > 0$, the definition of conditional probability implies that

$$\Pr(A_j | B) = \frac{\Pr(A_j \cap B)}{\Pr(B)}.$$

Bayes' law follows from the substitution of $\Pr(A_j \cap B) = \Pr(B | A_j) \Pr(A_j)$ for the numerator and $\Pr(B) = \sum_{i=1}^{k} \Pr(B | A_i) \Pr(A_i)$ for the denominator. □

8.4. Random Variables and Distributions. It is often convenient to use numerical representations of outcomes and events. Such representations are known as *random variables*. A real-valued random variable is simply a function that maps all possible outcomes into real numbers.

DEFINITION 12.33 *Let* $X : S \to \mathbb{R}$ *for some sample space S. Then X is a random variable that assigns a real number X(s) to each possible outcome* $s \in S$.

Using this definition of random variables, it is straightforward to define events as sets of real numbers and to define probability *distributions* over the random variables. A distribution is simply an assignment of probabilities to such events.

DEFINITION 12.34 *Let A be any subset of* $\mathbb{R}$ *and let* $\Pr(X \in A)$ *denote the probability that X is in A. Then* $\Pr(X \in A) = Pr\{s : X(s) \in A\}$. *A probability distribution of X is a specification of* $\Pr(X \in A)$ *for all* $A \subset \mathbb{R}$.

8.4.1. Discrete Distributions. A random variable X has a discrete distribution if it can take on only a finite number of outcomes: $x_1, x_2, \dots, x_k$. The set of all possible outcomes is the *support* of the distribution.

DEFINITION 12.35 *If a random variable has a discrete distribution, the probability function (pf)* f *of X is defined as* $f(x) = \Pr(X = x)$ *for any real number x.*

If x is not equal to one of the points in the support of X, then $f(x) = 0$. By the axioms of probability theory, $0 \le \sum_{i=1}^{k} f(x_i) \le 1$ and $0 \le f(x_i) \le 1$.

EXAMPLE 12.18 *The Uniform Distribution over Integers: Suppose that the value of X is equally likely to be one of k integers* $1, 2, 3, \dots, k$. *Then the pf is*

$$f(x) = \begin{cases} \frac{1}{k} \ for \ x = 1, \dots, k \\ 0 \ otherwise \end{cases}.$$

EXAMPLE 12.19 *The Binomial Distribution: Suppose an experiment succeeds with probability p and fails with probability* $1 - p$. *The pf for x successes out of n trials is given by*

$$f(x) = \begin{cases} \binom{n}{x} p^x (1-p)^{n-x} \text{ for } x = 0, \dots, n \\ 0 \text{ otherwise} \end{cases}$$

where $\binom{n}{x} = n!/(x!\,(n-x)!)$.

8.4.2. Continuous Distributions. Suppose that X takes values on a continuum. Then we say that X is a continuous random variable. If X is a continuous random variable, then there exists a nonnegative function f such that for any interval $A = [a, b]$

$$\Pr(X \in A) = \int_A f(x)dx = \int_a^b f(x)dx.$$

The function f is known as the probability density function (or pdf). It does not tell us the value of $Pr(X = x)$ (which is 0) but $f(x) = \lim_{\varepsilon \to 0} \Pr(X \in [x - \epsilon, x + \epsilon])$. Every pdf must satisfy the following:

$$f(x) \geq 0 \text{ for all } x$$

$$\int_{-\infty}^{\infty} f(x)dx = 1.$$

The set $X^s = \{x : f(x) > 0\}$ is known as the support of X.

EXAMPLE 12.20 *The Uniform Distribution on an Interval: Let a and b be two real numbers. Consider an experiment in which a point X is chosen from* $S = [a, b]$ *where the probability that X belongs to any subinterval is proportional to the length of that subinterval. This implies that the pdf must be the same on any point in S and 0 otherwise. Thus,* $\int_{-\infty}^{\infty} f(x)dx = \int_a^b f(x)dx = \int_a^b cdx = 1$. *Solving the integral for c, we obtain that* $c = 1/(b - a)$. *Thus, the pdf for the uniform distribution is*

$$f(x) = \begin{cases} \frac{1}{b-a} \text{ for } x \in [a, b] \\ 0 \text{ otherwise} \end{cases}.$$

8.4.3. The Cumulative Distribution Function. The *cumulative distribution function* (cdf) is a real-valued function that indicates for any real number x the probability that X takes on a value no greater than x:

$$F(x) = \Pr(X \le x).$$

For discrete distributions, $F(x) = \sum_{\{i : x_i < x\}} f(x_i)$. For continuous distributions, $F(x) = \int_{-\infty}^{x} f(\xi) d\xi$. Note that at any point in which F is differentiable, we have $F'(x) = f(x)$. Thus, continuous random variables with densities can be represented either by the pdf or by the cdf.

The following are some important properties of the cdf:

(1) $\Pr(X > x) = 1 - F(x)$.
(2) $\Pr(x_2 > X \ge x_1) = F(x_2) - F(x_1)$.
(3) F is nondecreasing (i.e., if $x_2 > x_1$ then $F(x_2) \ge F(x_1)$).
(4) $\lim_{x \to -\infty} F(x) = 0$ and $\lim_{x \to \infty} F(x) = 1$.
(5) F is always continuous from the right. It may be discontinuous from the left at x if x occurs with a positive probability. See Figure 12.8.

8.4.4. Bivariate Distributions. Sometimes we are concerned with the probabilities that two or more random variables, say X and Y, simultaneously take on certain values. One useful tool for analyzing two random variables is the joint distribution that characterizes the probability of pairs of realizations of X and Y.

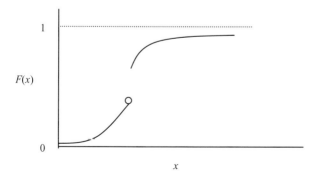

Figure 12.8. Discontinuous Cumulative Density Functions.

8.4.4.1. Discrete Bivariate Probability Functions. For the case of two discrete random variables, the bivariate probability function is given by

$$f(x, y) = \Pr\{X = x \text{ and } Y = y\}.$$

Let $x_1, \ldots, x_k$ and $y_1, \ldots, y_m$ be the support of X and Y, respectively; then $f(x, y)$ must satisfy the following properties:

(1) $\sum_{i=1}^{k} \sum_{j=1}^{m} f(x_i, y_j) = 1.$
(2) Let A be any set of combinations of $\{x_1, \ldots, x_k\}$ and $\{y_1, \ldots, y_m\}$; then $\Pr\{(x, y) \in A\} = \sum_{(x_i, y_j) \in A} f(x_i, y_j).$

8.4.4.2. Continuous Bivariate Density Functions. If X and Y are continuous random variables, the bivariate density is defined by

$$\Pr\{(x, y) \in A\} = \iint_A f(x, y)dxdy$$

for any $A \subset \mathbb{R}^2$. The bivariate pdf must satisfy the following properties:

(1) For any $(x, y) \in \mathbb{R}^2$, $f(x, y) \geq 0.$
(2) $\iint_{\mathbb{R}^2} f(x, y)dxdy = 1.$

8.4.4.3. Bivariate Distribution Function. The cdf can be generalized to bivariate distributions. The joint distribution function can be denoted by

$$F(x, y) = \Pr\{x \leq X \text{ and } y \leq Y\}.$$

We can use the joint distribution function to determine the probability that (x, y) lies in a rectangle $[a, b] \times [c, d]$

$$\begin{aligned}
\Pr(a &< X < b \ \& \ c < Y < d) \\
&= Pr(a < X < b \ \& \ Y < d) - Pr(a < X < b \ \& \ Y < c) \\
&= \Pr(X < b \ \& \ Y < d) - Pr(X < a \ \& \ Y < d) \\
&\quad - \Pr(aX < b \ \& \ Y < c) - Pr(X < a \ \& \ Y < c) \\
&= F(b, d) - F(a, d) - F(b, c) + F(a, c).
\end{aligned}$$

8.4.5. Marginal Distributions. Suppose we know the joint pdf of X and Y. We can generate the probability density of each of them individually. These distributions of the individual random variables are known as the marginal distributions. For discrete distributions, the marginal probability functions f_x and f_y are defined by

$$\Pr(X = x) = f_x(x) = \sum_y \Pr(x = X \text{ and } y = Y) = \sum_y f(x, y)$$

$$\Pr(Y = y) = f_y(y) = \sum_x \Pr(x = X \text{ and } y = Y) = \sum_x f(x, y).$$

For continuous random variables, the marginal density functions are

$$f_x(x) = \int_{-\infty}^{\infty} f(x, y) dy$$

$$f_y(y) = \int_{-\infty}^{\infty} f(x, y) dx.$$

8.5. Independent Random Variables. We know that if X and Y are independent random variables, then $\Pr(X = x \text{ and } Y = y) = \Pr(X = x) \Pr(Y = y)$. This implies that

$$F(x, y) = F_x(x) F_y(y)$$

where F_x and F_y are the marginal cdf's. It is also true that

$$f(x, y) = f_x(x) f_y(x)$$

where f_x and f_y are marginal probability (density) functions.

8.6. Conditional Distributions. Suppose that X and Y are not independent. Then we can define conditional distributions of X given Y and Y given X. The derivation of the conditional distributions follows directly from the definition of conditional probability given earlier. For the discrete case, the conditional probability functions $g_x(x|y)$ and

$g_y(y|x)$ are defined as follows:

$$g_x(x|y) = \Pr(X = x|Y = y) = \frac{\Pr(X = x \text{ and } Y = y)}{\Pr(Y = y)} = \frac{f(x, y)}{f_y(y)}$$

$$g_y(y|x) = \Pr(Y = y|X = x) = \frac{\Pr(X = x \text{ and } Y = y)}{\Pr(X = x)} = \frac{f(x, y)}{f_x(x)}.$$

For continuous random variables,

$$g_x(x|y) = \frac{f(x, y)}{f_y(y)}$$

$$g_y(y|x) = \frac{f(x, y)}{f_x(x)}.$$

8.7. The Expectation of a Random Variable. One of the most important features of any probability distribution is its *expectation* or central tendency. The expectation of a random variable is the average over all of the realizations weighted by the probability of the realizations. For discrete distributions, the expectation of X or $E(X)$ is defined as

$$E(X) = \sum_x x f(x).$$

For continuous distributions,

$$E(X) = \int_{-\infty}^{\infty} x f(x) dx = \int_{-\infty}^{\infty} x \, dF(x).$$

Often in this book, we are interested in expectations of functions of a random variable. Let $Y = r(X)$; then $E(Y) = \int_{-\infty}^{\infty} r(x) f(x) dx$.
  The expectation functions satisfy the following properties:

(1) If $Y = a + bX$, then $E(Y) = a + bE(X)$.
(2) If there exists a such that $Pr(X \geq a) = 1$, then $E(X) \geq a$. If there exists b such that $Pr(X \leq b) = 1$, $E(X) \leq b$.
(3) If $X_1, \ldots, X_n$ are random variables, $E(X_1 + \cdots + X_n) = E(X_1) + \cdots + E(X_n)$.
(4) If $X_1, \ldots, X_n$ are independent random variables, then $E\left(\prod_{i=1}^{n} X_i\right) - \prod_{i=1}^{n} E(X_i)$.

It is important to note that (4) does not hold if the random variables are not independent.

8.8. The Variance of a Random Variable. Another important property of a random variable is the extent to which it deviates from its expected value. One such measure is the variance, defined as

$$var(X) = \sigma_x^2 = E\left[(X - E(X))^2\right].$$

The variance function must satisfy a number of properties.

(1) If there exists c such that $\Pr(X = c) = 1$, $var(X) = 0$.
(2) For any constants a and b, $var(a + bX) = b^2 var(X)$.
(3) For any random variable X, $var(X) = E(X^2) - [E(X)]^2$.
(4) If $X_1, \ldots, X_n$ are independent random variables, then $var\left(\sum_{i=1}^{n} X_i\right) = \sum_{i=1}^{n} var(X_i)$.

8.9. The Median and the Mode. Two other important functions that help to summarize random variables are the median and the mode.

   The Median: Let F be the cdf of X. A point m is the median of X if and only if $Pr(X \le m) \ge .5$ and $Pr(X \ge m) \le .5$ or (for continuous distributions) $F(m) = .5$.

   The Mode: Let f be the pf or pdf of X. Then a number m is a mode of X if and only if $m \in \arg\max f(x)$.

8.10. Covariance and Correlation. Given a joint distribution over (X, Y), we are often interested in describing the relationship between X and Y. In particular, we want to know the extent to which they move together or covary. To measure this relationship, the covariance is defined as

$$cov(X, Y) = \sigma_{xy} = E\left[(X - \mu_x)(Y - \mu_y)\right]$$

where $\mu_x = E(X)$ and $\mu_y = E(Y)$.

   If X and Y move "together," the covariance is the expectation of a positive function and therefore positive. If X and Y move "against one another," the covariance is the expectation of a negative function and is therefore negative.

   The covariance has a scaling problem. Consider the covariance of X and $Z = aY + b$. It is straightforward to show that $\sigma_{xz} = a\sigma_{xy}$. Thus, the covariance depends on how variables are scaled. The correlation adjusts for this problem. Formally, the correlation between X and Y is

$$\rho_{xy} = \frac{\sigma_{xy}}{\sigma_x \sigma_y}.$$

Covariances and correlation coefficients satisfy the following properties:

(1) For any random variables X and Y with finite variances, $1 \geq \rho_{xy} \geq -1$.
(2) For any random variables X and Y, $\sigma_{xy} = E(XY) - \mu_x \mu_y$.
(3) For independent random variables X and Y with finite variances, $\sigma_{xy} = \rho_{xy} = 0$.
(4) For random variable X with a finite variance and $Y = aX + b$, $\rho_{xy} = 1$ if $a > 0$ and $\rho_{xy} = -1$ if $a < 0$.
(5) For any random variables X and Y with finite variances, $var(X + Y) = \sigma_x^2 + \sigma_y^2 + 2\sigma_{xy}$.
(6) If $X_1, \ldots, X_n$ are random variables with finite variances, $var(\sum_{i=1}^{n} X_i) = \sum_{i=1}^{n} \sigma_i^2 + 2\sum_{i=1}^{n} \sum_{j=i+1}^{n} \sigma_{ij}$.

8.11. Conditional Expectation. Often we are interested in computing expectations of random variables conditioned on the outcomes of other random variables. The conditional expectation function is defined as

$$E(Y|x) = \sum_y y g_y(y|x)$$

$$E(Y|x) = \int_{-\infty}^{\infty} y g_y(y/x) dy.$$

The conditional expectation is a function of X and has a distribution derived from the distribution of X. An important property of conditional expectations is the law of iterated expectations:

$$E(E(Y|X)) = E(Y).$$

Bibliography

Abreu, Dilip. 1988. "On the Theory of Infinitely Repeated Games with Discounting." *Econometrica* 56: 383–396.

Acemoglu, Daron, and James Robinson. 2005. *The Economic Origins of Democracy and Dictatorship.* New York: Oxford University Press.

Arrow, Kenneth J. 1951. *Social Choice and Individual Values.* New York: Wiley.

Ashworth, Scott, and Ethan Bueno de Mesquita. 2006. "Monotone Comparative Statics in Models of Politics." *American Journal of Political Science* 50(1): 214–231.

Austen-Smith, David, and Jeffrey Banks. 1988. "Elections, Coalitions, and Legislative Outcomes." *American Political Science Review* 82(2): 405–422.

Austen-Smith, David, and Jeffrey Banks. 1996. "Information Aggregation, Rationality, and the Condorcet Jury Theorems." *American Political Science Review* 90: 34–45.

Austen-Smith, David, and Jeffrey S. Banks. 1999. *Positive Political Theory I: Collective Preference.* Ann Arbor: University of Michigan Press.

Austen-Smith, David, and Jeffrey S. Banks. 2005. *Positive Political Theory II: Strategies and Structure.* Ann Arbor: University of Michigan Press.

Austen-Smith, David, and John R. Wright. 1992. "Competitive Lobbying for a Legislator's Vote." *Social Choice and Welfare* 9: 229–257.

Austen-Smith, David, and John R. Wright. 1994. "Counteractive Lobbying." *American Journal of Political Science* 38: 25–44.

Axelrod, Robert. 1970. *Conflict of Interest.* Chicago: Marham.

Axelrod, Robert. 1984. *The Evolution of Cooperation.* New York: Basic Books.

Banks, Jeffrey S. 1990. "Equilibrium Behavior in Bargaining Games." *American Journal of Political Science* 34(3): 599–614.

Banks, Jeffrey A. 1991. *Signaling Games in Political Science.* Chur, Switzerland: Harwood Academic.

Banks, Jeffrey, and Joel Sobel. 1987. "Equilibrium Selection in Signaling Games." *Econometrica* 55: 647–661.

Baron, David P. 1991. "Majoritarian Incentives, Pork Barrel Programs, and Procedural Control." *American Journal of Political Science* 35(1): 57–90.

Baron, David P., and John A. Ferejohn. 1989. "Bargaining in Legislatures." *American Political Science Review* 83(4): 1181–1206.

Baron, David P., and Adam Meirowitz. 2006. "Fully-Revealing Equilibria of Multiple-Sender Signaling and Screening Models." *Social Choice and Welfare* 26(3): 455–470.

Battaglini, Marco. 2002. "Multiple Referrals and Multidimensional Cheap Talk." *Econometrica* 70: 1379–1401.

Bellman, Richard. 1957. *Dynamic Programming*. Princeton, NJ: Princeton University Press.

Bendor, Jonathan, and Adam Meirowitz. 2004. "Spatial Models of Delegation." *American Political Science Review* 98(2): 293–310.

Berge, Claude. 1997. *Topological Spaces*. Mineola, NY: Dover.

Black, Duncan. 1958. *The Theory of Committees and Elections*. London: Cambridge University Press.

Border, Kim C. 1989. *Fixed Point Theorems with Applications to Economics and Game Theory*. New York: Cambridge University Press.

Brouwer, L. E. J. 1910. "Über Abbildung von Mannigfaltigkeiten." *Mathematische Annalen* 71: 97–115.

Calvert, Randall L. 1985. "Robustness of the Multidimensional Voting Model: Candidate Motivations, Uncertainty, and Convergence." *American Journal of Political Science* 29(1): 69–95.

Camerer, Colin F. 2003. *Behavioral Game Theory: Experiments in Strategic Interactions*. Princeton, NJ: Princeton University Press.

Cameron, Charles M. 1999. *Veto Bargaining: The Politics of Negative Power*. New York: Cambridge University Press.

Cameron, Charles M., and Nolan McCarty. 2004. "Models of Vetoes and Veto Bargaining." *Annual Review of Political Science* 7: 409–435.

Chiang, Alpha. 2004. *Fundamental Methods of Mathematical Economics*. New York: McGraw-Hill.

Clarke, Edward H. 1971. "Multi-Part Pricing of Public Goods." *Public Choice* 2: 19–33.

Cho, In-Koo, and David Kreps, 1987. "Signaling Games and Stable Equilibria." *Quarterly Journal of Economics* 102: 179–221.

Condorcet, Marquis de. (1785/1976). "Essay on the Application of Mathematics to the Theory of Decision-Making." Reprinted in K.M. Baker (ed.), *Condorcet: Selected Writtings*. Indianapolis: Bobbs-Merrill.

Cox, Gary, and Mathew D. McCubbins. 1994. *Legislative Leviathan*. Berkeley: University of California Press.

Debreu, Gerard. 1959. *The Theory of Value*. New Haven, CT: Yale University Press.

DeGroot, Morris, and Mark J. Schervish. 2001. *Probability and Statistics*. Boston: Pearson Addison Wesley.

Downs, Anthony. 1957. *An Economic Theory of Democracy* New York: Harper & Row.

Duggan, John, and Cesar Martinelli. 2001. "A Bayesian Model of Voting in Juries." *Games and Economic Behavior* 37: 259–294.

Echenique, Federico, 2002. "A Characterization of Strategic Complementarities." Working Papers 1142, California Institute of Technology, Division of the Humanities and Social Sciences.

Ellsberg, Daniel. 1961. "Risk, Ambiguity, and the Savage Axioms." *Quarterly Journal of Economics* 75: 643–669.

Epstein, David, and Sharyn O'Halloran. 1994. "Administrative Procedures, Information, and Agency Discretion." *American Journal of Political Science* 38(3): 697–722.

Epstein, David, and Peter Zemsky. 1995. "Money Talks: Deterring Quality Challengers in Congressional Elections." *American Political Science Review* 89(2): 295–308.

Fearon, James D. 1994. "Domestic Political Audiences and the Escalation of International Disputes." *American Political Science Review* 88(3): 577–592.

Fearon, James D. 1995. "Rationalist Explanations for War." *International Organization*, 49(3): 379–414.

Fearon, James D., and David D. Laitin. 1996. "Explaining Interethnic Cooperation." *American Political Science Review* 90(4): 715–735.

Fedderson, Timothy, and Wolfgang Pesendorfer. 1998. "Convicting the Innocent: The Inferiority of Unanimous Jury Verdicts Under Strategic Voting." *American Political Science Review* 92(1): 23–35.

Ferejohn, John. 1986. "Incumbent Performance and Electoral Control." *Public Choice* 50: 5–26.

Fudenberg, Drew, and Eric Maskin. 1986. "The Folk Theorem in Repeated Games with Discounting or Incomplete Information." *Econometrica* 54: 533–554.

Fudenberg, Drew, and Jean Tirole. 1991. *Game Theory.* Cambridge, MA: MIT Press.

Gailmard, Sean. 2005. "Menu Laws and Forbidden Actions: Choice of Instruments to Constrain Bureaucratic Discretion." Typescript, Northwestern University.

Gaughan, Edward. 1993. *Introduction to Analysis*, 4th ed. Pacific Grove, CA: Brooks Cole.

Gibbard, Alan. 1973. "Manipulation of Voting Schemes: A General Result." *Econometrica* 41(4): 587–602.

Gill, Jeff. 2004. *Essential Mathematics for Political and Social Research.* New York: Cambridge University Press.

Gilligan, Thomas, and Keith Krehbiel. 1987. "Collective Decision-Making and Standing Committees: An Informational Rationale for Restrictive Amendment Procedures." *Journal of Law, Economics, and Organization* 3(2): 287–335.

Gilligan, Thomas W., and Keith Krehbiel. 1989. "Asymmetric Information and Legislative Rules with a Heterogenous Committee." *American Journal of Political Science* 33(2): 459–490.

Green, Edward, and Rob Porter. 1984. "Noncooperative Collusion Under Imperfect Price Information." *Econometrica* 52(January): 87–100.

Groseclose, Timothy. 1996. "An Examination of the Market for Favors and Votes in Congress." *Economic Inquiry* 34: 320–340.

Groseclose, Timothy, and Nolan McCarty. 2000. "The Politics of Blame: Bargaining Before an Audience." *American Journal of Political Science* 45(1): 100–119.

Groves, Theodore. 1973. "Incentives in Teams." *Econometrica* 45: 617–631.

Harsanyi, John C. 1967–68. "Games with Incomplete Information Played by Bayesian Players." *Management Science* 14: 159–182, 320–334, 486–502.

Hotelling, Harold. 1929. "Stability in Competition." *Economic Journal* 39(153): 41–57.

Huber, John D., and Nolan McCarty. 2004. "Bureaucratic Capacity, Delegation, and Political Reform." *American Political Science Review* 98(3): 481–494.

Kahn, Kim F., and Patrick J. Kenney. 1999. *The Spectacle of U.S. Senate Campaigns.* Princeton, NJ: Princeton University Press.

Kahneman, Daniel, and Amos Tversky. 1979. "Prospect Theory: An Analysis of Decision Under Risk." *Econometrica* 47(2): 263–291.

Kakutani, Shizuo. 1941. "A Generalization of Brouwer's Fixed Point Theorem." *Duke Mathematical Journal* 8: 457–459.

Knight, Frank H. 1921. *Risk, Uncertainty, and Profit.* Boston: Houghton Mifflin.

Kolmogorov A. N., and S. V. Fomin. 1970. *Introductory Real Analysis.* New York: Dover.

Krehbiel, Keith. 1991. *Information and Legislative Organization.* Ann Arbor: University of Michigan Press.

Krehbiel, Keith. 2001. "Plausibility of Signals by Heterogeneous Committees." *American Political Science Review* 95: 453–458.

Krishna. Vijay. 2002. *Auction Theory.* San Diego: Academic Press.

Krishna, Vijay, and John Morgan. 1997. "An Analysis of the War of Attrition and the All-Pay Auction." *Journal of Economic Theory* 72: 343–362.

Krishna, Vijay, and John Morgan. 2001. "Asymmetric Information and Legislative Rules: Some Amendments." *American Political Science Review* 95(2): 435–452.

Lasswell, Harold D. 1936. *Politics: Who Gets What, When and How.* New York: McGraw Hill.

Matthews, Steven A. 1989. "Veto Threats: Rhetoric in a Bargaining Game." *Quarterly Journal of Economics* 104: 347–369.

McCarty, Nolan. 1997. "Presidential Reputation and the Veto." *Economics and Politics* 9: 1–27.

McCarty, Nolan. 2000a. "Proposal Rights, Veto Rights, and Political Bargaining." *American Journal of Political Science* 44(3): 506–522.

McCarty, Nolan. 2000b. "Presidential Pork: Executive Veto Power and Distributive Politics." *American Political Science Review* 94(1): 117–129.

McCarty, Nolan 2002. "Vetoes in the Early Republic." Working paper, Woodrow Wilson School, Princeton University.

McCarty, Nolan. 2004. "The Appointments Dilemma." *American Journal of Political Science* 48(3): 413–428.

McKelvey, Richard D. 1976. "Intransitivities in Multidimensional Voting Models and Some Implications for Agenda Control." *Journal of Economic Theory* 12: 472–482.

McKelvey, Richard D., and Richard Niemi. 1978. "Multistage Game Representation of Sophisticated Voting for Binary Procedures." *Journal of Economic Theory* 18: 1–22.

Meirowitz, Adam. 2002. "Informative Voting and Condorcet Jury Theorems with a Continuum of Types." *Social Choice and Welfare* 19: 219–236.

Meirowitz, Adam. 2004a. "Polling Games and Information Revelation in the Downsian Framework." *Games and Economic Behavior* 51: 464–489.

Meirowitz, Adam. 2004b. "Costly Action in Electoral Contests." Typescript, Princeton University.

Mertens, Jean-François, and Shmuel Zamir. 1985. "Formulation of Bayesian Analysis for Games with Incomplete Information." *International Journal of Game Theory* 14(1): 1–29.

Milgrom, Paul, Douglass North, and Barry Weingast. 1990. "The Role of Institutions in the Revival of Trade: The Medieval Law Merchant, Private Judges, and the Champagne Fairs." *Economics and Politics* 2: 1–23.

Morrow, James. 1994. *Game Theory for Political Scientists*. Princeton, NJ: Princeton University Press.

Moulin, Herve. 1980. "On Strategy-Proofness and Single Peakedness." *Public Choice* 35: 437–455.

Muthoo, Abhinay. 1999. *Bargaining Theory with Applications* New York: Cambridge University Press.

Myerson, Roger. 1981. "Optimal Auction Design." *Mathematics of Operations Research* 6: 68–73.

Nash, John C. 1950a. "The Bargaining Problem." *Econometrica* 18(2): 155–162.

Nash, John F. 1950b. "Equilibrium Points in N-Person Games." *Proceedings of the National Academy of Science* 36: 48–49.

Olson, Mancur. 1965. *The Logic of Collective Action: Public Goods and the Theory of Groups*. Cambridge, MA: Harvard University Press.

Ordeshoo K, Peter C. 1986. *Game Theory and Political Theory: An Introduction*. New York: Cambridge University Press.

Palfrey, Thomas R., and Howard Rosenthal. 1984. "Participation and the Provision of Discrete Public Goods: A Strategic Analysis." *Journal of Public Economics* 24(2): 171–193.

Palfrey, Thomas R., and Howard Rosenthal. 1988. "Private Incentives in Social Dilemmas: The Effects of Incomplete Information and Altruism." *Journal of Public Economics* 35: 309–332.

Palfrey, Thomas, and Sanjay Srivastava. 1989. "Mechanism Design with Incomplete Information: A Solution to the Implementation Problem." *Journal of Political Economy* 97(3): 668–691.

Plott, Charles R. 1967. "A Notion of Equilibrium and Its Possibility Under Majority Rule." *American Economic Review* 57: 787–806.

Powell, Robert. 1999. *In the Shadow of Power*. Princeton, NJ: Princeton University Press.

Primo, David. 2004. "Open vs. Closed Rules in Budget Legislation: A Result and an Application." Typescript, University of Rochester.

Riker, William. 1962. *The Theory of Coalitions*. New Haven, CT: Yale University Press.

Riley, John G., and William F. Samuelson. 1981. "Optimal Auctions." *American Economic Review* 71: 381–392.

Romer, Thomas, and Howard Rosenthal. 1978. "Political Resource Allocation, Controlled Agendas, and the Status Quo." *Public Choice* 33(1): 27–44.

Royden. H. L. 1988. *Real Analysis,* 3d ed. Englewood Cliffs, NJ: Prentice-Hall.

Rubinstein, Ariel. 1982. "Perfect Equilibrium in a Bargaining Model." *Econometrica* 50: 97–110.

Sattherwaite, Mark. 1975. "Strategy-Proofness and Arrow's Conditions: Existence and Correspondence Theorems for Voting Procedures and Social Welfare Functions." *Journal of Economics Theory* 10: 187–217.

Savage, Leonard. 1954. *The Foundations of Statistics.* New York: Wiley.

Selten, Reinhard. 1965. "Spieltheoretische Behandlung eines Oligopolmodells mit Nachfragentragheit." *Zeitschrift fur die gesamte Staatswissenschaft* 12: 201–324.

Shepsle, Kenneth. 1979. "Institutional Arrangements and Equilibrium in Multidimensional Voting Models." *American Journal of Political Science* 23(1): 27–59.

Shepsle, Kenneth A., and Barry R. Weingast. 1987. "The Institutional Foundations of Committee Power." *American Political Science Review* 81(1): 85–104.

Simon, Carl P., and Lawrence Blume. 1994. *Mathematics for Economists.* New York: W. W. Norton.

Spence, Michael. 1974. *Market Signaling.* Cambridge, MA: Harvard University Press.

Taylor, Michael. 1976. *Anarchy and Cooperation.* London: Wiley.

Topkis, Donald. M. 1998. *Supermodularity and Complementarity.* Princeton, NJ: Princeton University Press.

Von Neumann, John, and Oscar Morgenstern. 1944. *Theory of Games and Economic Behavior.* Princeton NJ: Princeton University Press.

Weingast, Barry R. 1997. "The Political Foundations of Democracy and the Rule of Law." *American Political Science Review* 91(2): 245–263.

Weingast, Barry R., and William J. Marshall. 1988. "The Industrial Organization of Congress; or, Why Legislatures, Like Firms, Are Not Organized as Markets." *Journal of Political Economy* 96(1): 132–163.

Whittman, Donald. 1977. "Candidates with Policy Preferences: A Dynamic Model." *Journal of Economic Theory* 14: 180–189.

Zhou, Lin. 1994. "The Set of Nash Equilibria of a Supermodular Game Is a Complete Lattice." *Games and Economic Behavior* 7: 295–300.

Index

3423